Eustace

Eustace

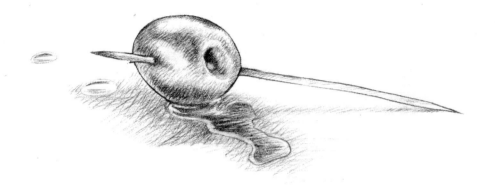

S. J. Harris

Jonathan Cape
London

To Clare
with love

Thank you

Clare for gently nudging me towards
the cartoon novel and for your
help, companionship and love.
Mum, Dad, Michelle
Rick Dickerson & Paul Beynon,
                    Alan Graham
Gill Green, Mike Wood, Jonathan Wood
                    Aunty Anne
Farah Thompson, Clare Williams
Dan Franklin, Steven Messer
            & all at Random House
Wowbagger, Shazz & all at h2g2
Angoulême chums of 2003
Miz for the initial spark
everyone who provided
            encouragement, support
                    & friendship
anyone who has helped the book
    along its merry way since I
    wrote these acknowledgements
... and my apologies to anyone
I've failed to mention here that
                I should have.

Finally, a special thank you to
my Great Aunts & Uncles.

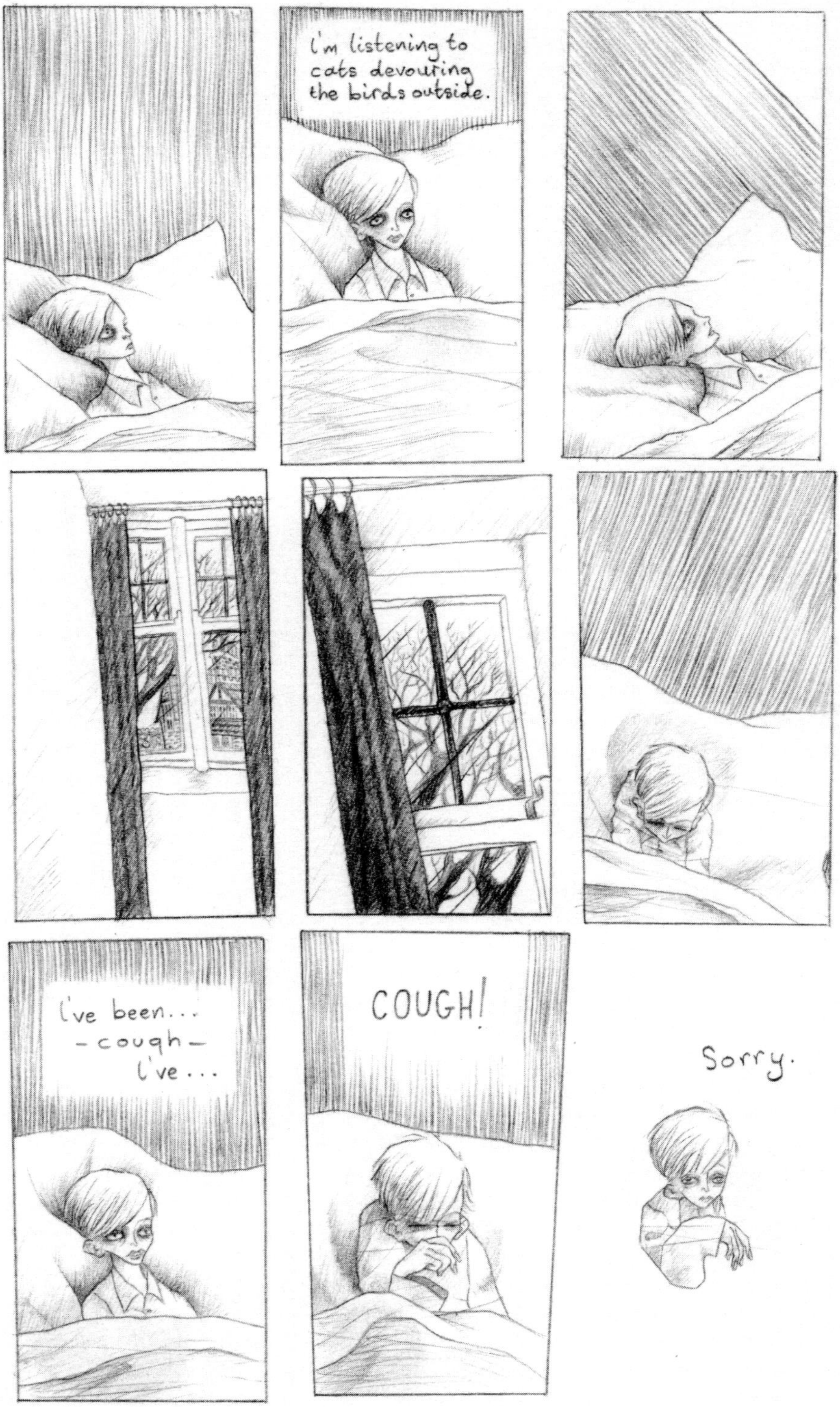
I'm listening to cats devouring the birds outside.
I've been... -cough- I've...
COUGH!
Sorry.

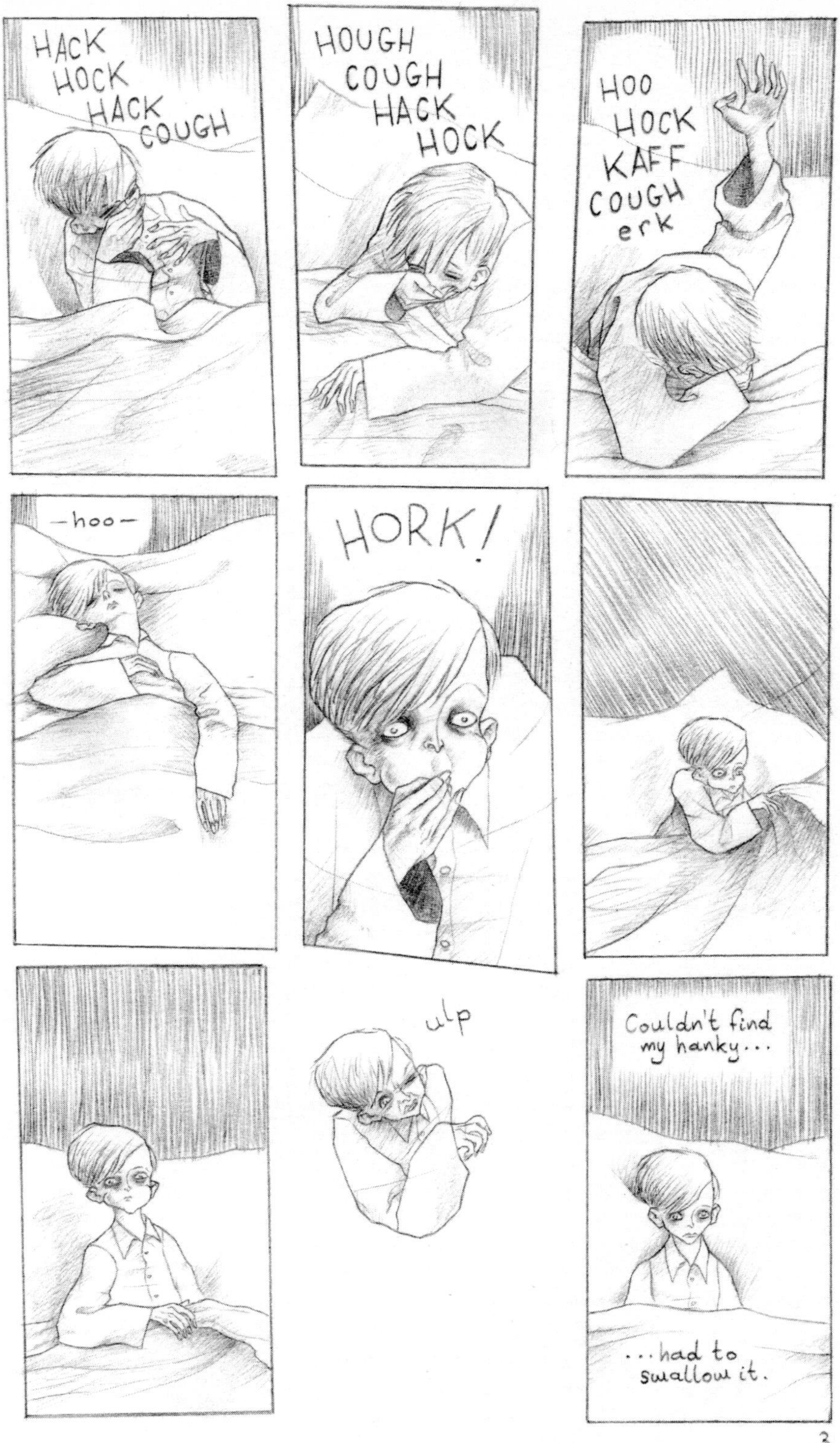
HACK
HOCK
HACK
COUGH
HOUGH
COUGH
HACK
HOCK
HOO
HOCK
KAFF
COUGH
erk
-hoo-
HORK!
ulp
Couldn't find my hanky...
...had to swallow it.

Eustace

It's quite hard work being ill. All this coughing is exhausting. Yesterday I coughed into my soup and some soup went into my eye.

Luckily it was tepid.

Hopefully Mother will bring the cough medicine when she brings me my soup for lunch today.

The soup's rotten but I like the medicine.

The medicine's quite scrummy.

−cough−
I've been quite poorly.

The dead were standing over me, gently blowing my hair.

Or perhaps it was Aunties.

I have
all these
Aunties
you see.

They are not
just Aunties
but
Great Aunties.

Like the War.

They visit sometimes.

When the Aunties
visit I know that
I must be really
quite poorly
indeed.

They can smell
illness from thirty
miles away.

And cake.
When they smell
that I'm at my
weakest and
can't resist their
attack...

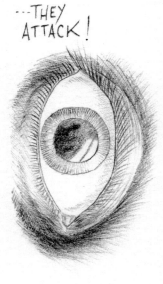

...THEY
ATTACK!

Isn't nature
horrid?

7

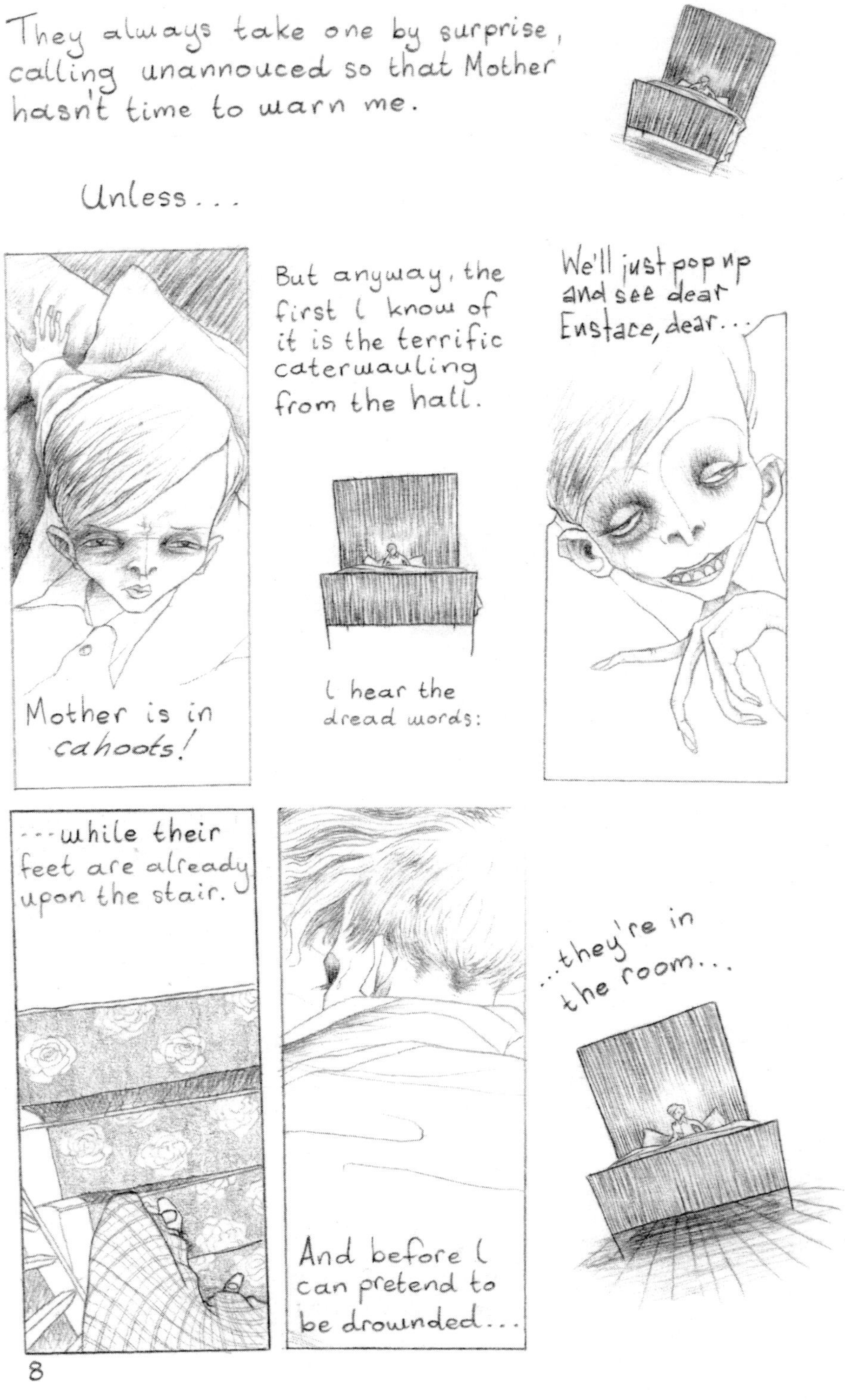
They always take one by surprise, calling unannouced so that Mother hasn't time to warn me.
Unless...
Mother is in cahoots!
But anyway, the first I know of it is the terrific caterwauling from the hall.
I hear the dread words:
We'll just pop up and see dear Eustace, dear...
...while their feet are already upon the stair.
And before I can pretend to be drowned...
...they're in the room...

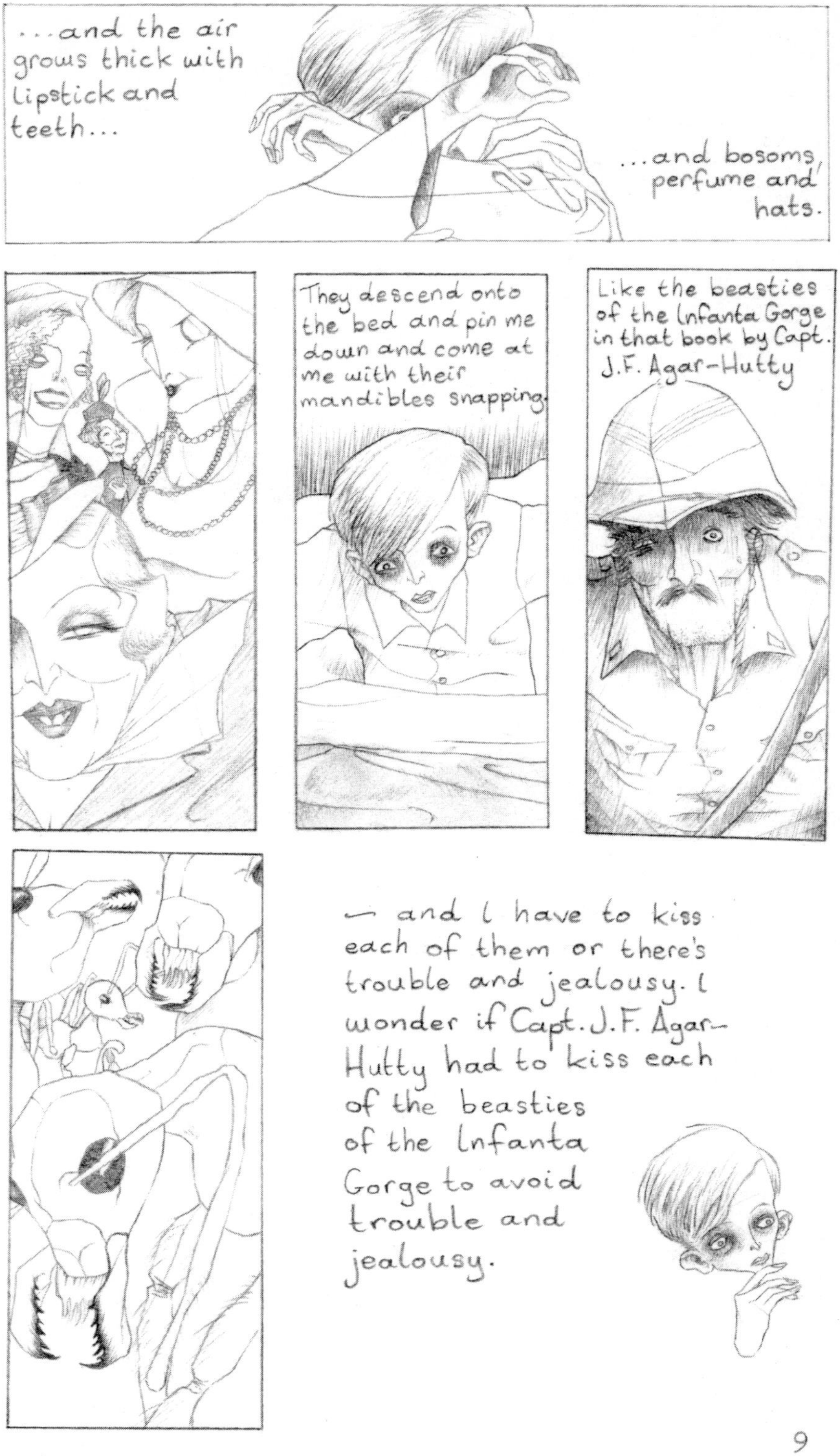
...and the air grows thick with lipstick and teeth...
...and bosoms, perfume and hats.
They descend onto the bed and pin me down and come at me with their mandibles snapping.
Like the beasties of the Infanta Gorge in that book by Capt. J.F. Agar-Hutty
— and I have to kiss each of them or there's trouble and jealousy. I wonder if Capt. J.F. Agar-Hutty had to kiss each of the beasties of the Infanta Gorge to avoid trouble and jealousy.

But actually, if you're quick, it is better to kiss an Aunty before she can kiss you. I've drawn a diagram to explain the method.

METHOD FOR KISSING AUNTIES

1. WAIT TILL YOU SEE THE PINKS OF HER GUMS.

2. POUNCE.

Kissing an Aunty is quite nice really. Their cheeks are soft and powdery like Turkish Delight but without as much icing sugar.

But if they get you first it is a horrible business.

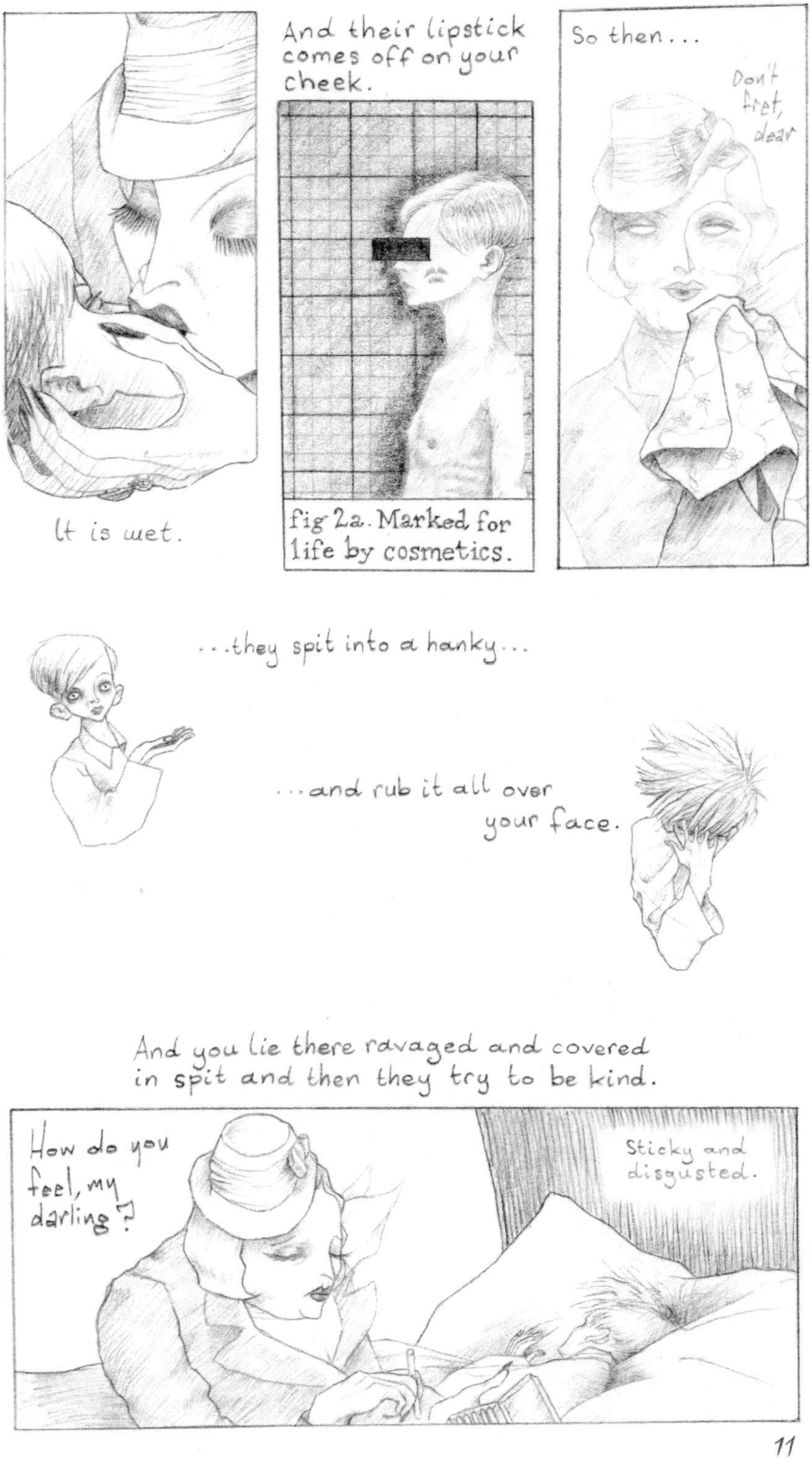

It is wet.
And their lipstick comes off on your cheek.
fig 2a. Marked for life by cosmetics.
So then...
Don't fret, dear
...they spit into a hanky...
...and rub it all over your face.
And you lie there ravaged and covered in spit and then they try to be kind.
How do you feel, my darling?
Sticky and disgusted.

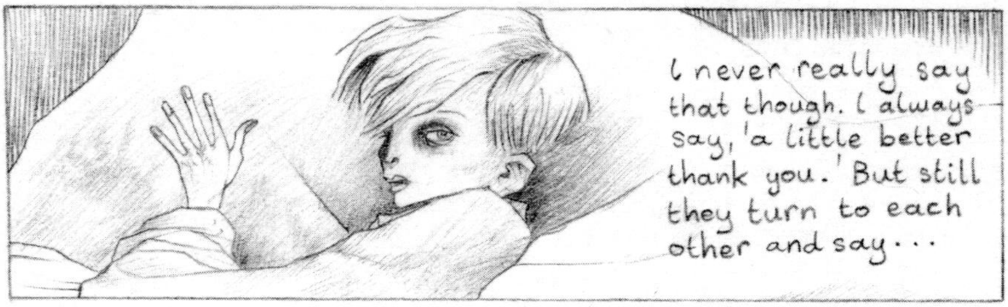
I never really say that though. I always say, 'a little better thank you.' But still they turn to each other and say...

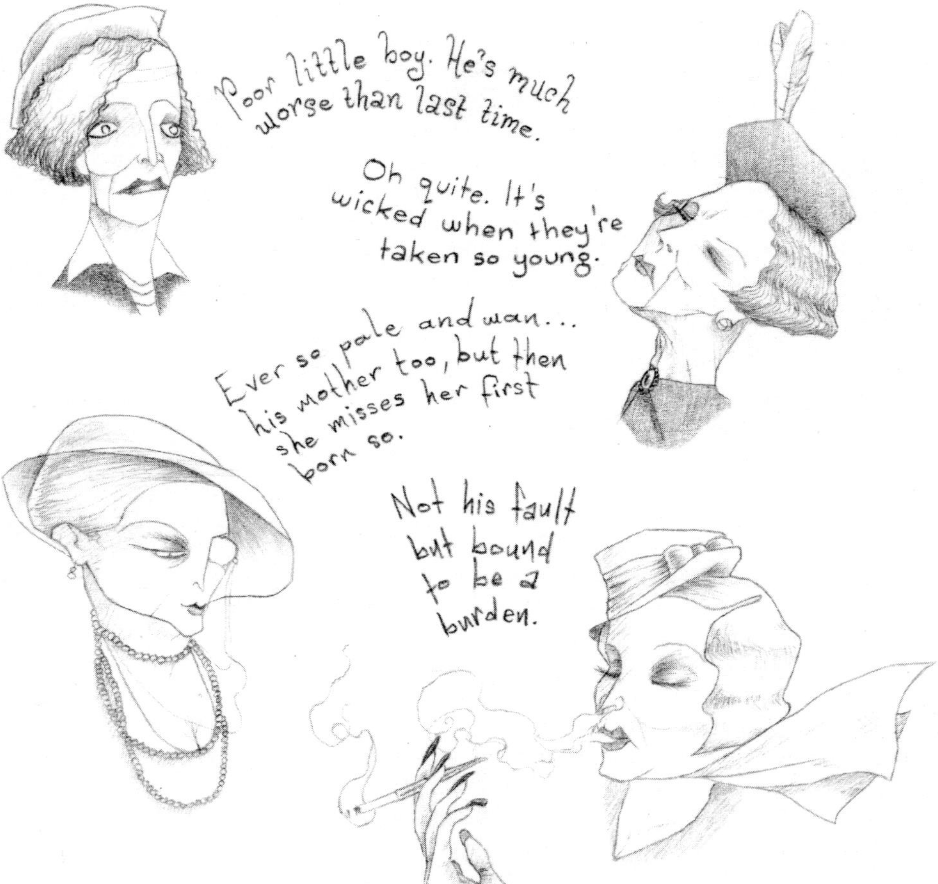
Poor little boy. He's much worse than last time.
Oh quite. It's wicked when they're taken so young.
Ever so pale and wan... his mother too, but then she misses her first born so.
Not his fault but bound to be a burden.

To hear them talk you'd think I wouldn't last till tea-time.

Still, it's nice to have the attention.

In fact, it's a bit disappointing when they talk about something else...

...like Aunty Cyrille whom I think is the best one. I don't see her very often. They all think she is barmy because she worships Bertrand Russell and once had tea with Moholy-Nagy at the Bauhaus.

Imagine if they knew that she'd posed for Schiele!

Or else they discuss a feud. There's always a feud going on but no one ever knows the dickens why.

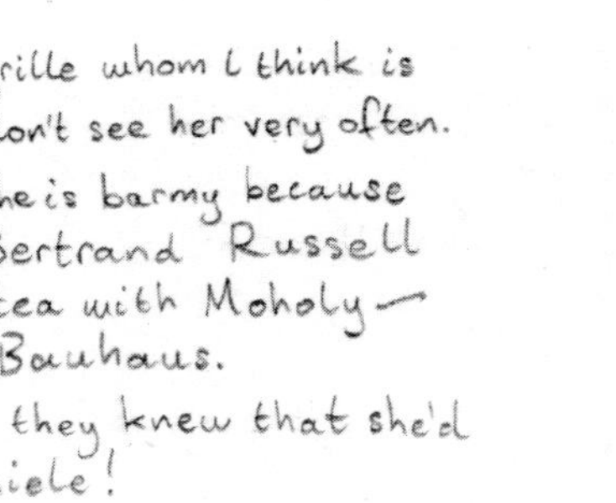

No one has spoken to Aunty Euphemia for years. She's a nice Irish lady. I've only met her once, she seemed a little sad but Uncle Lucien's a Lord, you know, so it must be because no one talks to her.

13

But most of the time I don't know what they're talking about...

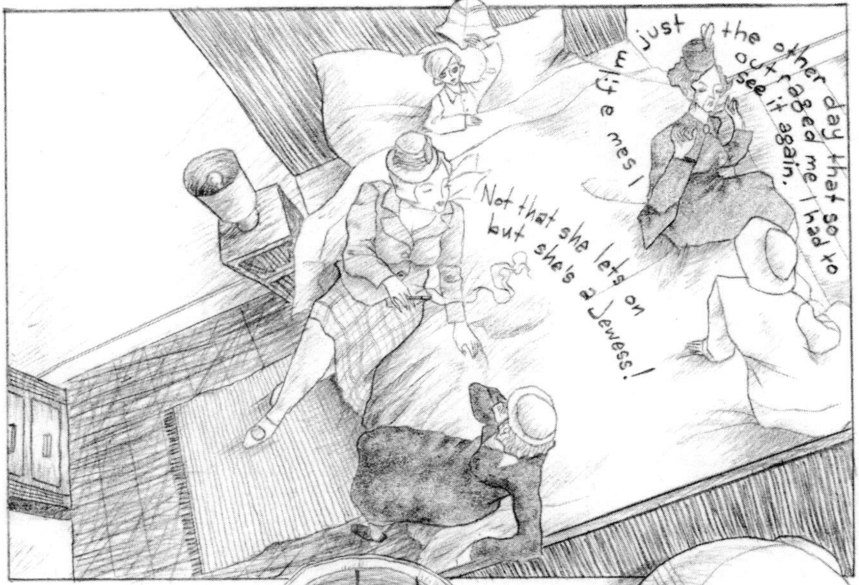
just the other day that so outraged me I had to see it again.
Not that she lets on but she's a Jewess!

...and so I steel myself to examine the species with dispassionate scientific rigour, as Capt. J.F. Agar-Hutty would say. What follows are some of my findings...

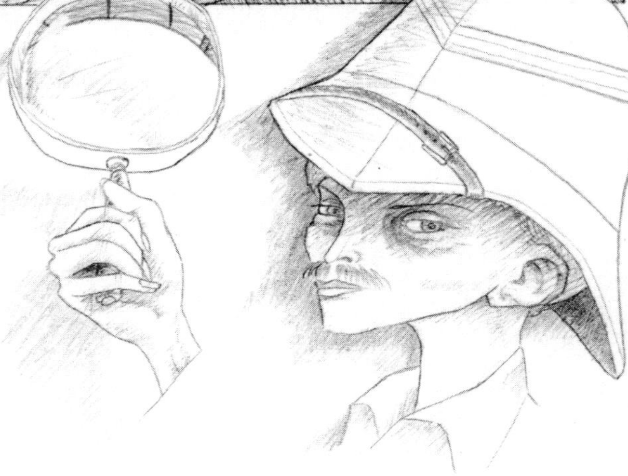

OBSERVATIONS ON SOME PHYSICAL ATTRIBUTES OF AUNTIES
BY Capt. Eustace

1.

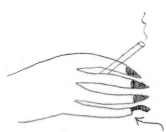

FUNNY LITTLE FINGERNAIL OF
AUNTY NIN. HARD TO BE
DISPASSIONATE AS GIVES ME
WILLIES.

2.

WHEN THEY TUT A LOT OF
SPIT FLIES ABOUT. THEY TUT A
LOT. I IMAGINE THEY COULD
FILL A GHASTLY BATH WITH THE
STUFF IN A SINGLE AFTERNOON.

3.

CREASES AT TOP OF BOSOM
POSSIBLY CAUSED BY YEARS
OF CRUSHING GREAT NEPHEWS
INTO IT.

4.

AUNTY GADD'S EAR-RING
(LEFT SIDE). IS THAT A
SETTEE STUD?

5.

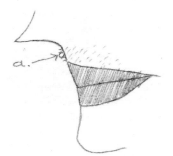

SUNLIGHT SHOWS UP THESE LITTLE MOUSTACHES THEY
HAVE. THEY USE THEM FOR CATCHING CAKE CRUMBS (a.)
ISN'T NATURE MIRACULOUS?

When it is time for the Aunties to go downstairs for tea with Mother, if I'm still alive they all try to slip me a sixpence without any of the others seeing — and I try not to look like I'm expecting anything...

They each press it into my hand...

...close my fingers over it and pat my fingers...

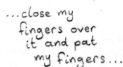

...and it is our big secret.

'Course, they all kiss me again while they're at it but it's worth it for a sixpence. Then all of a sudden they're gone and you'd never know they'd been there except for the perfume in the air and the spit drying on my cheek and the sixpences glowing in my palm.

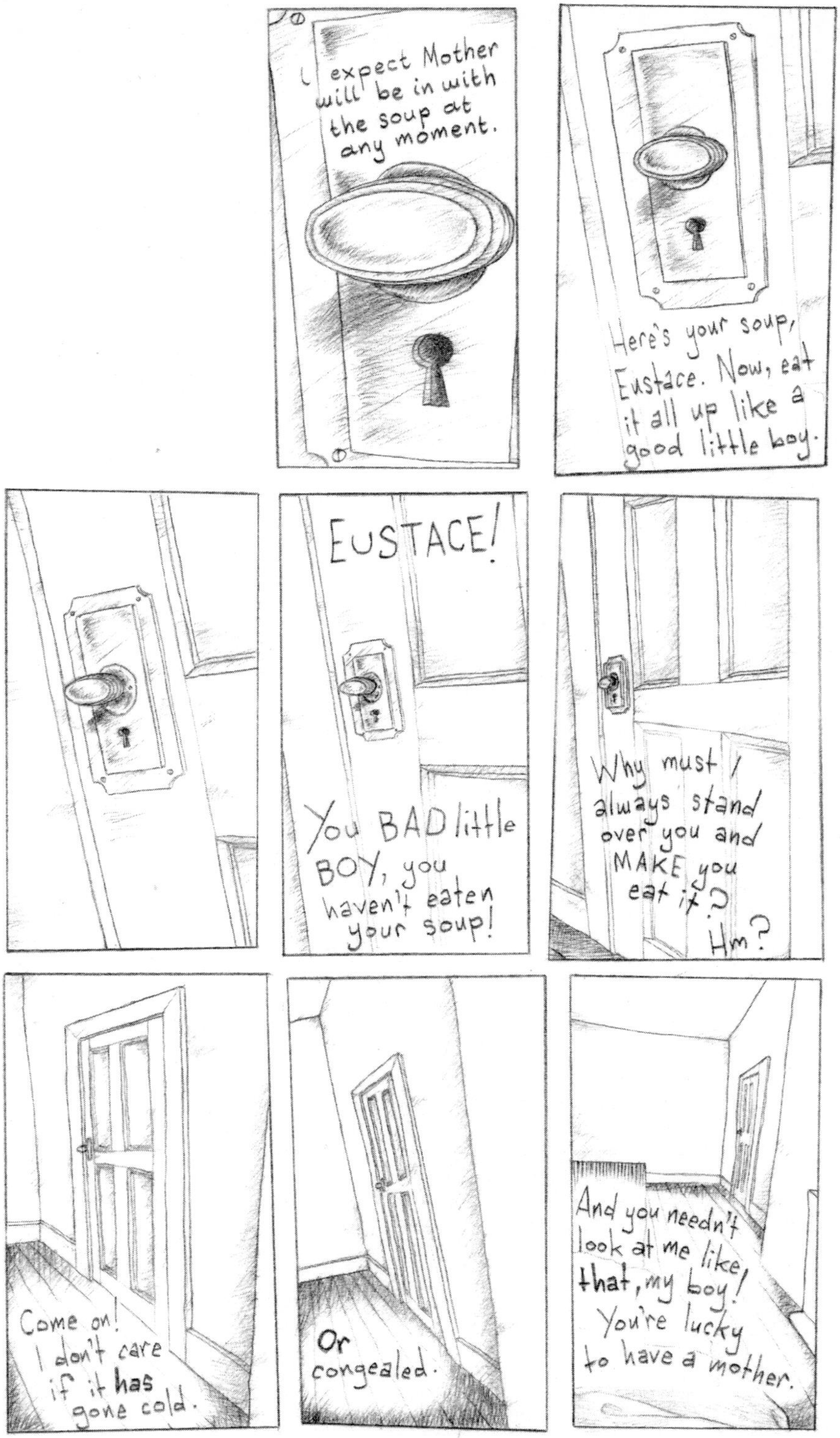
I expect Mother will be in with the soup at any moment.
Here's your soup, Eustace. Now, eat it all up like a good little boy.
EUSTACE!
You BAD little BOY, you haven't eaten your soup!
Why must I always stand over you and MAKE you eat it? Hm?
Come on! I don't care if it **has** gone cold.
Or congealed.
And you needn't look at me like **that**, my boy! You're lucky to have a mother.

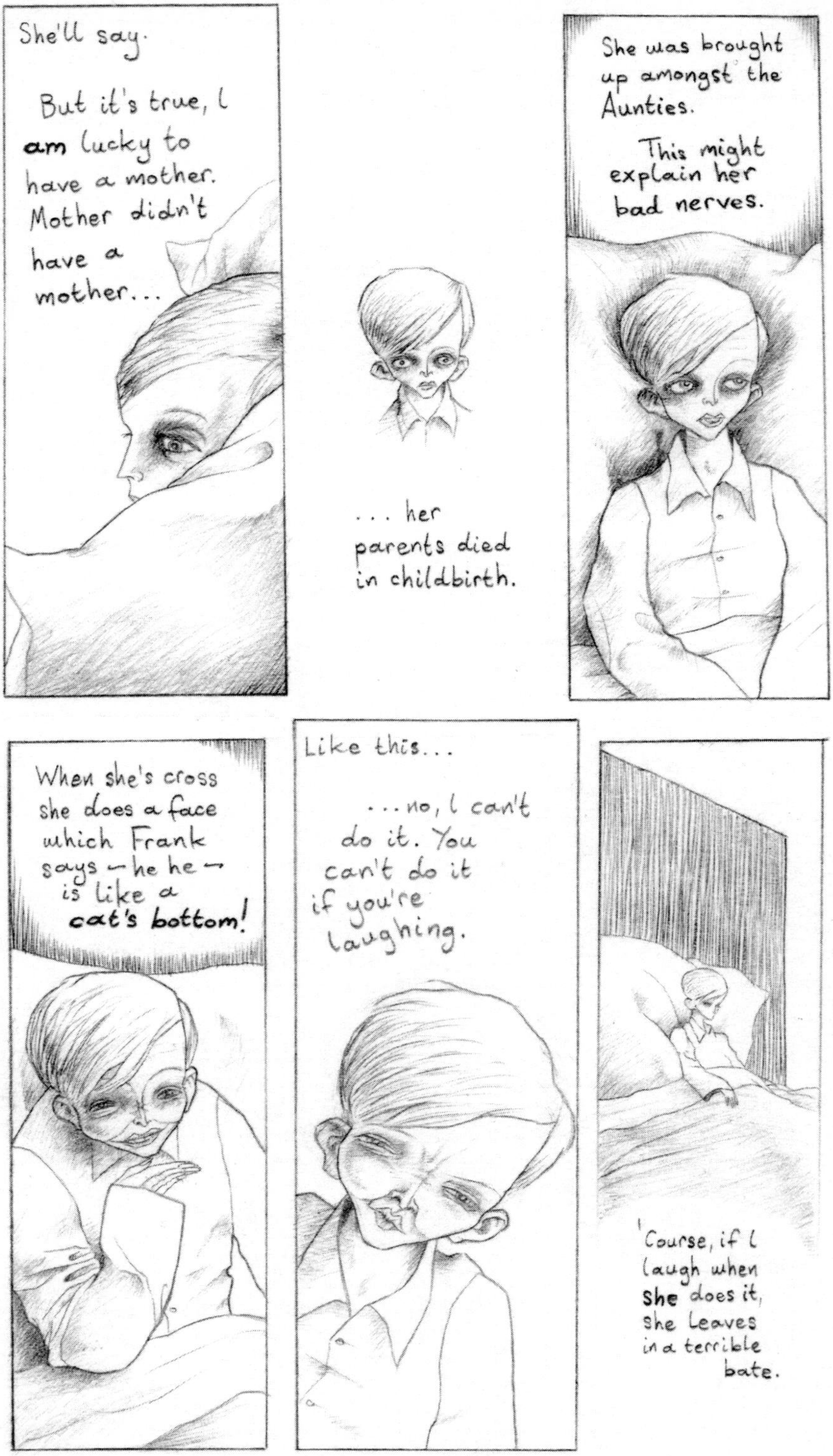
She'll say.
But it's true, I **am** lucky to have a mother. Mother didn't have a mother...
...her parents died in childbirth.
She was brought up amongst the Aunties.
This might explain her bad nerves.
When she's cross she does a face which Frank says – he he – is like a **cat's bottom!**
Like this...
...no, I can't do it. You can't do it if you're laughing.
'Course, if I laugh when **she** does it, she leaves in a terrible bate.

She'll be here
at any moment.

Almost
immediately
I expect.

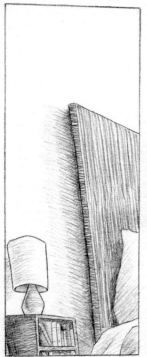

If Frank
were here
he'd have
someone
bring me
some soup.

But he's
in the
army
now.

Um, no.
That doesn't
look right
does it?

How about
this?

Well,
whatever the
uniform, I'm
sure he looks
splendid in it.

21

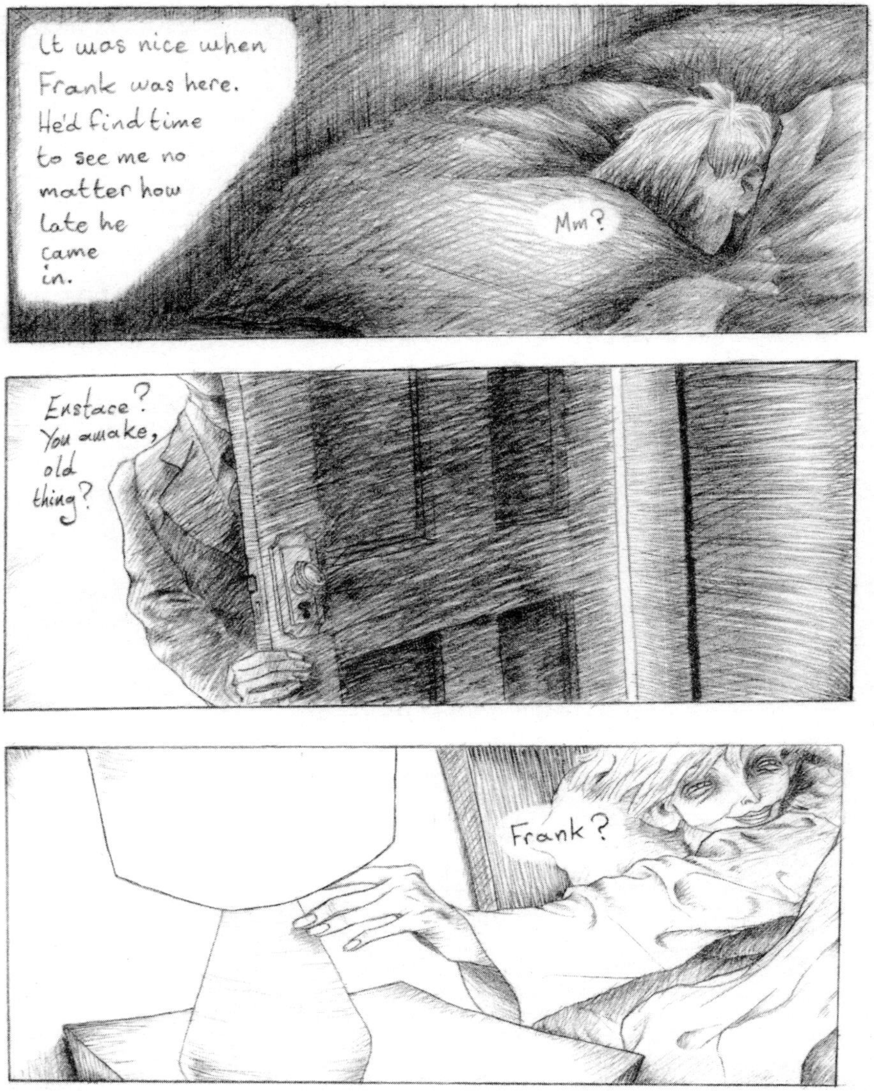
It was nice when Frank was here. He'd find time to see me no matter how late he came in.
Mm?
Eustace? You awake, old thing?
Frank?

We'd say silly things to one another and laugh at the silly things the other one would say.

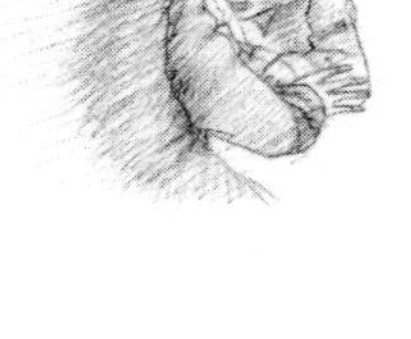

Usually I'd make myself ill
with hilarity.

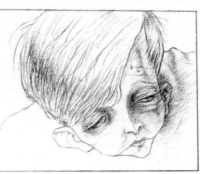

But Frank would
always come to my
rescue straight away.

Hold hard,
old
fellow
and I'll
fetch
Mother.
Shan't be
a tick.

After I'd been
sick he would
stroke my hair
and make me
feel better.

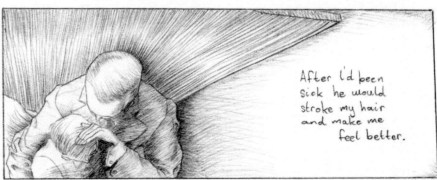

Until
Mother would
come back all
cross with the
empty bucket.

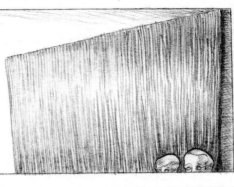

Eustace! Frank! What are you doing there, huddled together like SCHOOLGIRLS! It's really most unseemly.

Oh Mother, I'm just comforting the kid. He's been sick.

I'm all too intimate with the details, Frank. And if you make him sick again **you** can clear it up.

Now don't take on so, darling. I'll put away the bucket; you go downstairs like a good girl and I'll make you a nice martini.

Night night, Eustace.

24

French
Onion

Lobster
Bisque

Mulligatawny

Brown
Windsor

Bouillabaisse

Vichyssoise

All soups which are too rich
for the likes of my sensitive
innards.

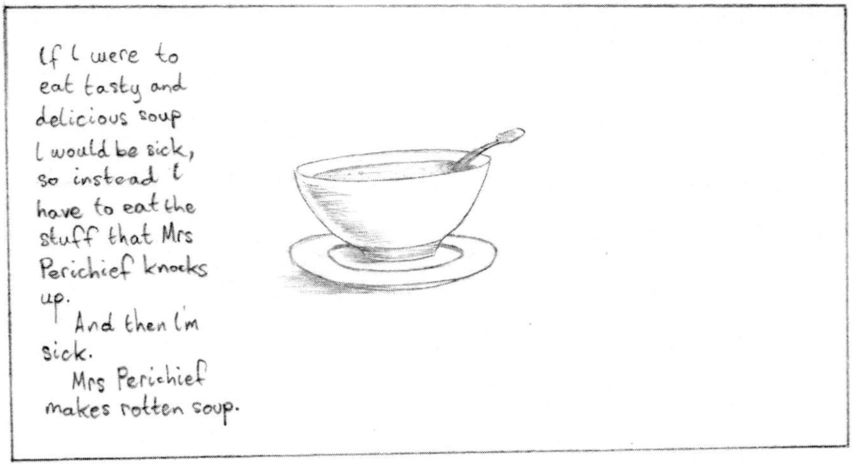
If I were to eat tasty and delicious soup I would be sick, so instead I have to eat the stuff that Mrs Perichief knocks up.
And then I'm sick.
Mrs Perichief makes rotten soup.

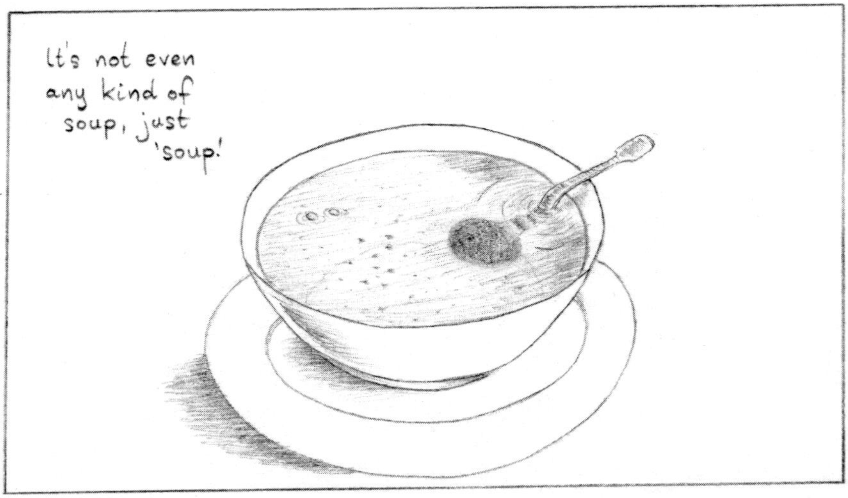
It's not even any kind of soup, just 'soup.'

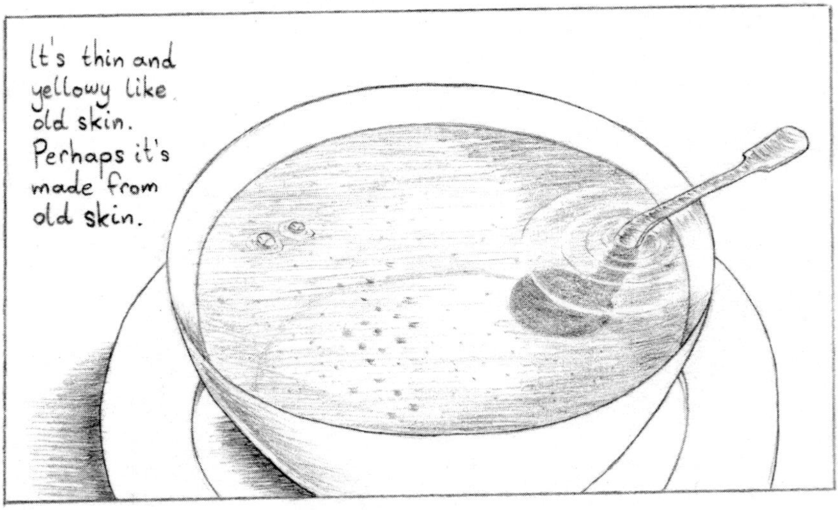
It's thin and yellowy like old skin. Perhaps it's made from old skin.

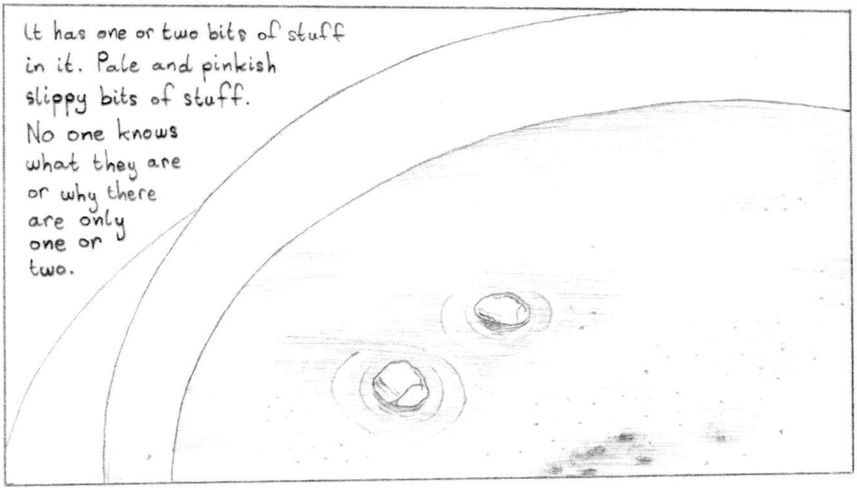
It has one or two bits of stuff in it. Pale and pinkish slippy bits of stuff.
No one knows what they are or why there are only one or two.

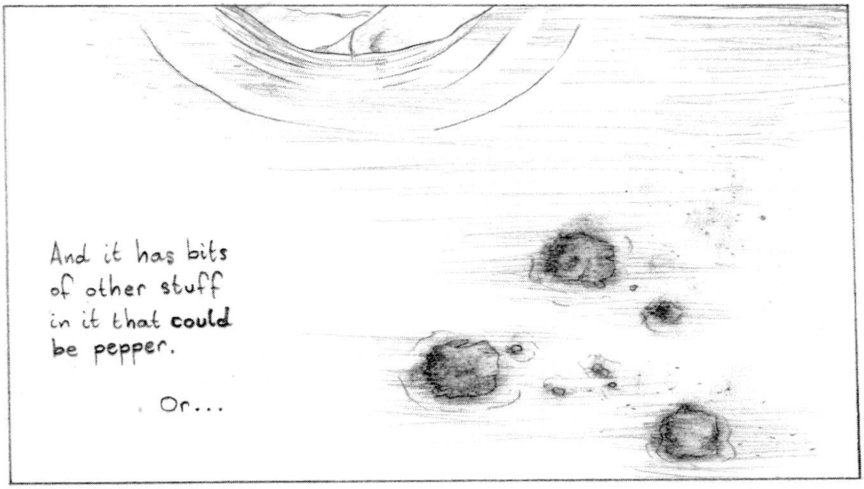
And it has bits of other stuff in it that **could** be pepper.
Or...

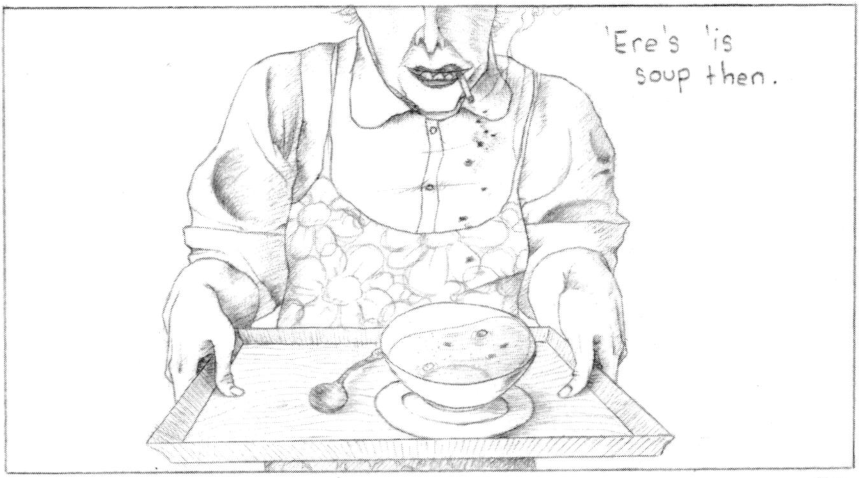
'Ere's 'is soup then.

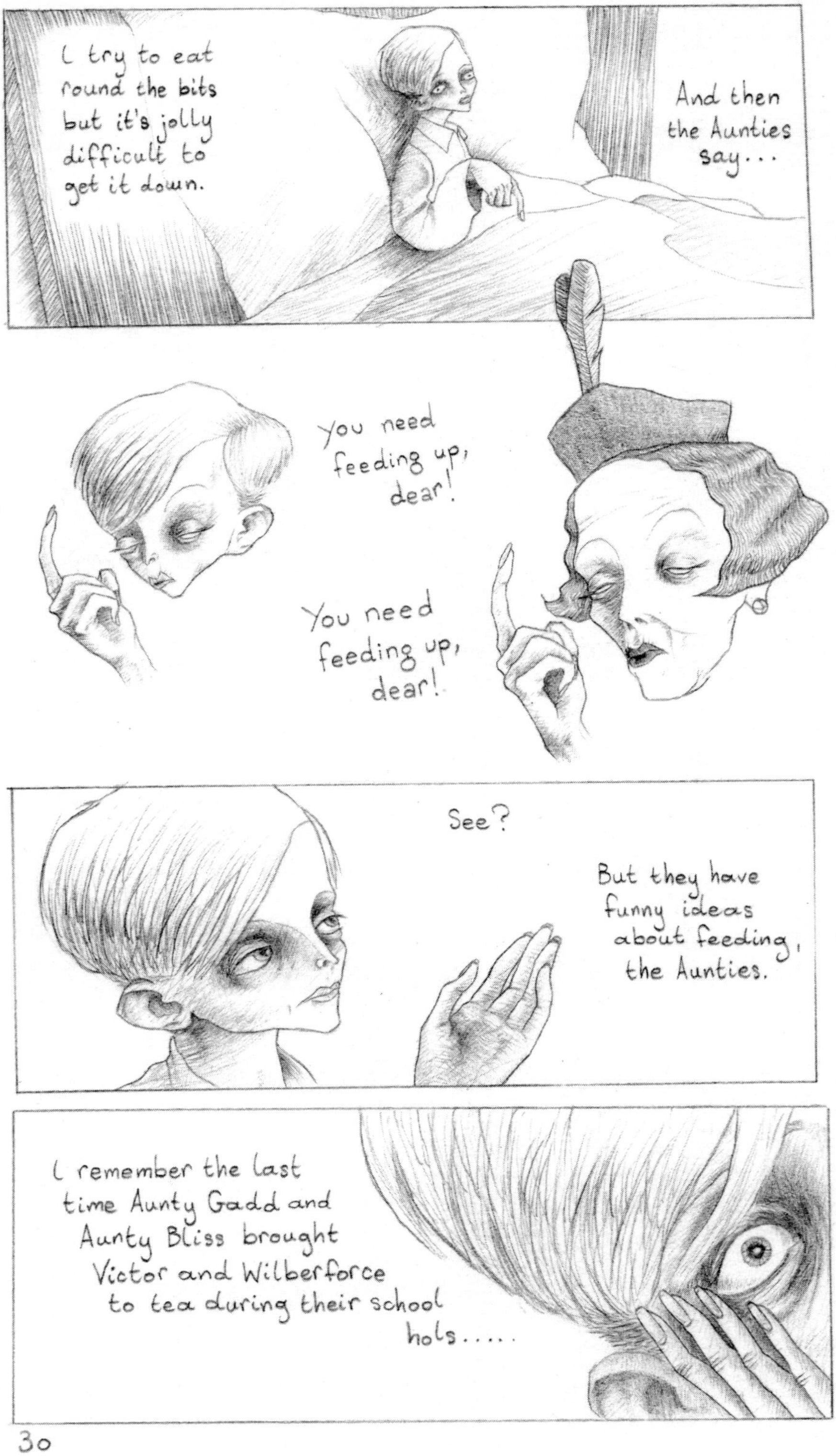
I try to eat round the bits but it's jolly difficult to get it down.
And then the Aunties say...
You need feeding up, dear!
You need feeding up, dear!
See?
But they have funny ideas about feeding, the Aunties.
I remember the last time Aunty Gadd and Aunty Bliss brought Victor and Wilberforce to tea during their school hols.....

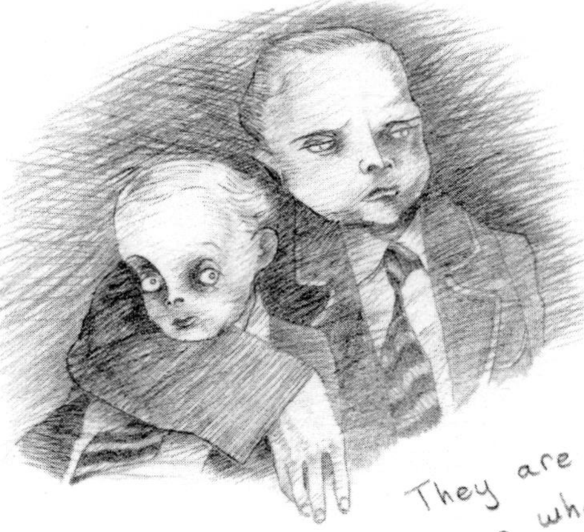

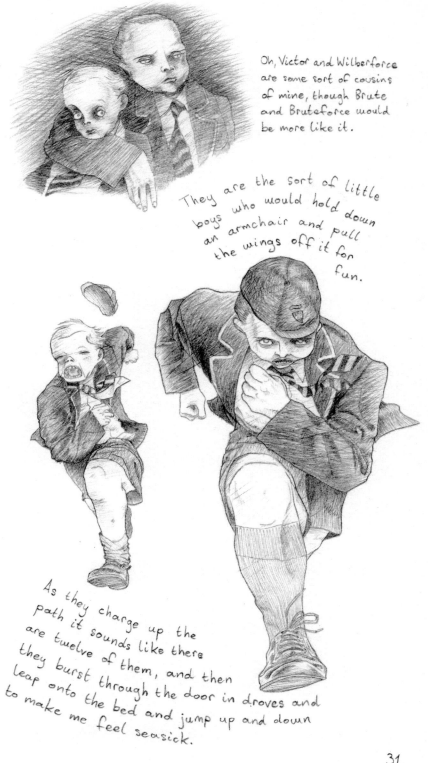

Oh, Victor and Wilberforce are some sort of cousins of mine, though Brute and Bruteforce would be more like it.

They are the sort of little boys who would hold down an armchair and pull the wings off it for fun.

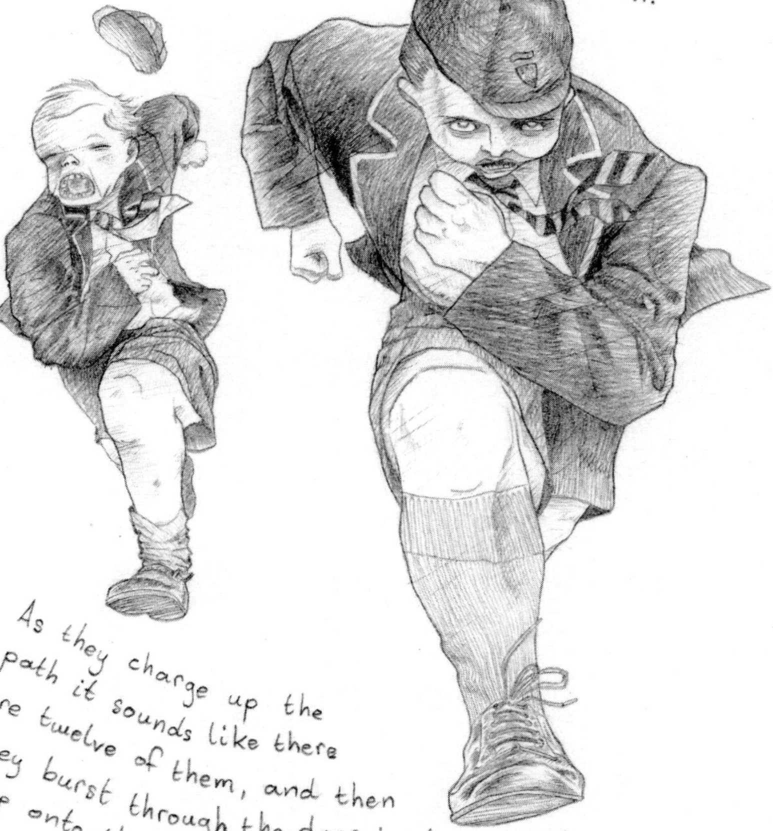

As they charge up the path it sounds like there are twelve of them, and then they burst through the door in droves and leap onto the bed and jump up and down to make me feel seasick.

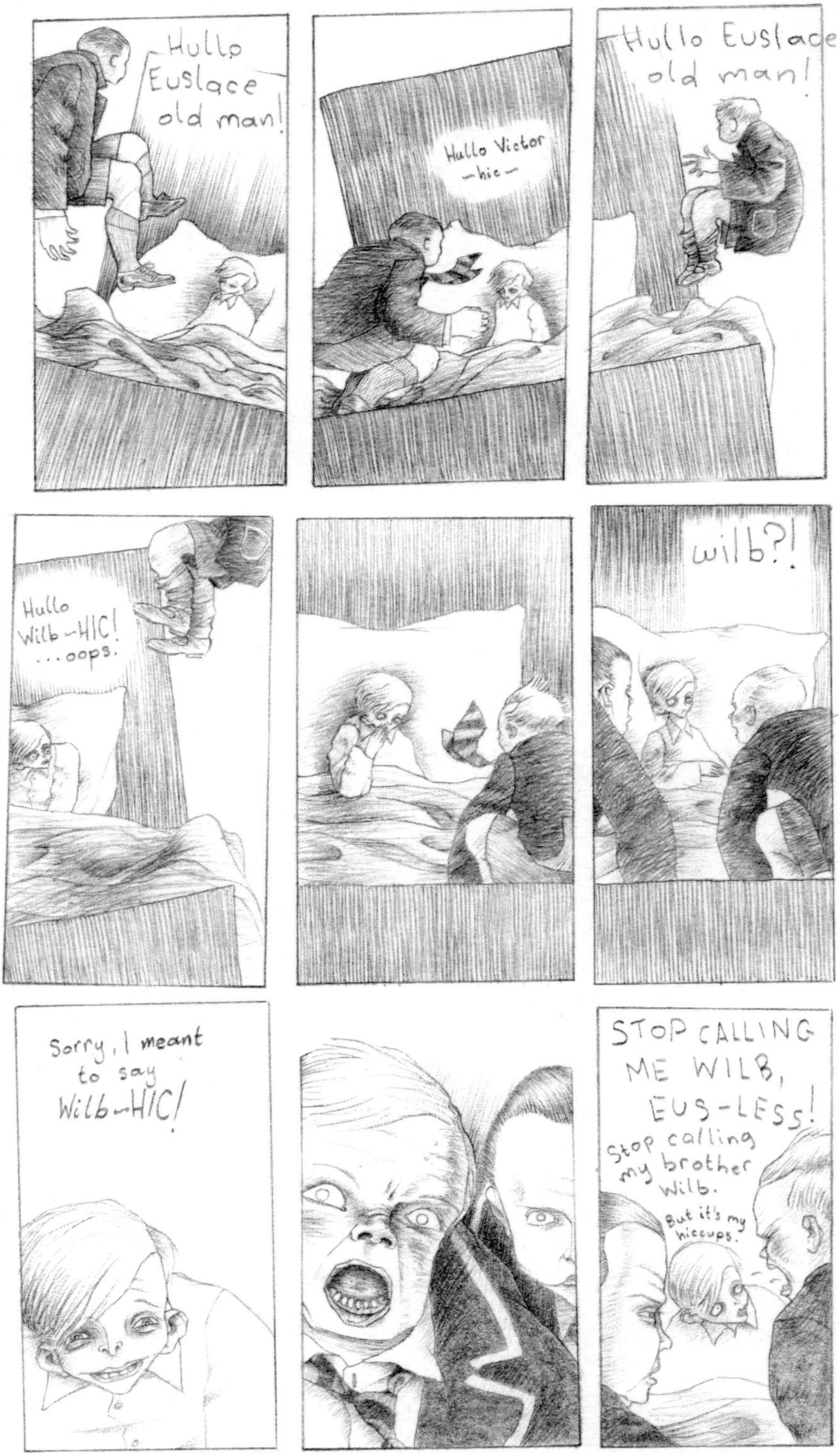
Hullo Euslace old man!
Hullo Victor —hic—
Hullo Euslace old man!
Hullo Wilb—HIC! ...oops.
wilb?!
Sorry, I meant to say Wilb—HIC!
STOP CALLING ME WILB, EUS-LESS!
Stop calling my brother Wilb.
But it's my hiccups.

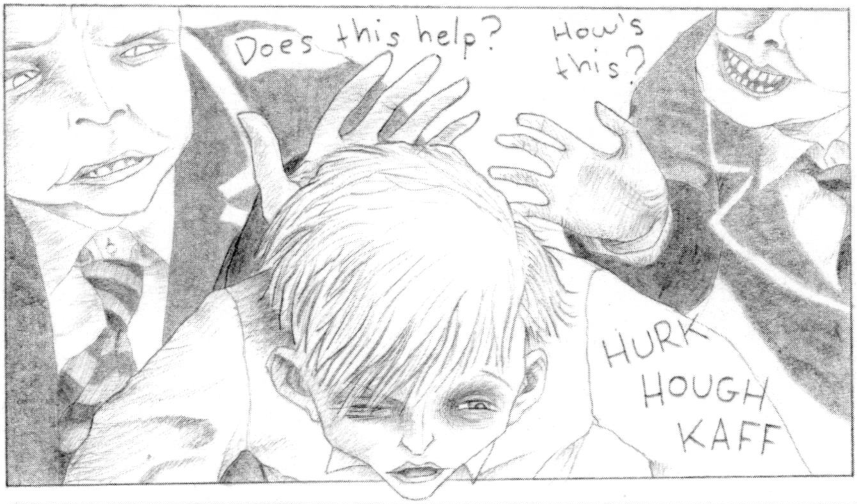
Does this help?
How's this?
HURK
HOUGH
KAFF

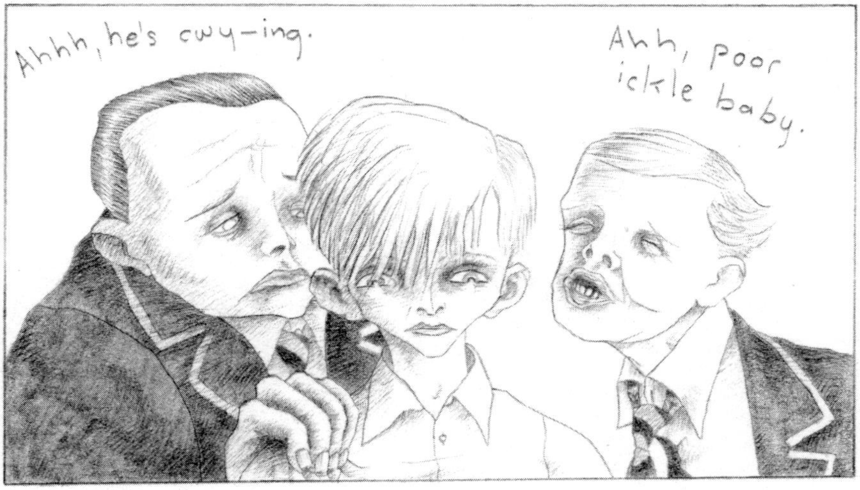
Ahhh, he's cwy-ing.
Ahh, poor ickle baby.

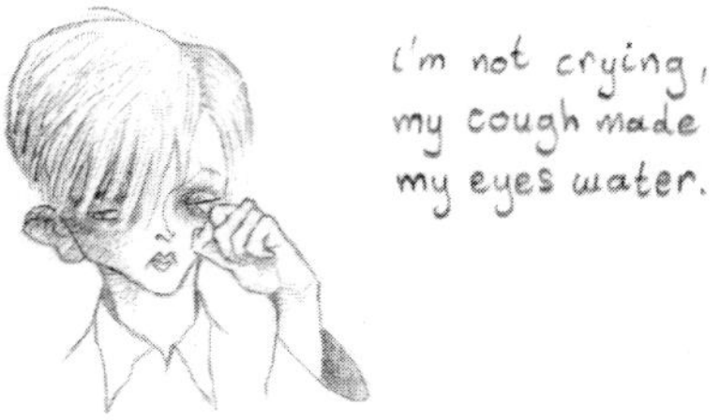
i'm not crying,
my cough made
my eyes water.

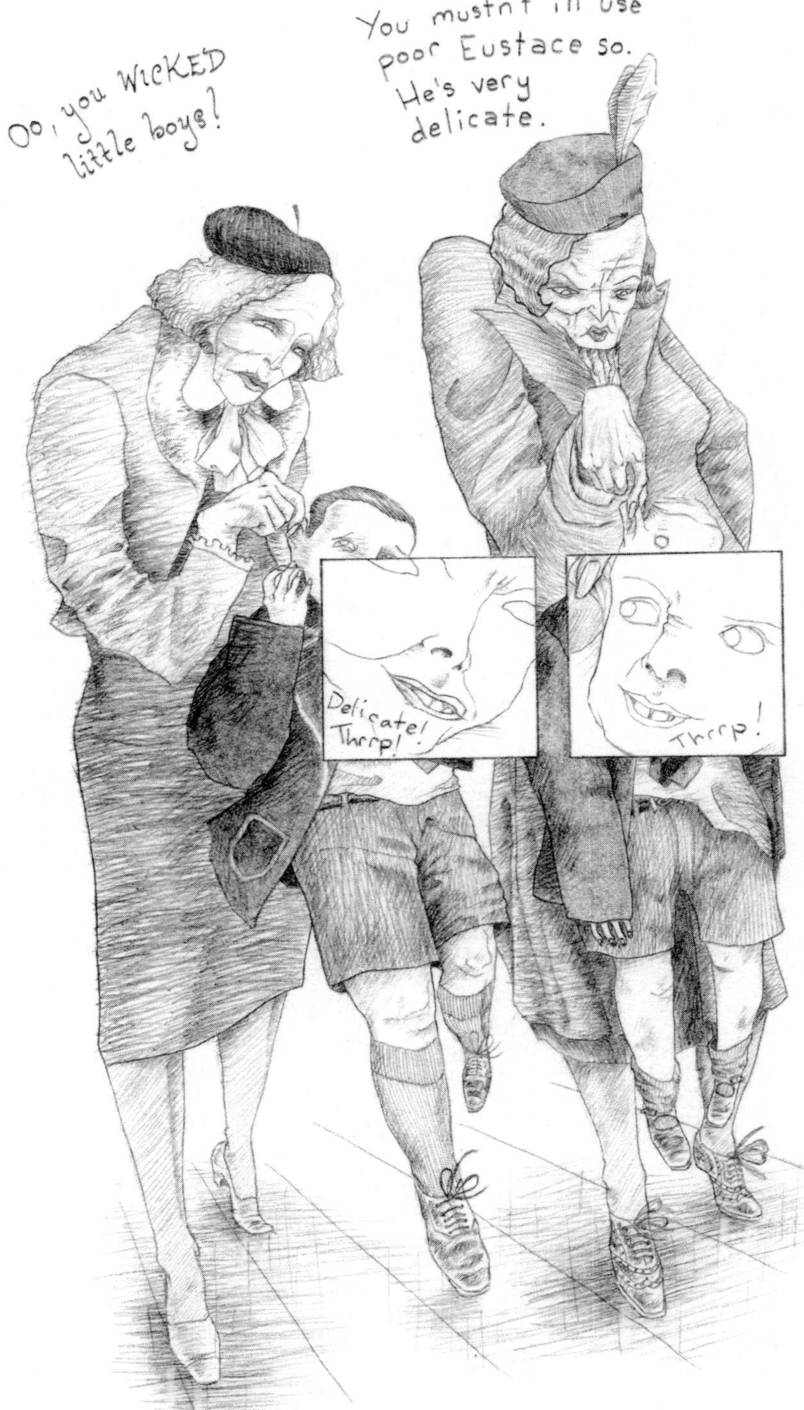
Oo, you WICKED little boys!
You mustn't ill use poor Eustace so. He's very delicate.
Delicate! Thrrp!
Thrrp!

I thought delicate was good but the Aunties seemed much more pleased with Victor and Wilberforce.

Such lusty lads!

Eustace is quite the loner; he simply isn't used to such health and vigour.

They certainly are healthy, just look at the legs on them!

Yes, just look at them! 'Rude health' I think they call it. I call it obscene.

But worse was to come.

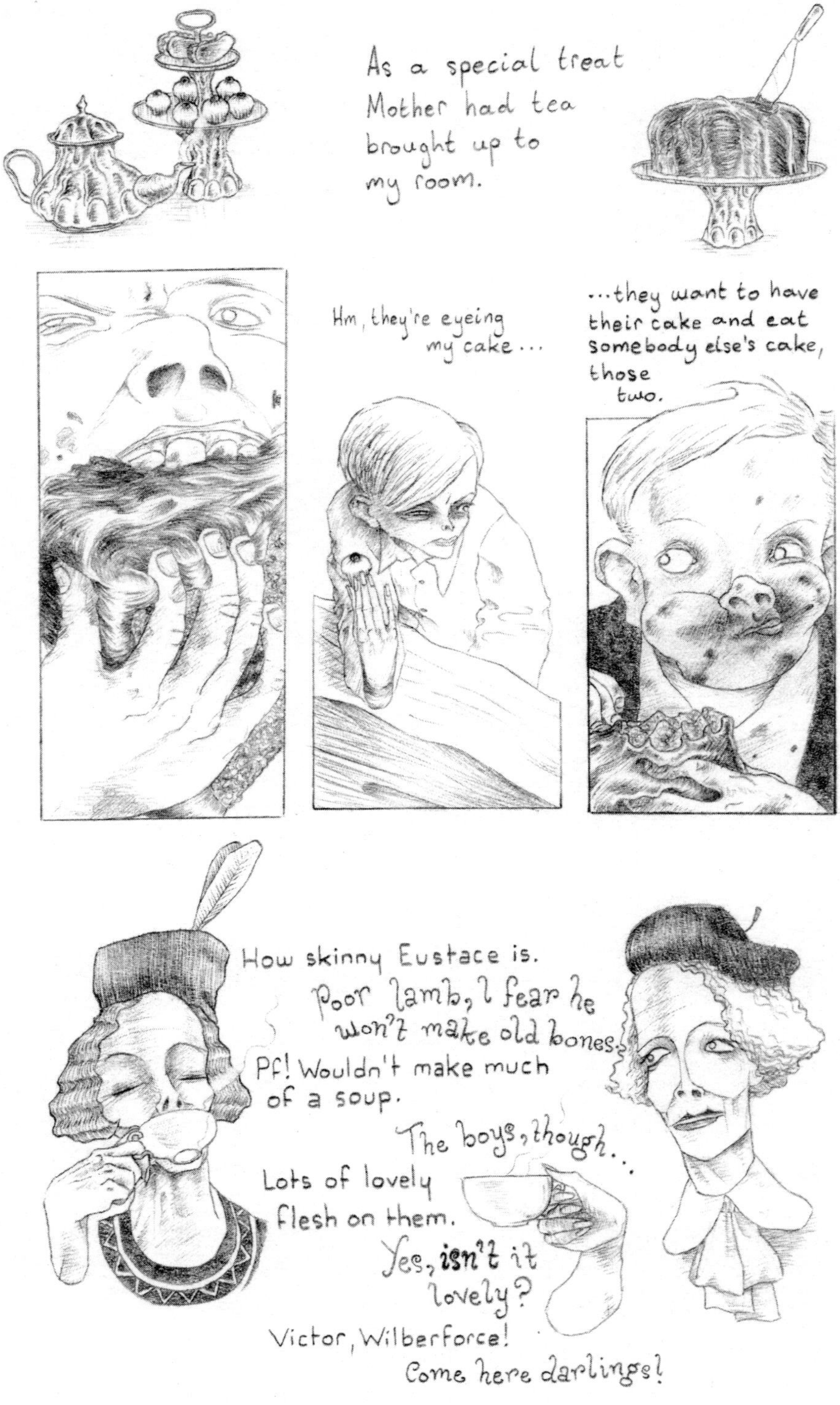
As a special treat Mother had tea brought up to my room.
Hm, they're eyeing my cake...
...they want to have their cake and eat somebody else's cake, those two.
How skinny Eustace is.
Poor lamb, I fear he won't make old bones.
Pf! Wouldn't make much of a soup.
The boys, though...
Lots of lovely flesh on them.
Yes, isn't it lovely?
Victor, Wilberforce! Come here darlings!

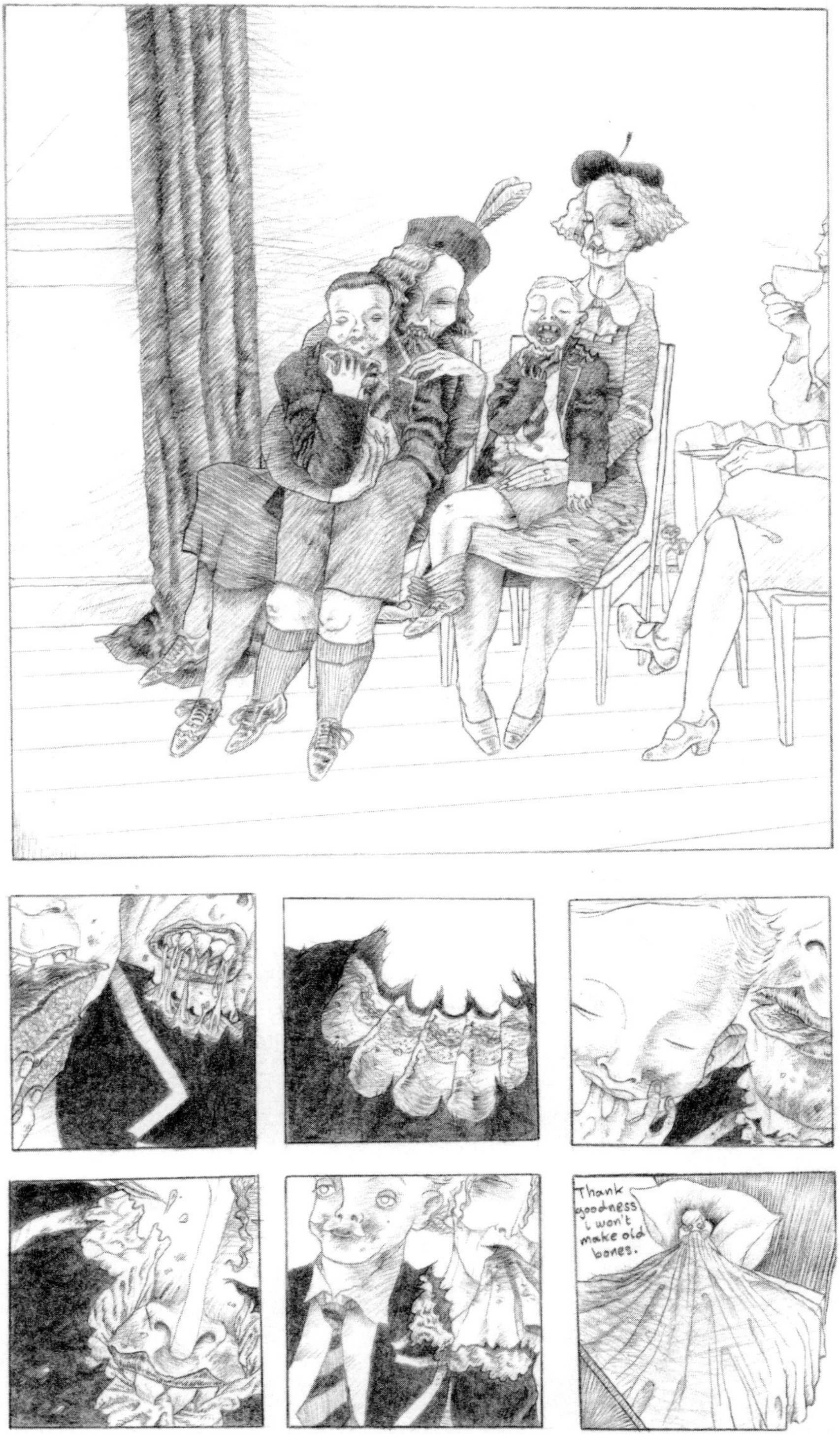
Thank goodness I won't make old bones.

Many things about the Aunties suddenly became clear...

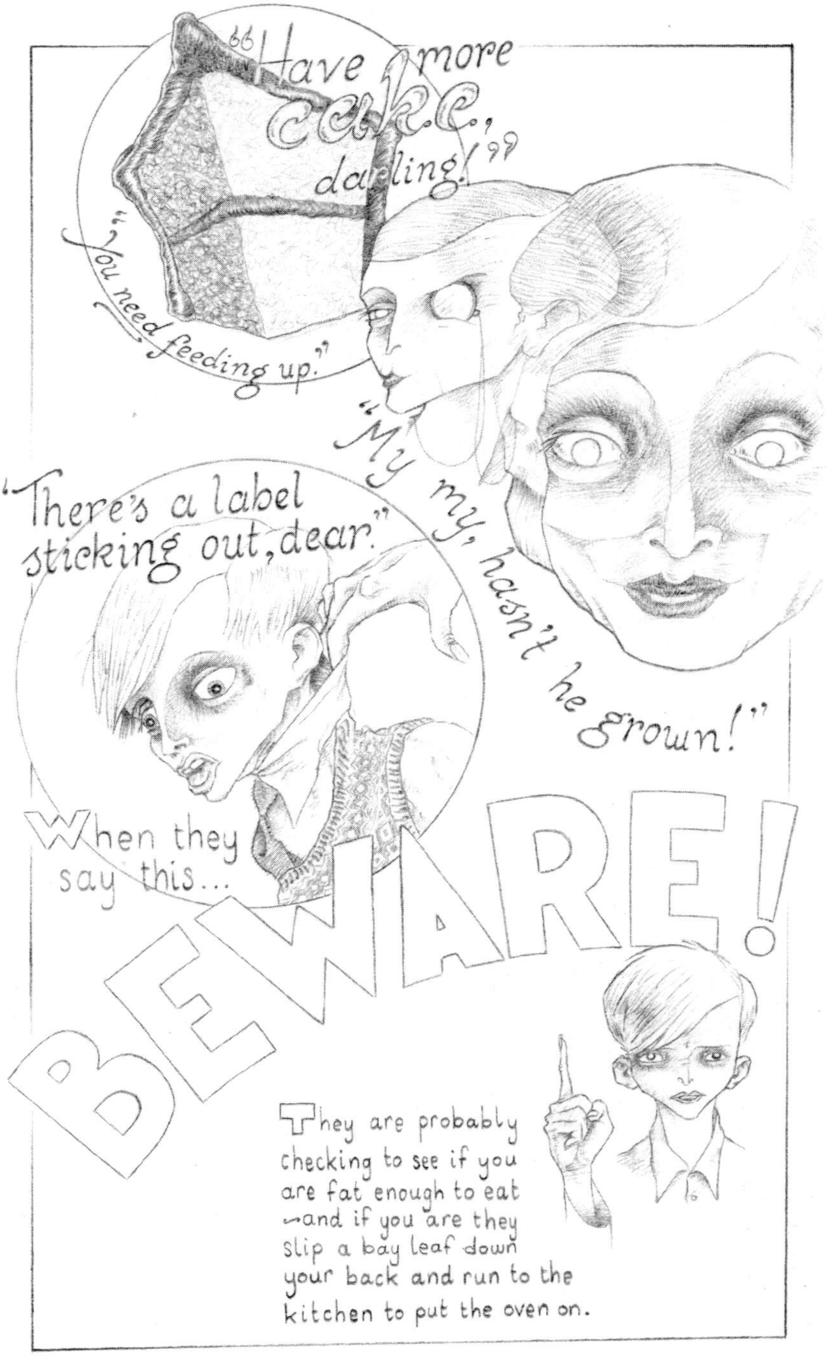
"Have more cake, darling!"
"You need feeding up."
"My my, hasn't he grown!"
"There's a label sticking out, dear."
When they say this...
BEWARE!
They are probably checking to see if you are fat enough to eat – and if you are they slip a bay leaf down your back and run to the kitchen to put the oven on.

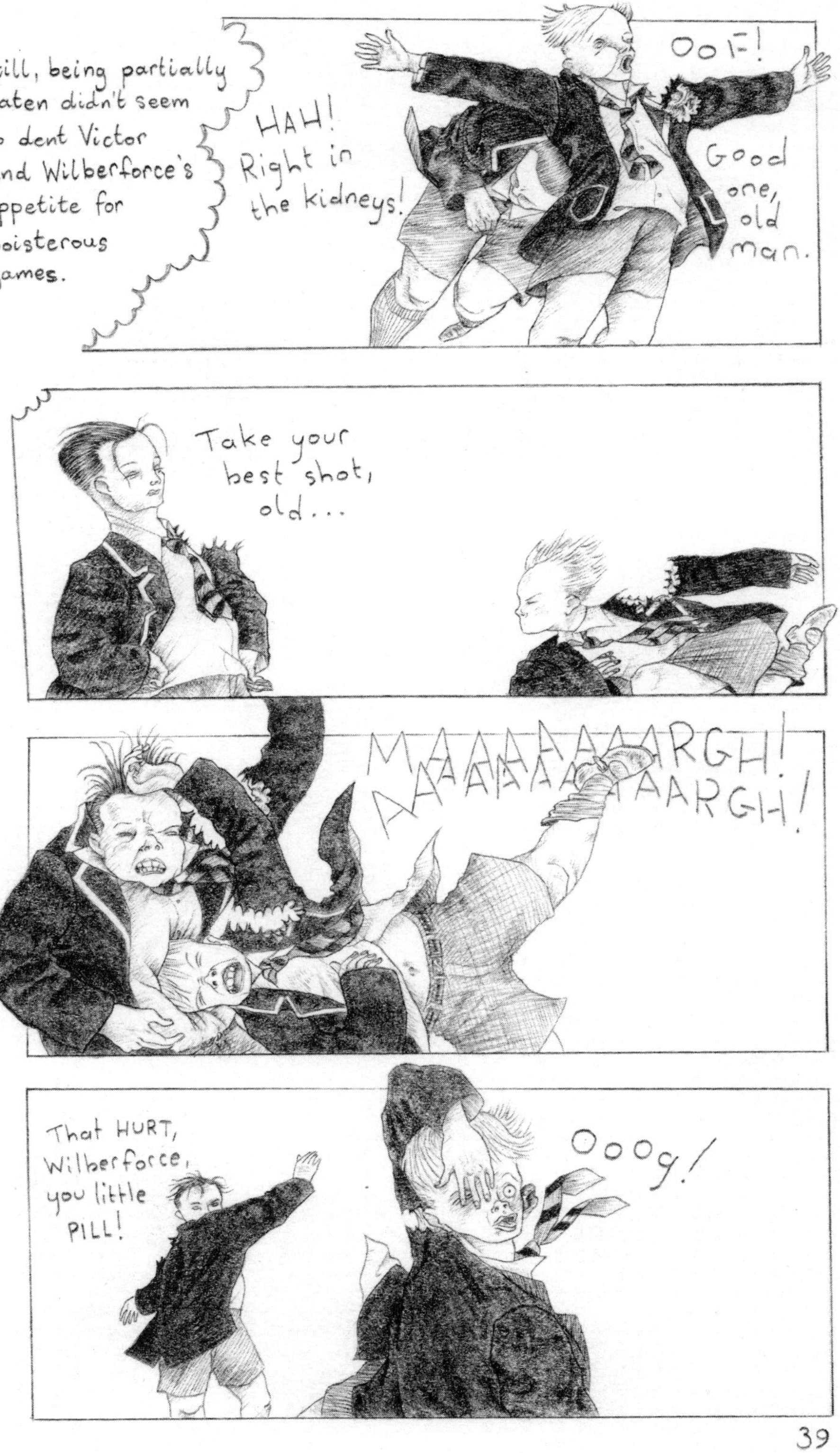

Still, being partially eaten didn't seem to dent Victor and Wilberforce's appetite for boisterous games.
HAH! Right in the kidneys!
OOF!
Good one, old man.
Take your best shot, old...
MAAAAAAARGH!
AAAAAAAAAARGH!
That HURT, Wilberforce, you little PILL!
Ooog!

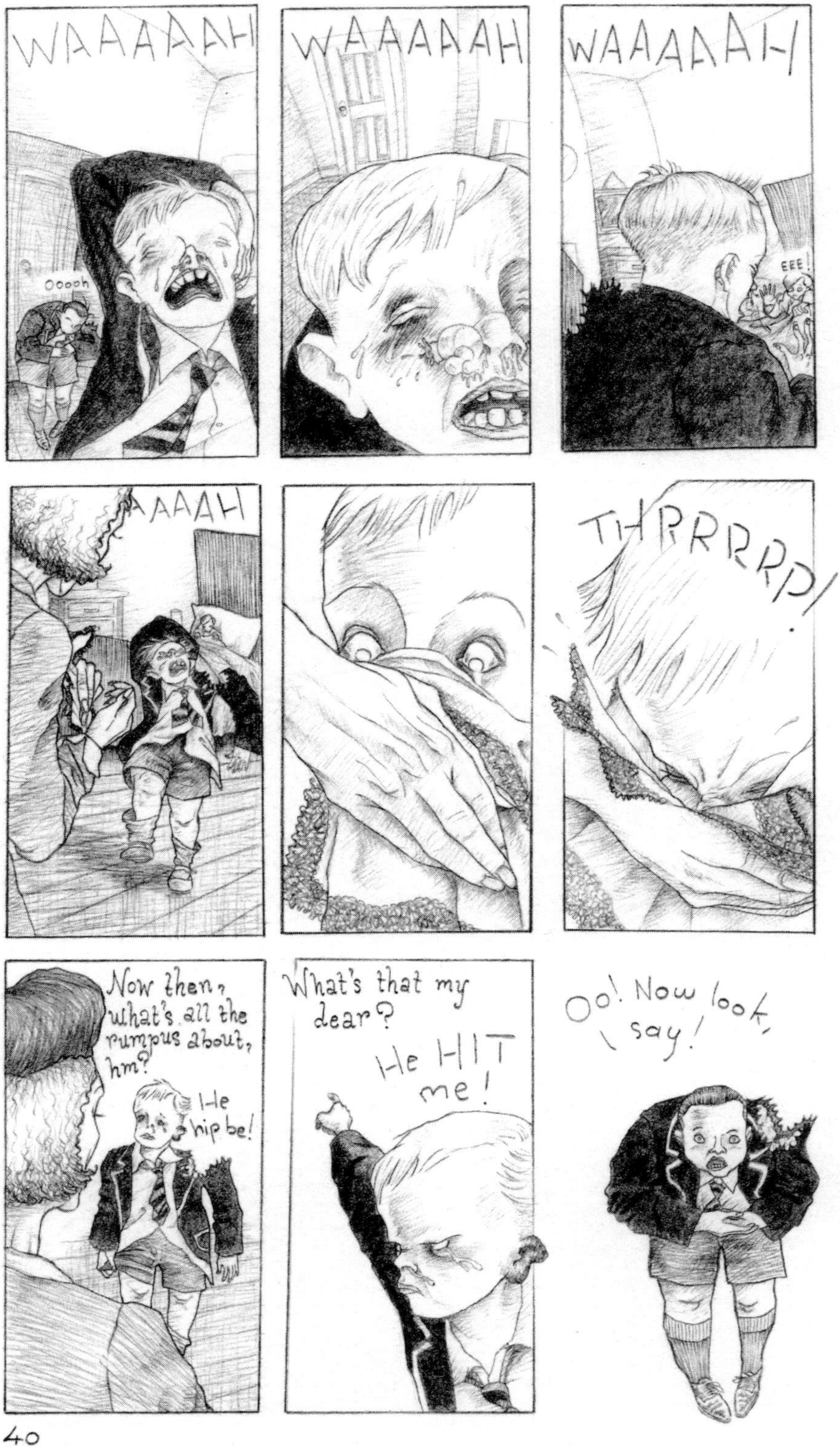
WAAAAAH
Ooooh
WAAAAAH
WAAAAAH
EEE!
AAAAH
THRRRRP!
Now then, what's all the rumpus about, hm?
He hip be!
What's that my dear?
He HIT me!
Oo! Now look, I say!

He hit me he hit me!

VICTOR! How dare you strike this child?

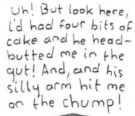

Uh! But look here, I'd had four bits of cake and he head-butted me in the gut! And, and his silly arm hit me on the chump!

Don't tell me to look here! YOU'RE MEANT TO SAY 'GOOD ONE OLD MAN!' ...like a man!

snrffll, blib blib blib...

...blup.

41

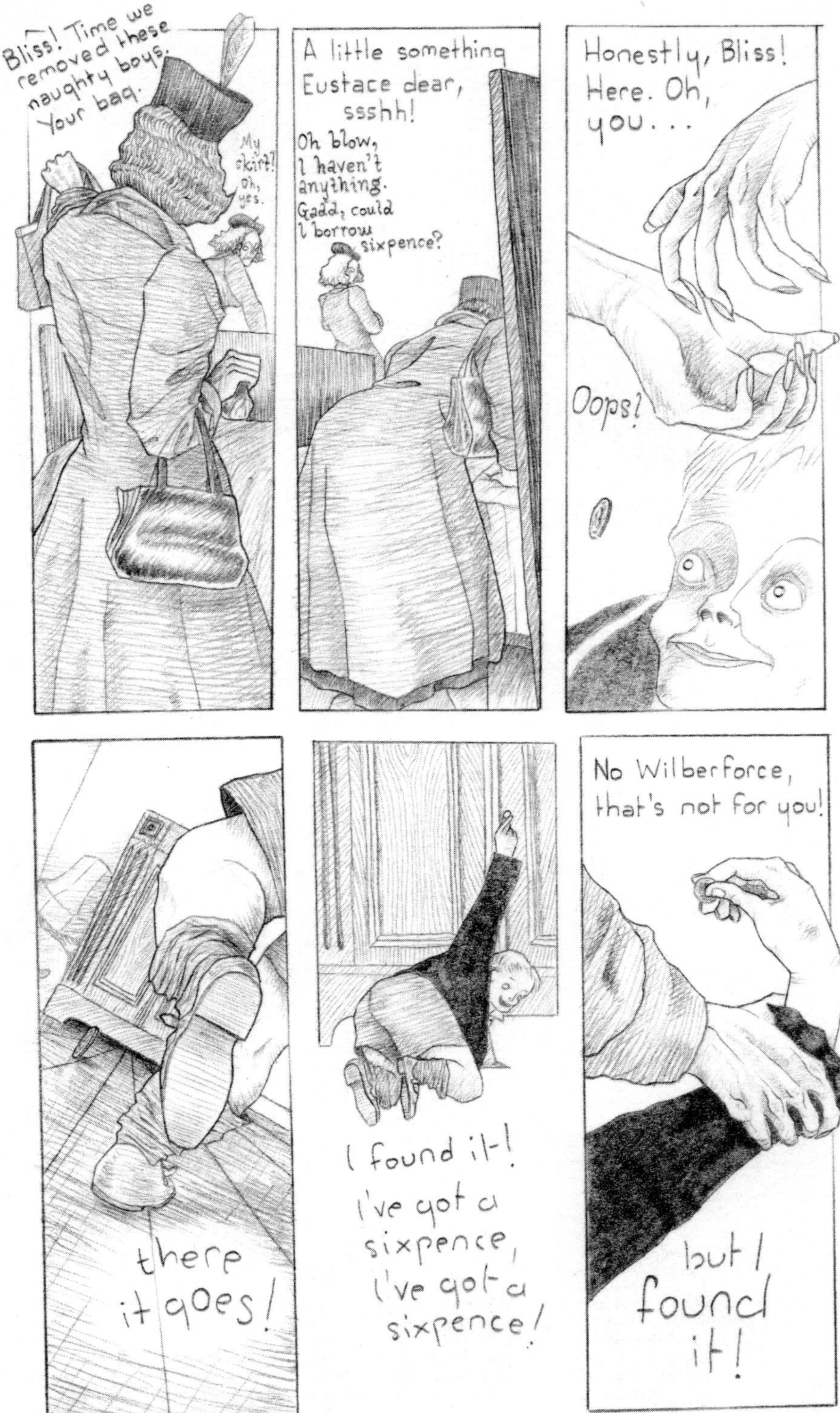
Bliss! Time we removed these naughty boys. Your bag.
My skirt? Oh, yes.
A little something Eustace dear, ssshh!
Oh blow, I haven't anything. Gadd, could I borrow sixpence?
Honestly, Bliss! Here. Oh, you...
Oops?
there it goes!
I found it! I've got a sixpence, I've got a sixpence!
No Wilberforce, that's not for you!
but I found it!

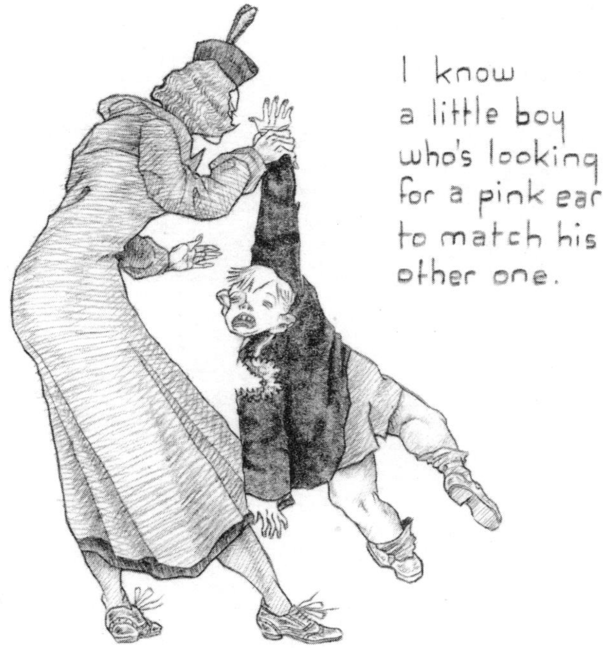
I know
a little boy
who's looking
for a pink ear
to match his
other one.

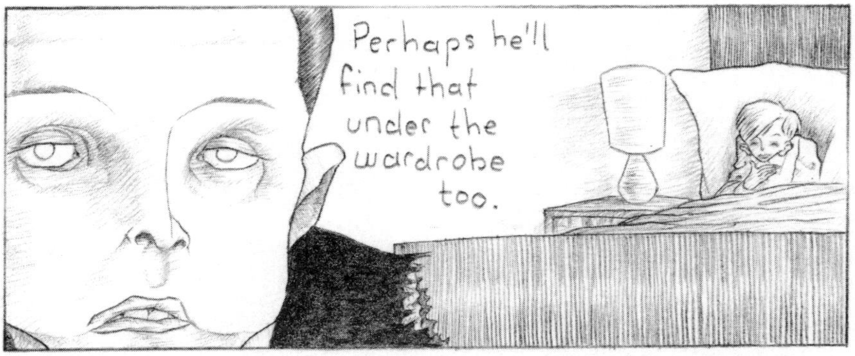
Perhaps he'll
find that
under the
wardrobe
too.

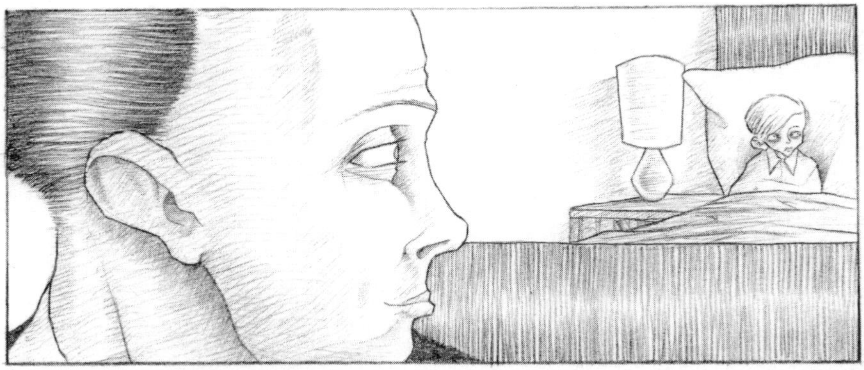

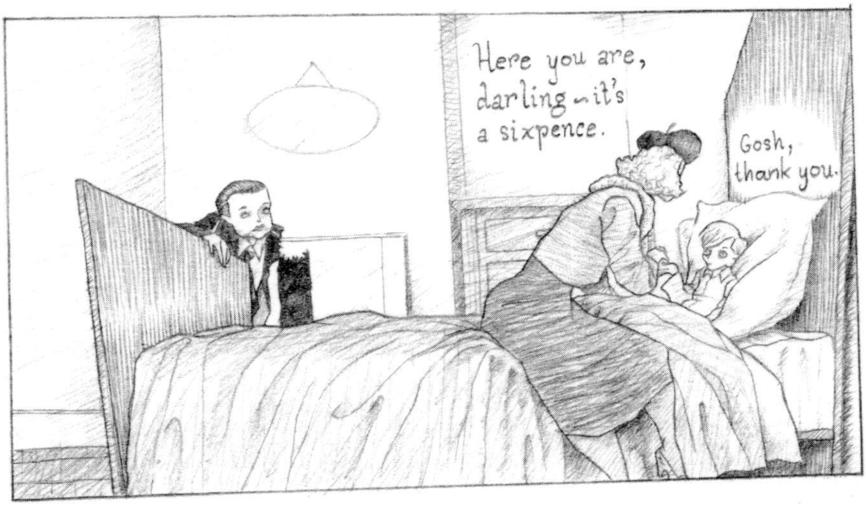
Here you are, darling – it's a sixpence.
Gosh, thank you.

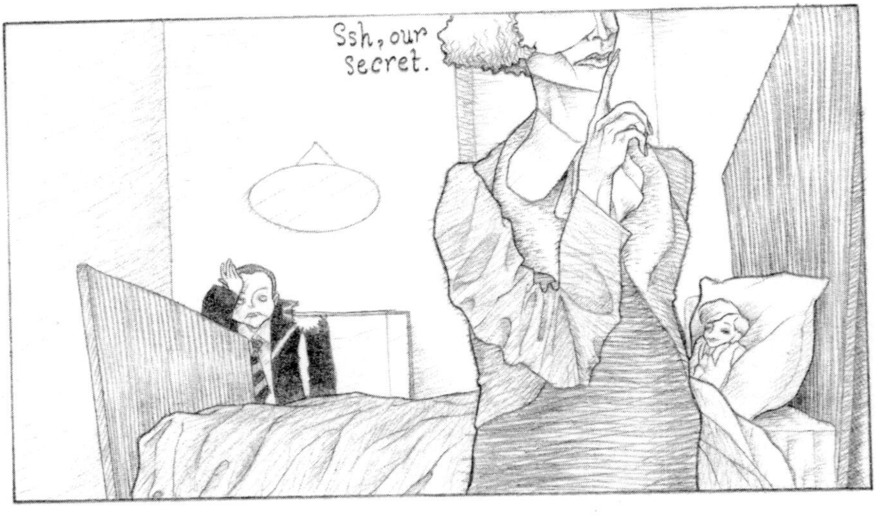
Ssh, our secret.

Then suddenly, within about half an hour they were gone.

I don't know if the Aunties ever finished Victor and Wilberforce.

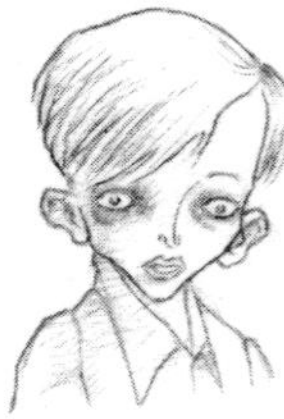

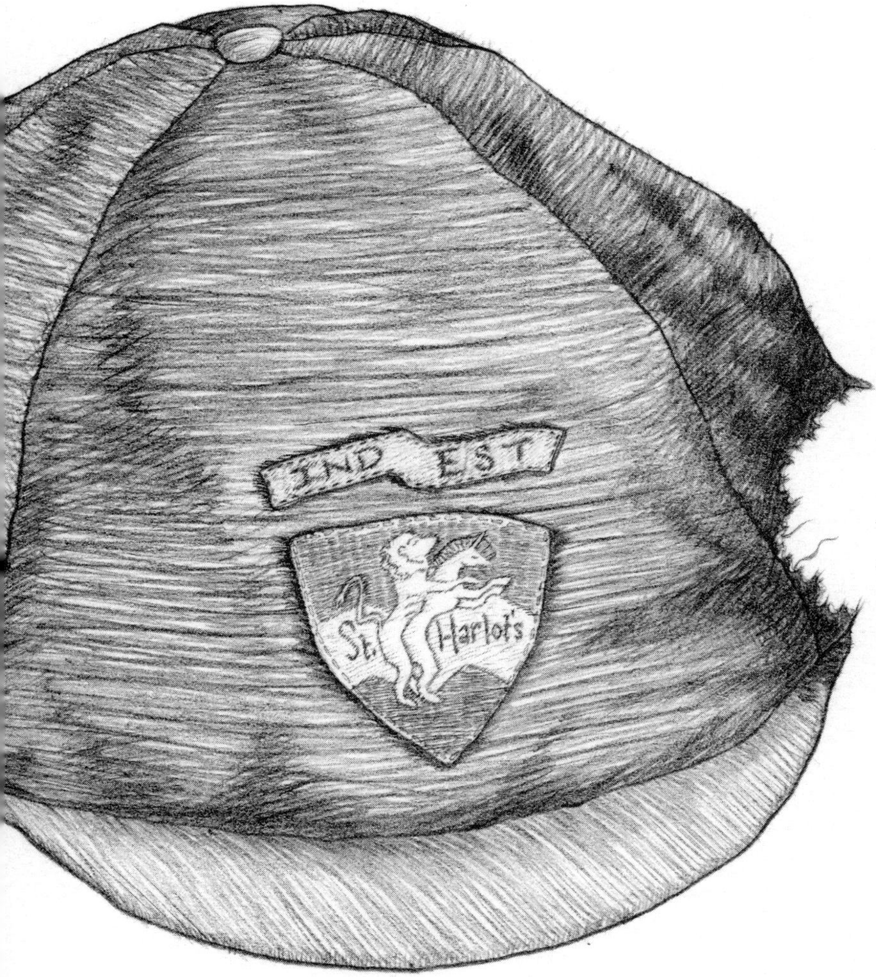
St. Harlot's

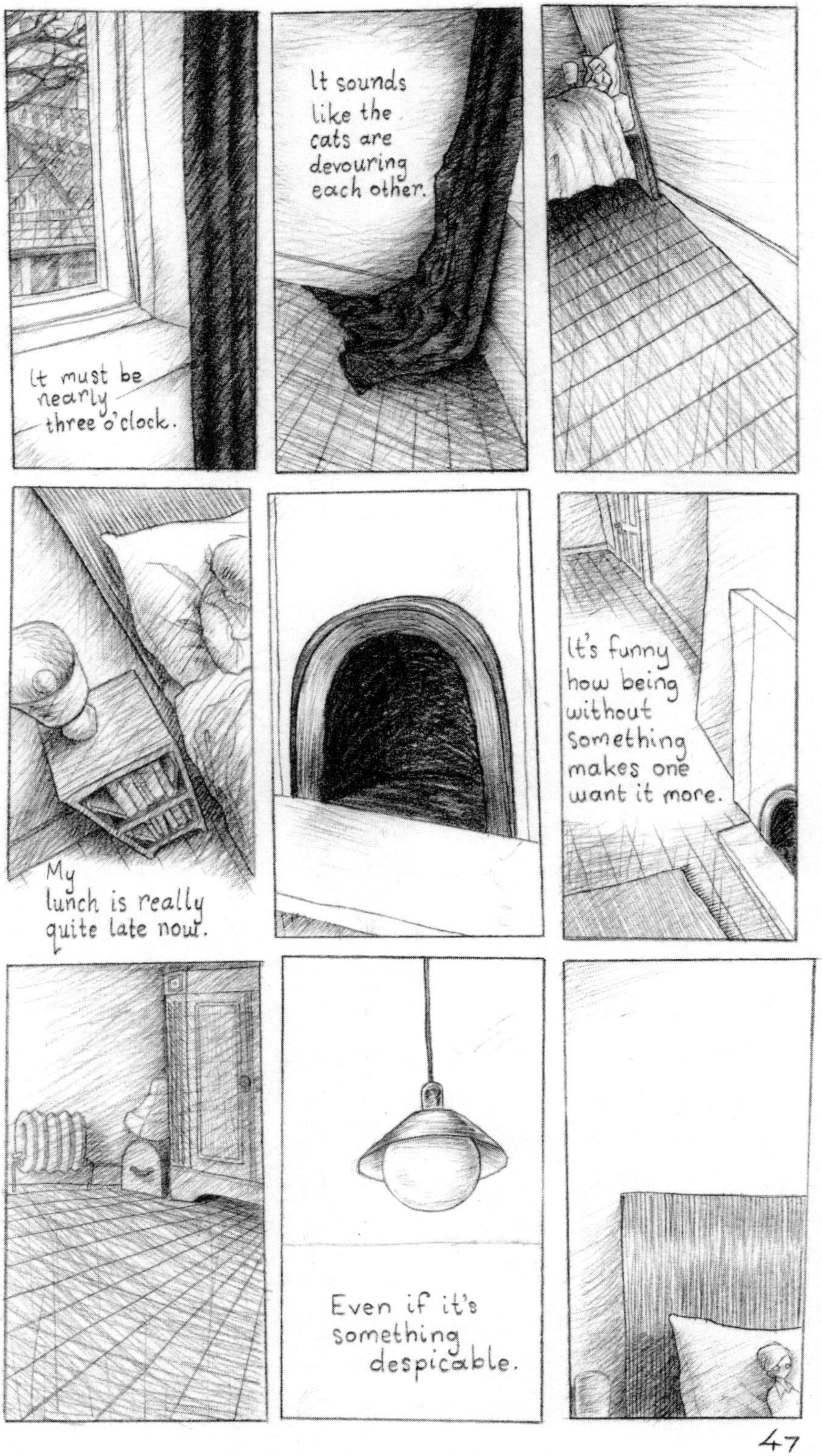
It must be nearly three o'clock.
It sounds like the cats are devouring each other.
My lunch is really quite late now.
It's funny how being without something makes one want it more.
Even if it's something despicable.

Perhaps Mother is ill.

It's not like her to be ill.

Ill-tempered, certainly.

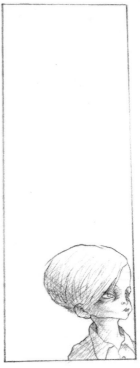

But that's just her bad nerves.

And she has medicine for those.

Now, Father...

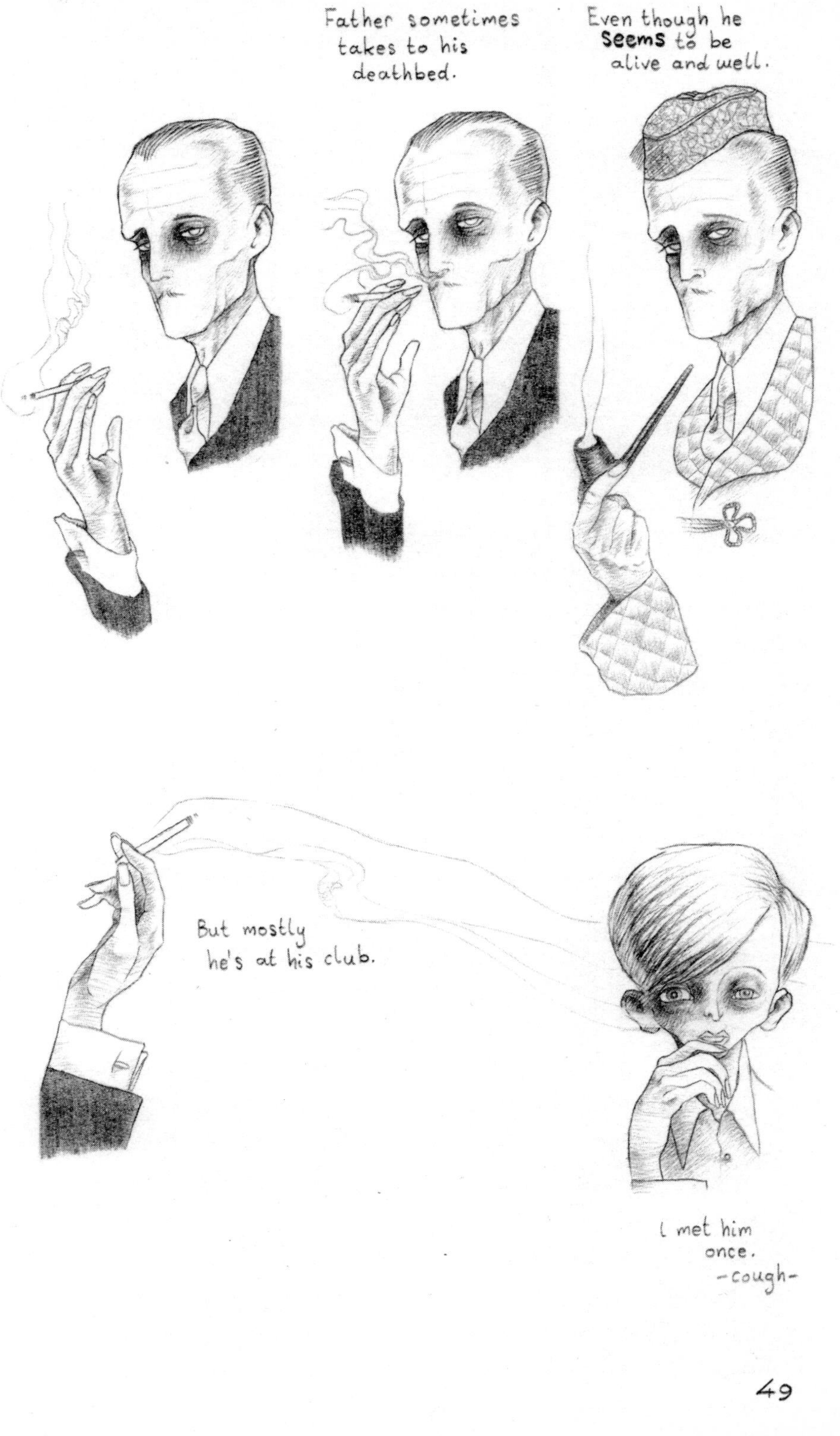
Father sometimes takes to his deathbed.
Even though he **seems** to be alive and well.
But mostly he's at his club.
I met him once.
-cough-

I was well enough to go downstairs. Mother even said she'd have Mrs Perichief bring me some cocoa in the back sitting room.

The trouble was that to get to the back sitting room...

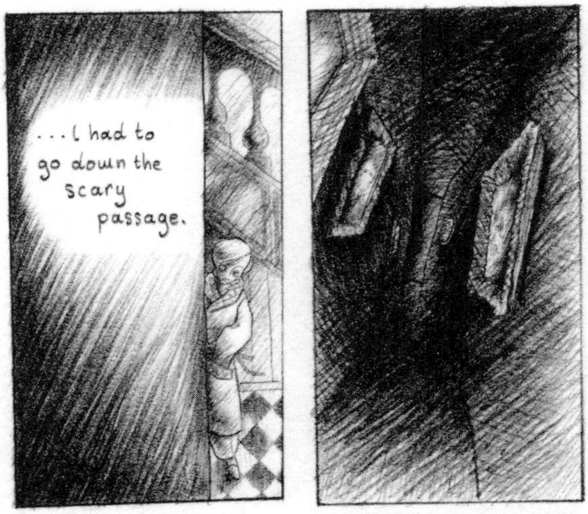
...I had to go down the scary passage.

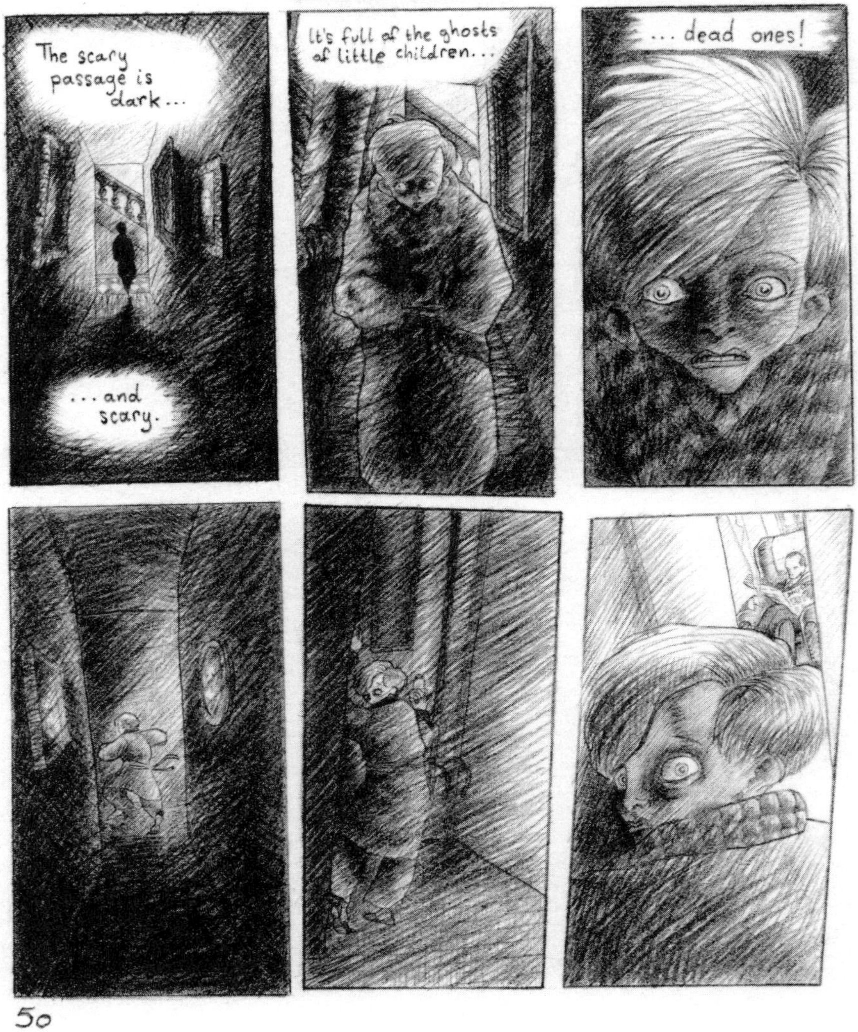
The scary passage is dark...
...and scary.
It's full of the ghosts of little children...
... dead ones!

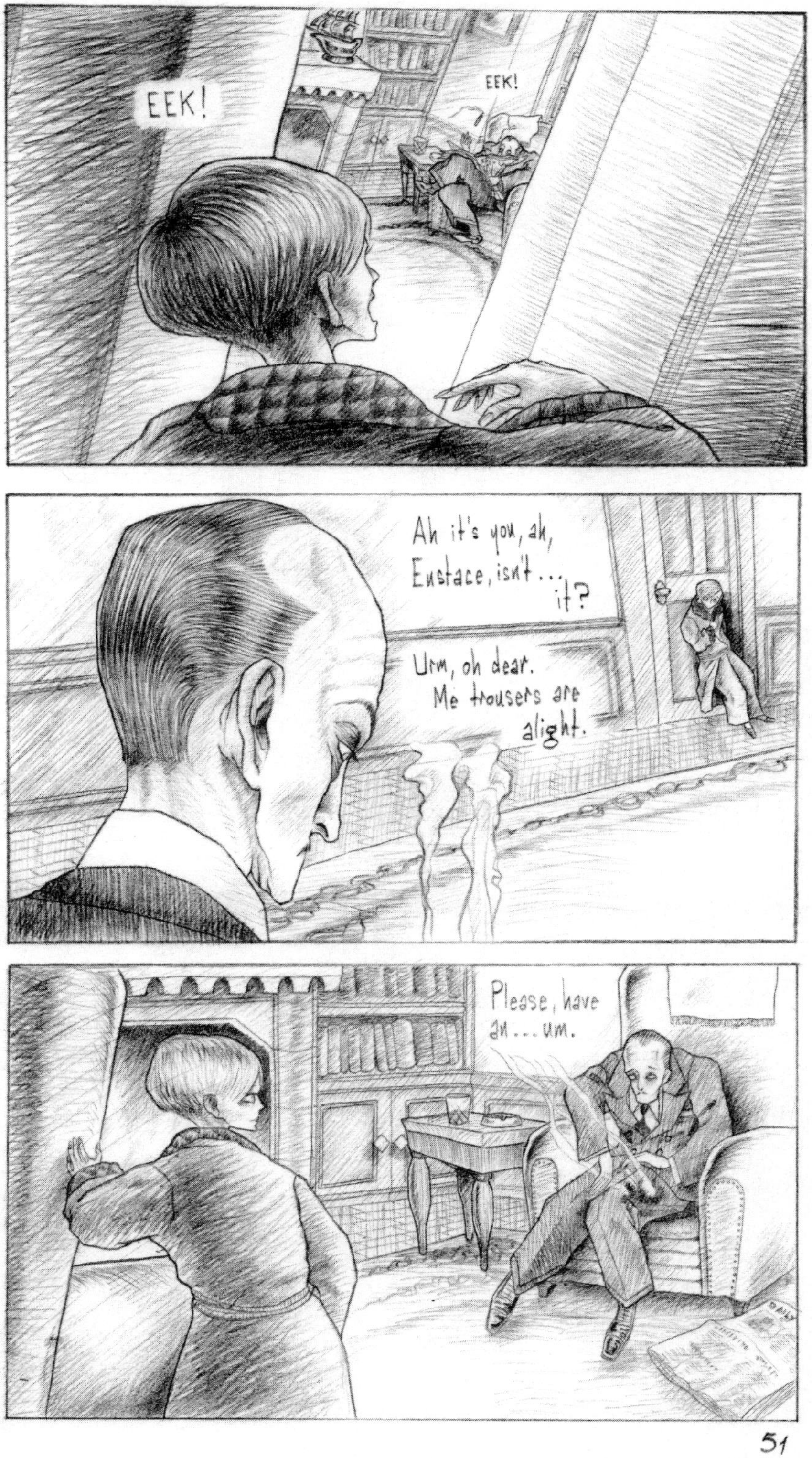
EEK!
EEK!
Ah it's you, ah, Eustace, isn't... it?
Urm, oh dear. Me trousers are alight.
Please, have an...um.

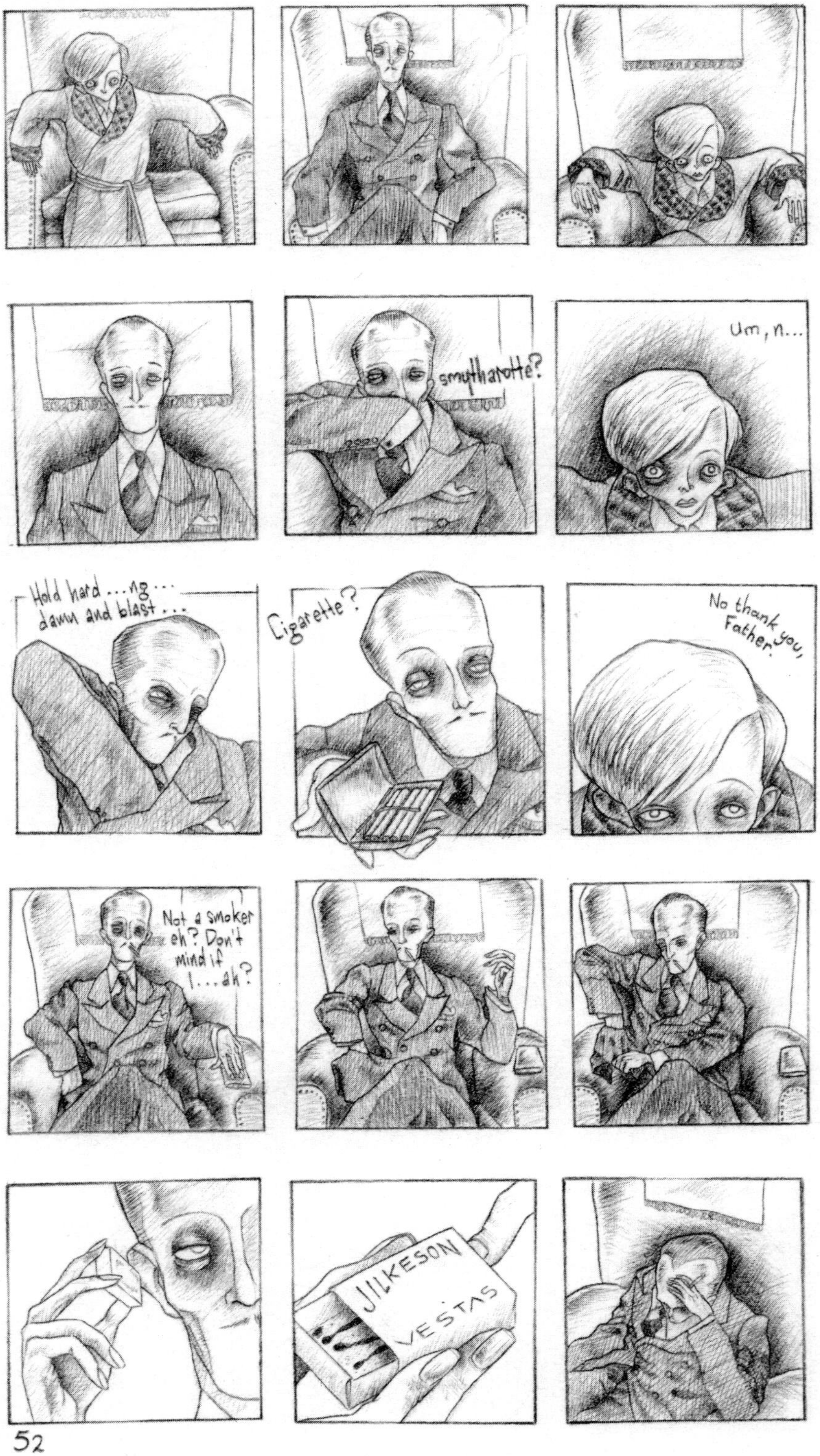
smuthharotte?
Um, n...
Hold hard ...ng ... damn and blast ...
Cigarette?
No thank you, Father.
Not a smoker eh? Don't mind if I ... ah?
JILKESON
VESTAS

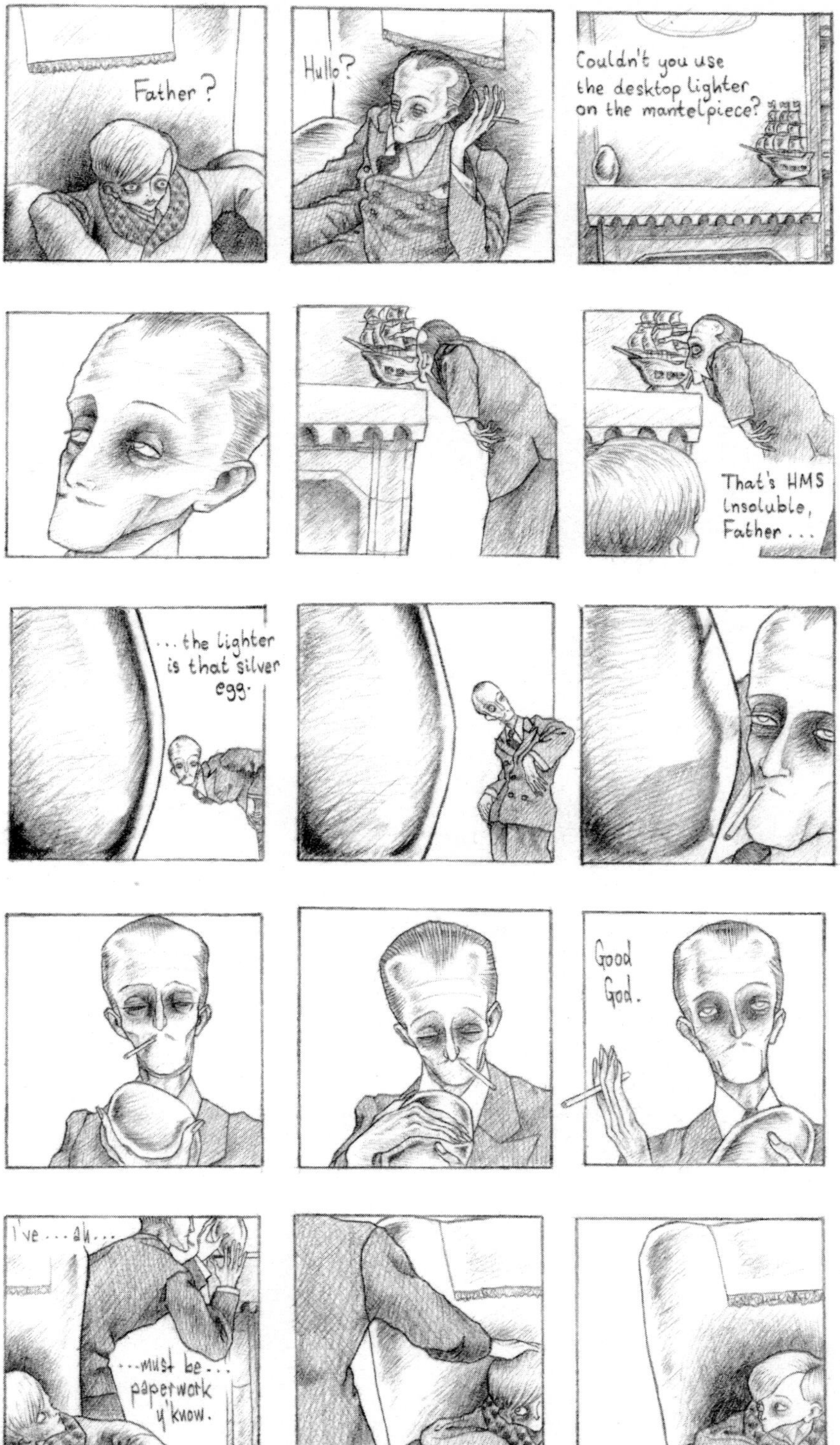
Father?
Hullo?
Couldn't you use the desktop lighter on the mantelpiece?
That's HMS Insoluble, Father...
...the lighter is that silver egg.
Good God.
I've...ah...
...must be... paperwork y'know.

After he'd gone I heard
Julian Tinkler and his
Droitwich Bambinos
playing 'Whoops Mrs
Fentiman, Didn't See
You There' coming
from the radiogram
in Father's study.

After a little while
Mrs Perichief brought
me my cocoa and
I gazed out of
the French windows
and watched the
wind blow little
old ladies across
the garden hedges.

But presently something
bad happened...

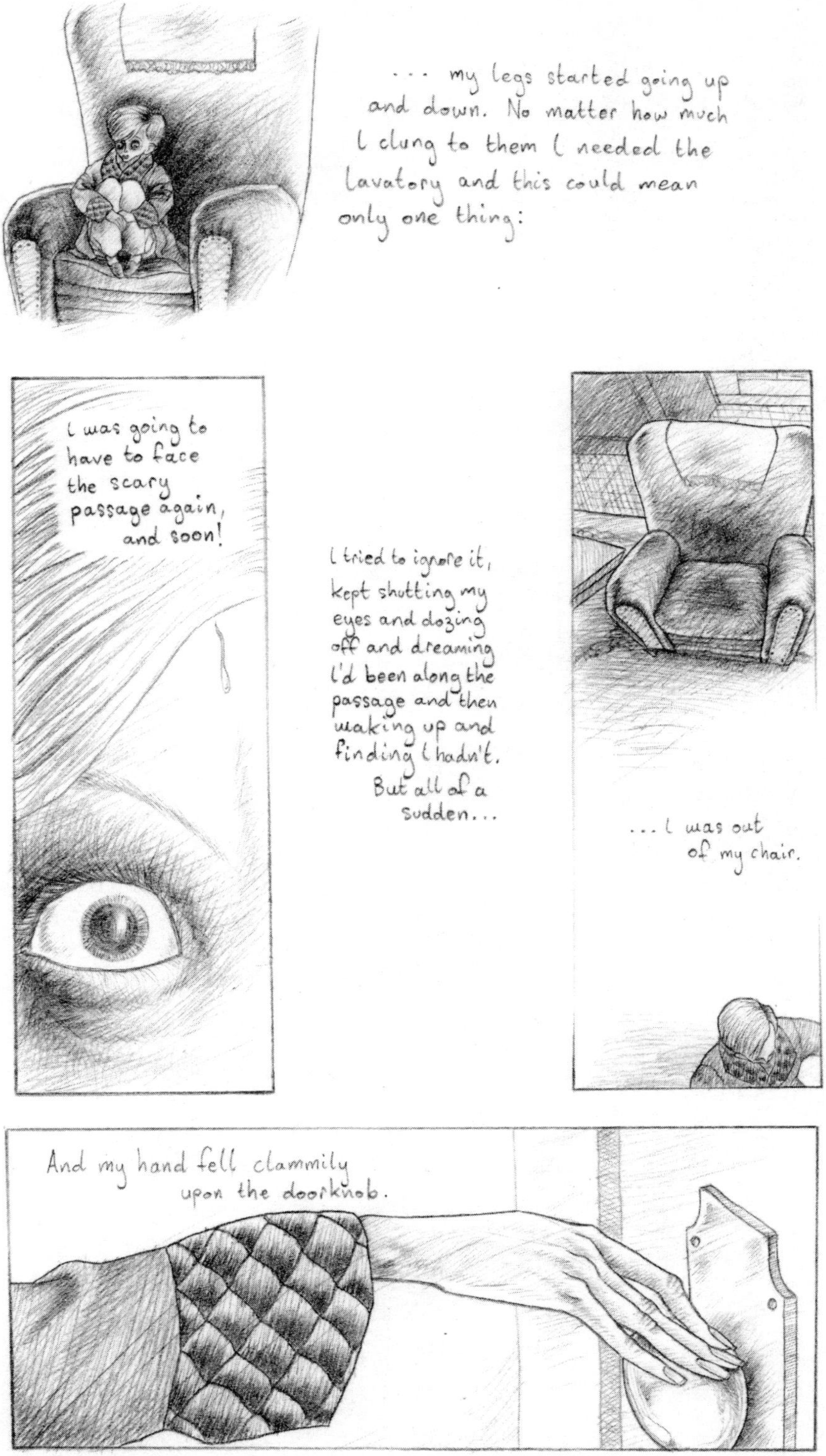
... my legs started going up and down. No matter how much I clung to them I needed the lavatory and this could mean only one thing:
I was going to have to face the scary passage again, and soon!
I tried to ignore it, kept shutting my eyes and dozing off and dreaming I'd been along the passage and then waking up and finding I hadn't. But all of a sudden...
... I was out of my chair.
And my hand fell clammily upon the doorknob.

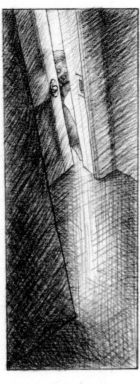

The passage looked cold and blue like a thing drowned at sea.

The portraits on the walls pretended not to look at me...

...but I knew they were only waiting.

If I could just get into the lavatory by the garden door...

Phew, made it alive!

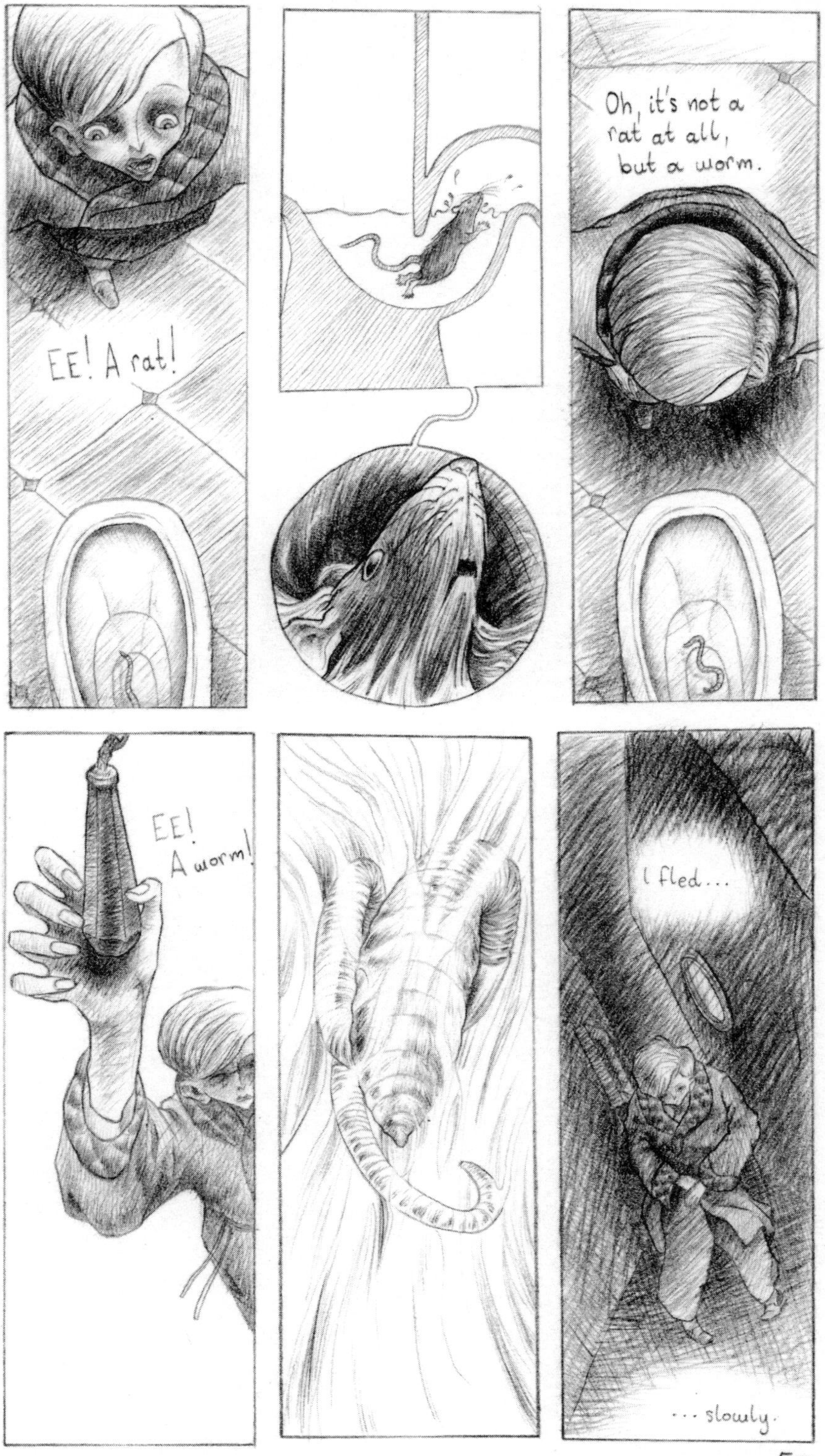
EE! A rat!
Oh, it's not a rat at all, but a worm.
EE! A worm!
I fled...
...slowly.

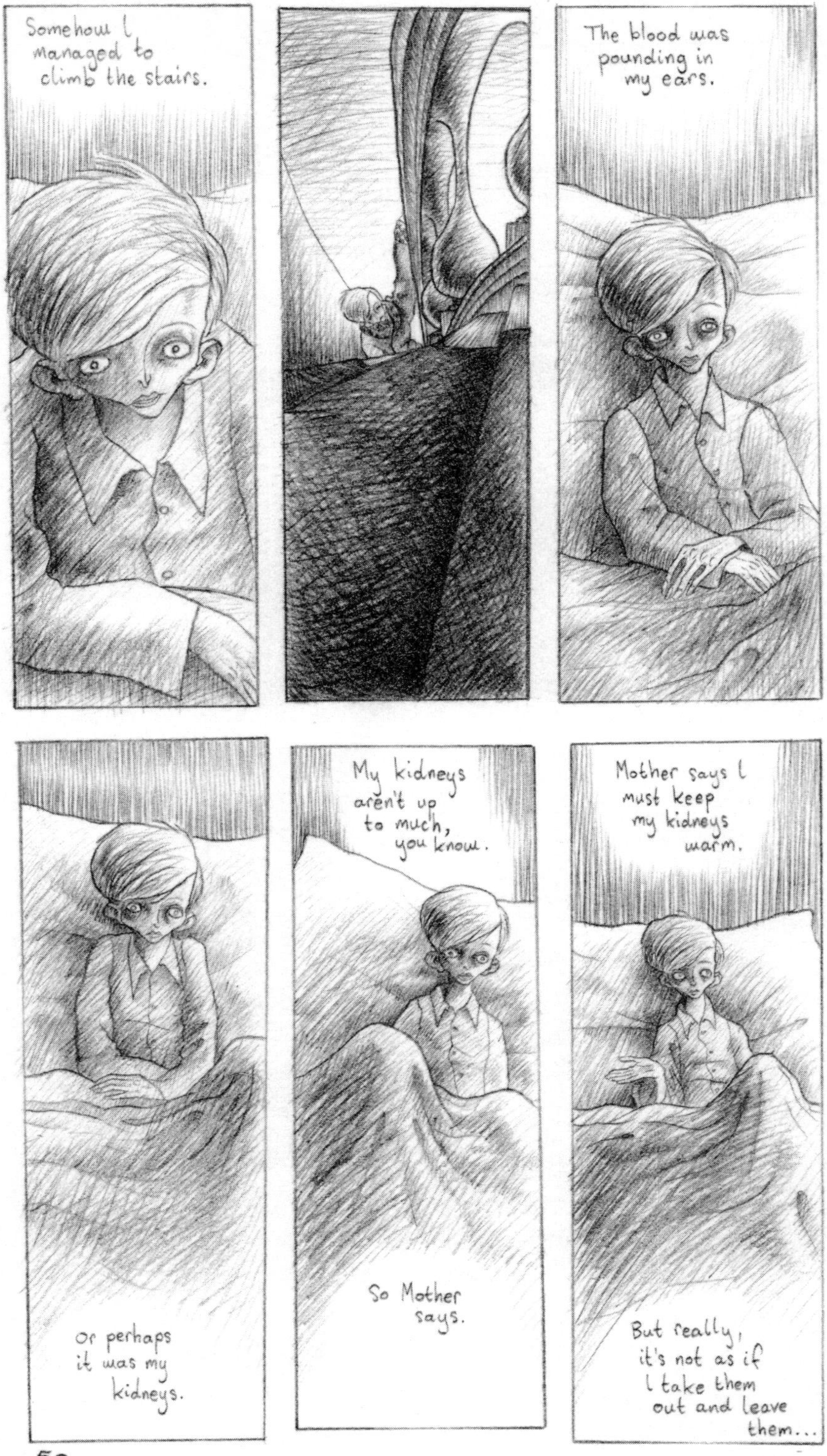
Somehow I managed to climb the stairs.
The blood was pounding in my ears.
Or perhaps it was my kidneys.
My kidneys aren't up to much, you know.
So Mother says.
Mother says I must keep my kidneys warm.
But really, it's not as if I take them out and leave them...

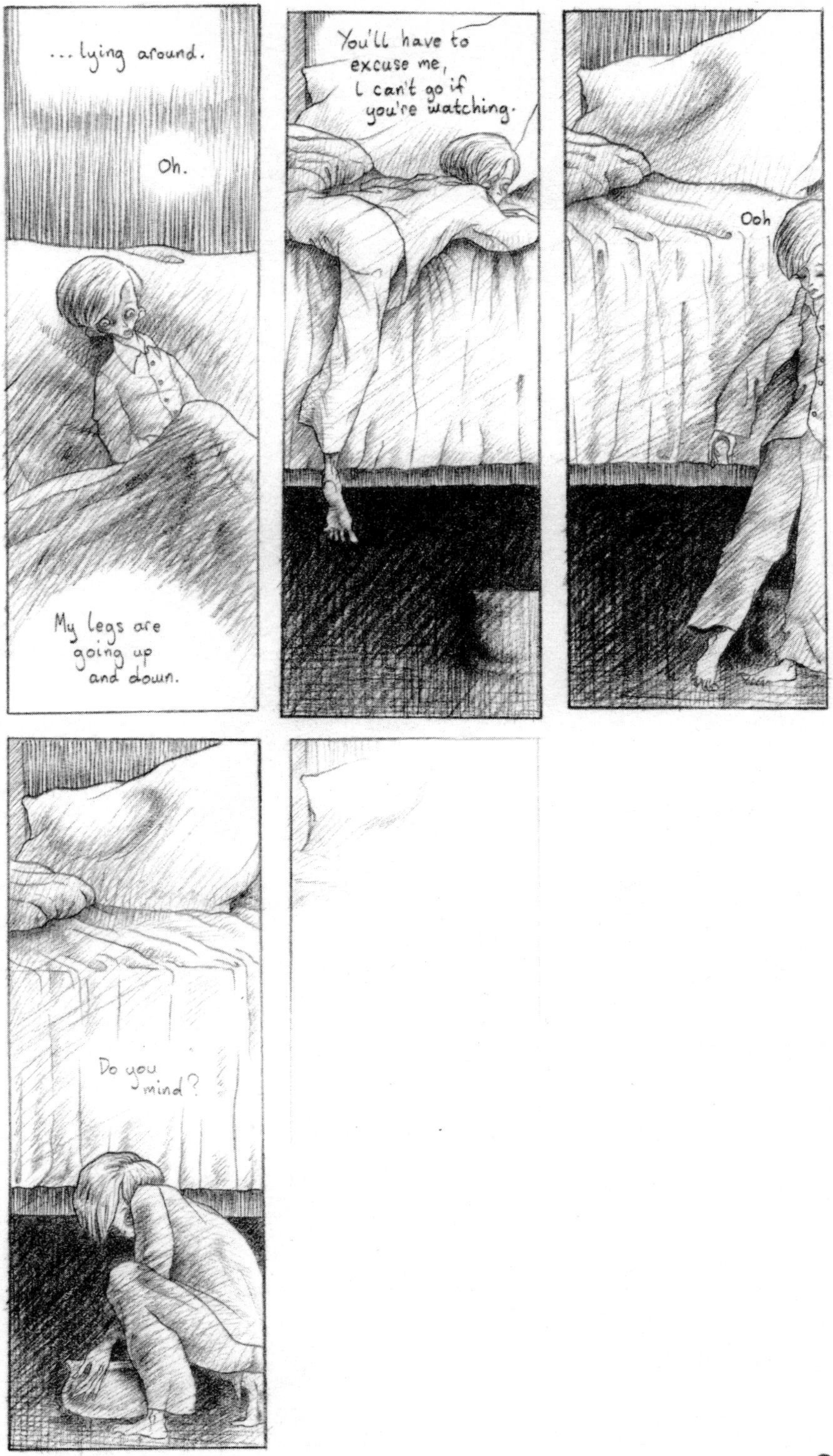
...lying around.
Oh.
My legs are going up and down.
You'll have to excuse me, I can't go if you're watching.
Ooh
Do you mind?

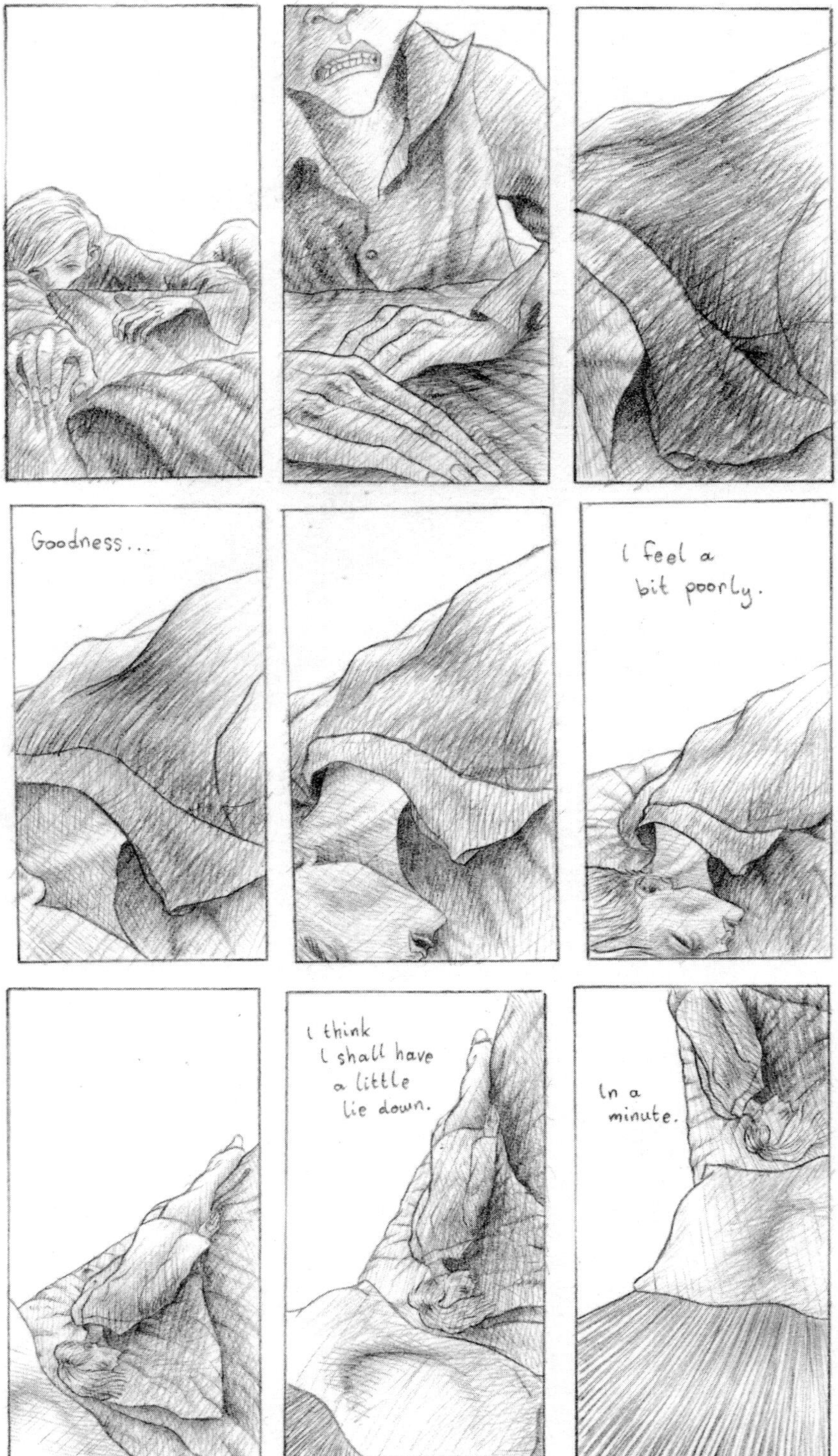
Goodness...
I feel a bit poorly.
I think I shall have a little lie down.
In a minute.

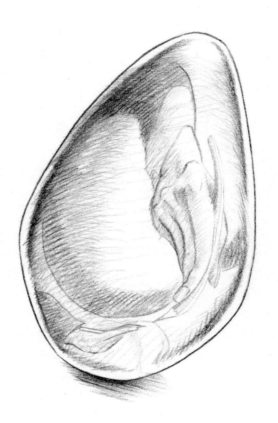

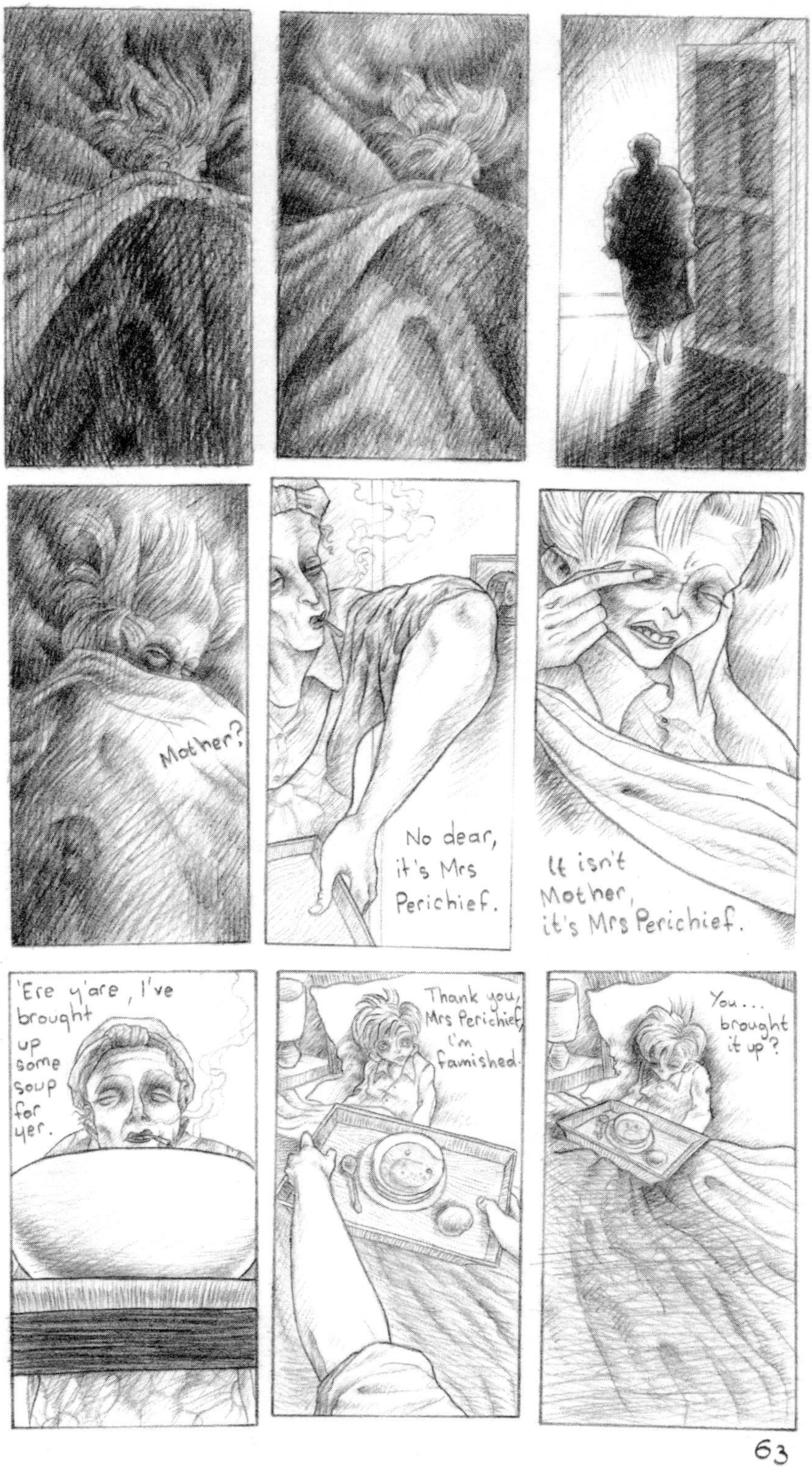
Mother?
No dear, it's Mrs Perichief.
It isn't Mother, it's Mrs Perichief.
'Ere y'are, I've brought up some soup for yer.
Thank you, Mrs Perichief, I'm famished.
You... brought it up?

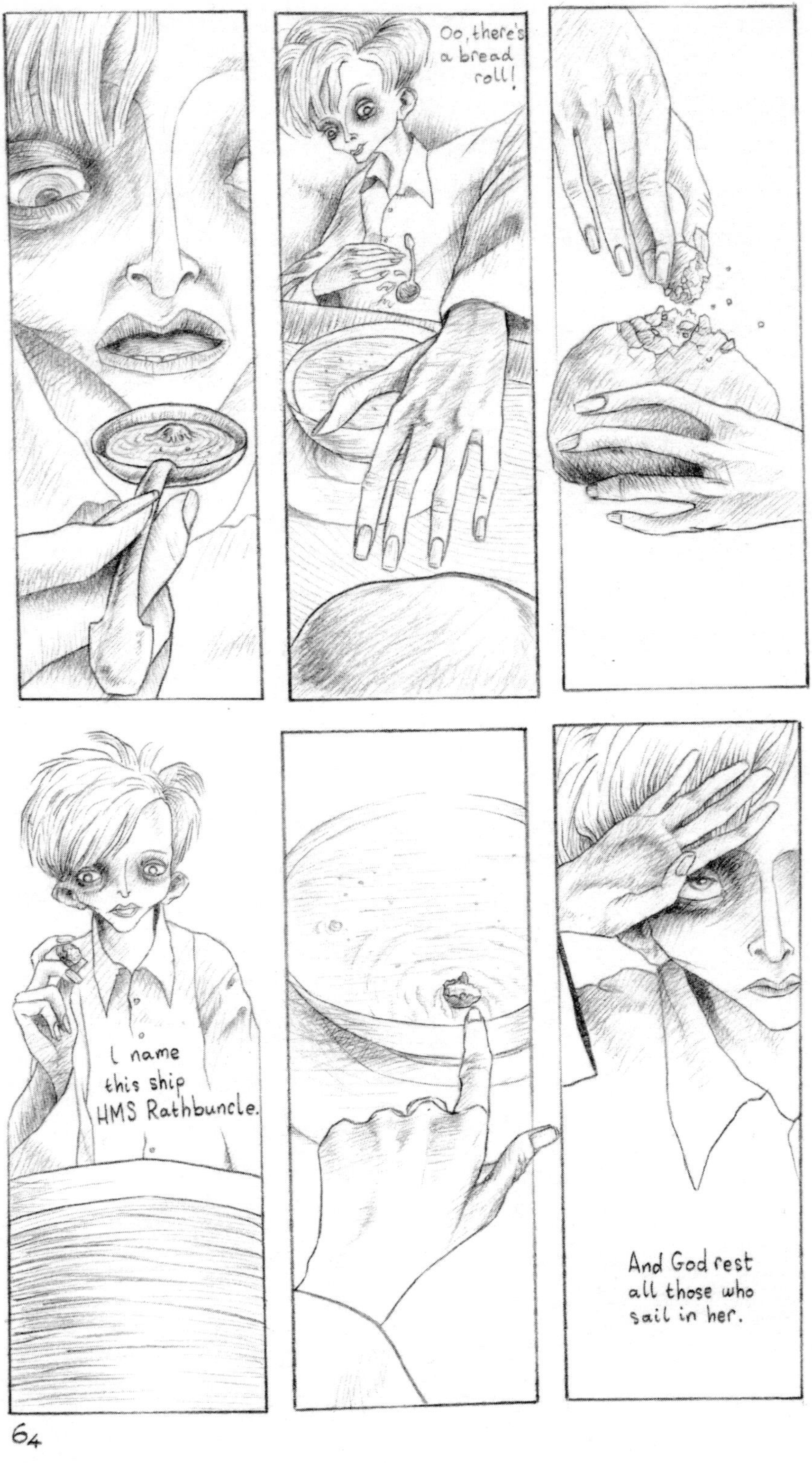
Oo, there's a bread roll!
I name this ship HMS Rathbuncle.
And God rest all those who sail in her.

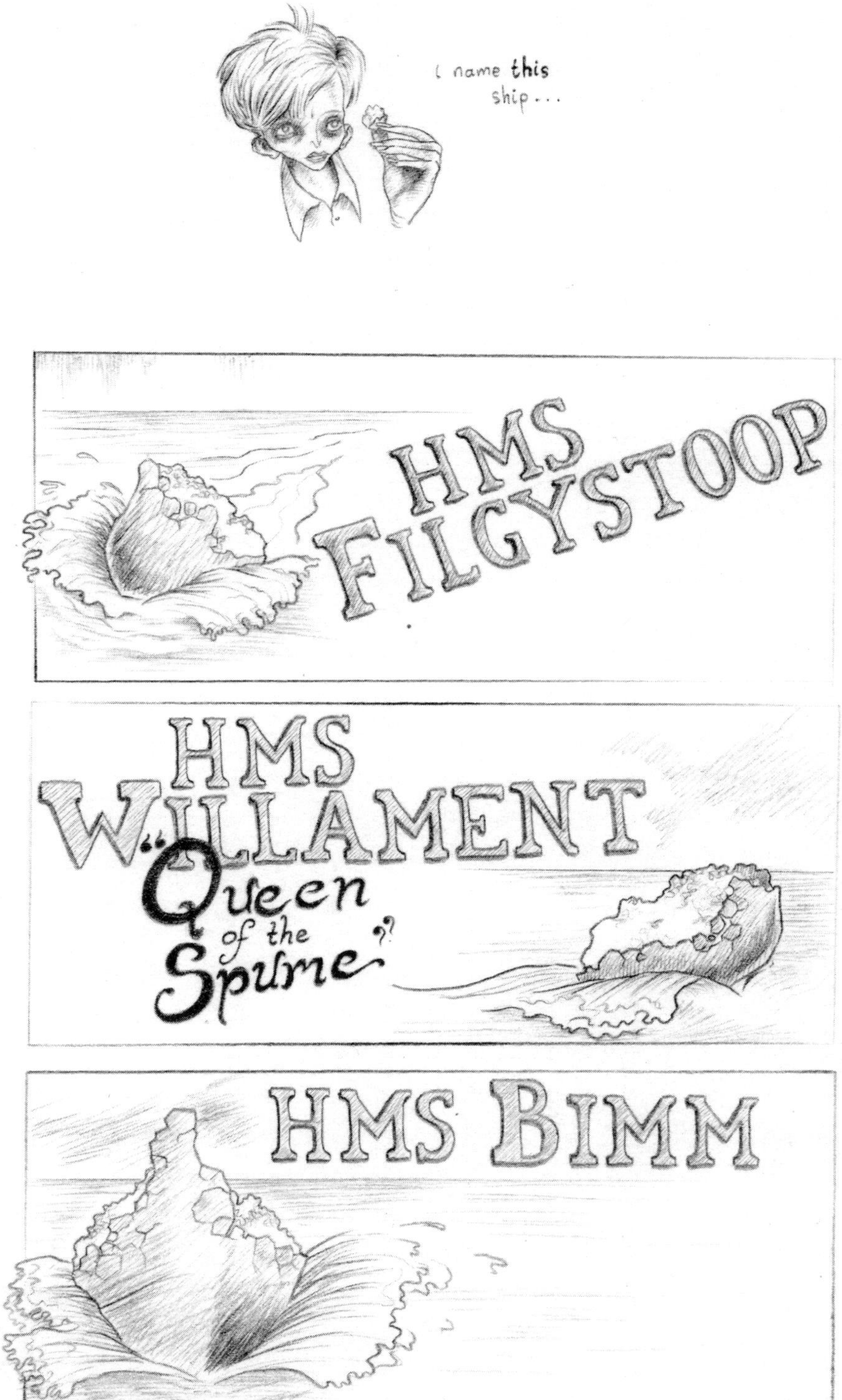

I name this ship...
HMS FILGYSTOOP
HMS WILLAMENT
"Queen of the Spume"
HMS BIMM

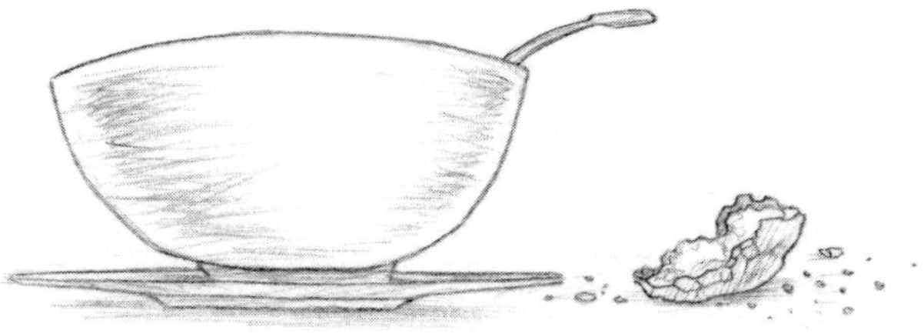

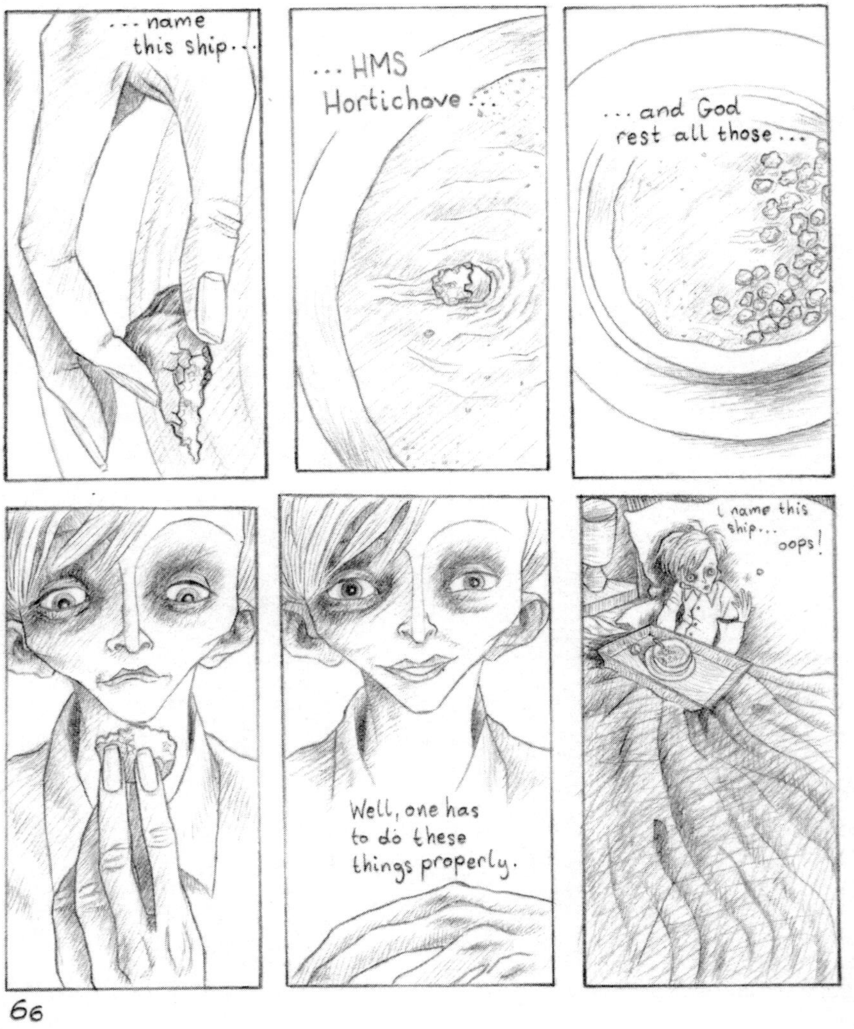
...name this ship...
...HMS Hortichove...
...and God rest all those...
Well, one has to do these things properly.
I name this ship... oops!

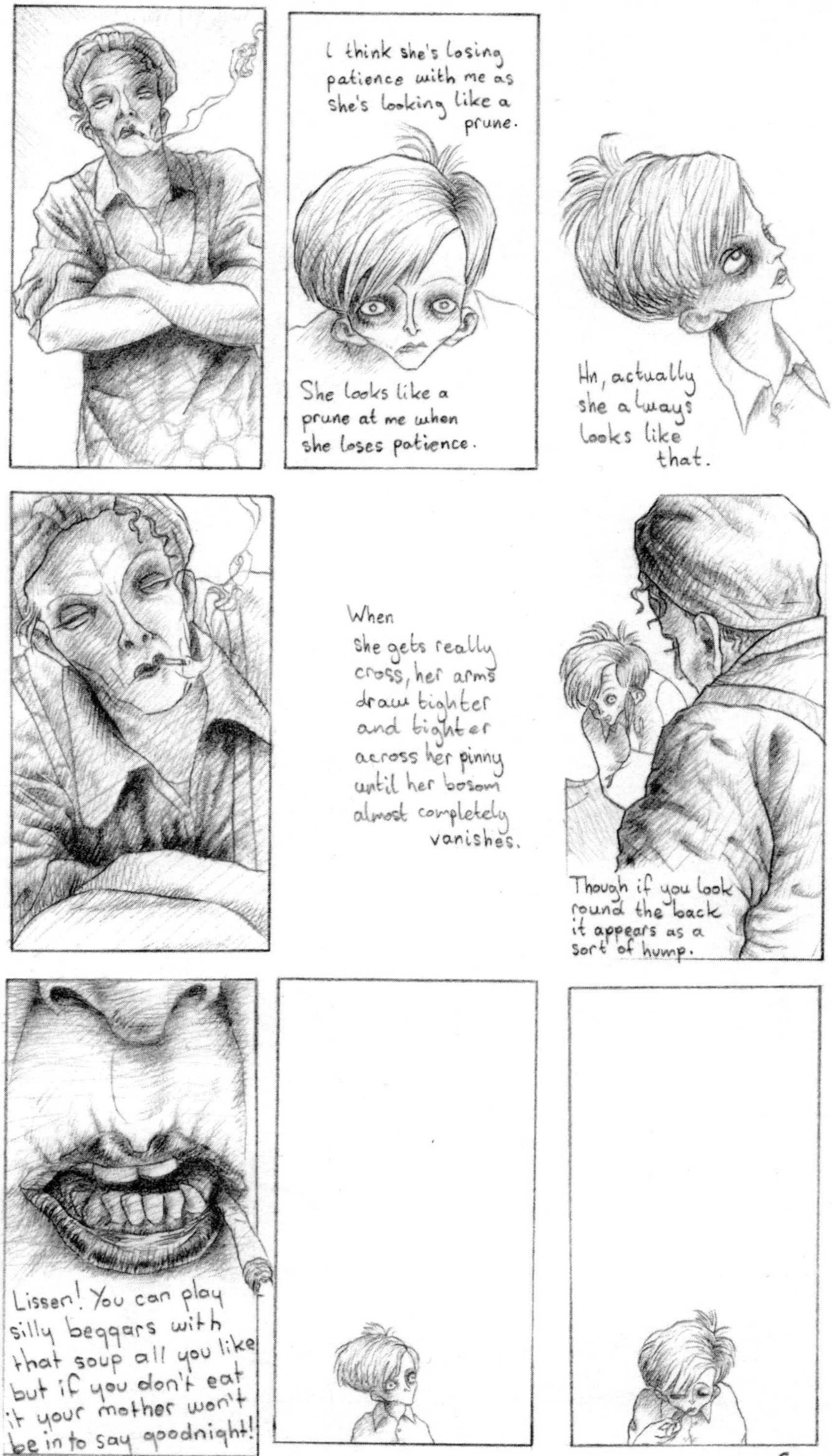
I think she's losing patience with me as she's looking like a prune.
She looks like a prune at me when she loses patience.
Hn, actually she always looks like that.
When she gets really cross, her arms draw tighter and tighter across her pinny until her bosom almost completely vanishes.
Though if you look round the back it appears as a sort of hump.
Lissen! You can play silly beggars with that soup all you like but if you don't eat it your mother won't be in to say goodnight!

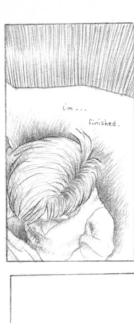

I'm...

finished.

There's just the bread roll Armada lying wrecked on the ocean floor with the loss of all souls.

God rest...

Yer not wastin' that roll.

I feel a bit poorly.

Are y'actually goin' ter be sick?

Right. 'Ere's your bucket.

Will Mother be along shortly?

I did eat all my soup.

No. Sorry dear, she went to bed with one of 'er 'eads an hour ago.

G'night dear.

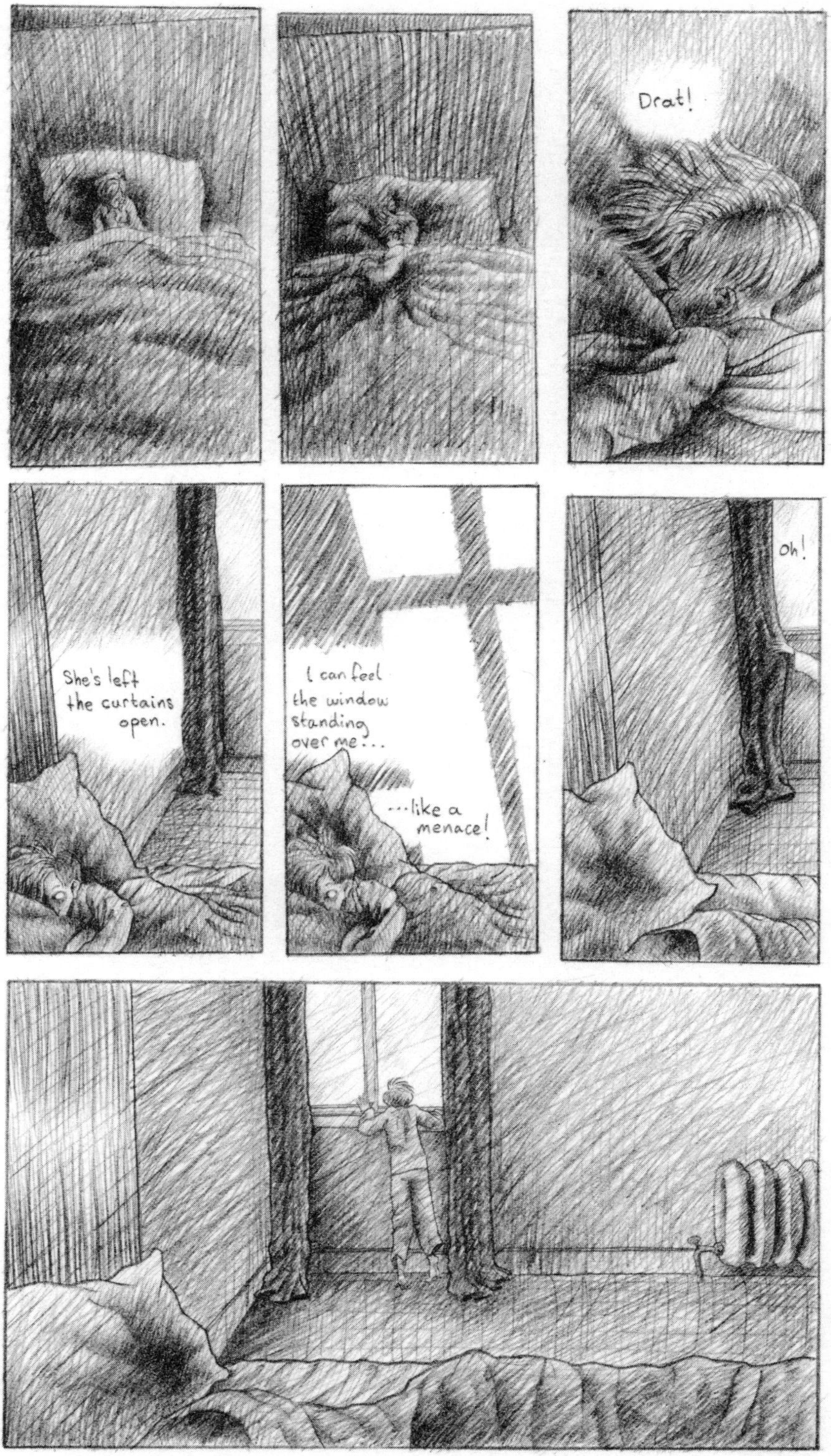
Drat!
She's left the curtains open.
I can feel the window standing over me...
...like a menace!
Oh!

The trees look like
giants' thumbprints
pressing mauve bruises
into the sky. Over
there I can see a
soup-coloured
rectangle of light,
and another the
colour of pea
soup.

I think I've stood
here too long.

   The cold sweat is
upon me ... I feel
like ... like a
damp windowpane.

   Better...
         back to...

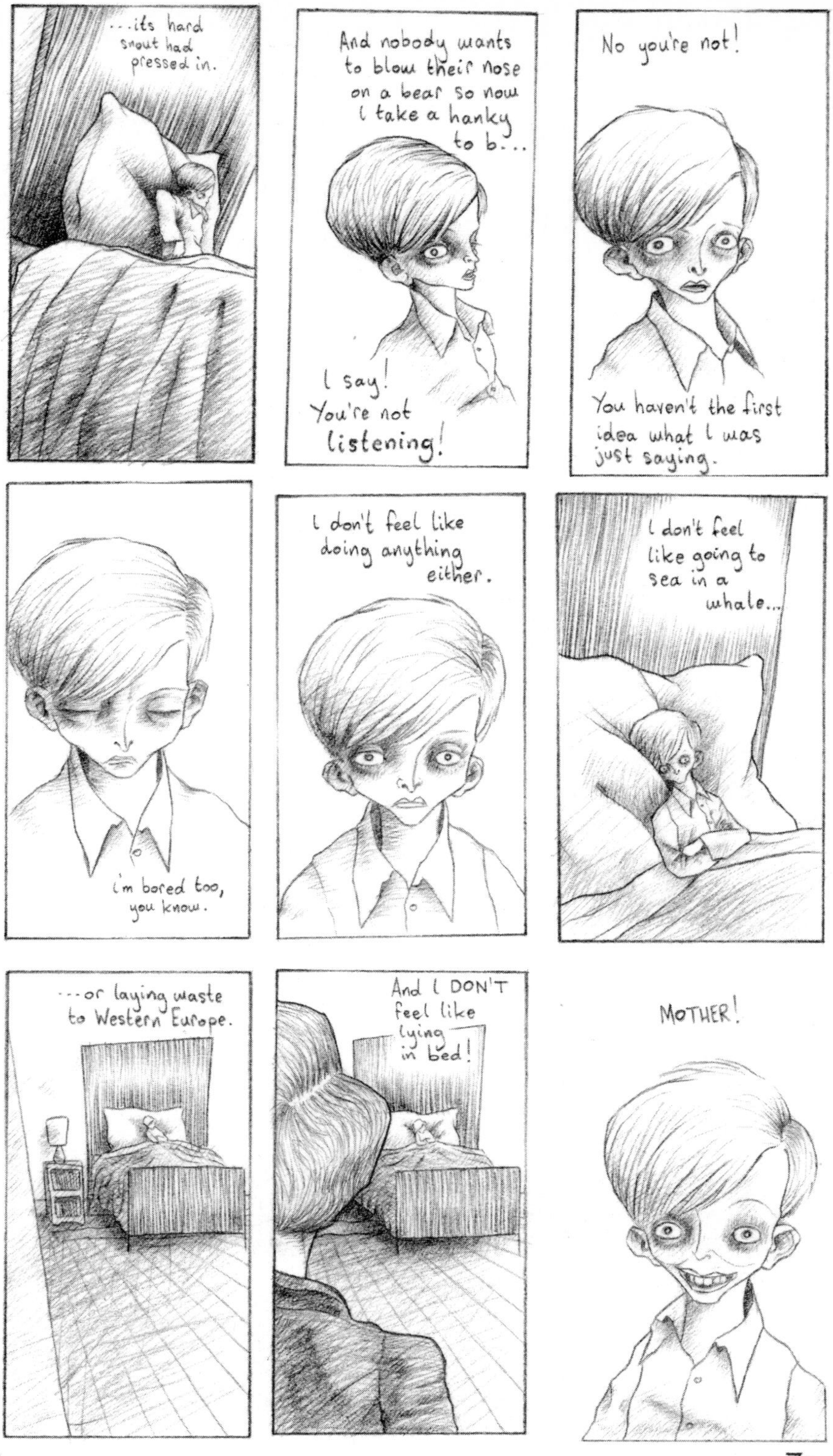
...its hard snout had pressed in.
And nobody wants to blow their nose on a bear so now I take a hanky to b...
I say! You're not listening!
No you're not!
You haven't the first idea what I was just saying.
I'm bored too, you know.
I don't feel like doing anything either.
I don't feel like going to sea in a whale...
...or laying waste to Western Europe.
And I DON'T feel like lying in bed!
MOTHER!

Hm?

Ah,
Eustace.

Eustace, I've brought
you some soup.

And you needn't make
that face.

Eat it all up
like a good
boy...

...and you
may get out
of bed
afterwards.

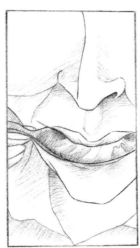

Mother, I've finished my soup. May I get up now?

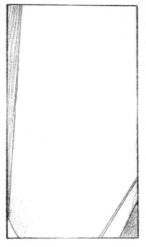

No, Eustace, don't be ridiculous, you're far too weak to get up.

But your Great Aunts and Uncles are coming to see you this afternoon and you're to have a bath.

Mrs Perichief will carry you down. I'll be along presently to wash your hair.

Let's be 'avin you then.

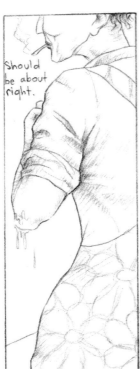

Hm.

Righto, off with yer togs!

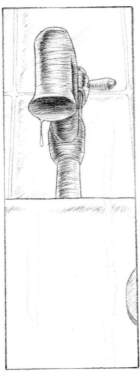

Should be about right.

'Course, I lost all feeling in me elbows years ago.

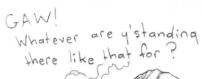

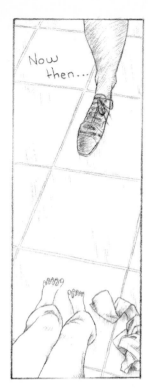

Now then...

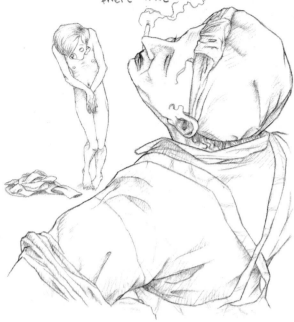

GAW!
Whatever are y'standing there like that for?

I'm not int'restid in your little winkle.

I 'as been married, y'know. Hupsy daisy.

'Ave a nice bath, dear. And Gawd 'elp all those 'oo sail in 'er.

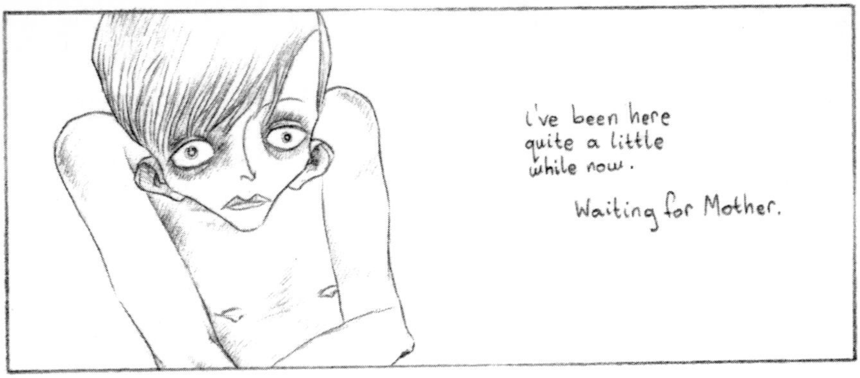
I've been here
quite a little
while now.
Waiting for Mother.

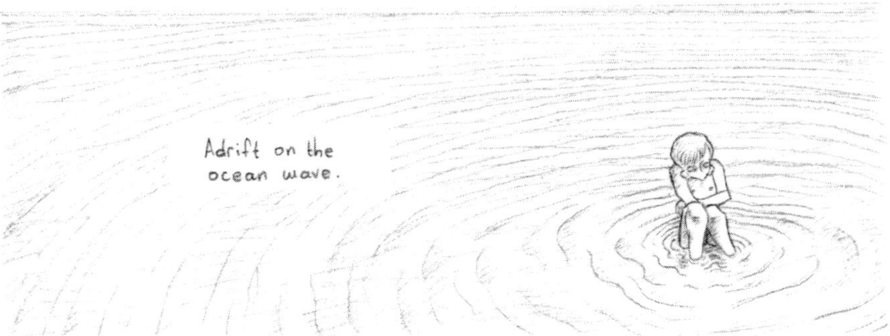
Adrift on the
ocean wave.

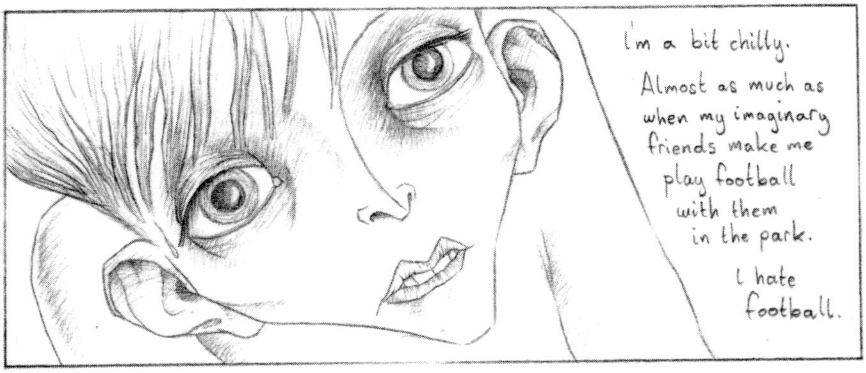
I'm a bit chilly.
Almost as much as when my imaginary friends make me play football with them in the park.
I hate football.

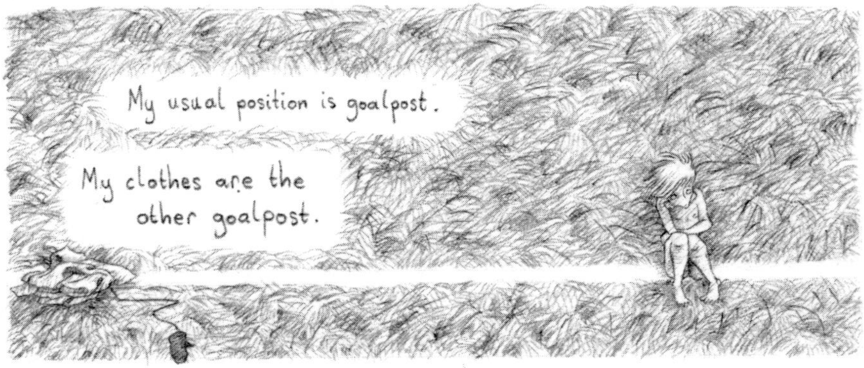
My usual position is goalpost.
My clothes are the other goalpost.

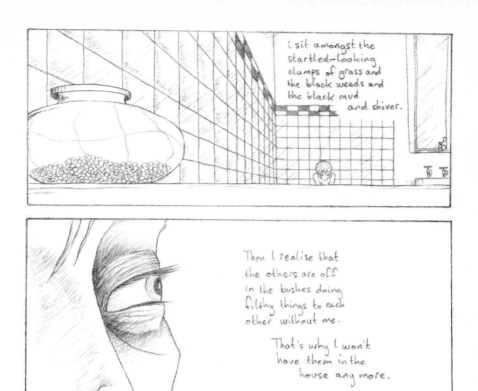

I sit amongst the startled-looking clumps of grass and the black weeds and the black mud and shiver.

Then I realise that the others are off in the bushes doing filthy things to each other without me.

That's why I won't have them in the house any more.

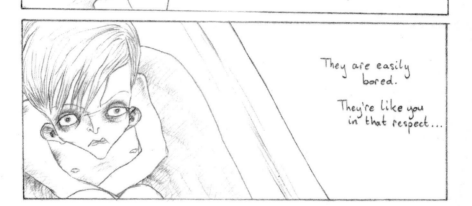

They are easily bored.

They're like you in that respect...

...except they're real!

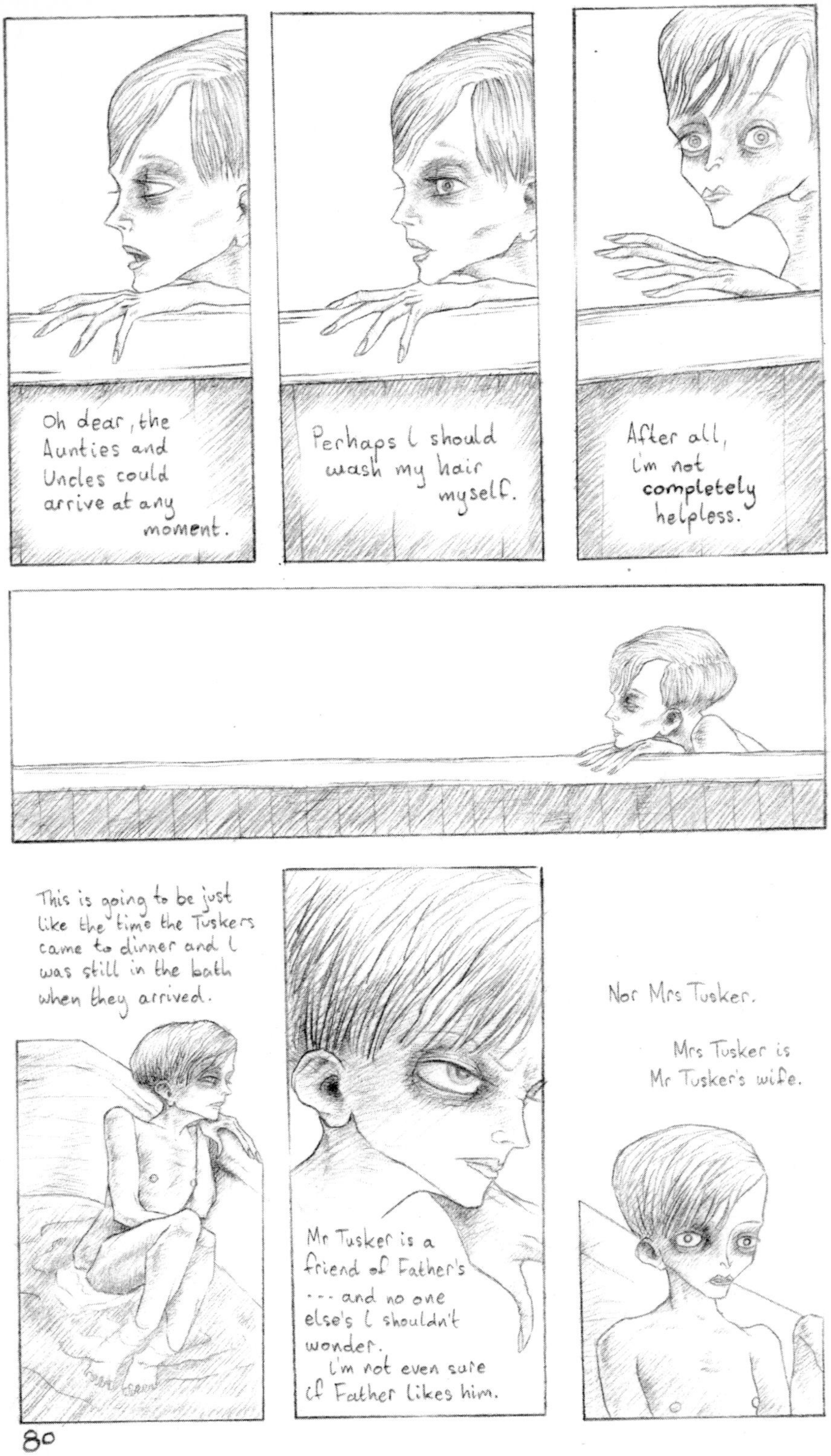

Oh dear, the Aunties and Uncles could arrive at any moment.
Perhaps I should wash my hair myself.
After all, I'm not **completely** helpless.
This is going to be just like the time the Tuskers came to dinner and I was still in the bath when they arrived.
Mr Tusker is a friend of Father's
... and no one else's I shouldn't wonder.
I'm not even sure if Father likes him.
Nor Mrs Tusker.
Mrs Tusker is Mr Tusker's wife.

Anyway,
there came a cretinous and
jolly knocking at the door
and then they were in the
hall and I heard their voices
through the floor. It sounded
like a wildebeest doing
something unspeakable
to a monkey.

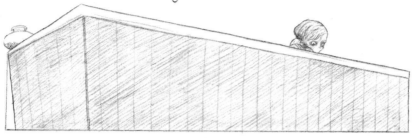

Nyee yee ya kam kam
EEK EEK EEK!

Oob onk ponk
fnorp onk
PAH FWAH
FWAH!

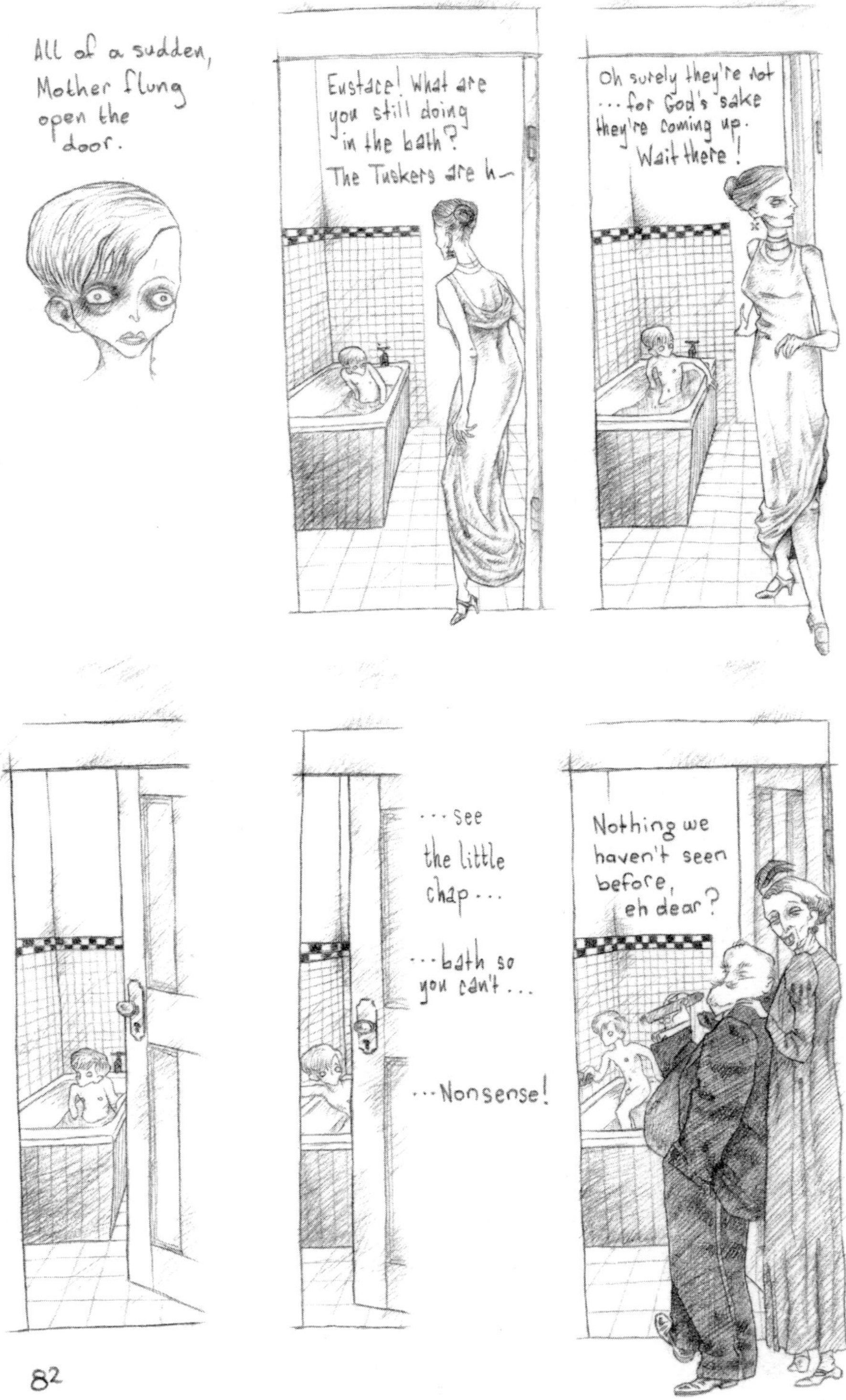

All of a sudden, Mother flung open the door.
Eustace! What are you still doing in the bath? The Tuskers are h—
Oh surely they're not ...for God's sake they're coming up. Wait there!
...see the little chap...
...bath so you can't...
...Nonsense!
Nothing we haven't seen before, eh dear?

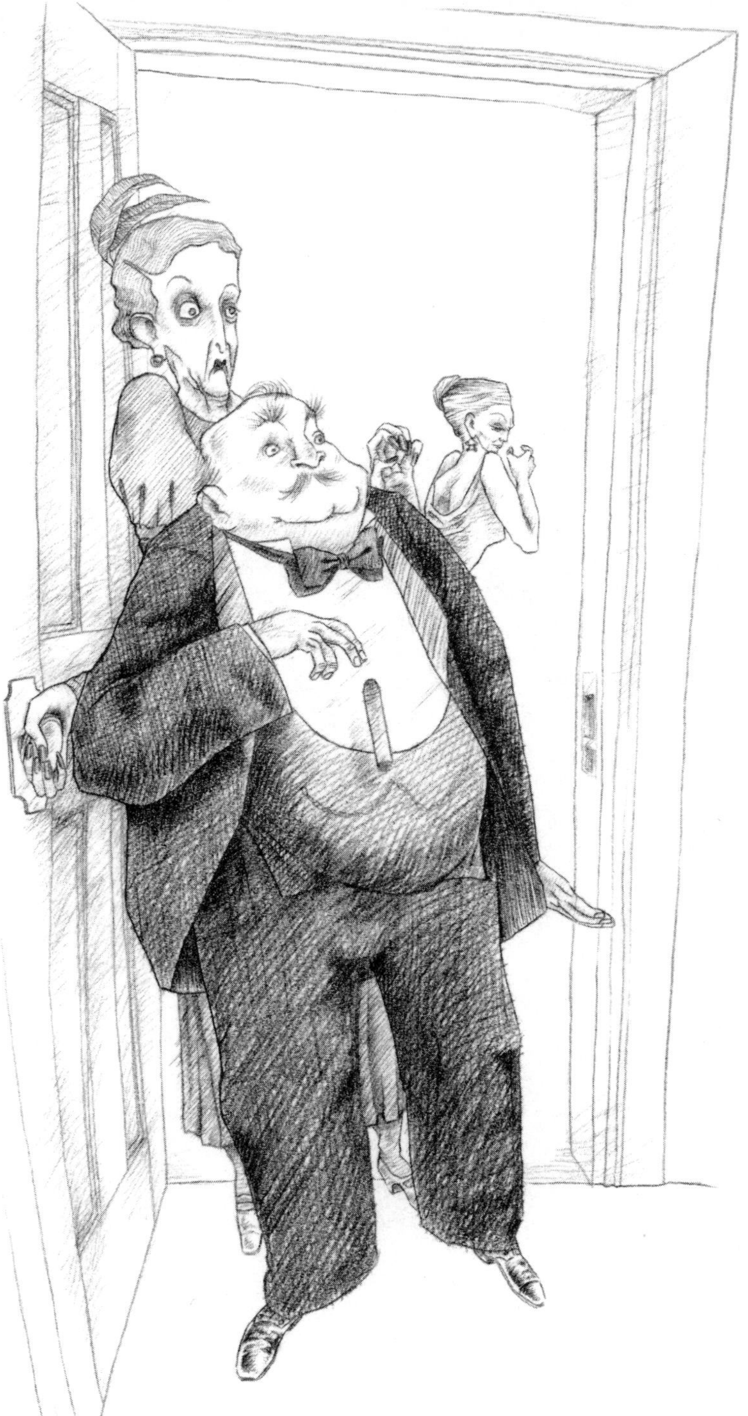

It wasn't my fault. I've always been taught to stand up when a lady enters the room.

No one told me what to do if you're in the **nude** at the time.

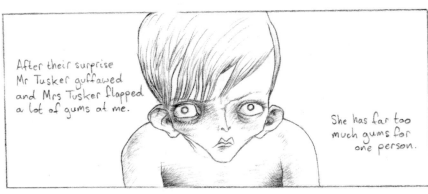

After their surprise Mr Tusker guffawed and Mrs Tusker flapped a lot of gums at me.

She has far too much gums for one person.

Perhaps it was the way I held the loofah.

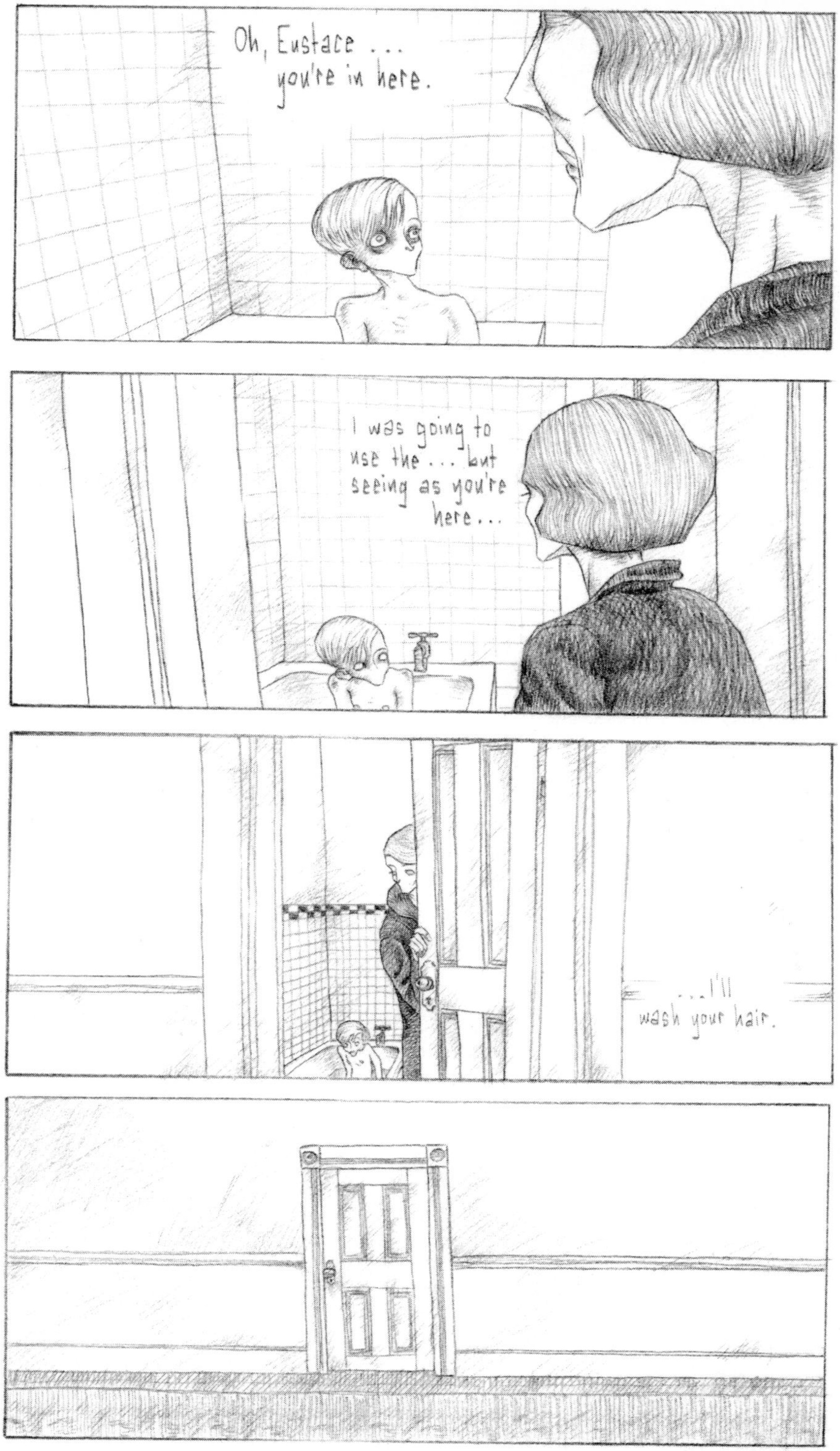
Oh, Eustace ...
you're in here.
I was going to use the ... but seeing as you're here ...
...I'll wash your hair.

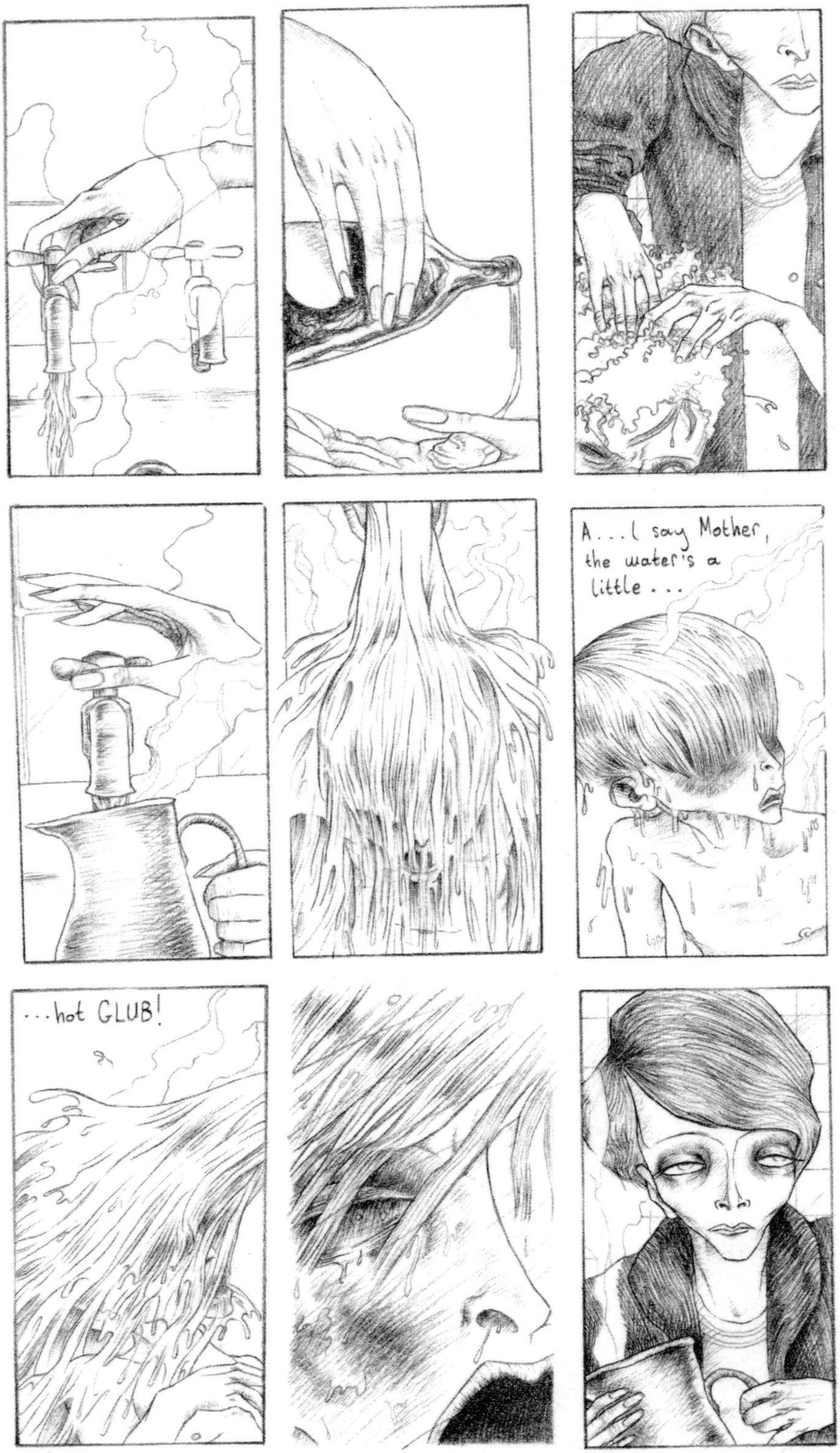
A . . . I say Mother, the water's a little . . .
. . . hot GLUB!

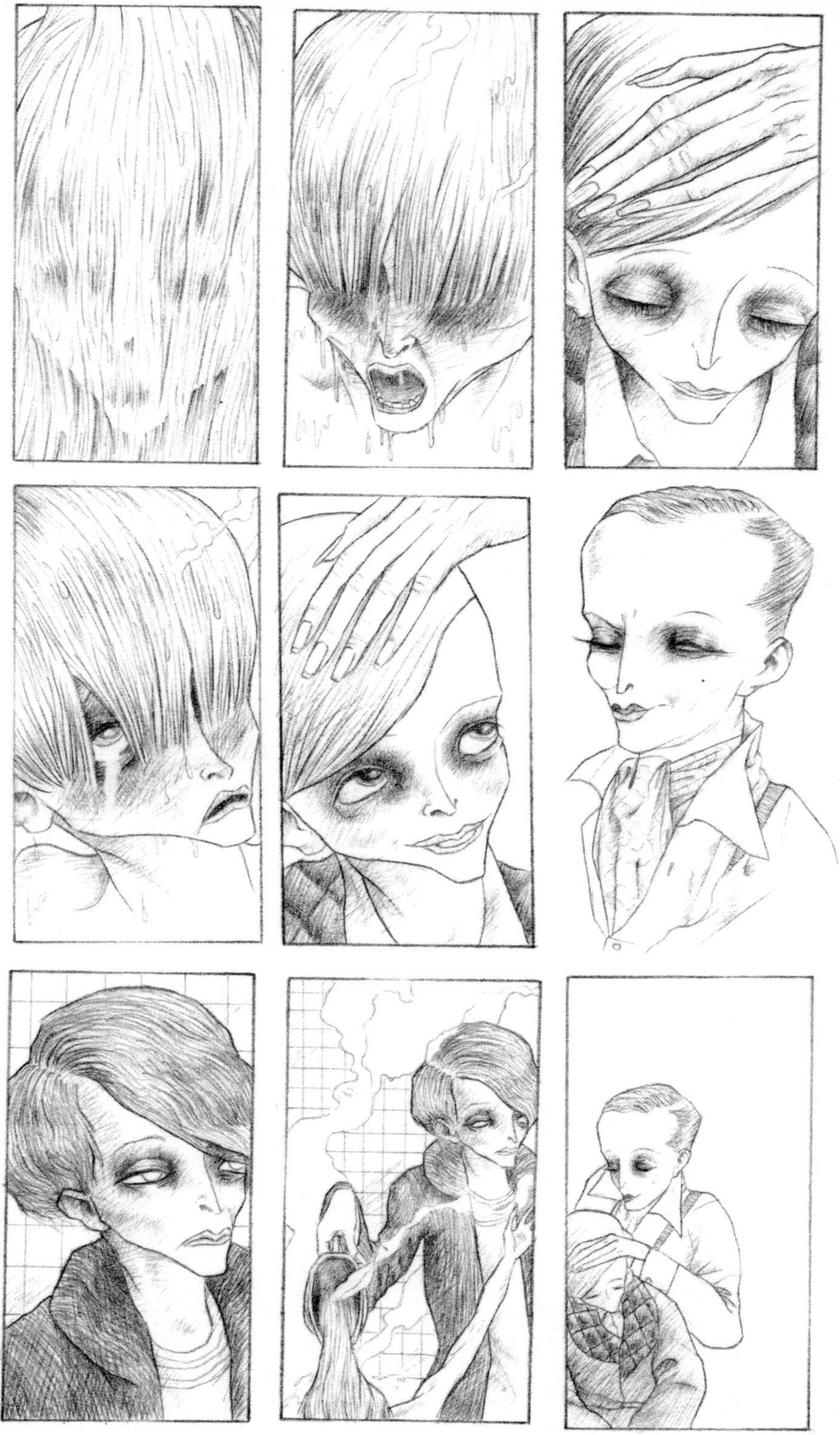

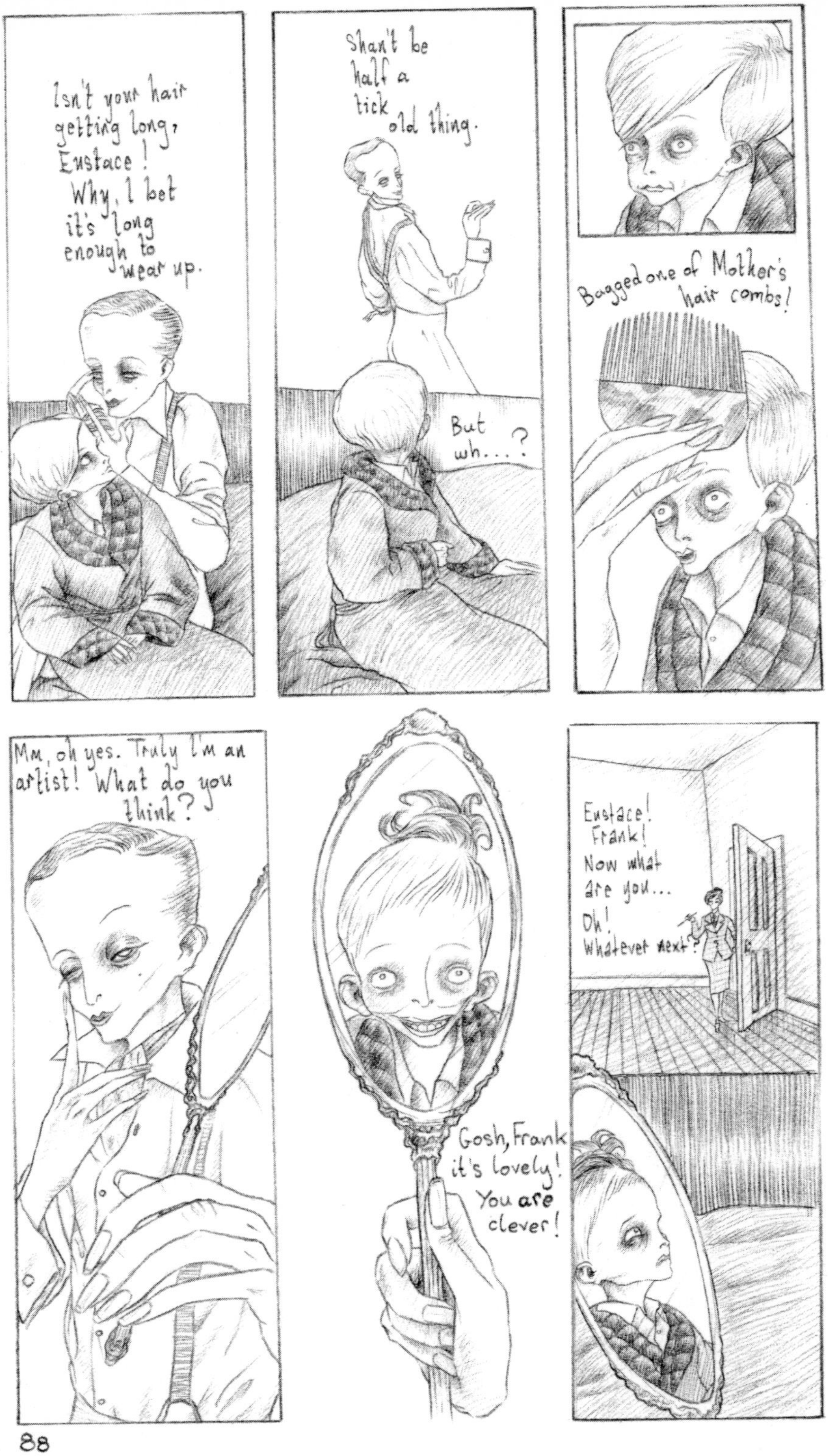
Isn't your hair getting long, Eustace! Why, I bet it's long enough to wear up.
Shan't be half a tick old thing.
But wh...?
Bagged one of Mother's hair combs!
Mm, oh yes. Truly I'm an artist! What do you think?
Gosh, Frank it's lovely! You are clever!
Eustace! Frank! Now what are you... Oh! Whatever next?

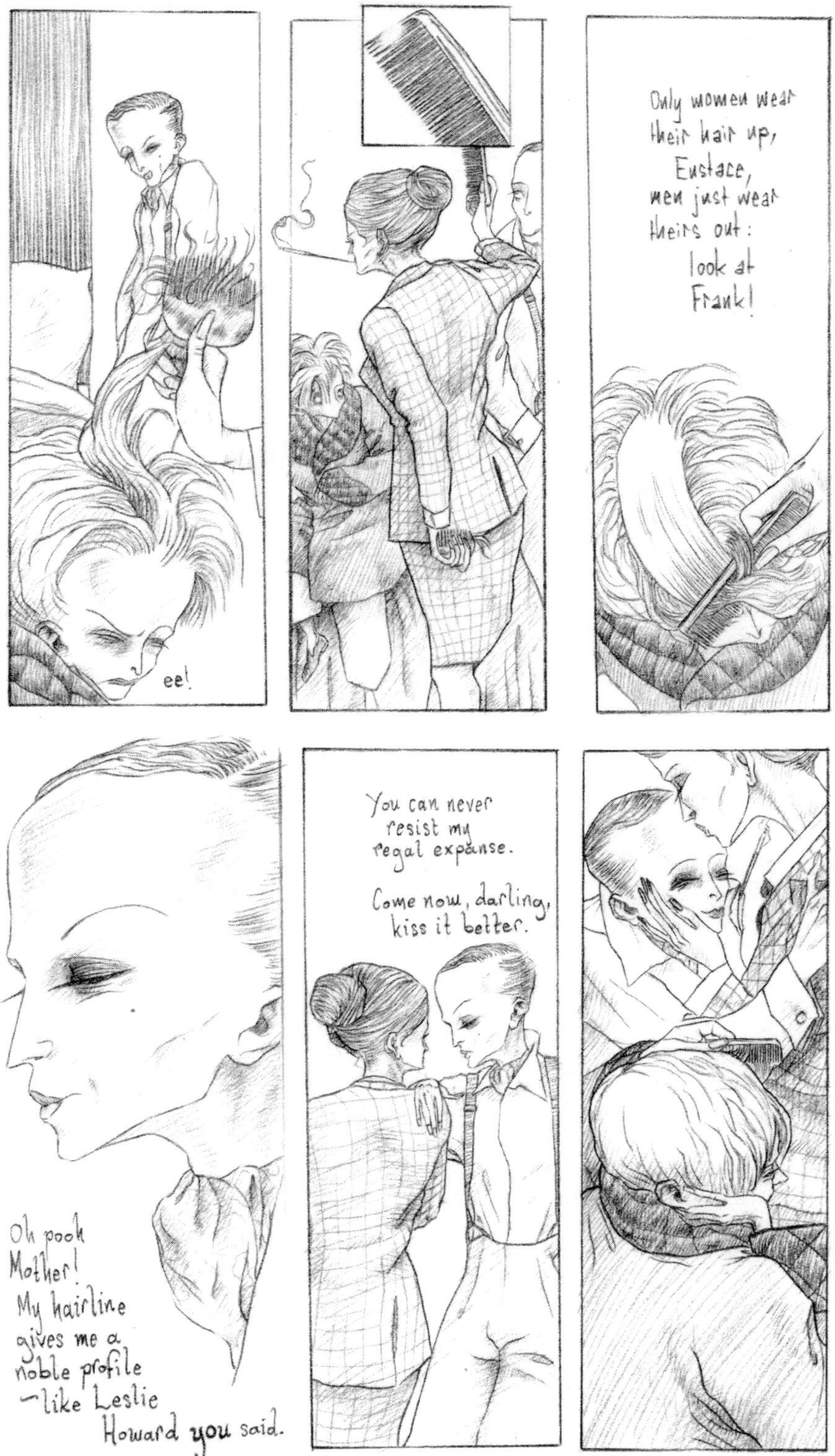
ee!
Only women wear their hair up, Eustace, men just wear theirs out: look at Frank!
Oh pooh Mother! My hairline gives me a noble profile —like Leslie Howard you said.
You can never resist my regal expanse.
Come now, darling, kiss it better.

I'm in clean pyjamas
and sheets and blankets.

I feel... hrrgh...

I feel scrubbed
raw inside and
out.

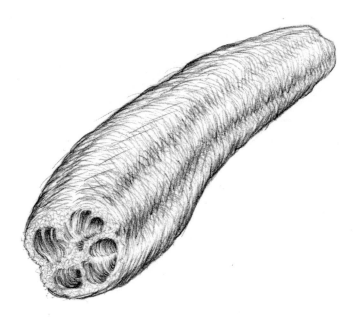

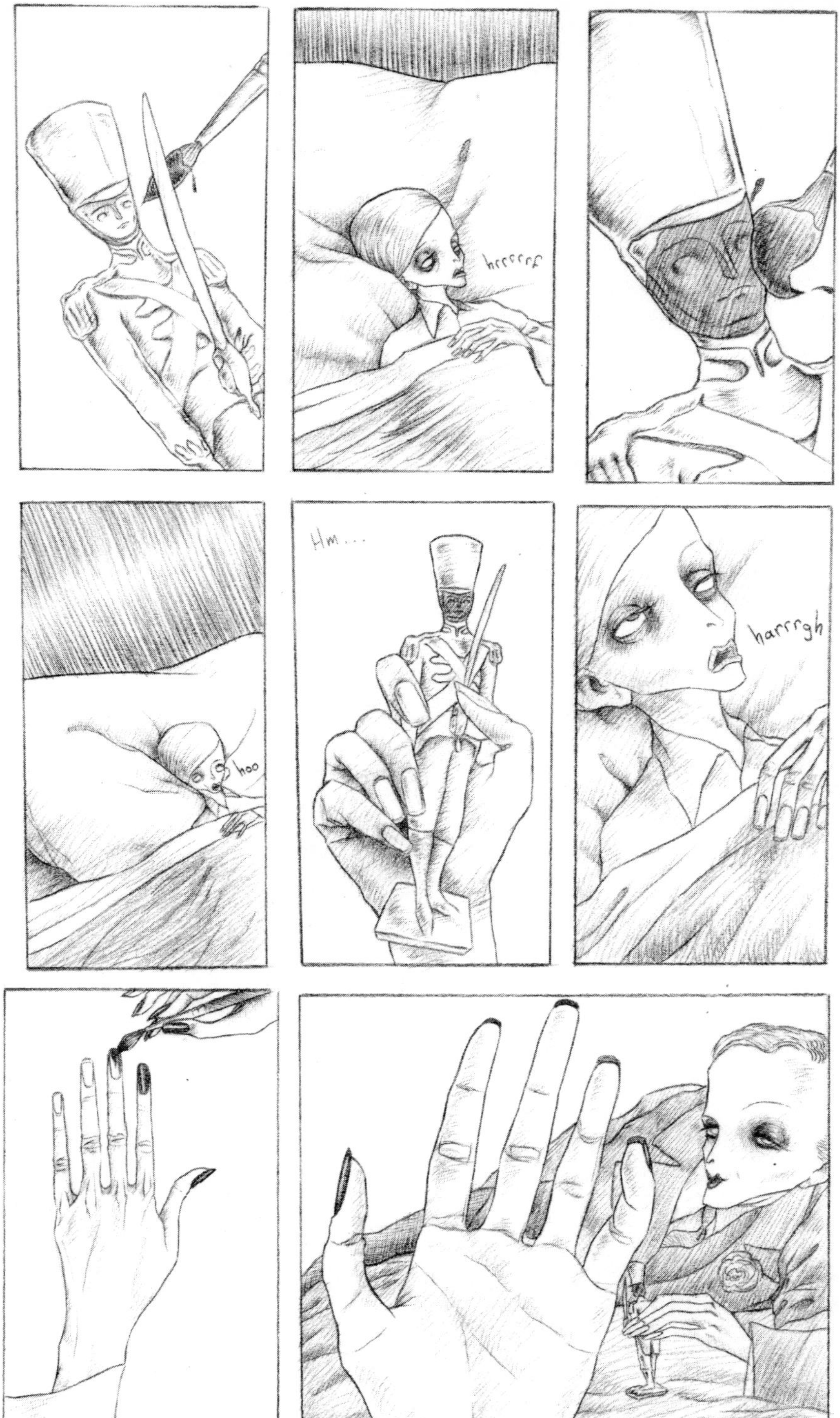
hrrrrrf
hoo
Hm...
harrrgh

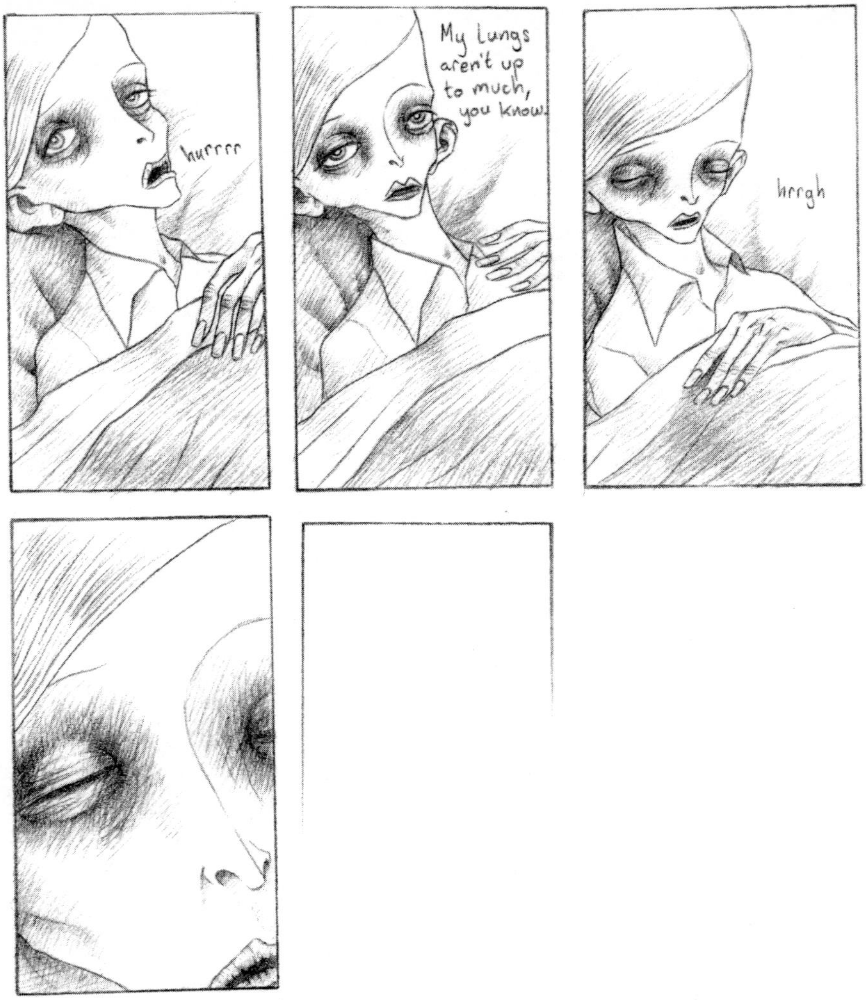
hurrrr
My lungs aren't up to much, you know.
hrrgh

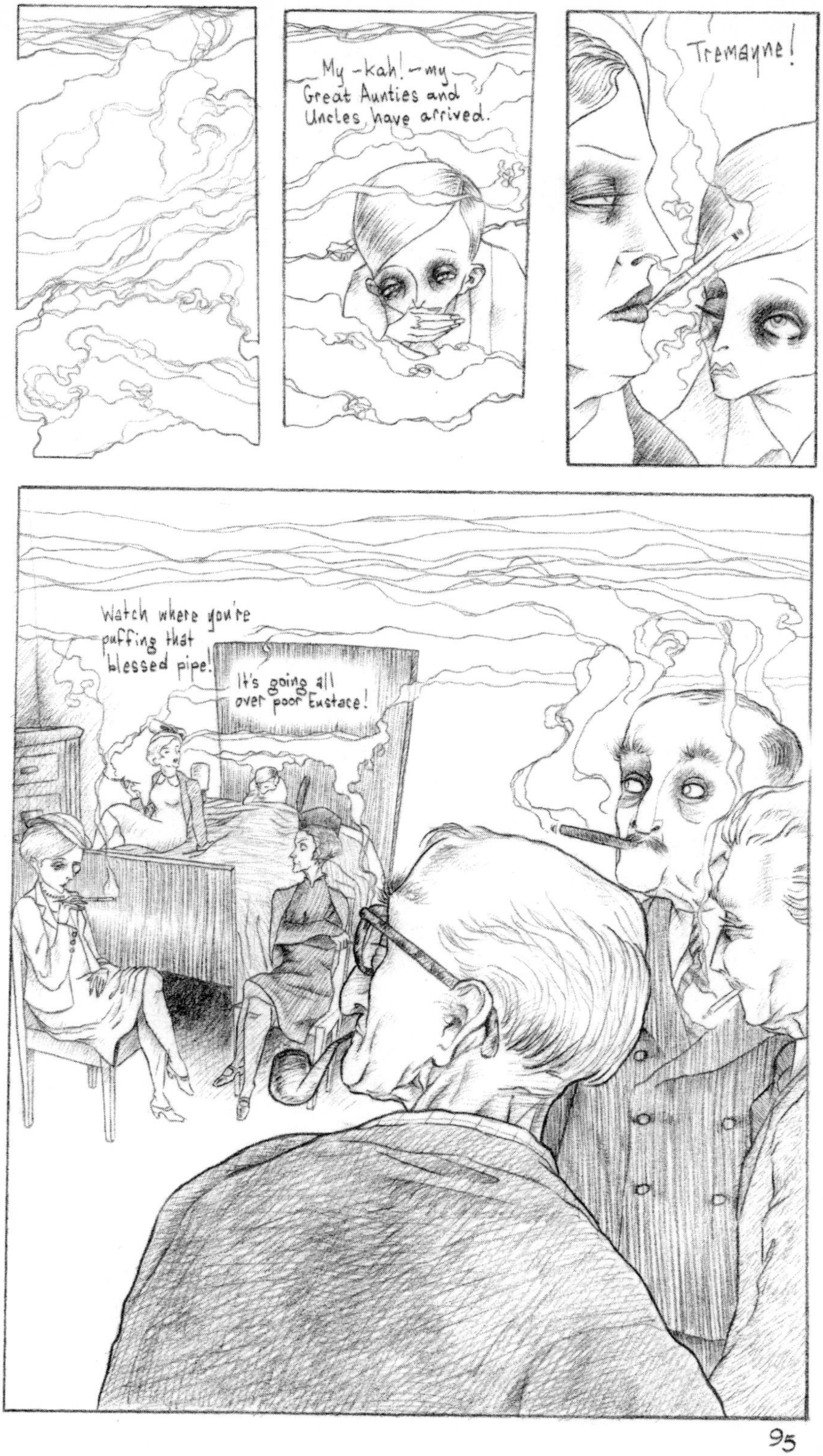
My-kah!—my Great Aunties and Uncles have arrived.
Tremayne!
Watch where you're puffing that blessed pipe!
It's going all over poor Eustace!

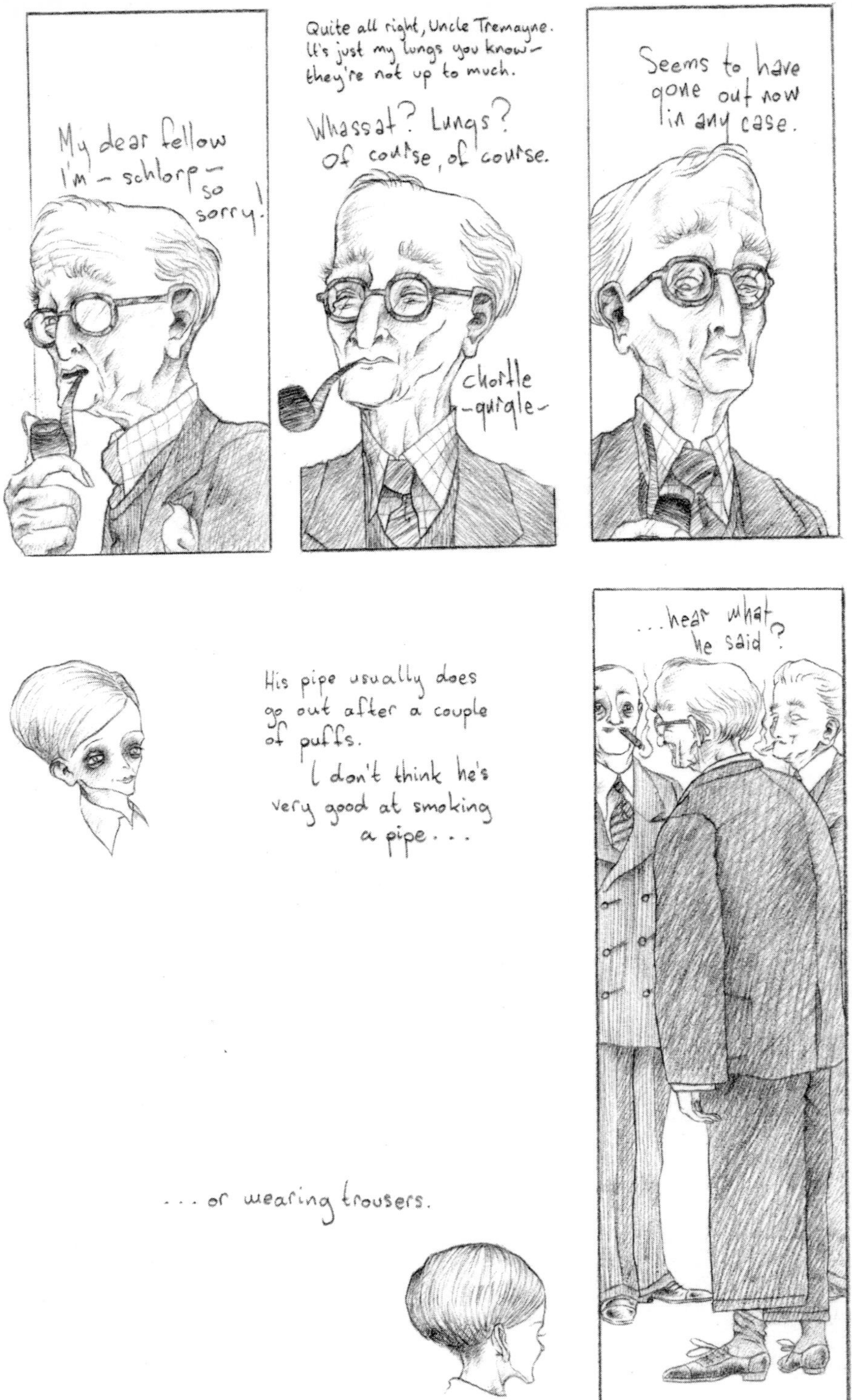
My dear fellow I'm – schlorp – so sorry!
Quite all right, Uncle Tremayne. It's just my lungs you know – they're not up to much.
Whassat? Lungs? Of course, of course.
chortle –gurgle–
Seems to have gone out now in any case.
His pipe usually does go out after a couple of puffs.
I don't think he's very good at smoking a pipe . . .
. . . hear what he said?
. . . or wearing trousers.

The Uncles are an almost entirely different species from the Aunties.

Uncle Lucien's not, he's their brother and couldn't help being related to them.

But the other Uncles **chose** to marry the Aunties!

Hoh hoh, that's a good one eh, Athol? His lungs!

Mostly they're a furrier beast than the Aunties.

He does come out with them!

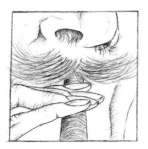

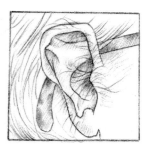

I did say **mostly** furrier.

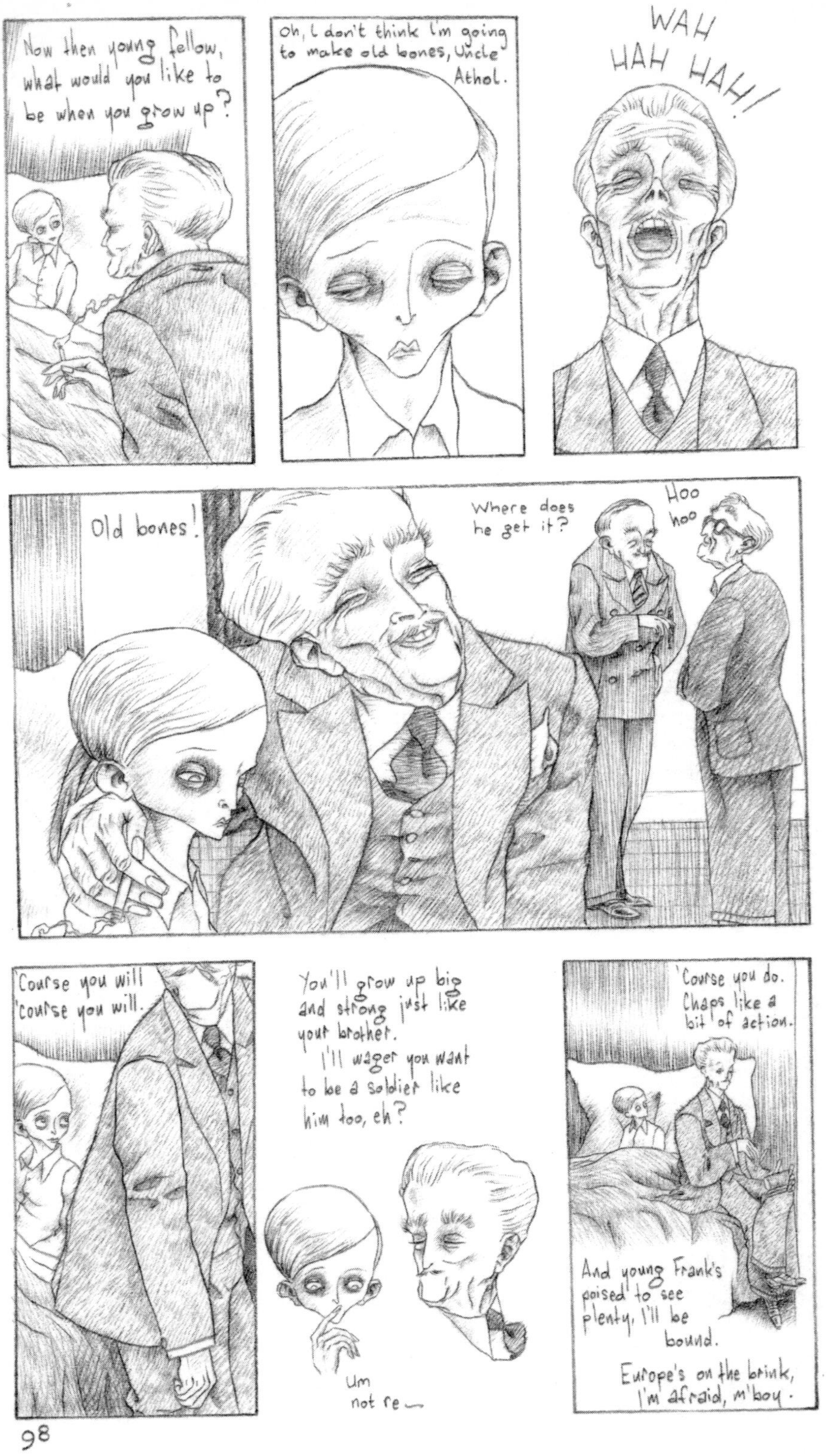
Now then young fellow, what would you like to be when you grow up?
Oh, I don't think I'm going to make old bones, Uncle Athol.
WAH HAH HAH HAH!
Old bones!
Where does he get it?
Hoo hoo
'Course you will 'course you will.
You'll grow up big and strong just like your brother.
I'll wager you want to be a soldier like him too, eh?
Um not re—
'Course you do. Chaps like a bit of action.
And young Frank's poised to see plenty, I'll be bound.
Europe's on the brink, I'm afraid, m'boy.

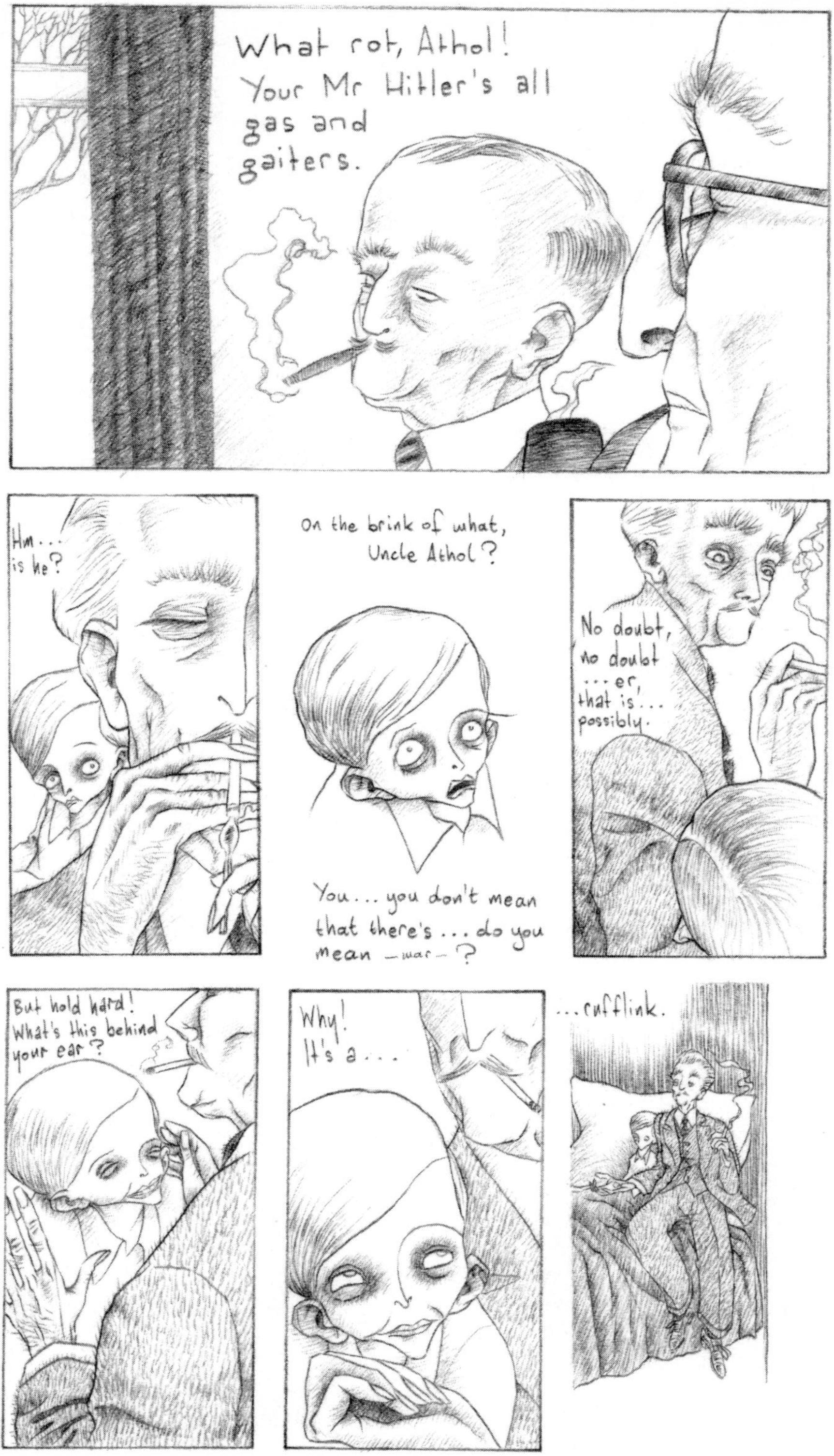
What rot, Athol! Your Mr Hitler's all gas and gaiters.
Hm... is he?
On the brink of what, Uncle Athol?
You... you don't mean that there's... do you mean —war—?
No doubt, no doubt ...er, that is!... possibly.
But hold hard! What's this behind your ear?
Why! It's a...
...cufflink.

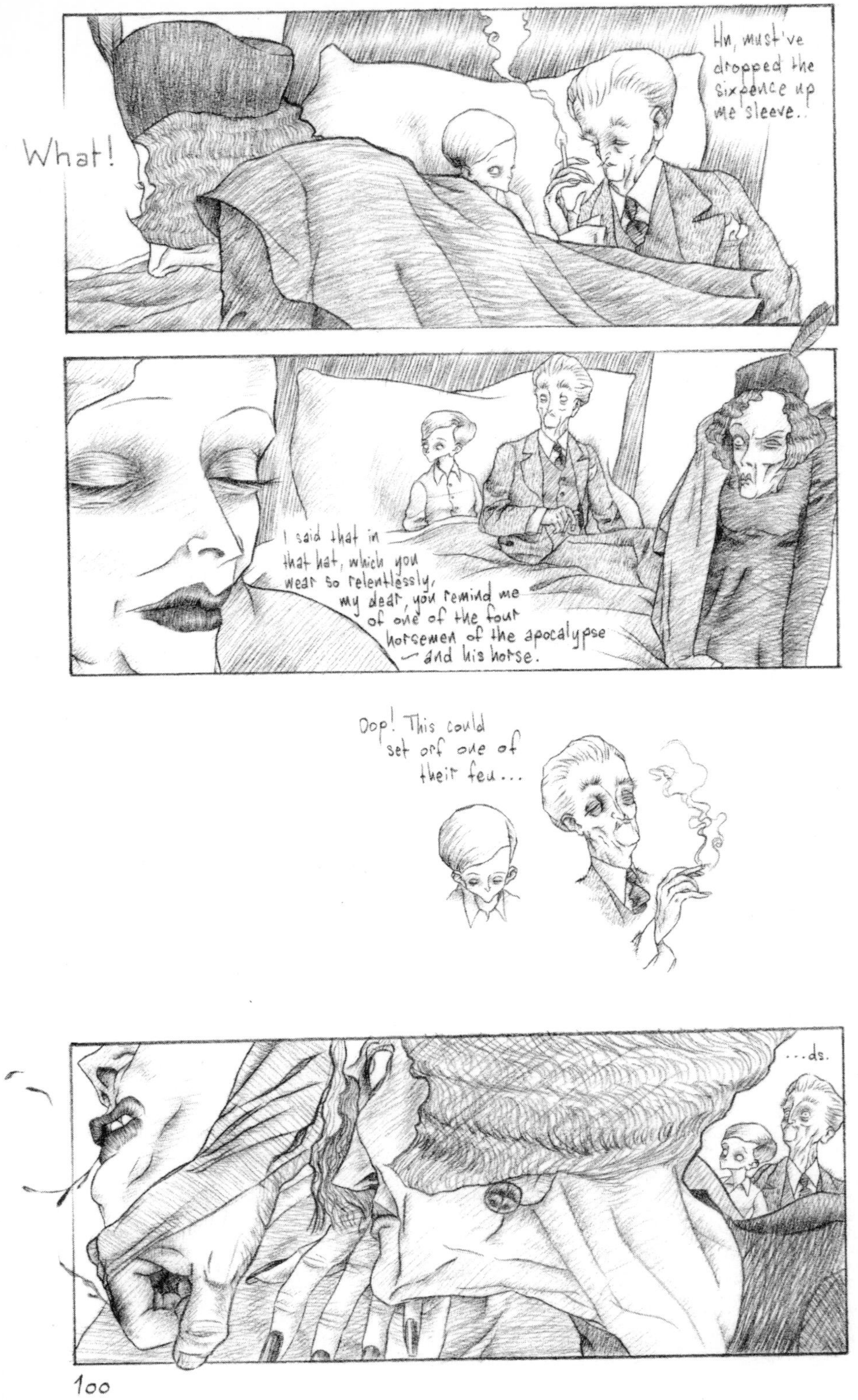
What!
Hn, must've dropped the sixpence up me sleeve..
I said that in that hat, which you wear so relentlessly, my dear, you remind me of one of the four horsemen of the apocalypse — and his horse.
Oop! This could set orf one of their feu...
...ds.

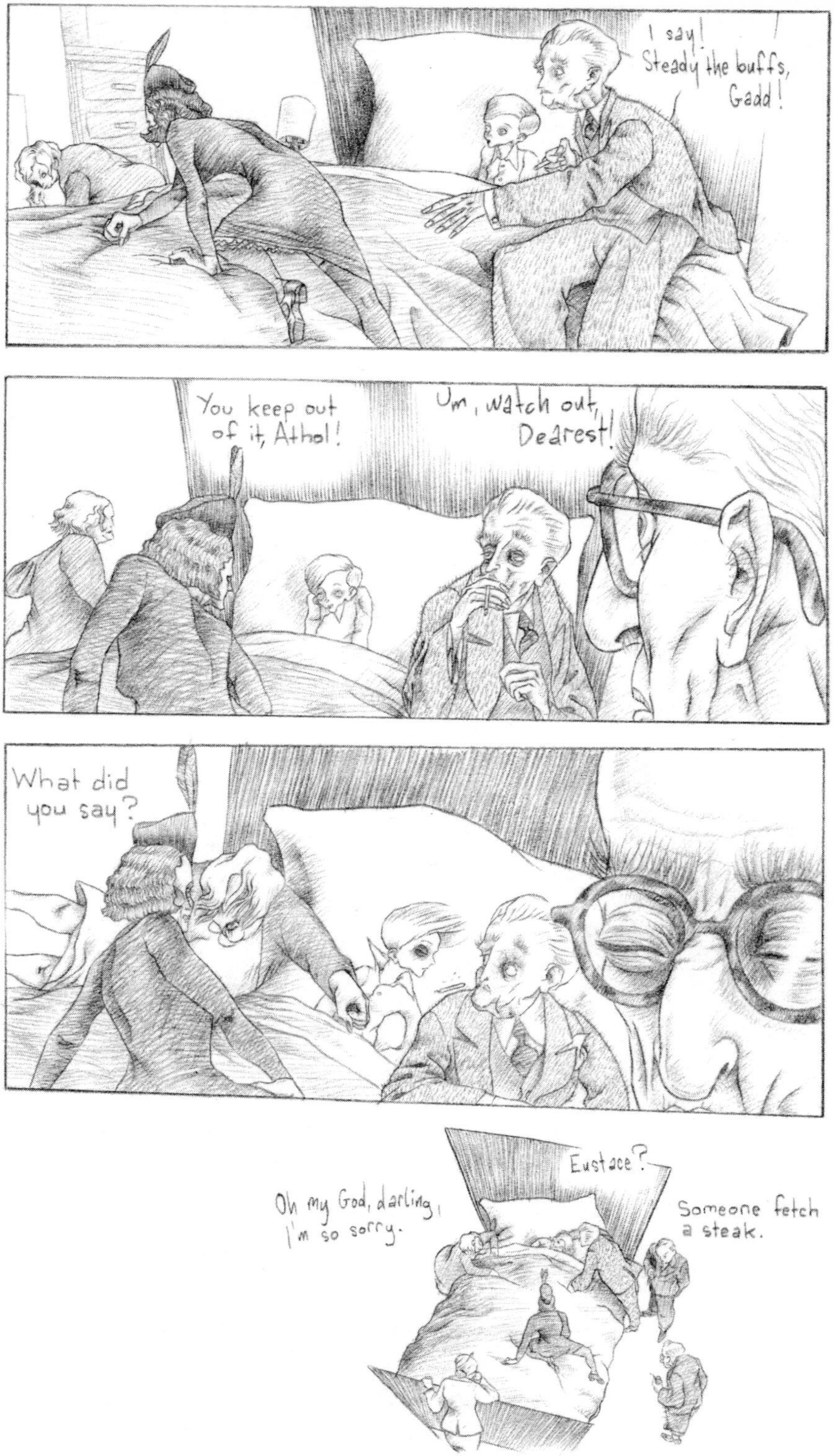
I say! Steady the buffs, Gadd!
You keep out of it, Athol!
Um, watch out, Dearest!
What did you say?
Eustace?
Oh my God, darling, I'm so sorry.
Someone fetch a steak.

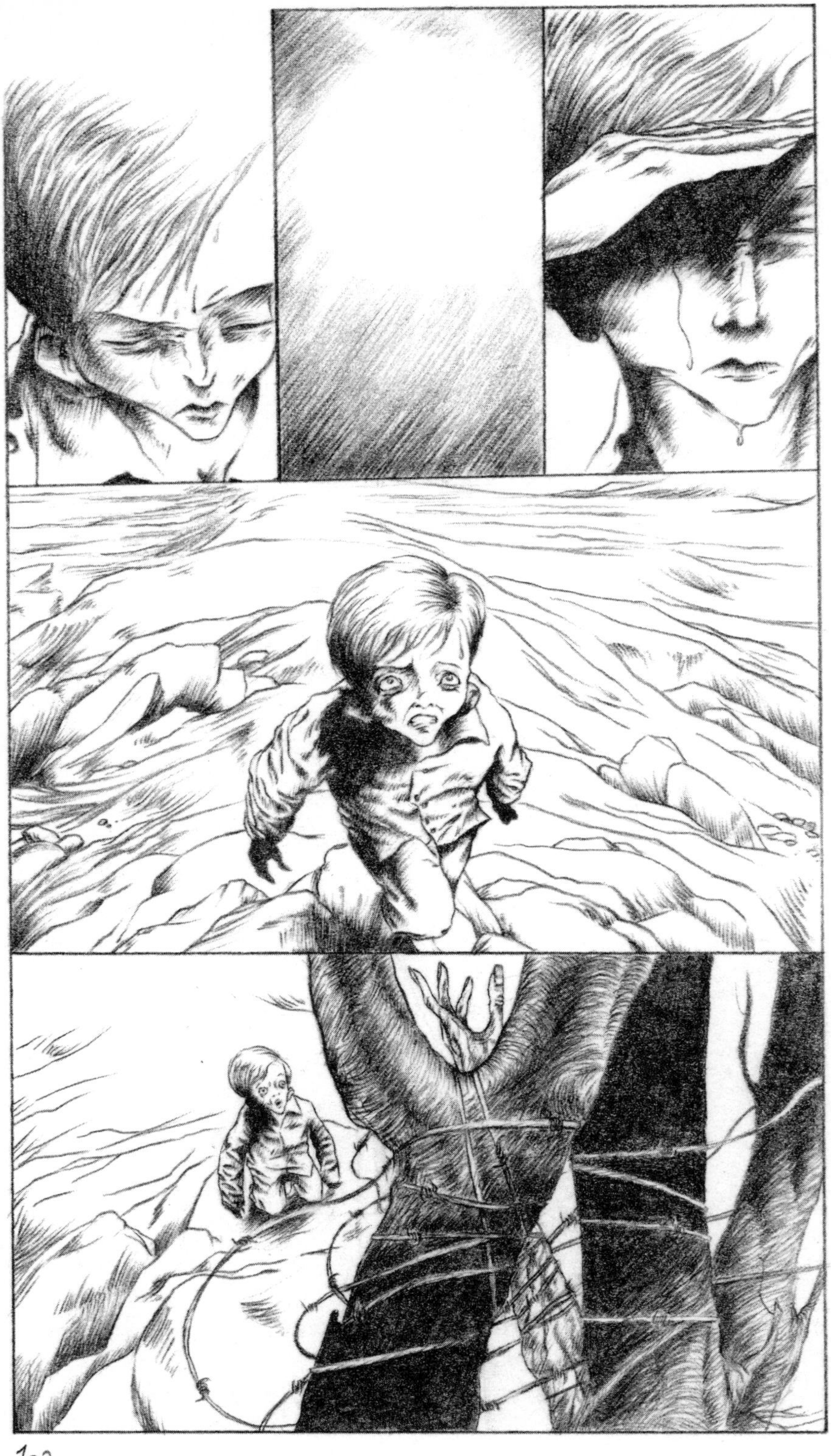

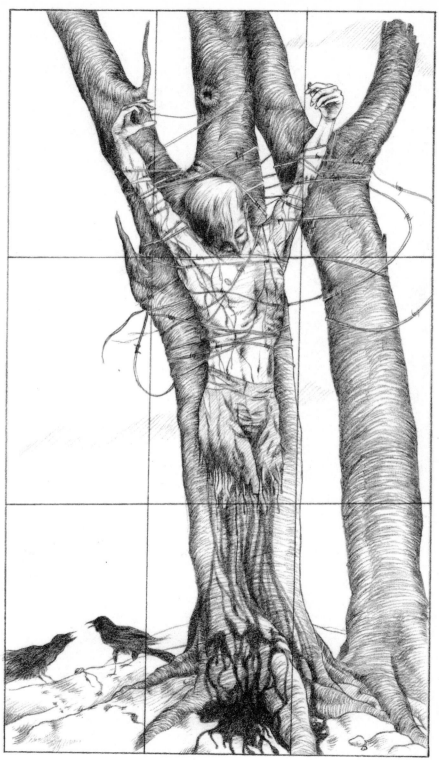

103

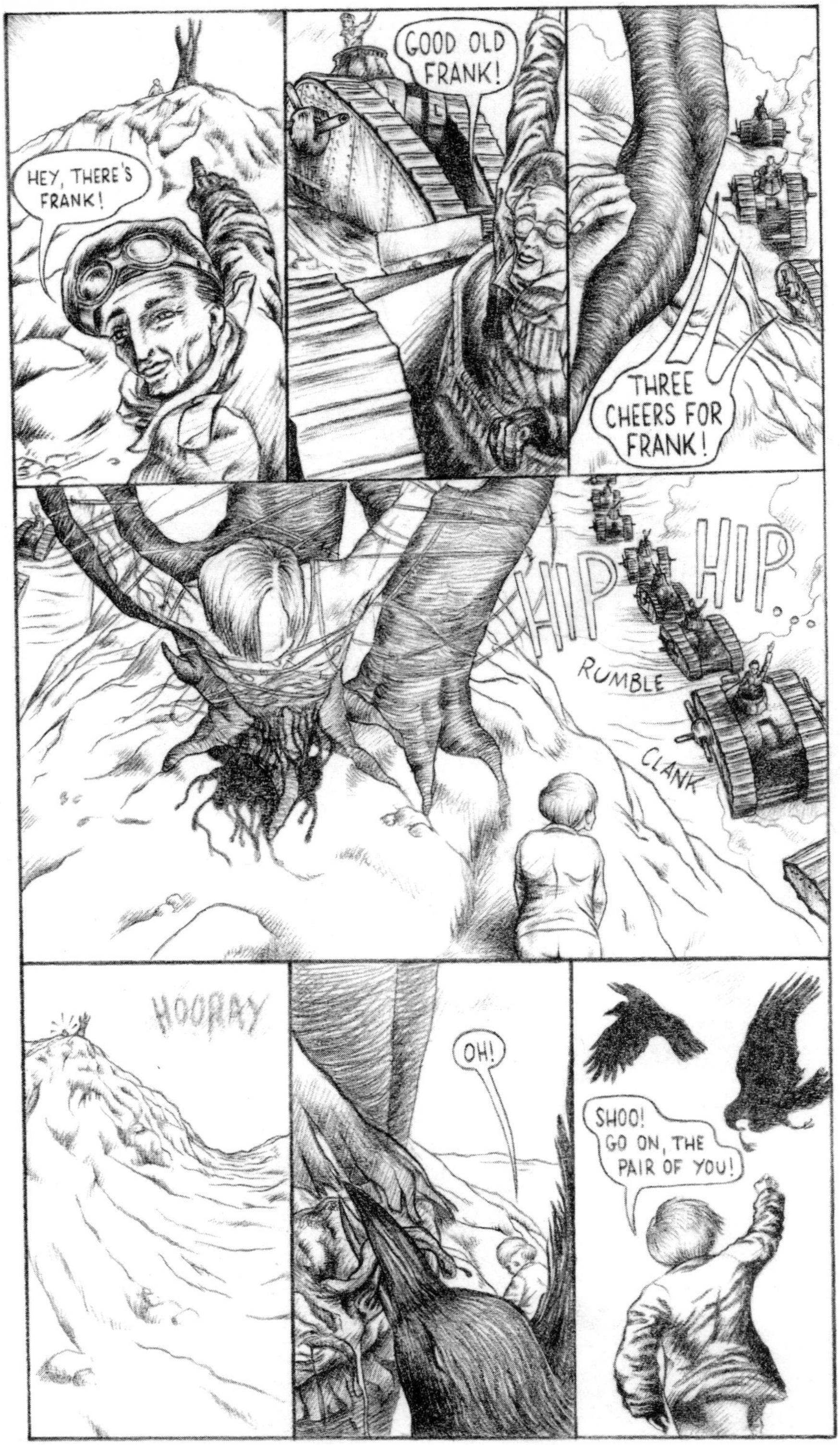
HEY, THERE'S FRANK!
GOOD OLD FRANK!
THREE CHEERS FOR FRANK!
HIP HIP...
RUMBLE
CLANK
HOORAY
OH!
SHOO! GO ON, THE PAIR OF YOU!

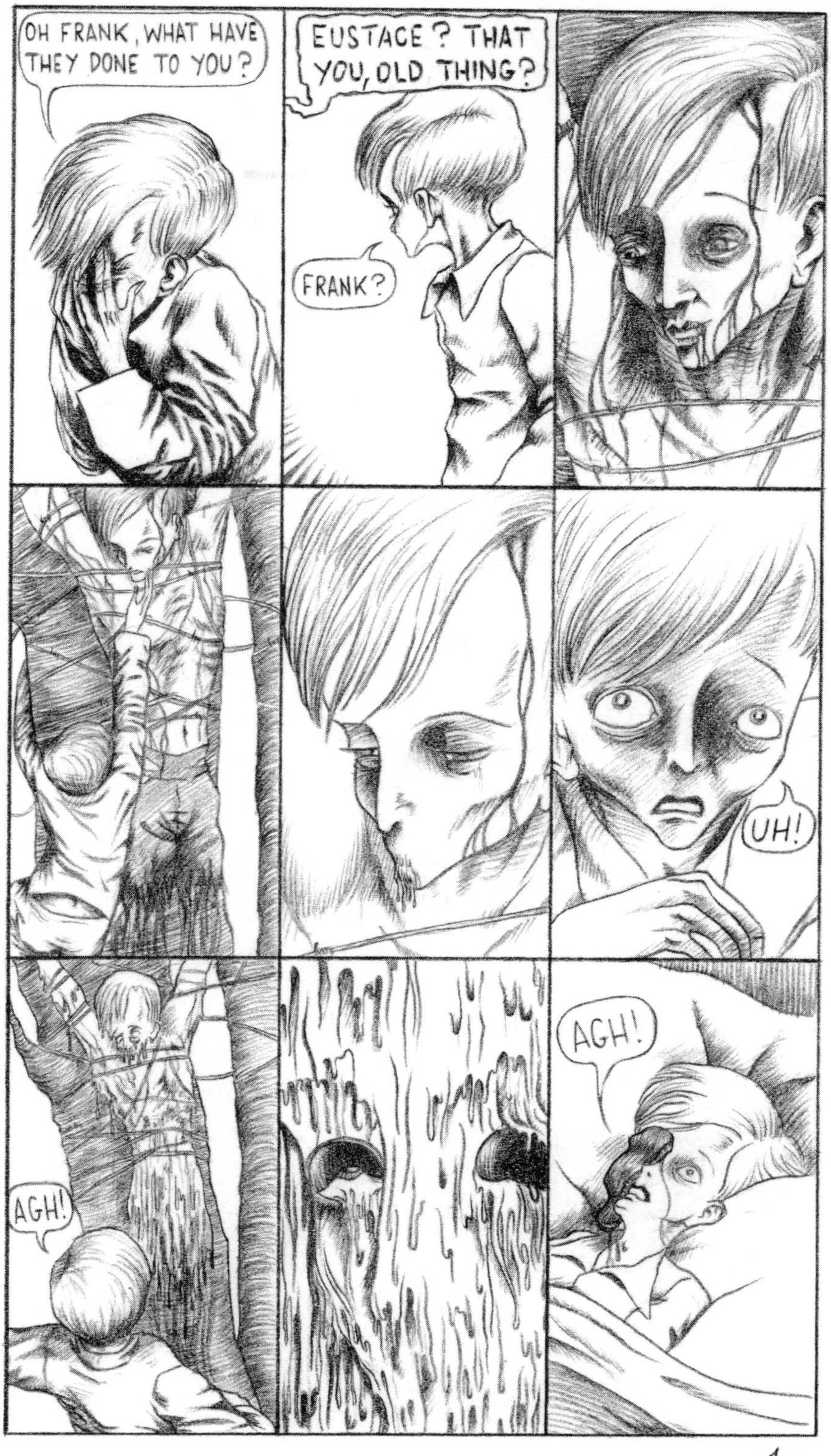
OH FRANK, WHAT HAVE THEY DONE TO YOU?
EUSTACE? THAT YOU, OLD THING?
FRANK?
UH!
AGH!
AGH!

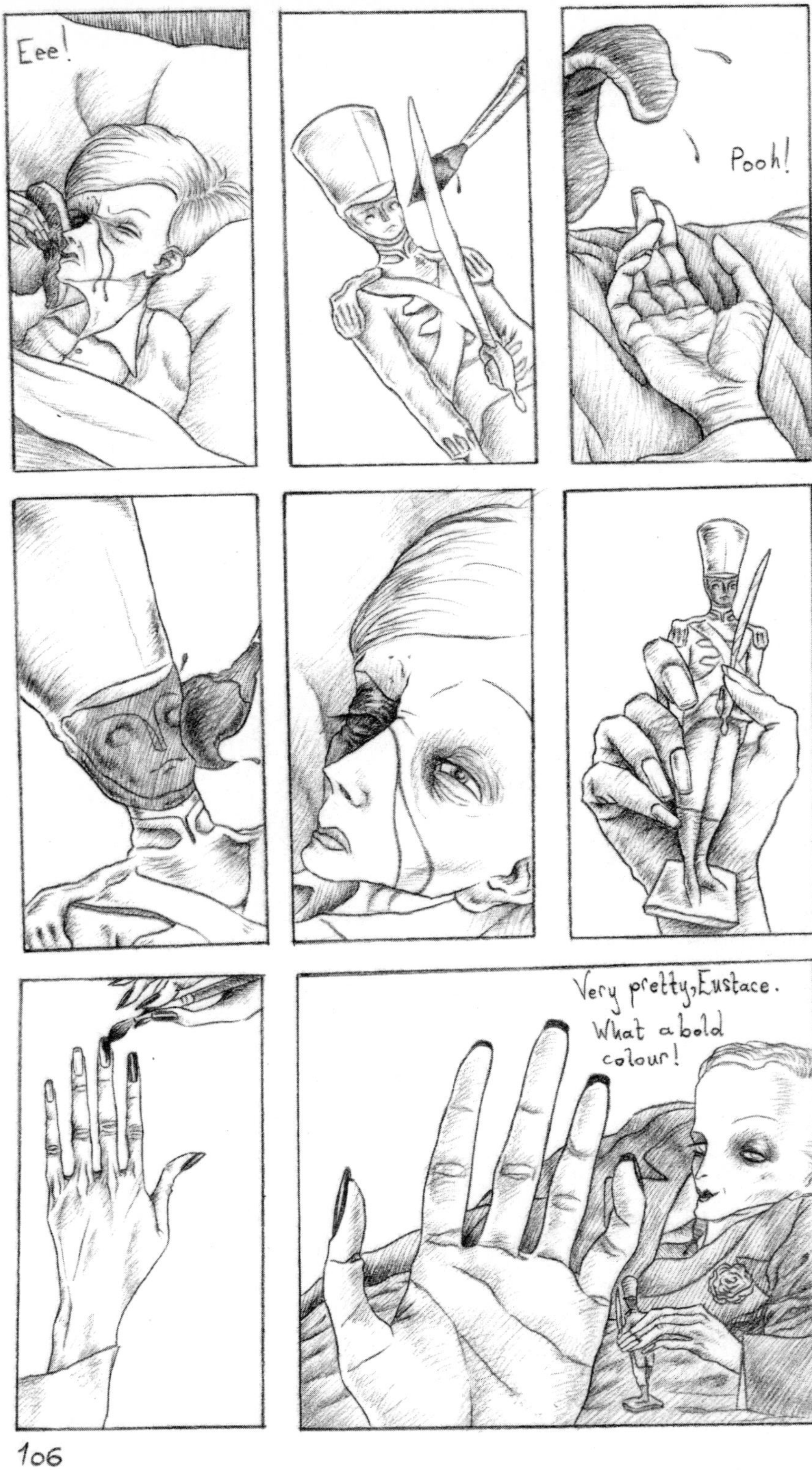
Eee!
Pooh!
Very pretty, Eustace.
What a bold colour!

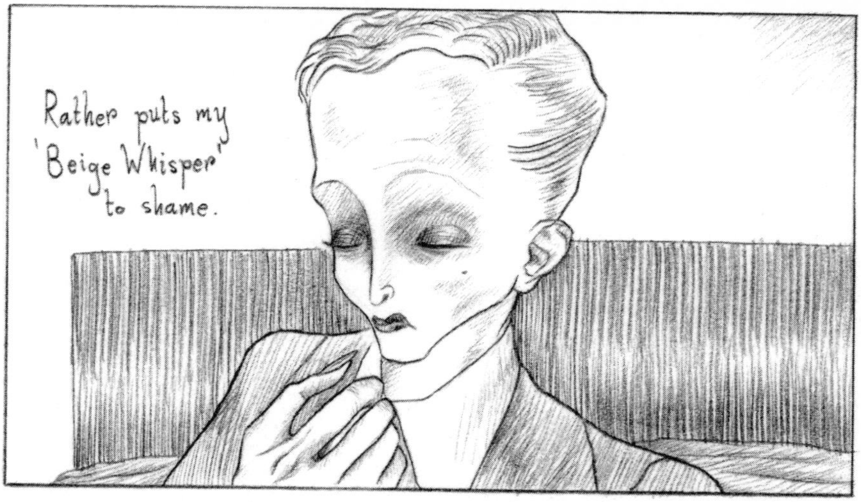
Rather puts my 'Beige Whisper' to shame.

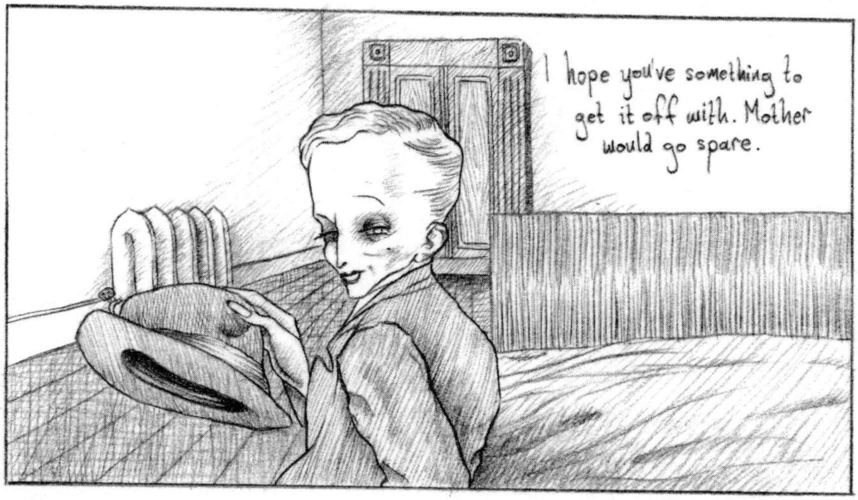
I hope you've something to get it off with. Mother would go spare.

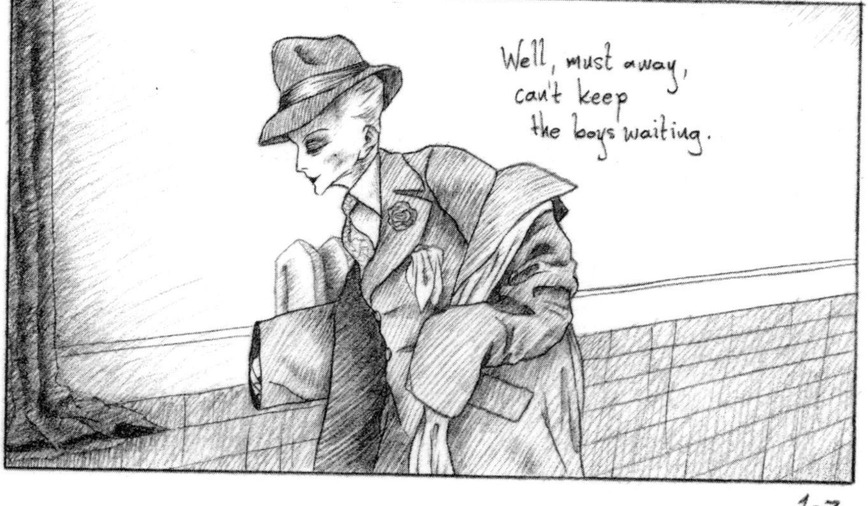
Well, must away, can't keep the boys waiting.

Bon soir
old thing,
I may be
some time...
    I hope!

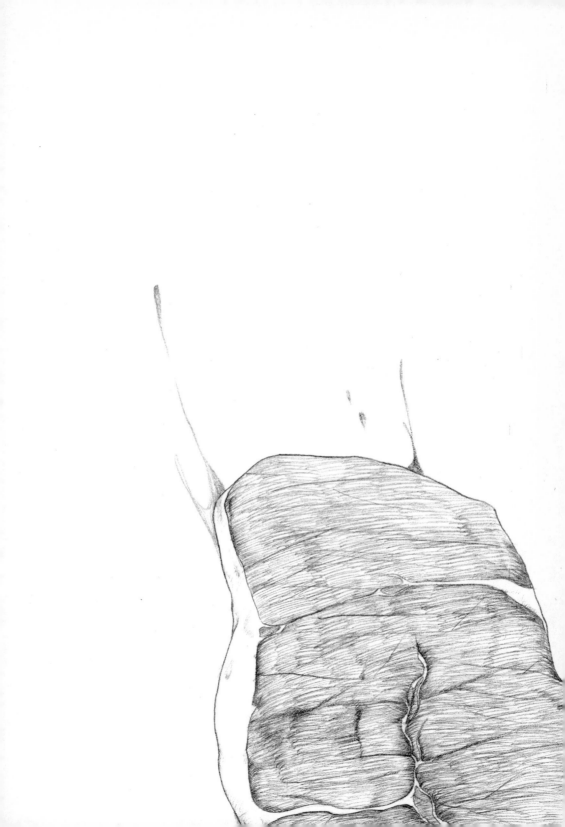

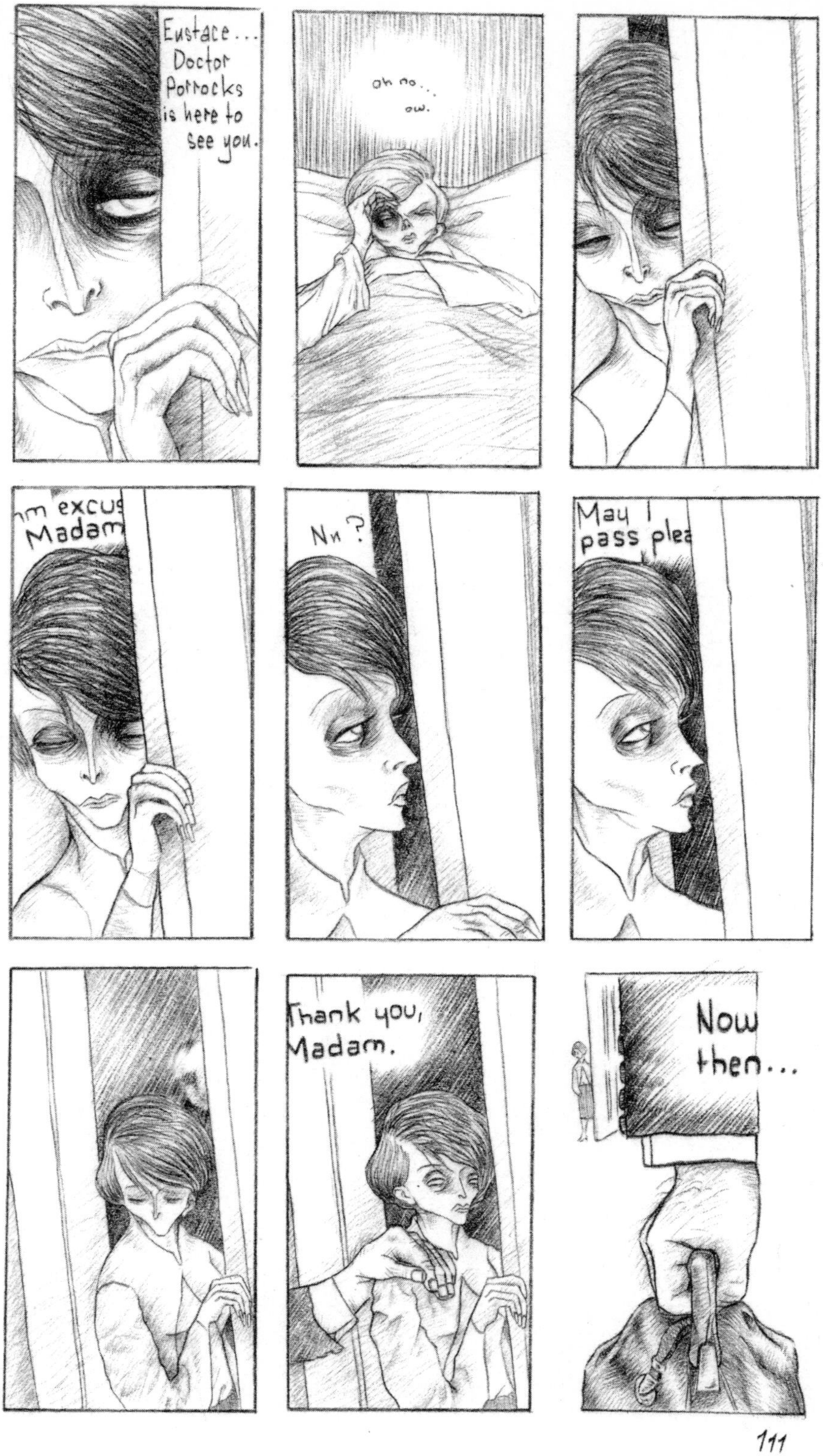
Eustace...
Doctor Porrocks is here to see you.
oh no...
ow.
hm excus
Madam
Nn?
May I
pass plea
Thank you, Madam.
Now then...

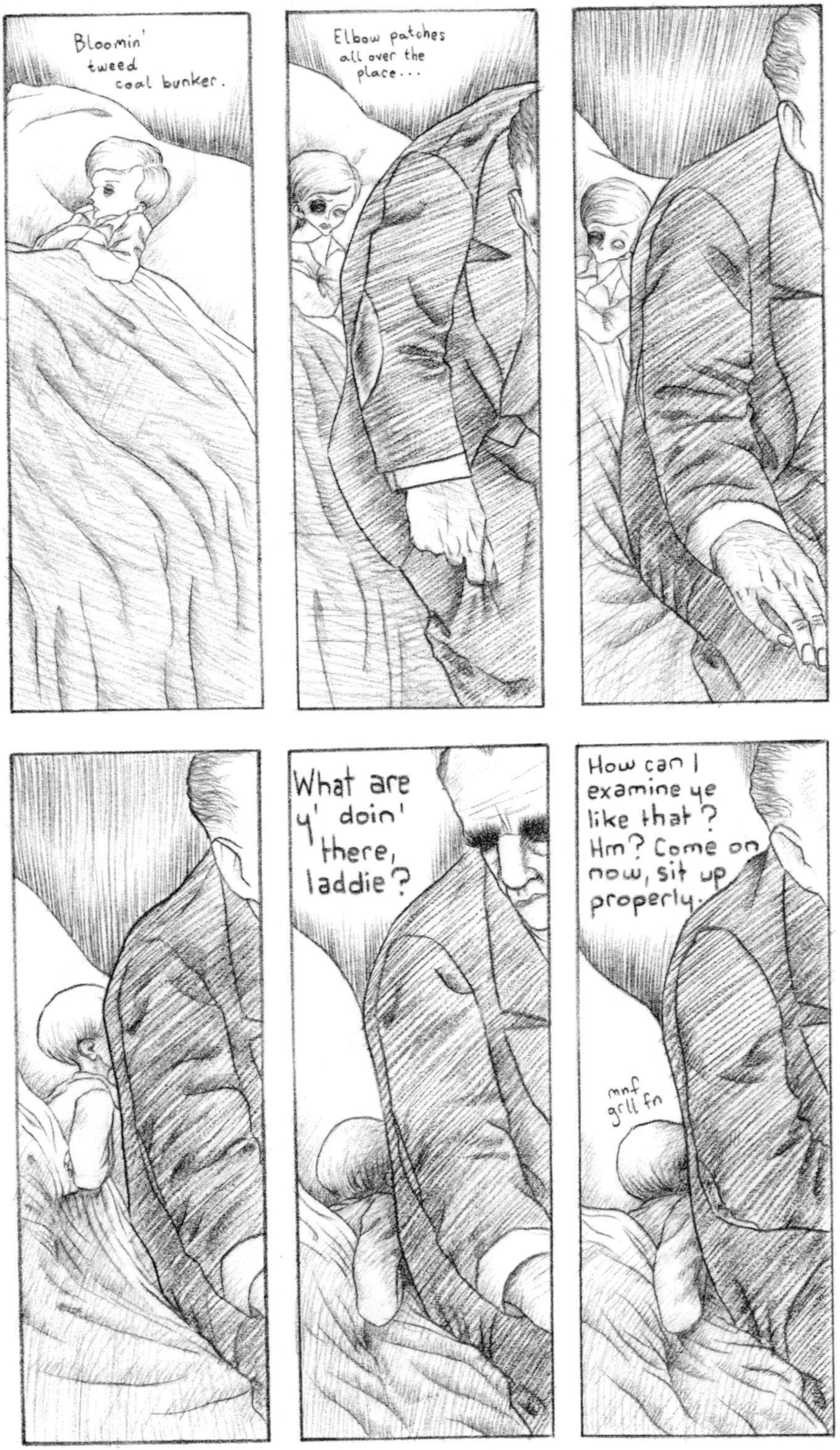
Bloomin' tweed coal bunker.
Elbow patches all over the place...
What are y' doin' there, laddie?
How can I examine ye like that? Hm? Come on now, sit up properly...
mnf grll fn

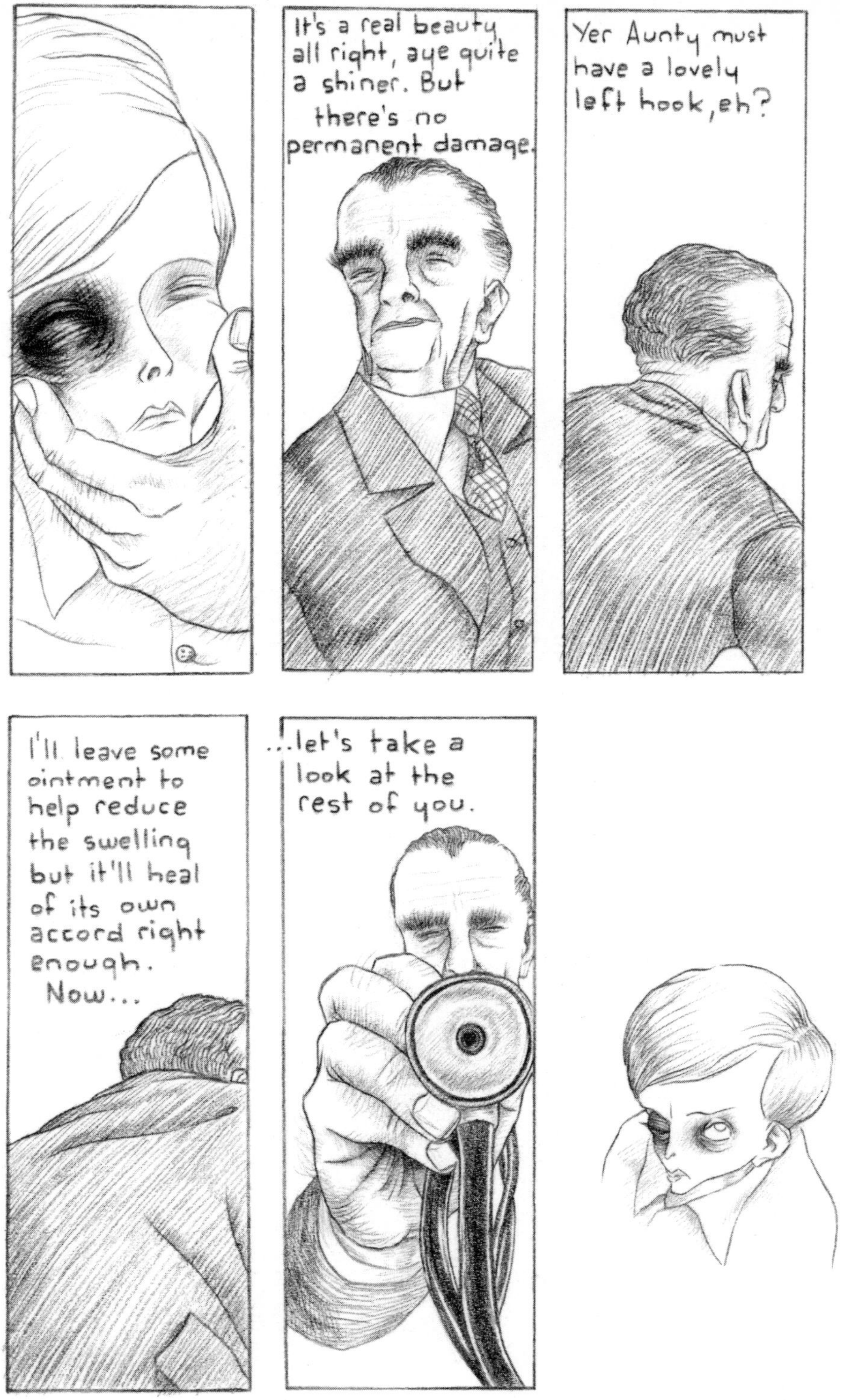
It's a real beauty all right, aye quite a shiner. But there's no permanent damage.
Yer Aunty must have a lovely left hook, eh?
I'll leave some ointment to help reduce the swelling but it'll heal of its own accord right enough. Now...
...let's take a look at the rest of you.

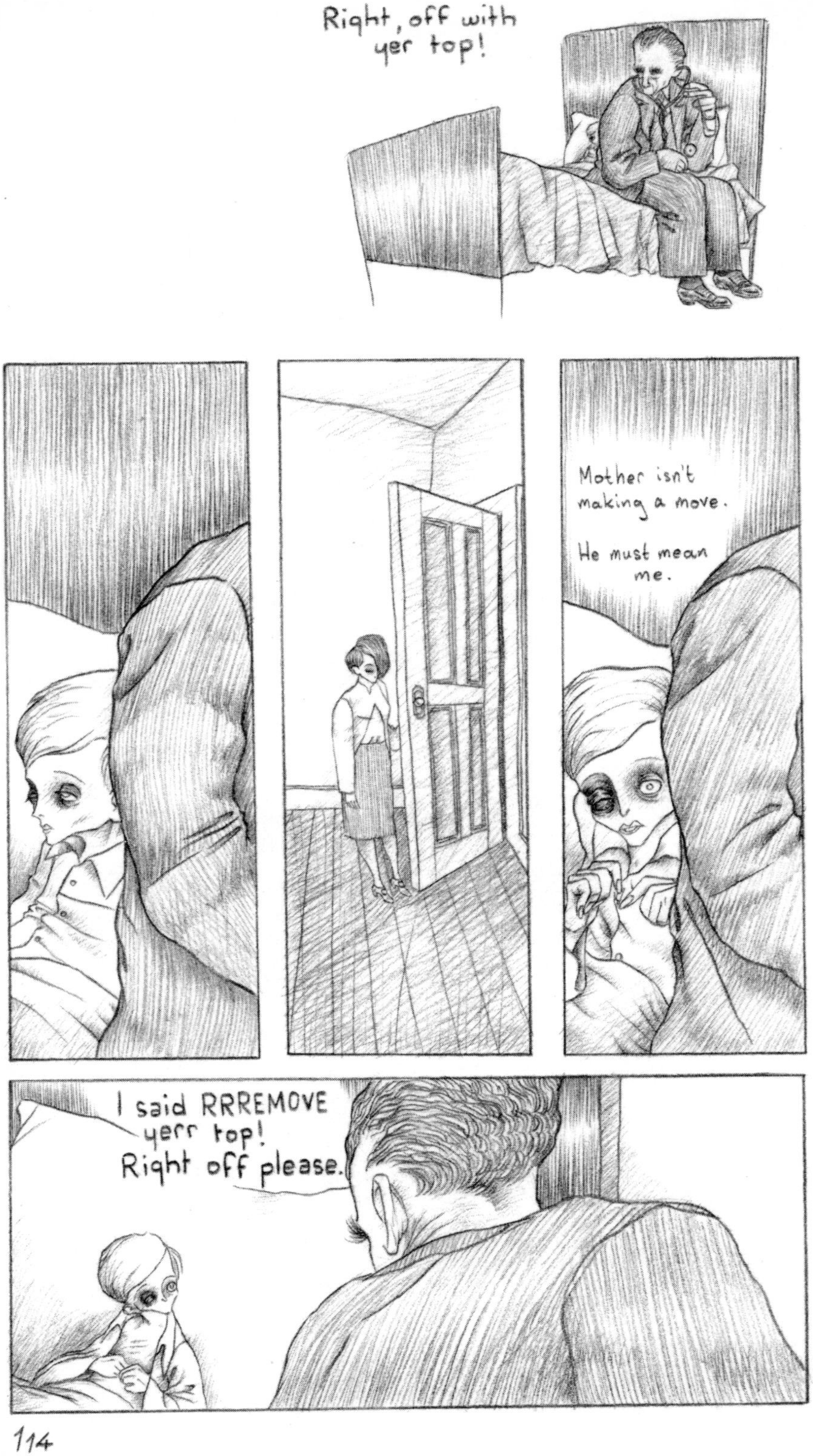
Right, off with yer top!
Mother isn't making a move.
He must mean me.
I said RRREMOVE yerr top! Right off please.

Hep!

Dearie me what a feeble specimen. Now, this will be a little chilly.

Hm, I canna hear anything. Are you holding yer breath?

Oo, do you know, I was!

Fer goodness... let's try again. Now, BRRRRREEEATHE!

Phew, it's exhausting work this breathing, isn't it? Can I stop now?

Oh NO laddie, it's my job to see to it that you don't do that!

Um, how are my lungs, Doctor? Not up to much, I expect.

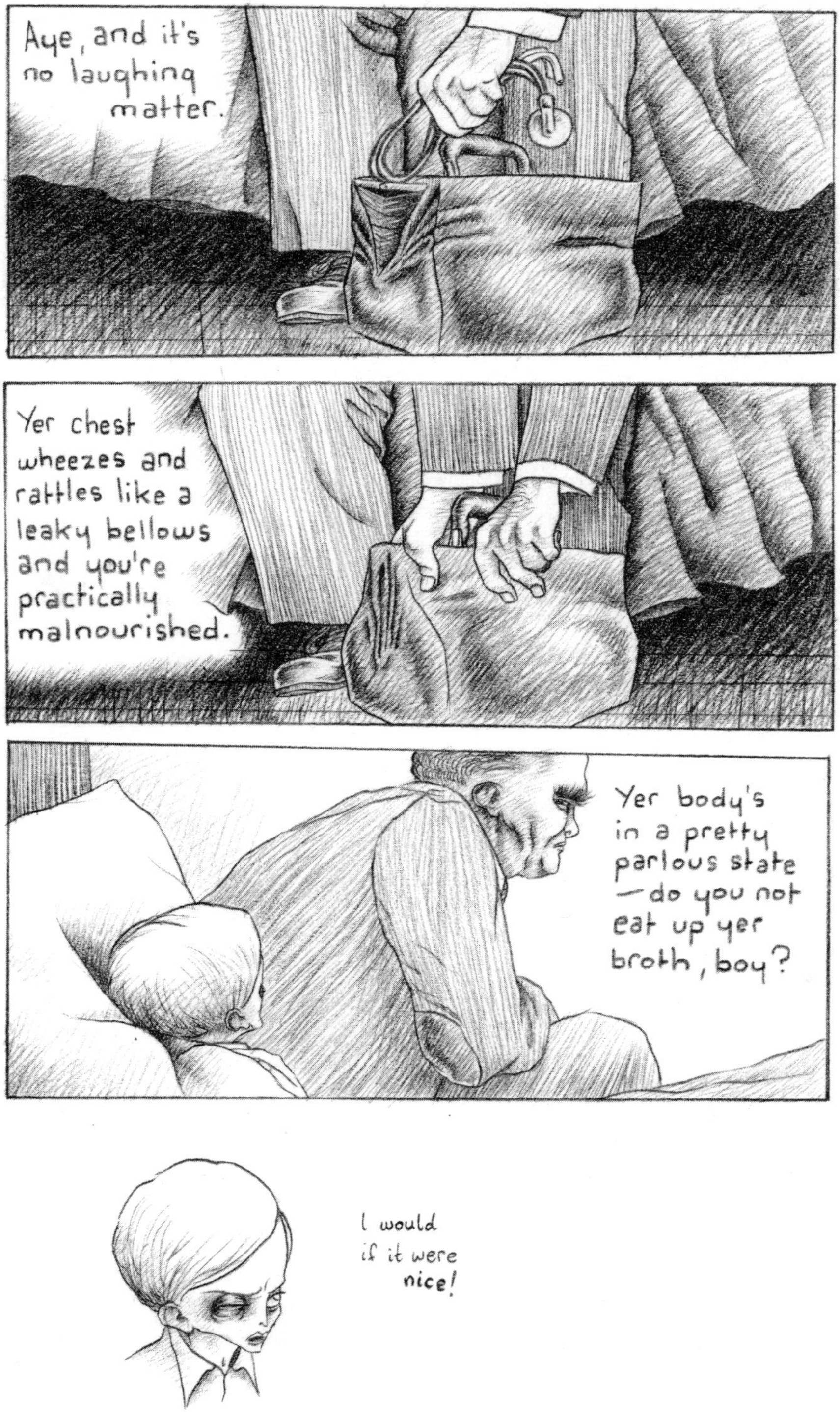
Aye, and it's no laughing matter.
Yer chest wheezes and rattles like a leaky bellows and you're practically malnourished.
Yer body's in a pretty parlous state — do you not eat up yer broth, boy?
I would if it were nice!

NICE?!

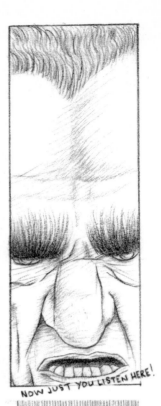

NOW JUST YOU LISTEN HERE!

THERE ARE MEN OOT ON THE STREET DYIN' FOR WANT O' BROTH. D'YE THINK THEY'D CARE ABOOT ITS NICENESS?

AND WHAT'S MORE, THAT POO-ER, BRAVE, NOBLE WOMAN OVER THERE — YER MOTHER! — HAS JUST ABOOT WORRIED HERSEL' SICK —

AYE, SICK TO THE CORE OVER YOU.

SO JUST YOU BE A MAN AND EAT UP YER BROTH — THOUGH IT MAKES YE GAG TO DO IT — FOR THE WORKING MAN, AYE, AND FOR YER MOTHER, SO'S YE CAN BE WELL AND STRONG FOR HER.

YE KEN?

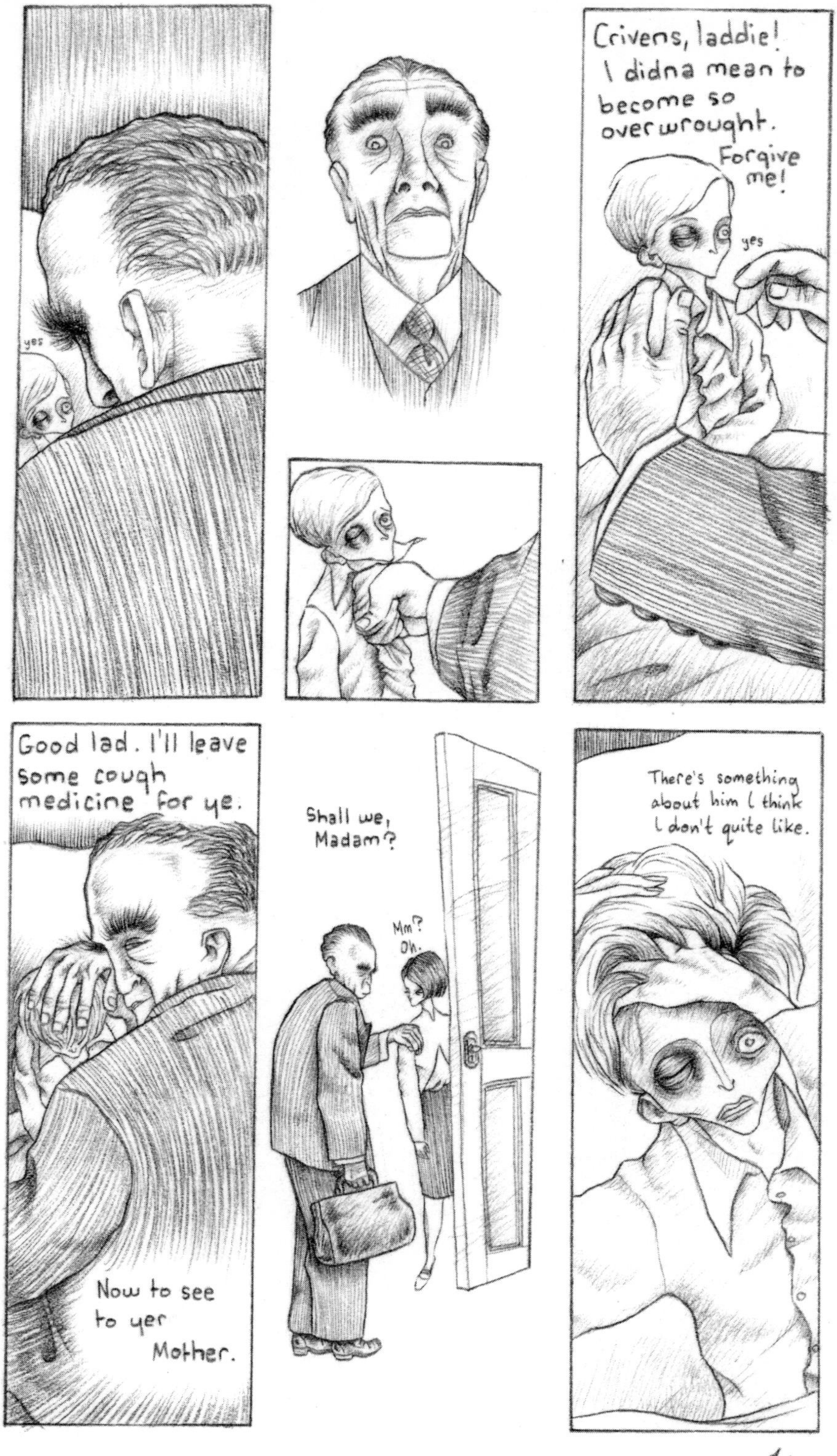

yes
Crivens, laddie! I didna mean to become so overwrought.
Forgive me!
yes
Good lad. I'll leave some cough medicine for ye.
Now to see to yer Mother.
Shall we, Madam?
Mm? Oh.
There's something about him I think I don't quite like.

I like my cough medicine though.

It is scrummy.

It is thick black stuff a bit like treacle and a bit like liquorice and a bit like the stuff that comes out of Uncle Tremayne's pipe.

Only it is scrummy.

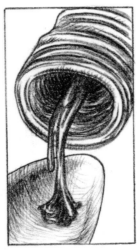

It takes an age to pour and when Mother takes the spoon out of my mouth my top lip goes with it and the medicine burns warmly and makes me happy. It's the best thing about being ill.

If only he'd left it with me, instead of Mother.

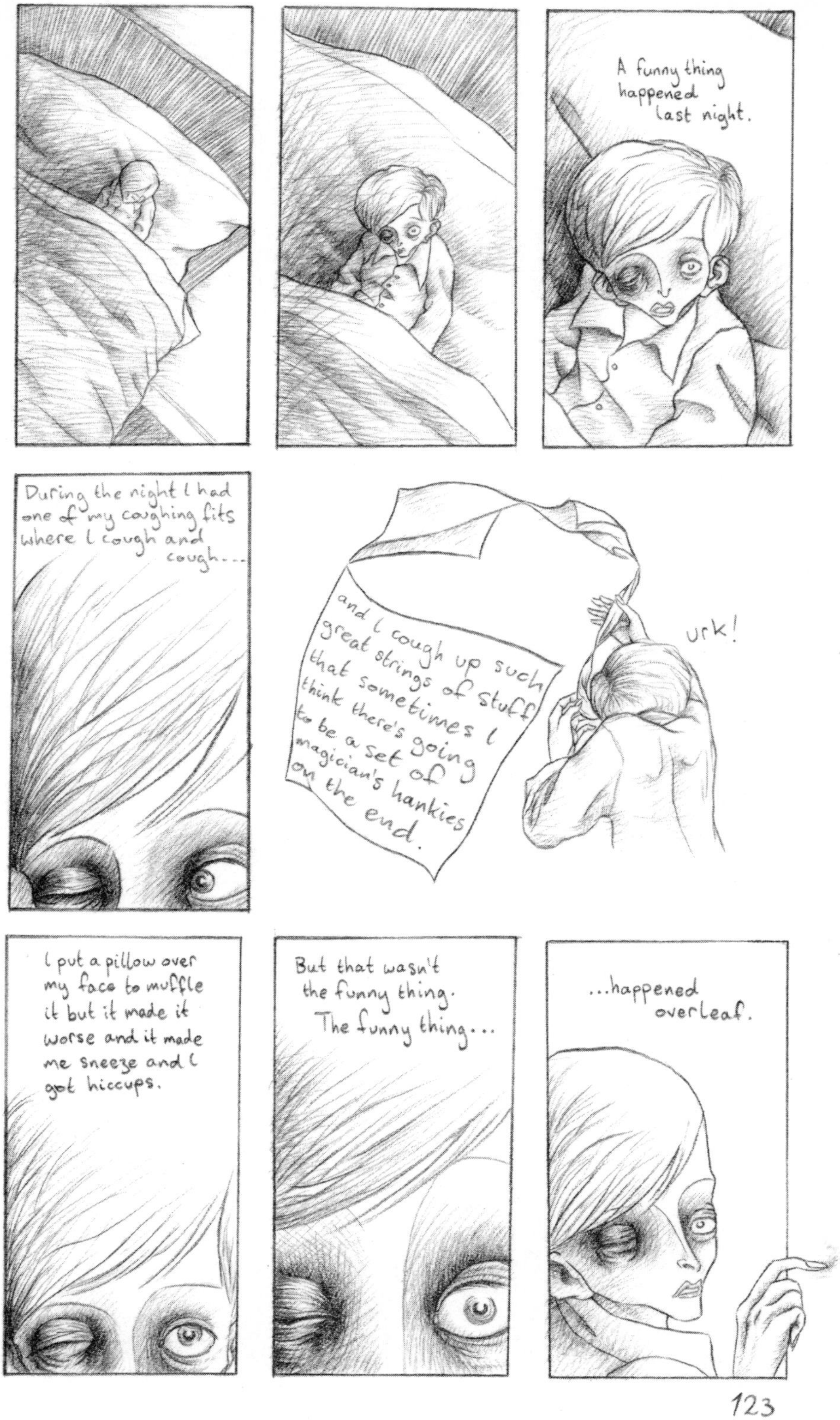
A funny thing happened last night.
During the night I had one of my coughing fits where I cough and cough...
and I cough up such great strings of stuff that sometimes I think there's going to be a set of magician's hankies on the end.
urk!
I put a pillow over my face to muffle it but it made it worse and it made me sneeze and I got hiccups.
But that wasn't the funny thing.
The funny thing...
...happened overleaf.

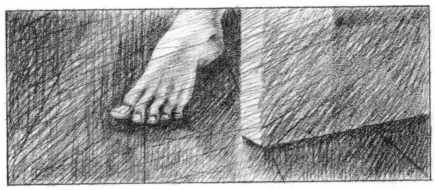

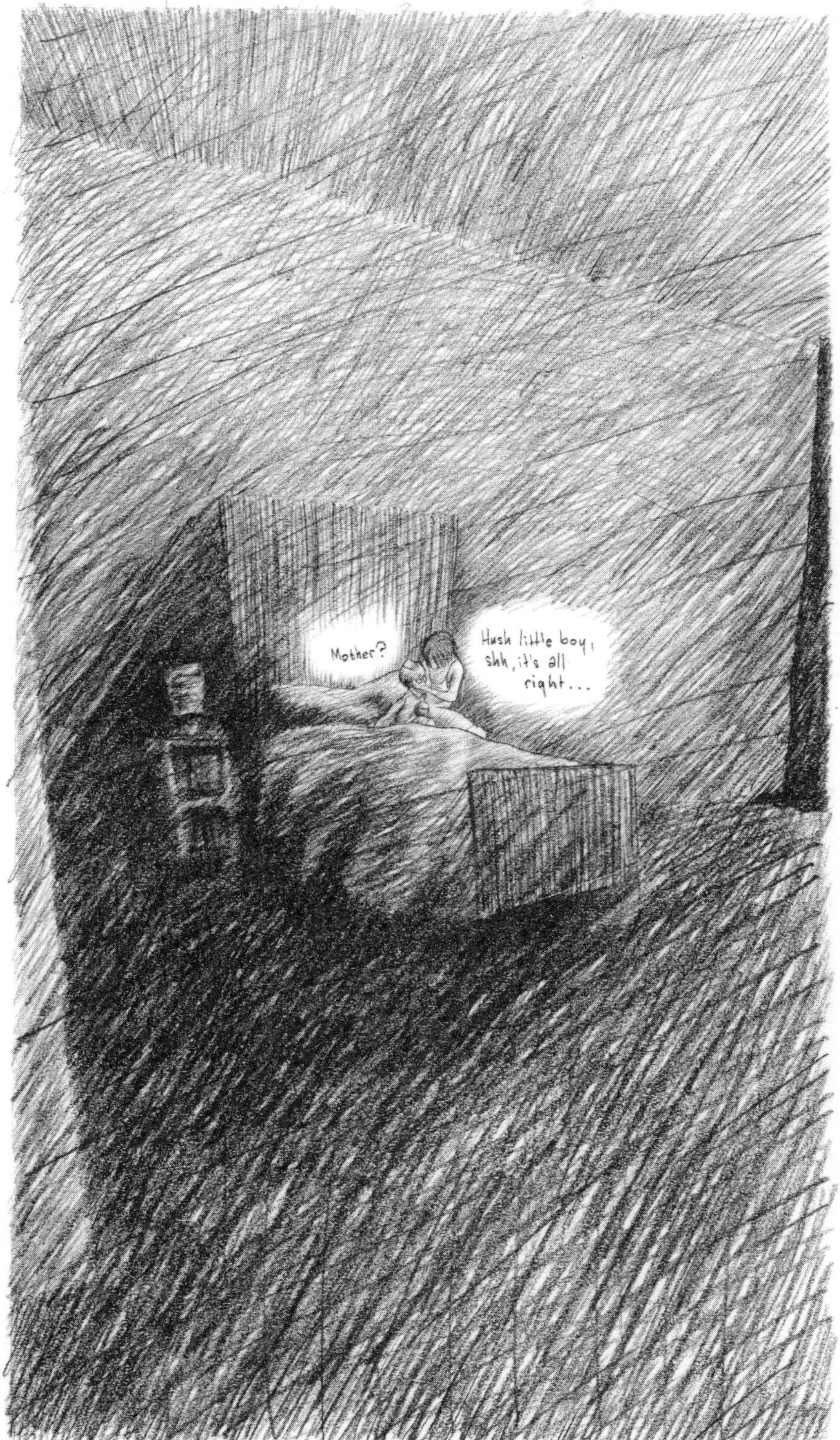
Mother?
Hush little boy, shh, it's all right...

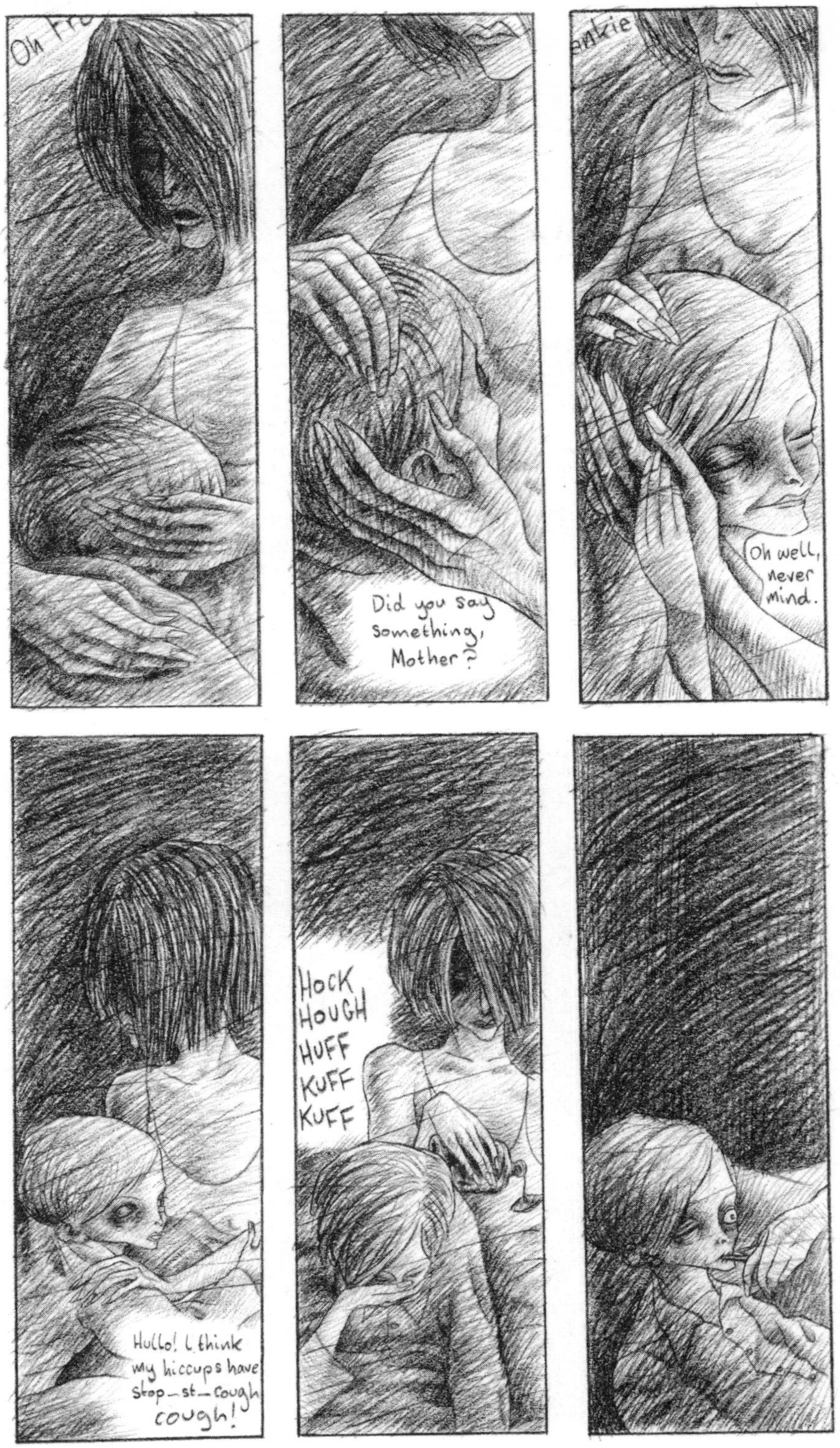
Oh Fr
Did you say something, Mother?
ankie
Oh well, never mind.
Hullo! I think my hiccups have stop_st_cough cough!
HOCK HOUGH HUFF KUFF KUFF

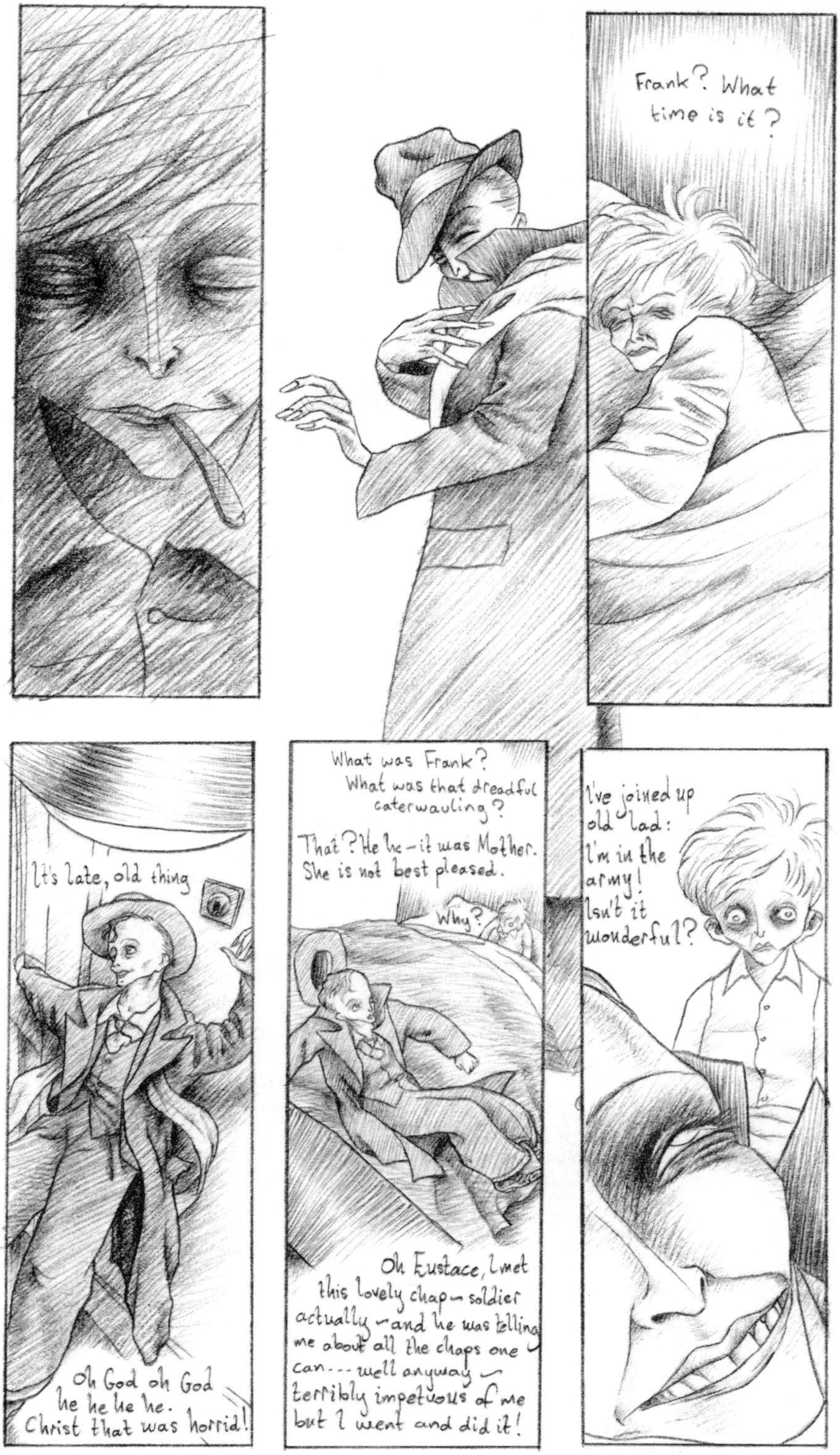
Frank? What time is it?
It's late, old thing
Oh God oh God he he he he. Christ that was horrid!
What was Frank? What was that dreadful caterwauling?
That? He he – it was Mother. She is not best pleased.
Why?
Oh Eustace, I met this lovely chap – soldier actually – and he was telling me about all the chaps one can... well anyway – terribly impetuous of me but I went and did it!
I've joined up old lad: I'm in the army! Isn't it wonderful?

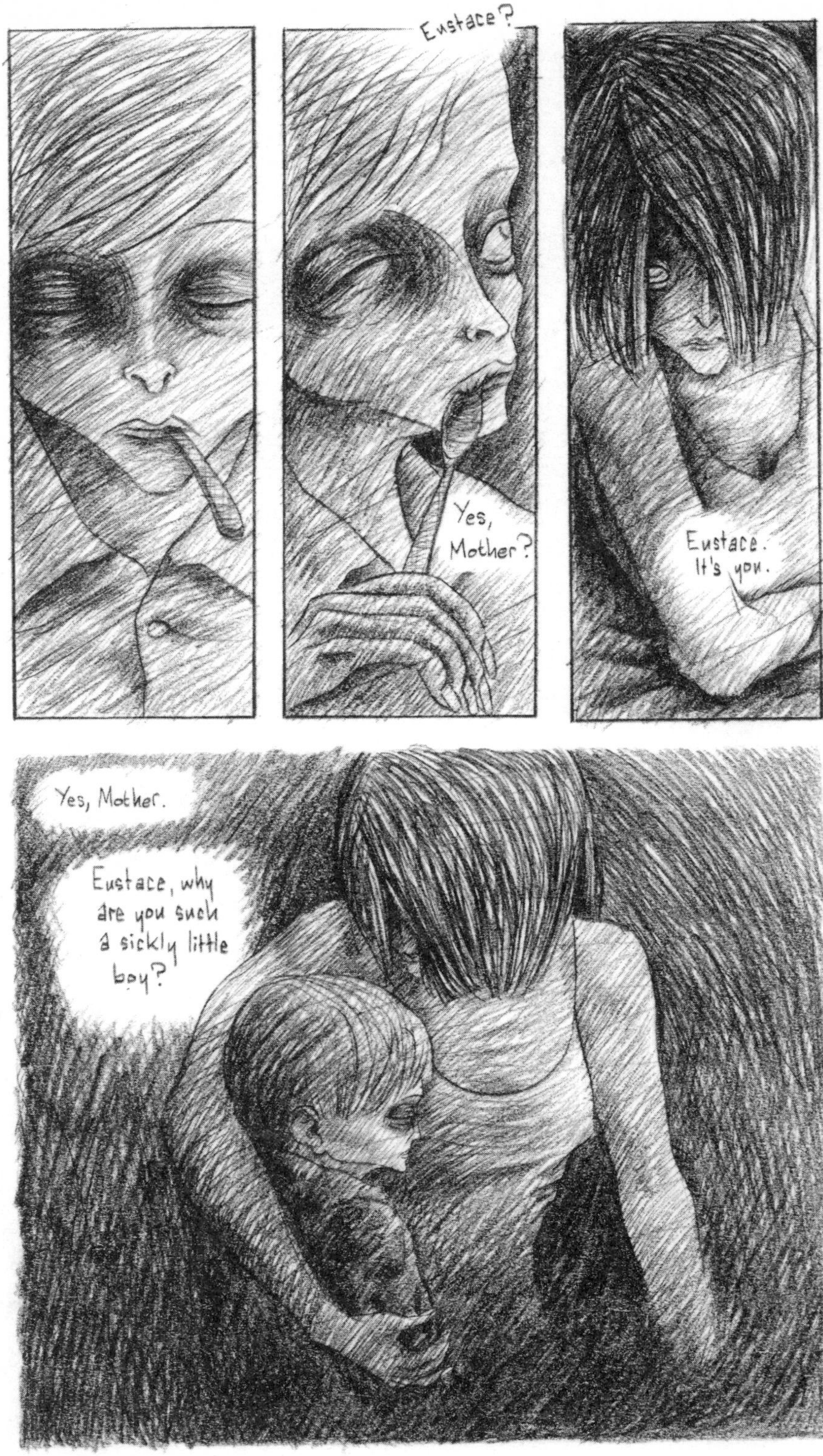
Eustace?
Yes, Mother?
Eustace. It's you.
Yes, Mother.
Eustace, why are you such a sickly little boy?

I don't know,
Mother.

I'll try harder
not to be —

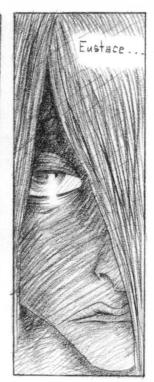

Eustace...

Yes, Mother?

You must...
forgibm...
must...

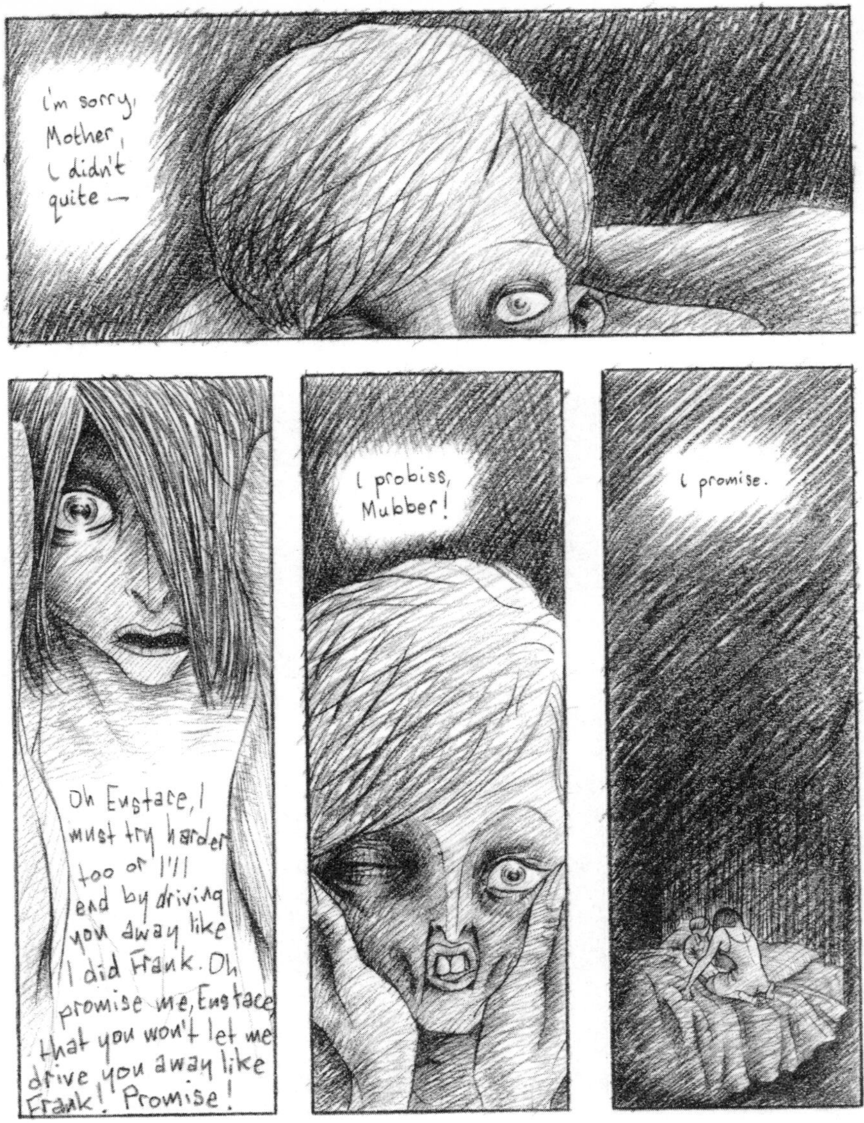
i'm sorry, Mother, I didn't quite –
Oh Eustace, I must try harder too or I'll end by driving you away like I did Frank. Oh promise me, Eustace, that you won't let me drive you away like Frank! Promise!
I probiss, Mubber!
I promise.
I meant it too. Good Lord, I'm only eight; where did she think I was going to go?

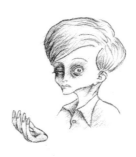

She started to say something else but petered out at the end like the talking sailor doll I used to have that said 'A life on the ocean wave' when you pulled a string on his back until I took him into the bath with me and he said 'A bibbly bobbly bottle of rum' and never spoke again.

Then she picked her way ever so carefully between the tiny bits of light and dust on the floor and left the room.

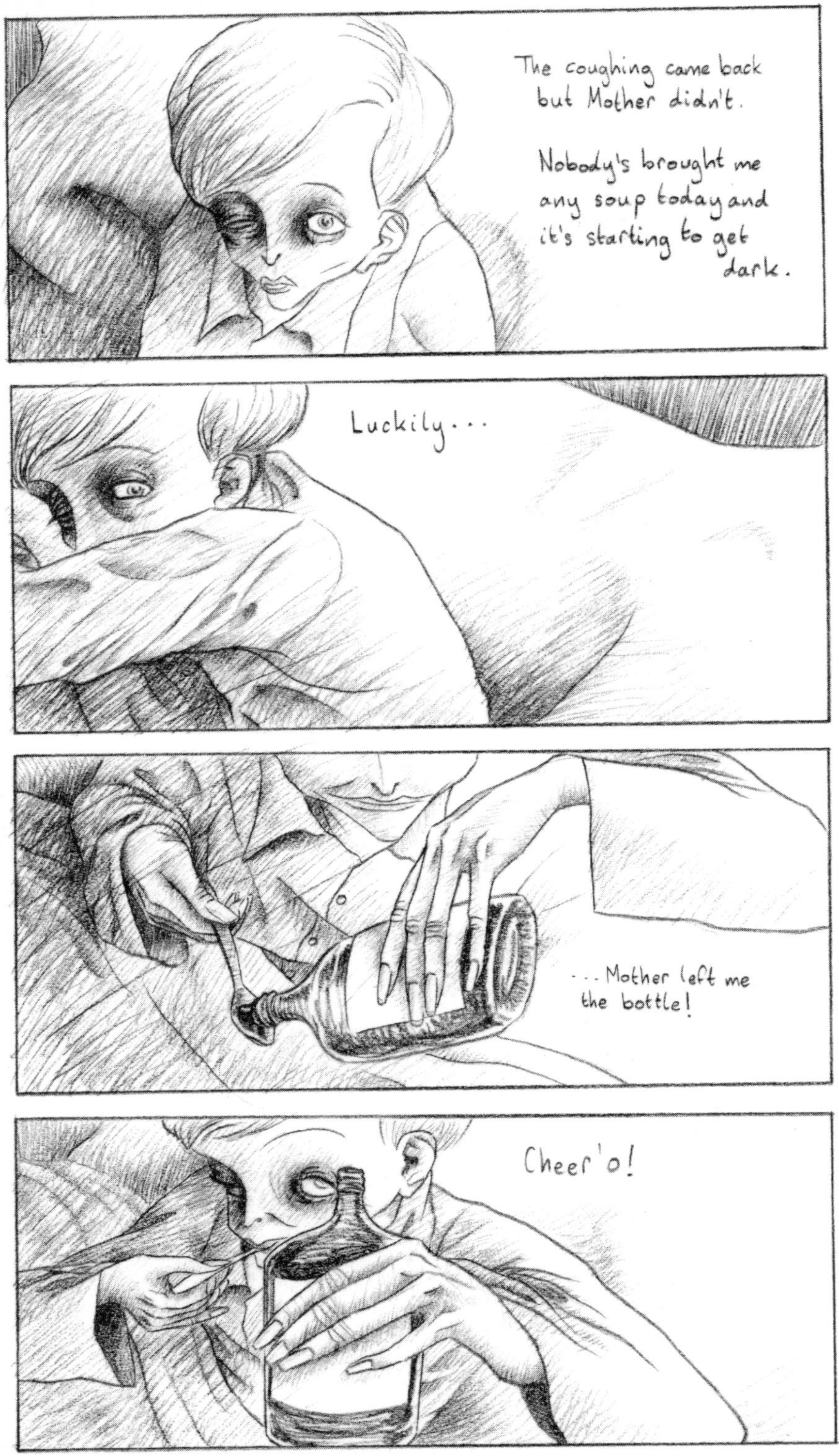
The coughing came back but Mother didn't.
Nobody's brought me any soup today and it's starting to get dark.
Luckily...
...Mother left me the bottle!
Cheer'o!

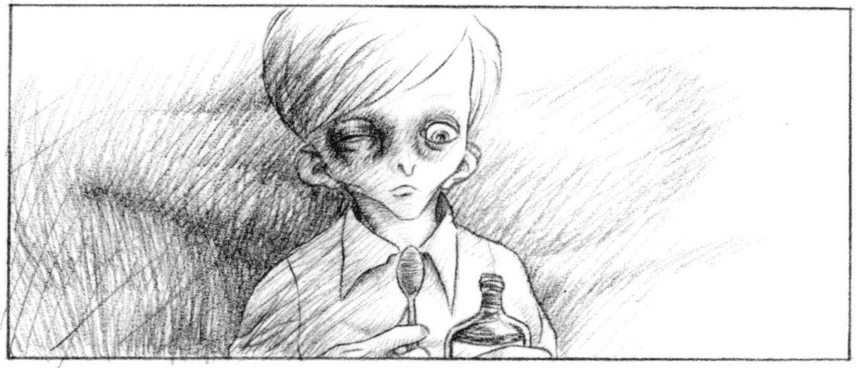

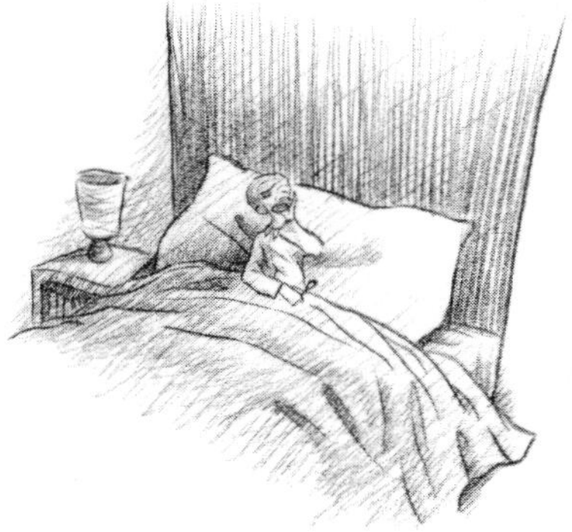

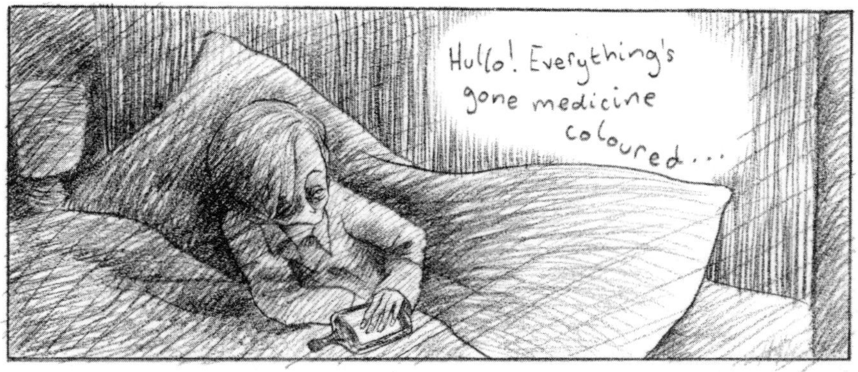
Hullo! Everything's gone medicine coloured...

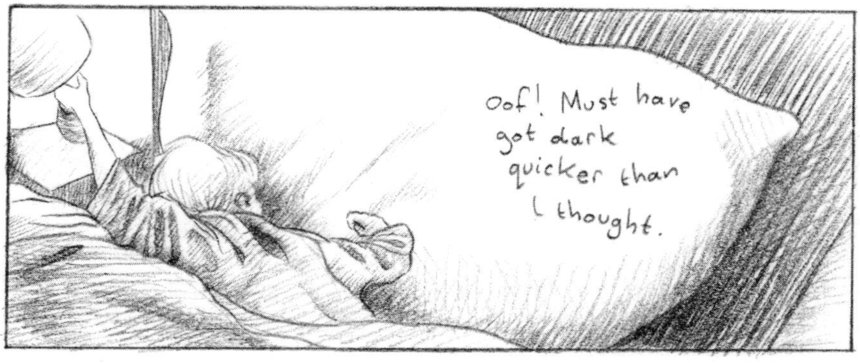
Oof! Must have got dark quicker than I thought.

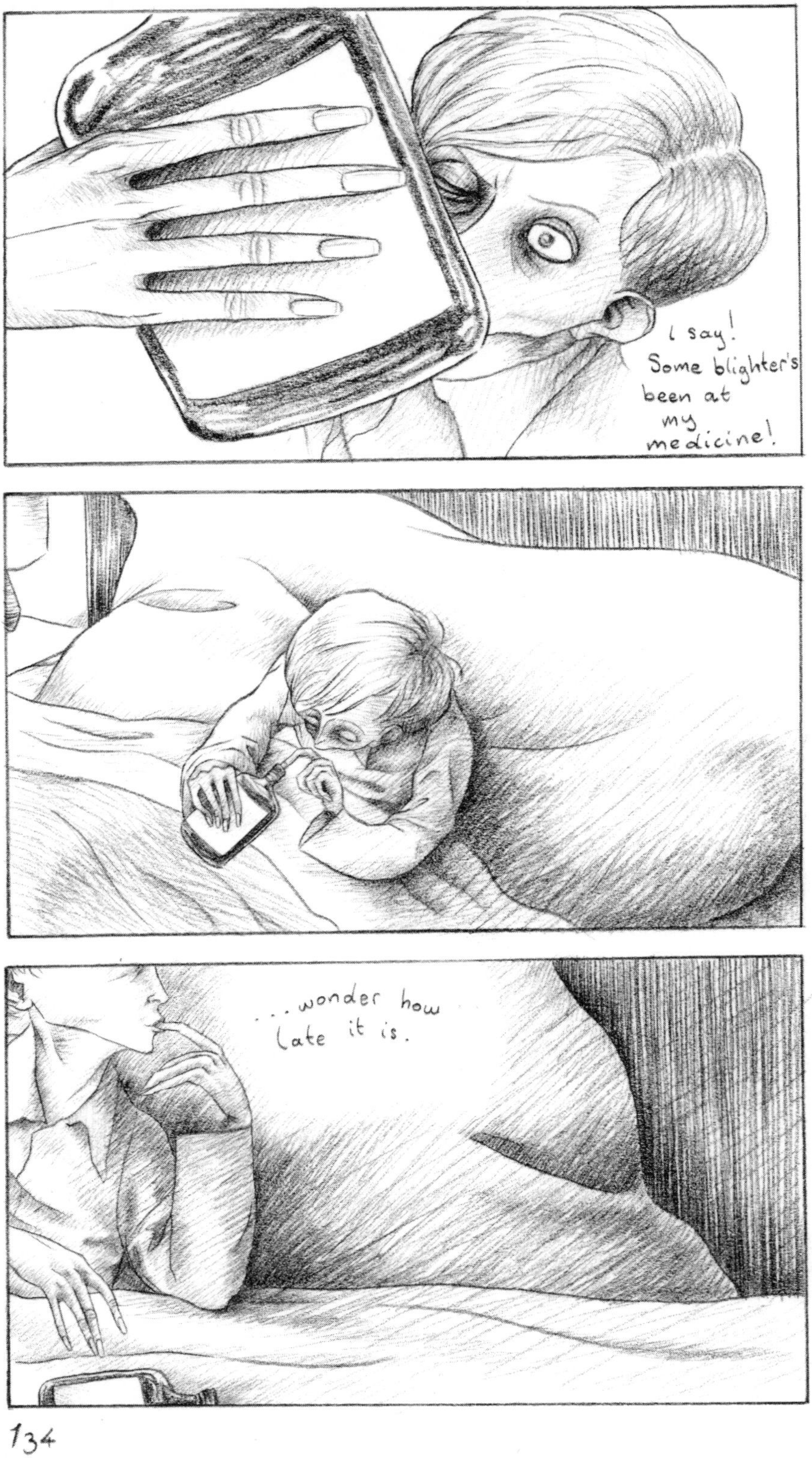
I say! Some blighter's been at my medicine!
...wonder how late it is.

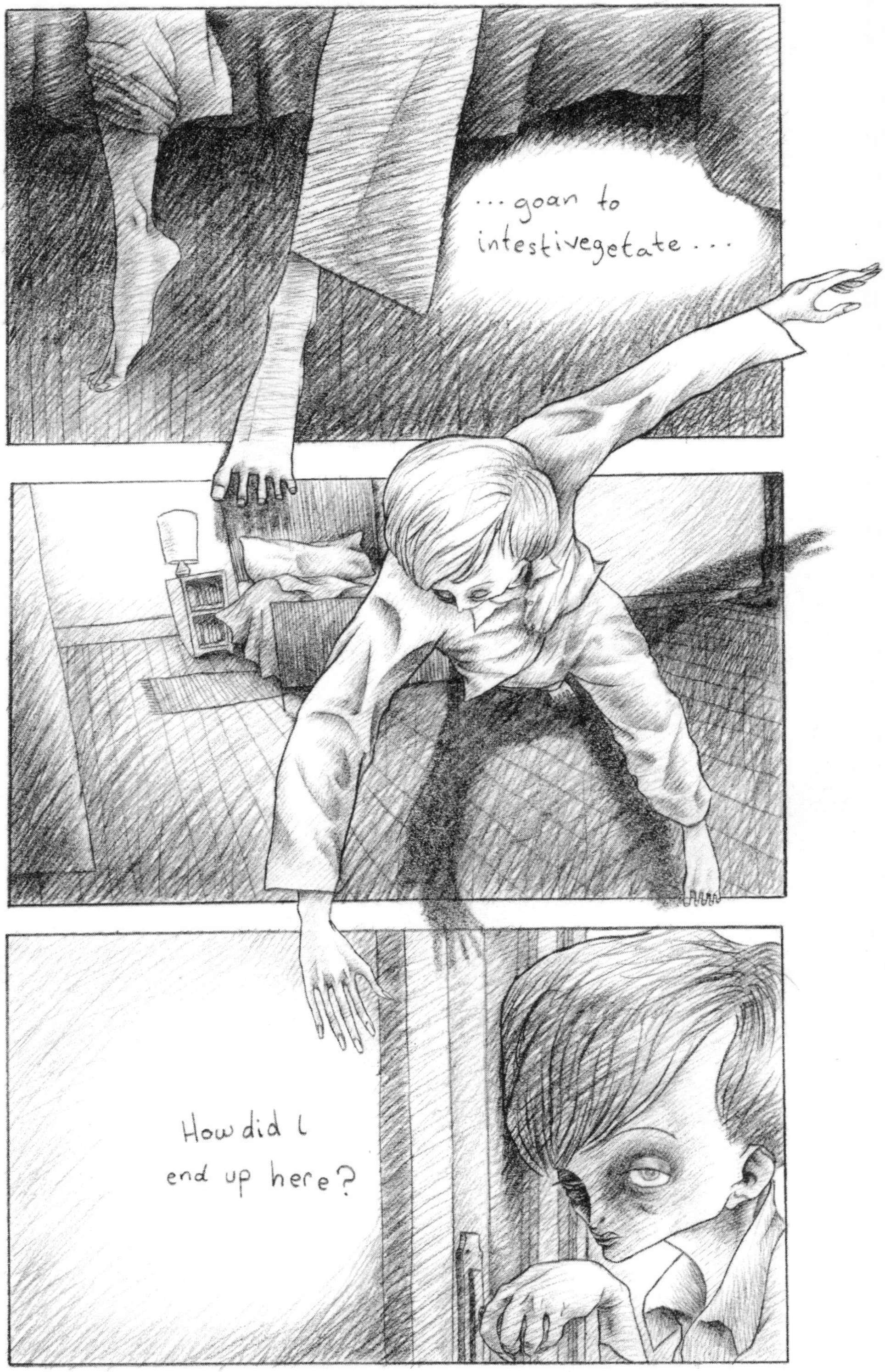
...goan to intestivegetate...
How did I end up here?

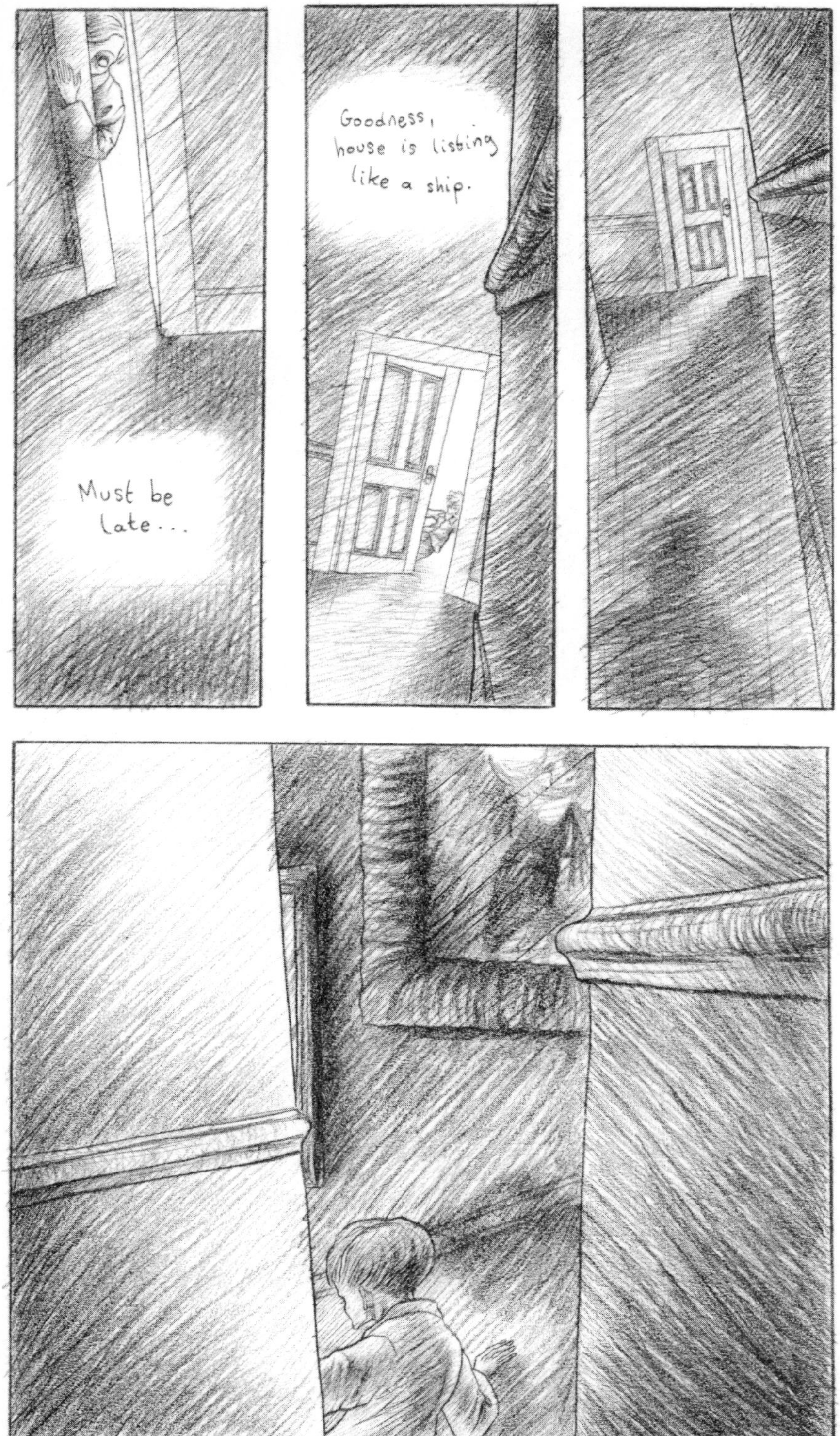
Must be late...
Goodness, house is listing like a ship.

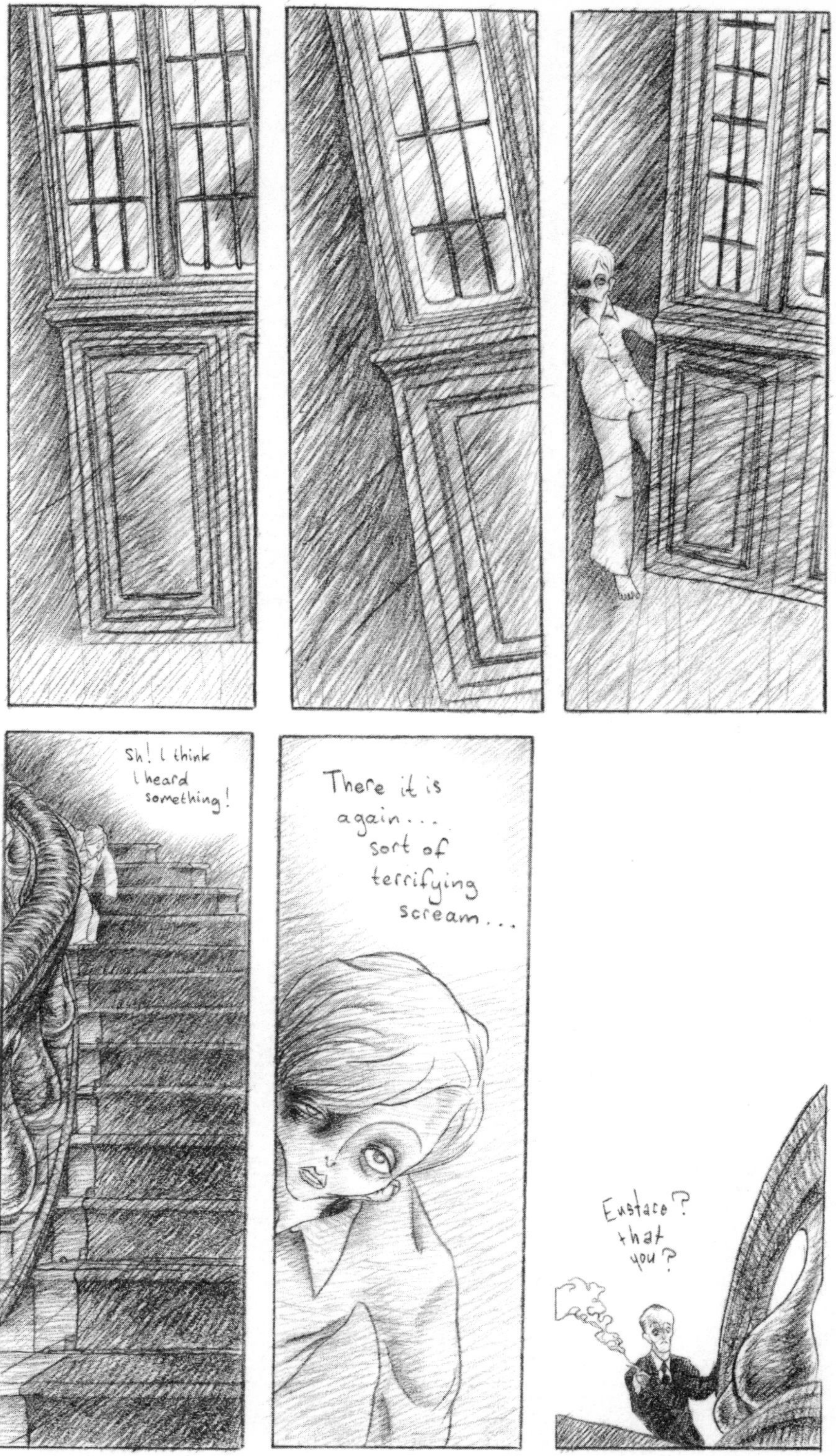
Sh! I think I heard something!
There it is again... sort of terrifying scream...
Eustace? that you?

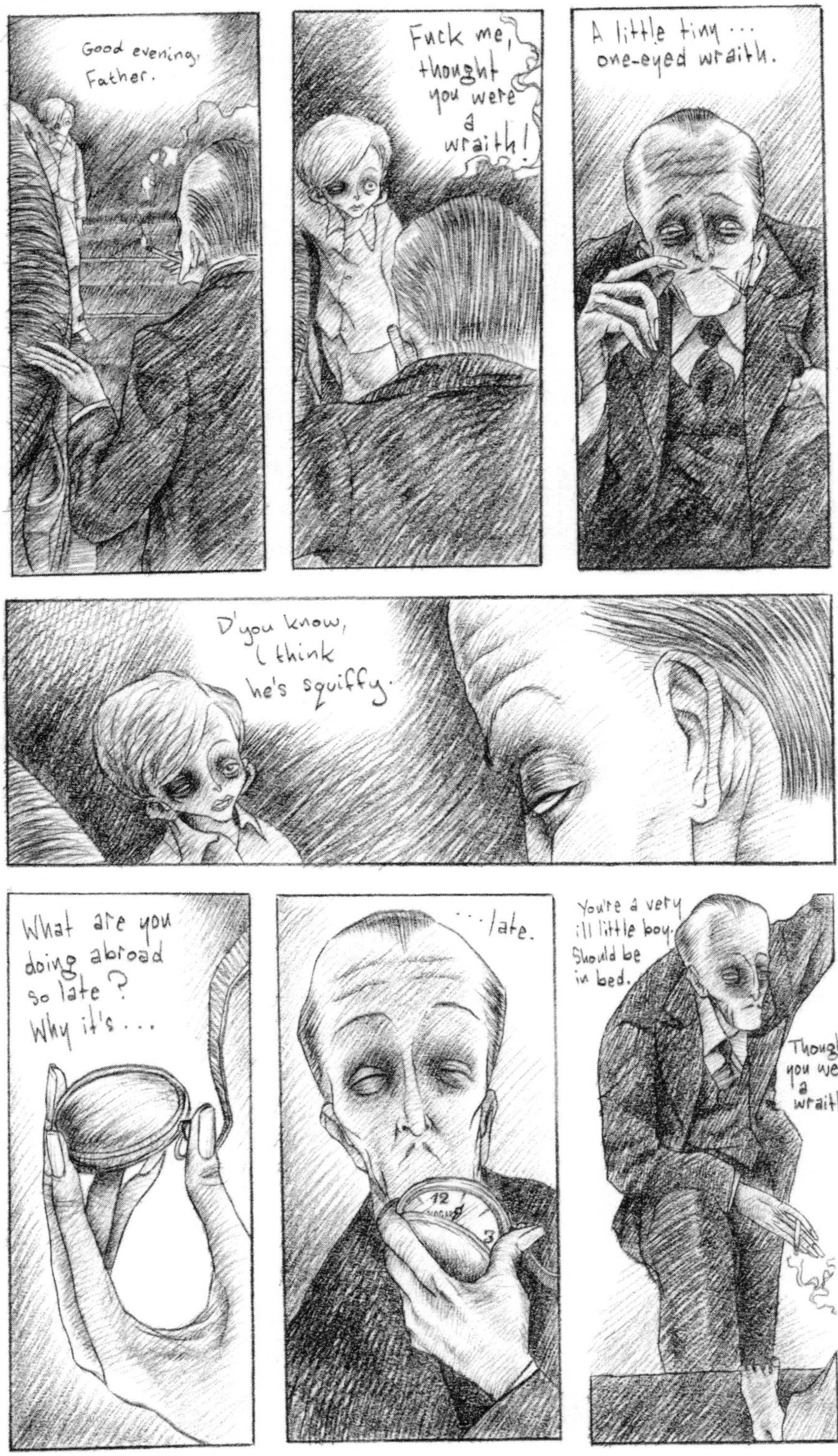
Good evening, Father.
Fuck me, thought you were a wraith!
A little tiny ... one-eyed wraith.
D'you know, I think he's squiffy.
What are you doing abroad so late? Why it's ...
... late.
You're a very ill little boy. Should be in bed.
Thought you were a wraith.

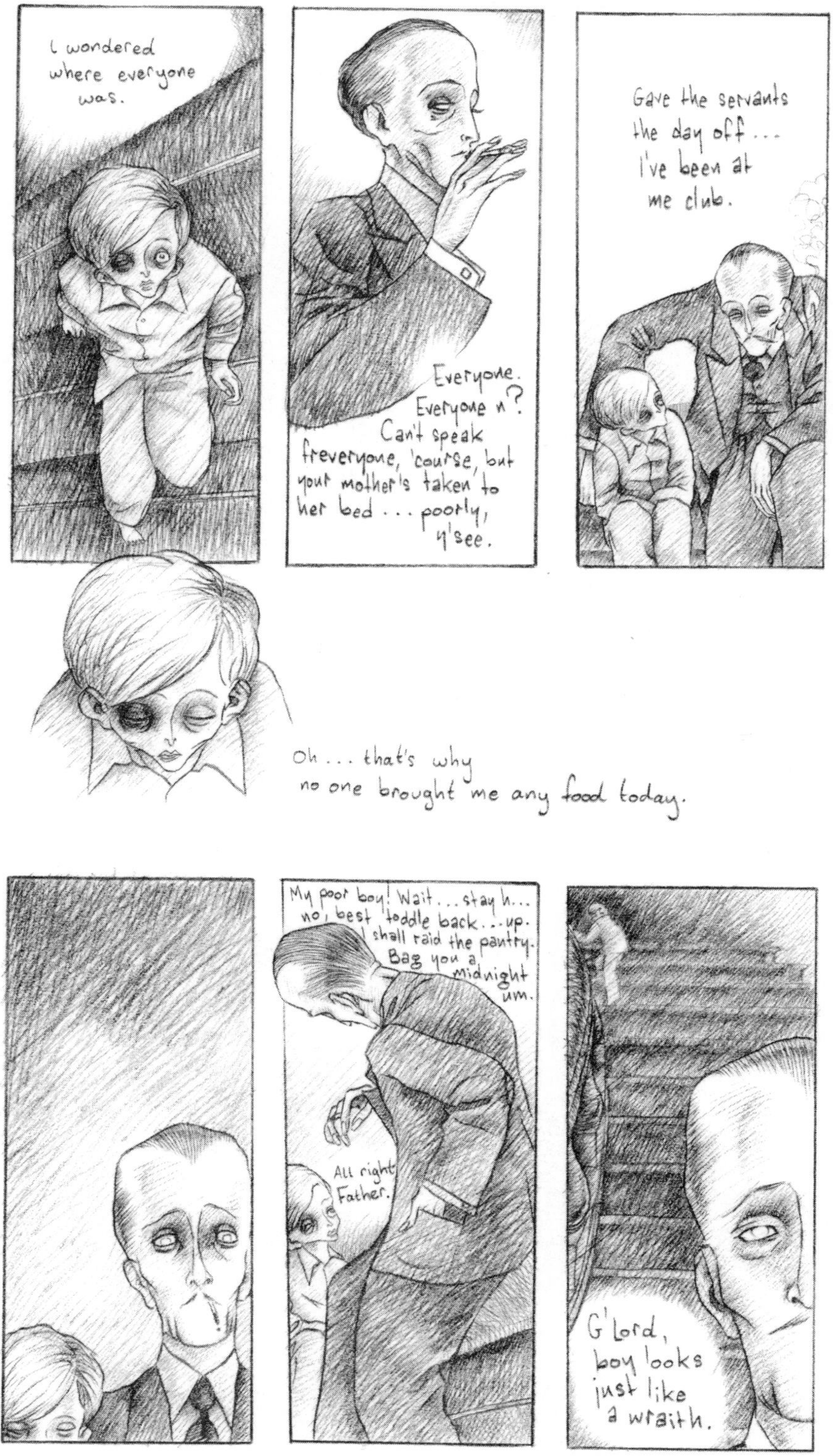

I wondered where everyone was.
Everyone. Everyone n? Can't speak freveryone, 'course, but your mother's taken to her bed . . . poorly, y'see.
Gave the servants the day off . . . I've been at me club.
Oh . . . that's why no one brought me any food today.
My poor boy! Wait . . . stay h . . . no, best toddle back . . . up. I shall raid the pantry. Bag you a midnight um.
All right Father.
G'Lord, boy looks just like a wraith.

Father's taking an awfully long time.

Hullo, is this the place?

Ah yes, so it is, so it mm.

Apologies for the ...ah... delay. I got ... had no idea there were so many ...rooms.

Not much in the ... either. But here ...

...it's a sandwich. Some kind of meat ...I suppose.

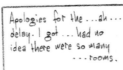

Though it's more jelly and gristle than meat ...really.

Shocking state of ... um ...affairs. In the pantry.

Thank you, Father. Oh. It's soggy.

140

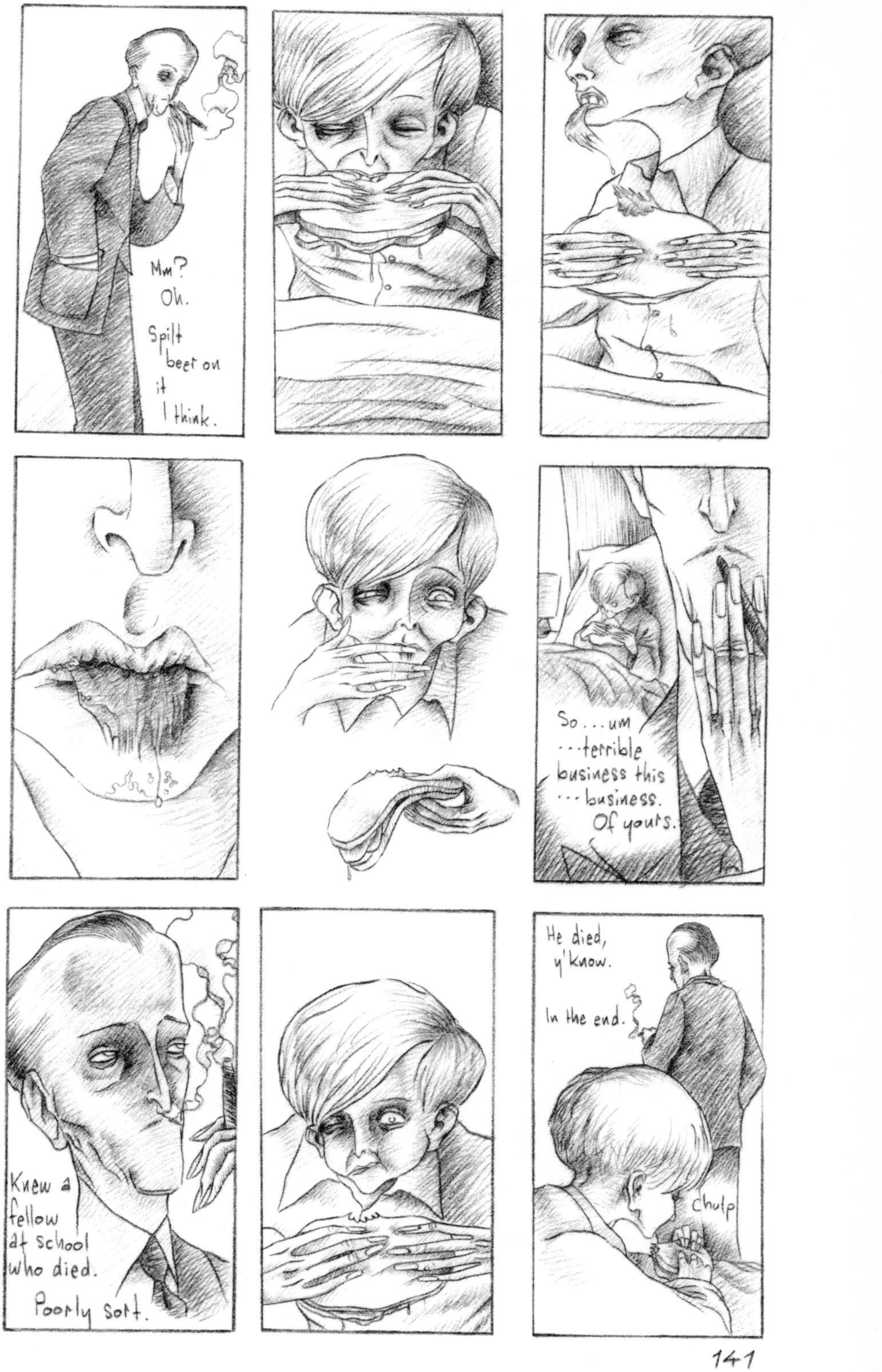
Mm?
Oh.
Spilt beer on it I think.
So . . . um . . . terrible business this . . . business. Of yours.
Knew a fellow at school who died.
Poorly sort.
He died, y'know.
In the end.
Chulp

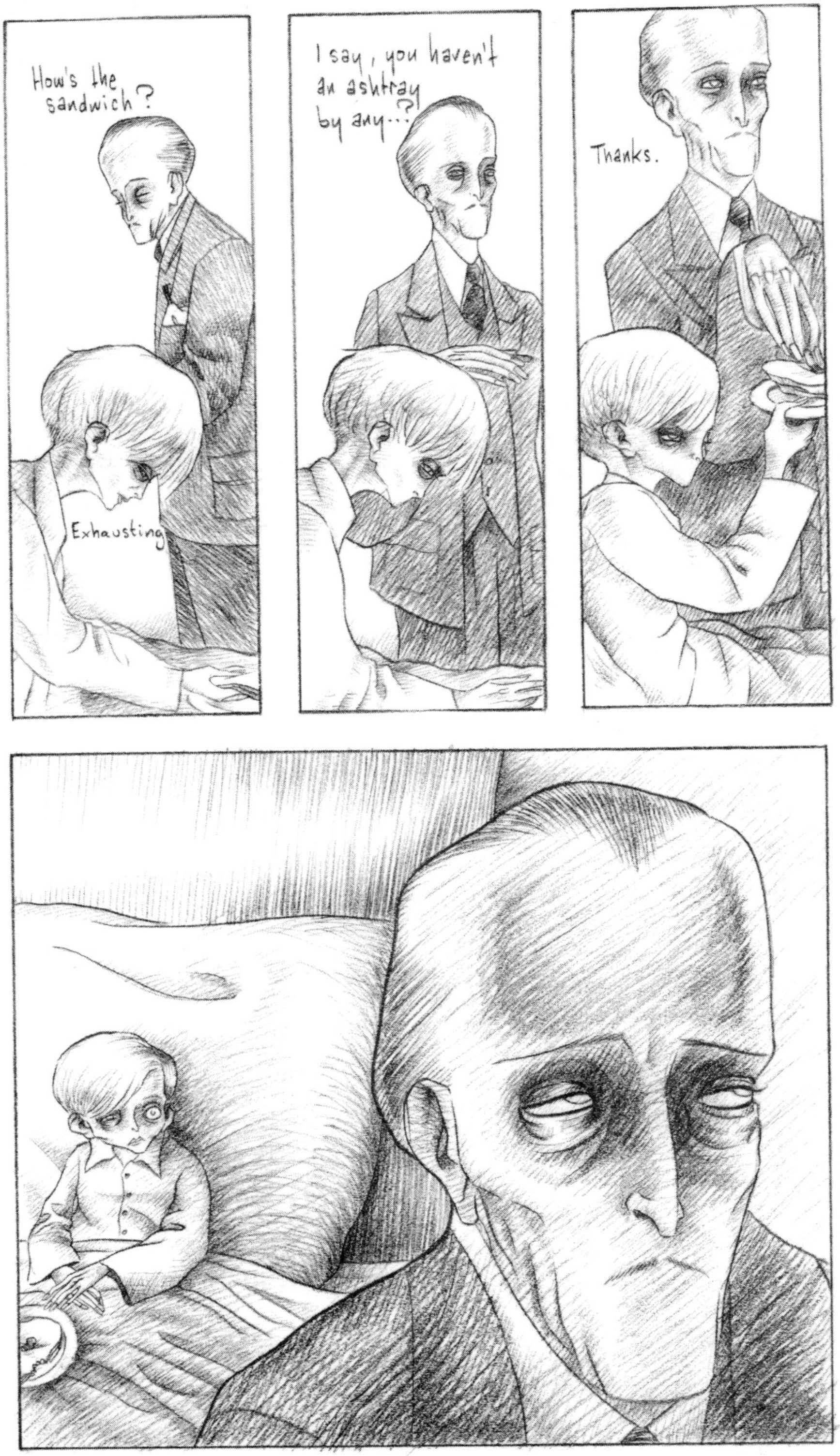
How's the sandwich?
Exhausting
I say, you haven't an ashtray by any...?
Thanks.

Well...

Suppose I ought to be joining your mother in — um — bed.

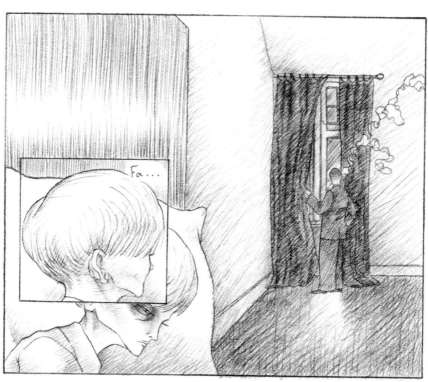

Fa...

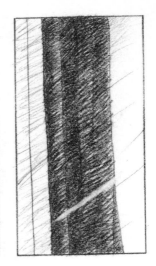

Father . . .
    goodnight ?

Oh . . .
yes, rather.

G'night
m'boy.
Sleep . . .

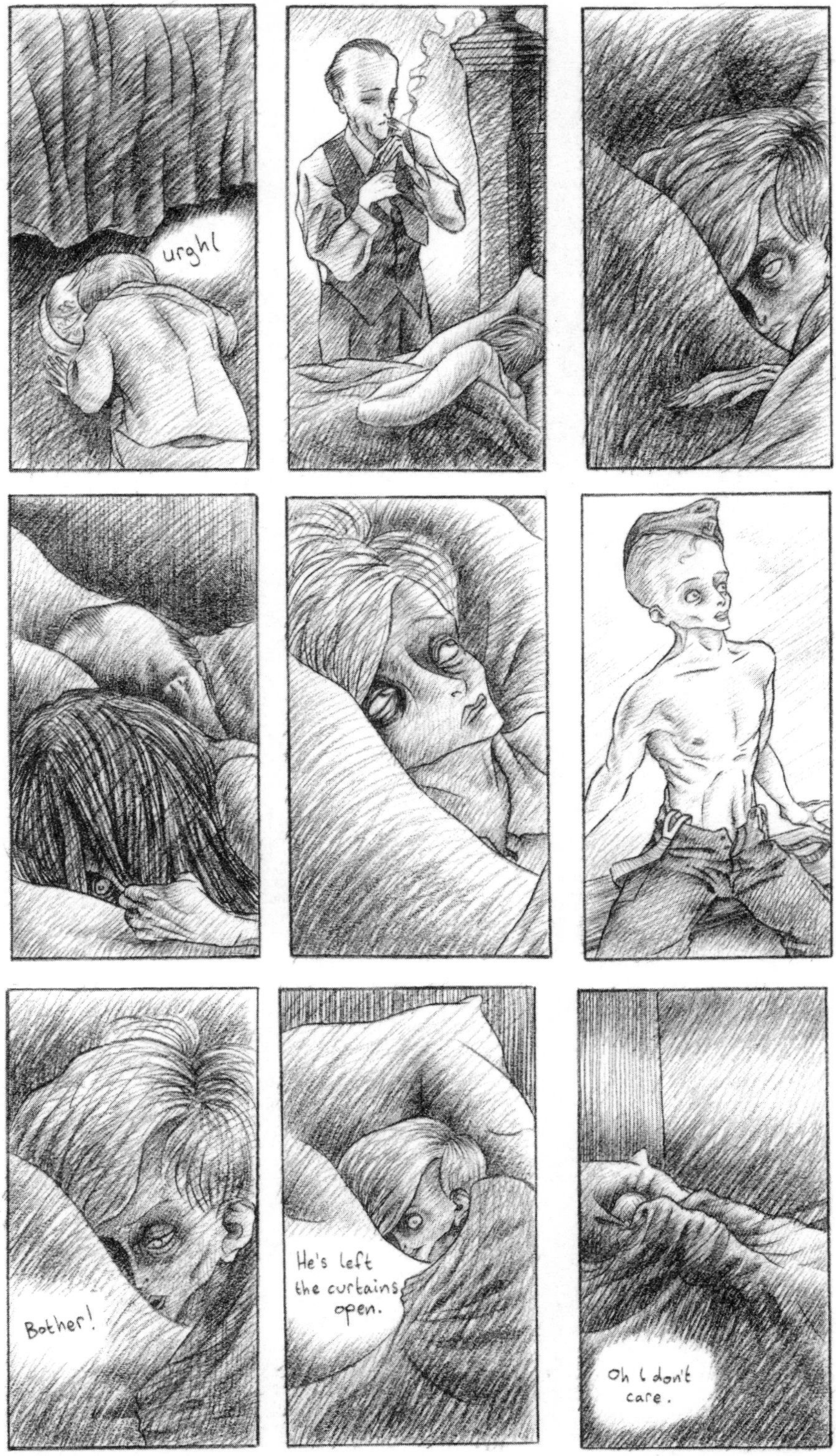
urghl
Bother!
He's left the curtains open.
Oh I don't care.

146

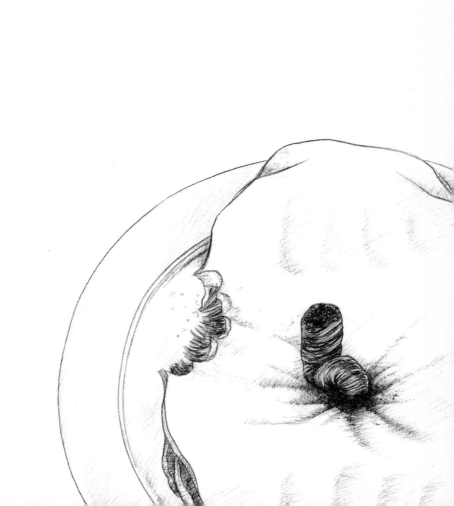

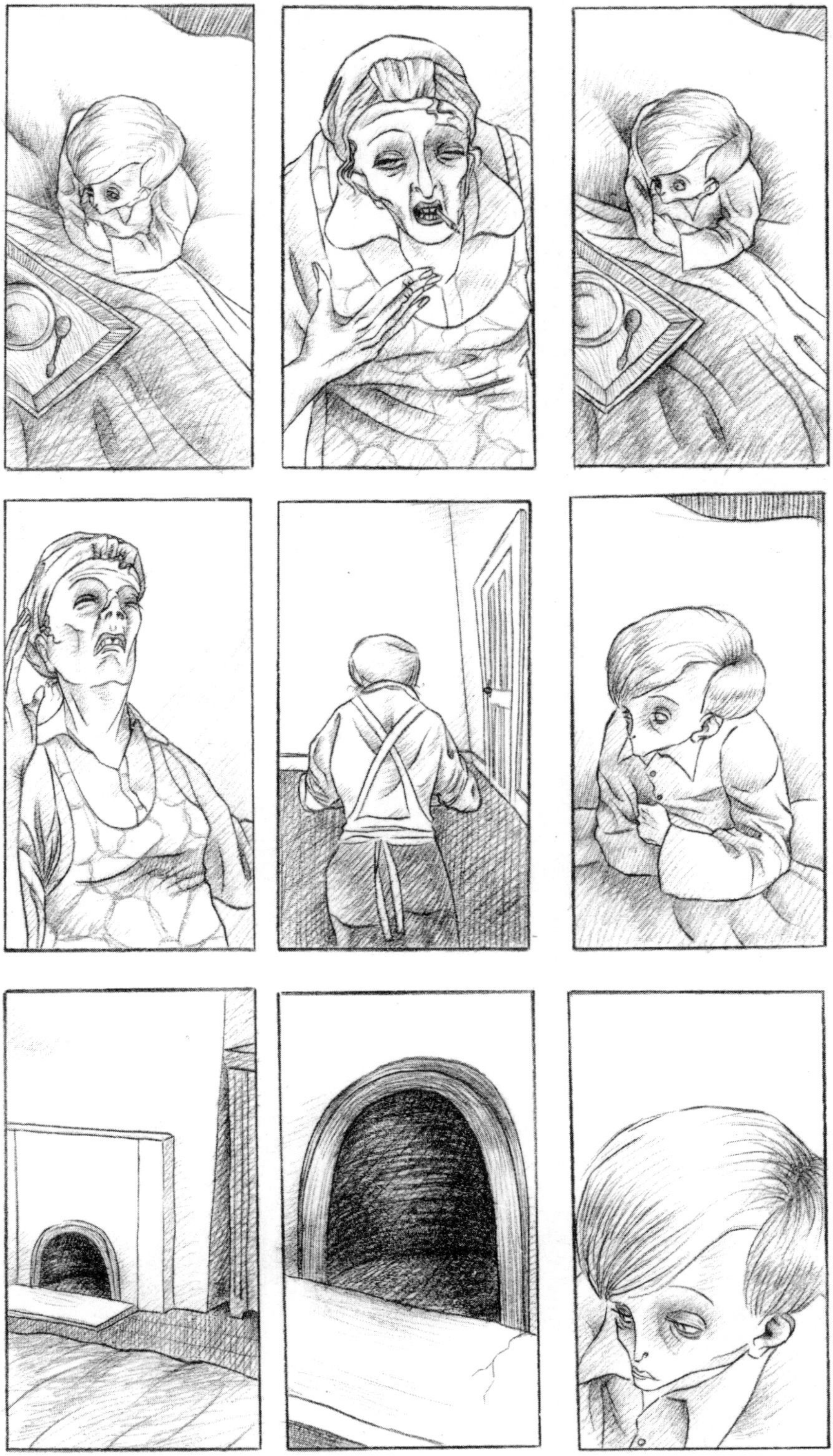

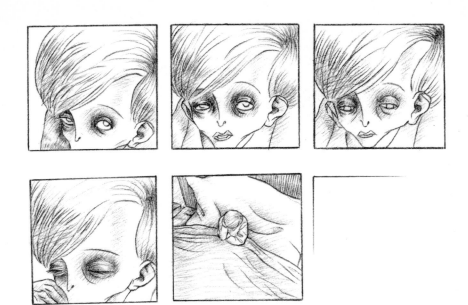

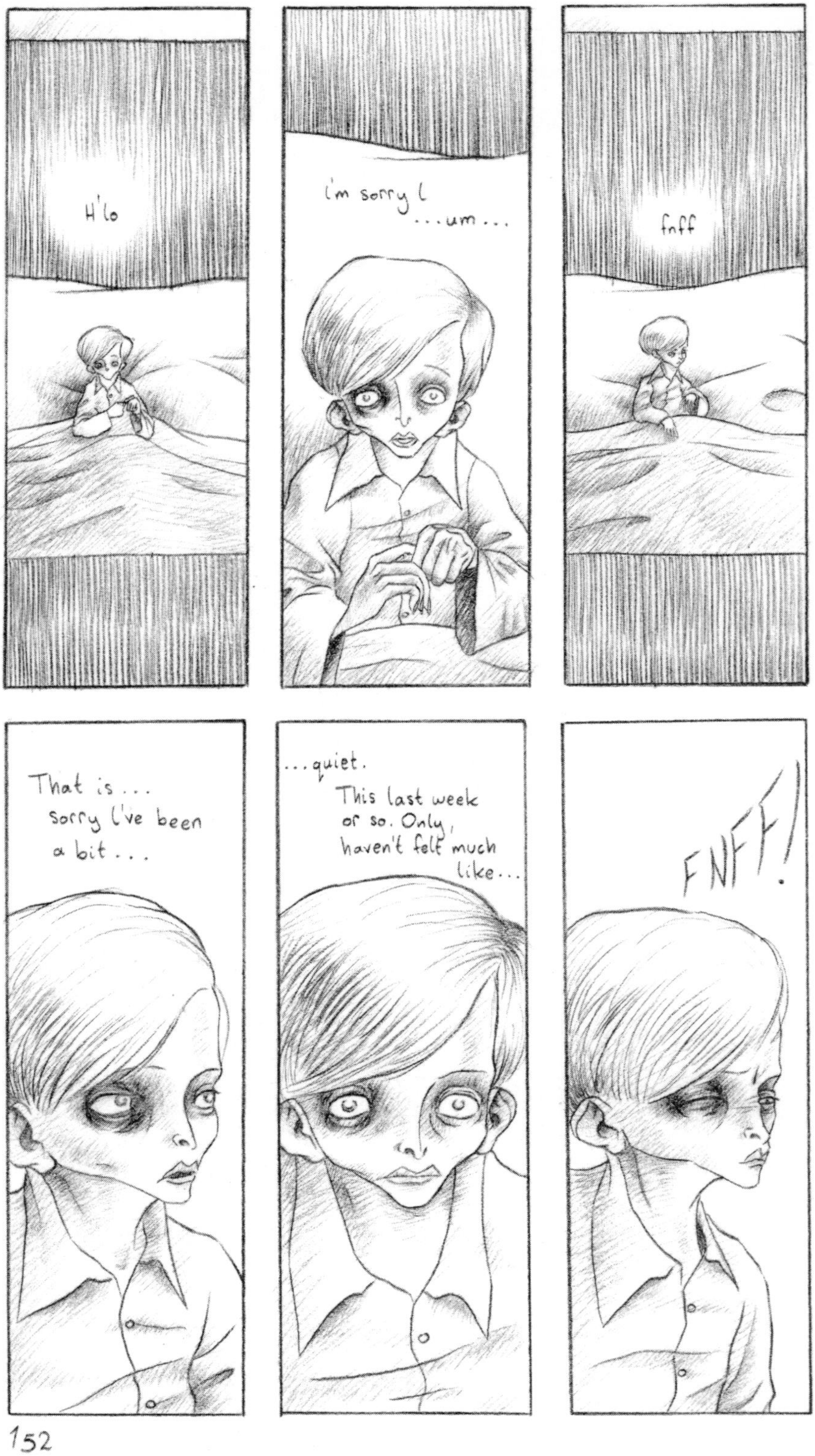
H'lo
i'm sorry I ...um...
fnff
That is ... sorry I've been a bit ...
...quiet.
This last week or so. Only, haven't felt much like...
FNFF!

Do you know, I'm sure I can smell smoke!

Pipe smoke! Like Uncle Tremayne's only... nice.

It seems to be coming from under the bed.

There's a man under my bed smoking a pi...

153

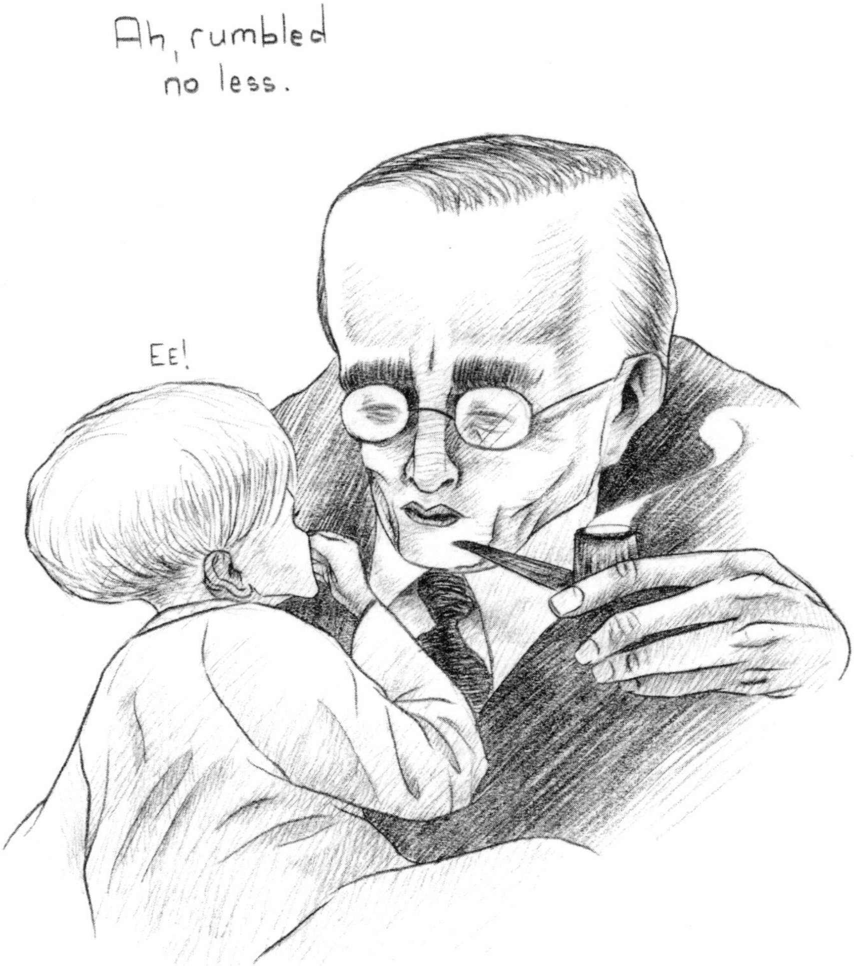
Ah, rumbled no less.
EE!

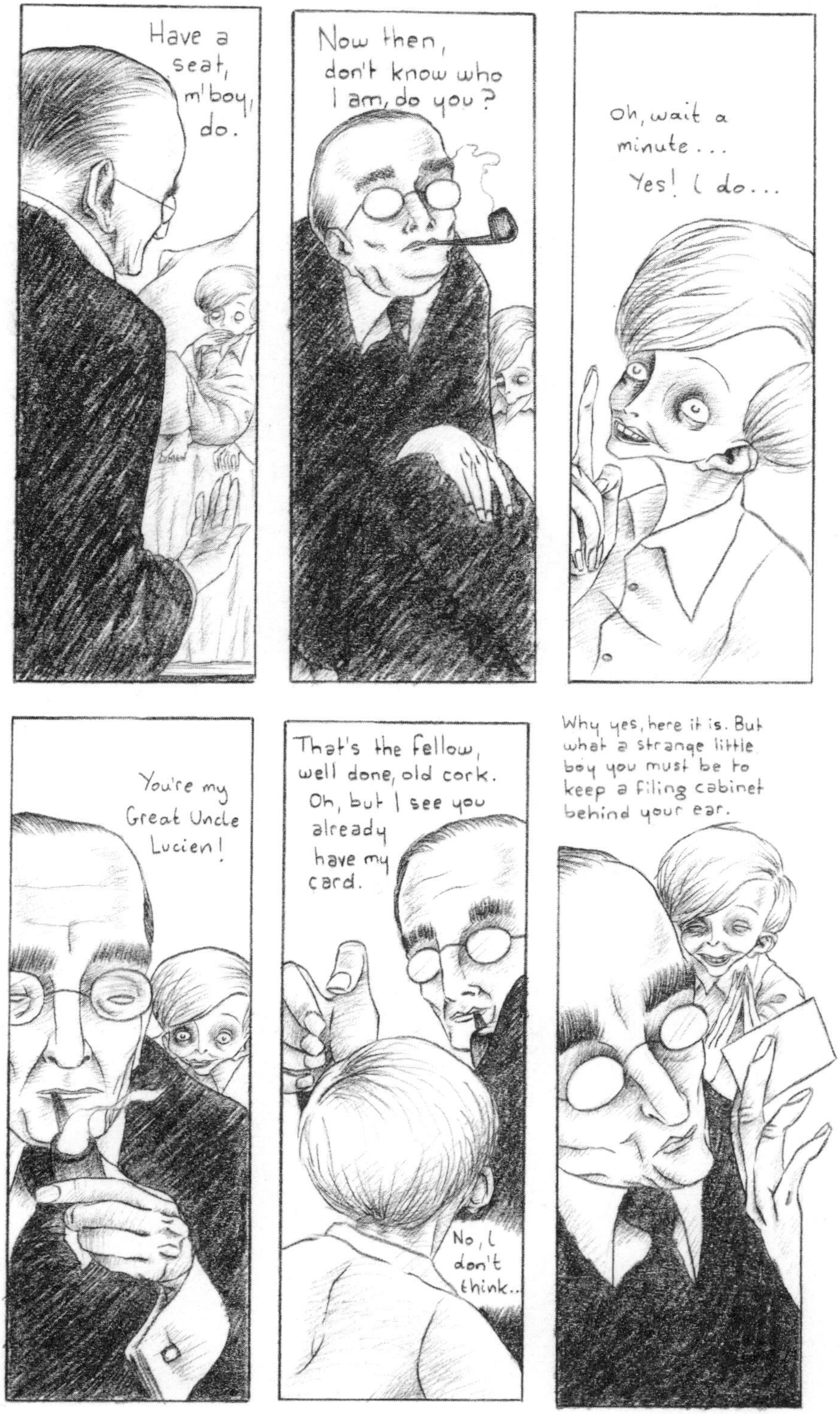
Have a seat, m'boy, do.
Now then, don't know who I am, do you?
Oh, wait a minute... Yes! I do...
You're my Great Uncle Lucien!
That's the fellow, well done, old cork. Oh, but I see you already have my card.
No, I don't think..
Why yes, here it is. But what a strange little boy you must be to keep a filing cabinet behind your ear.

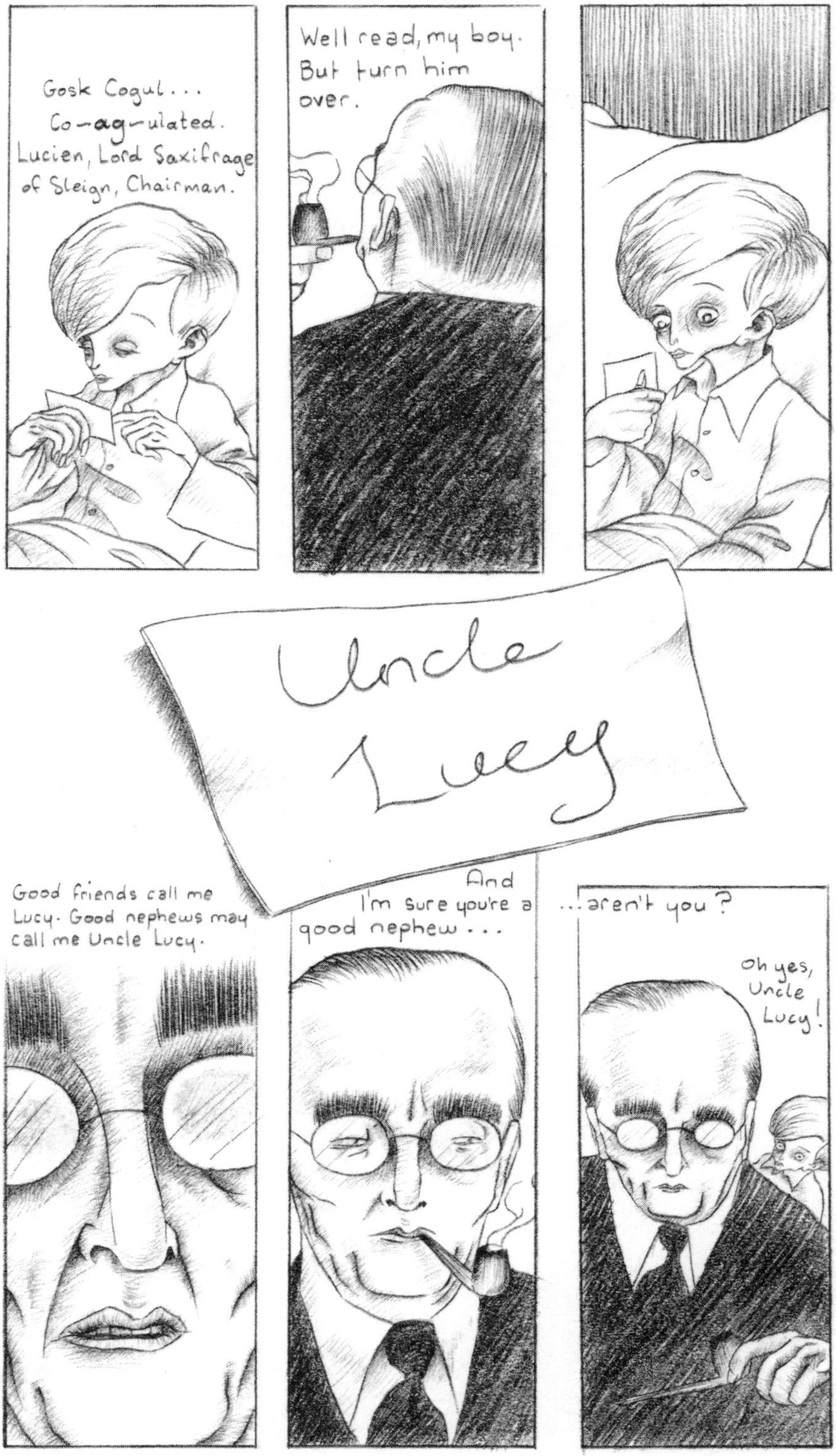
Gosk Cogul...
Co-ag-ulated.
Lucien, Lord Saxifrage of Sleign, Chairman.
Well read, my boy. But turn him over.
Uncle Lucy
Good friends call me Lucy. Good nephews may call me Uncle Lucy.
And I'm sure you're a good nephew...
...aren't you?
Oh yes, Uncle Lucy!

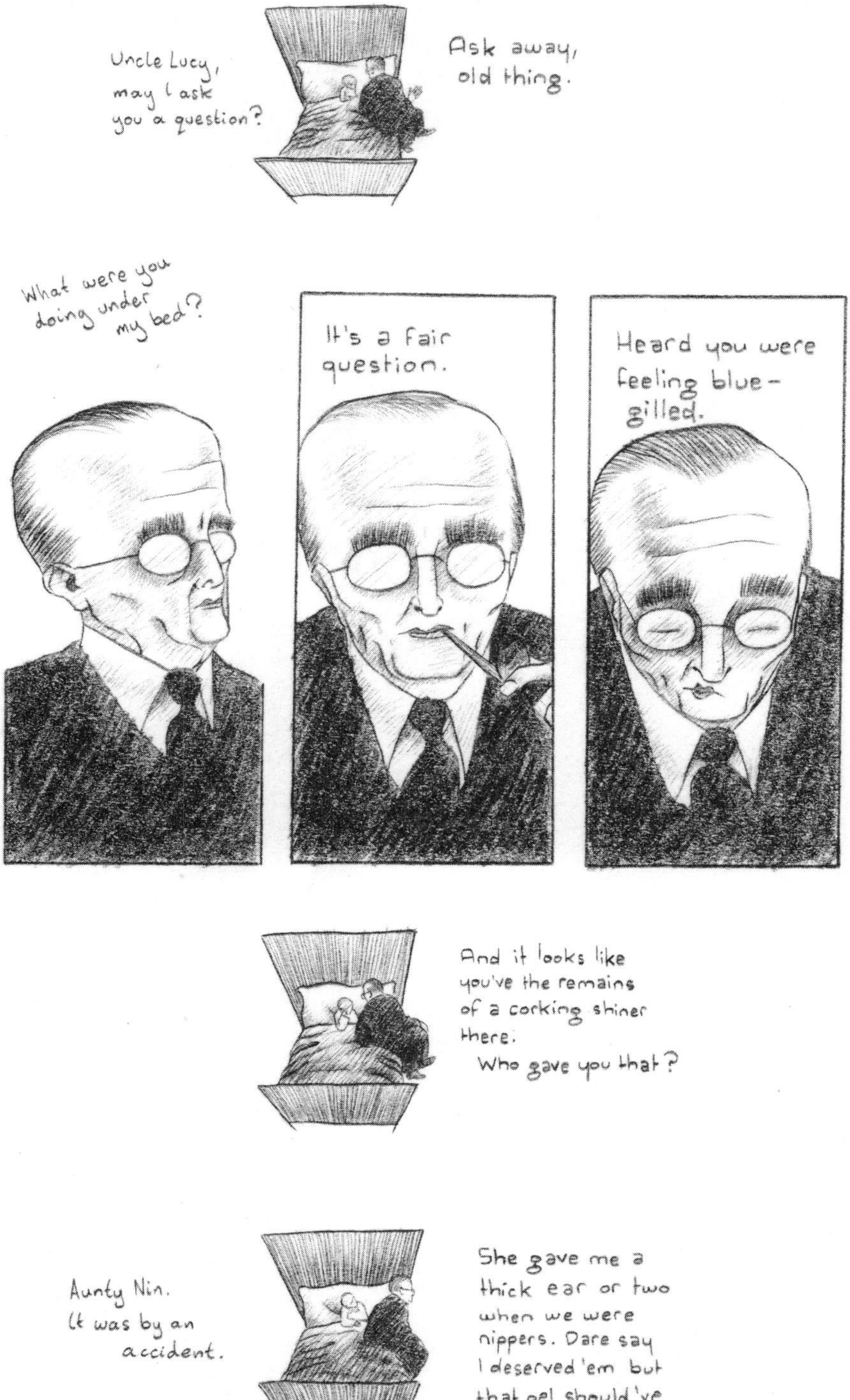
Uncle Lucy, may I ask you a question?
Ask away, old thing.
What were you doing under my bed?
It's a fair question.
Heard you were feeling blue-gilled.
And it looks like you've the remains of a corking shiner there.
Who gave you that?
Aunty Nin. It was by an accident.
She gave me a thick ear or two when we were nippers. Dare say I deserved 'em but that gel should've been a prizefighter.

Anyway, anyway, what with your illness thought I ought to pay my...ah, to see you.

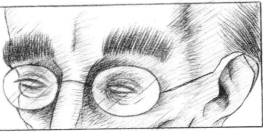

But...but you couldn't very well see me very well from under the bed... could you?

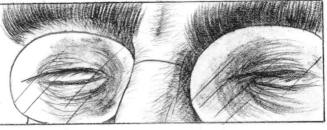

Nothing escapes you, old cork, does it?

Quite right.

Actually, I'm lying doggo. Wanted by the police.

Gosh! Whatever for?

Fraud and embezzlement.

158

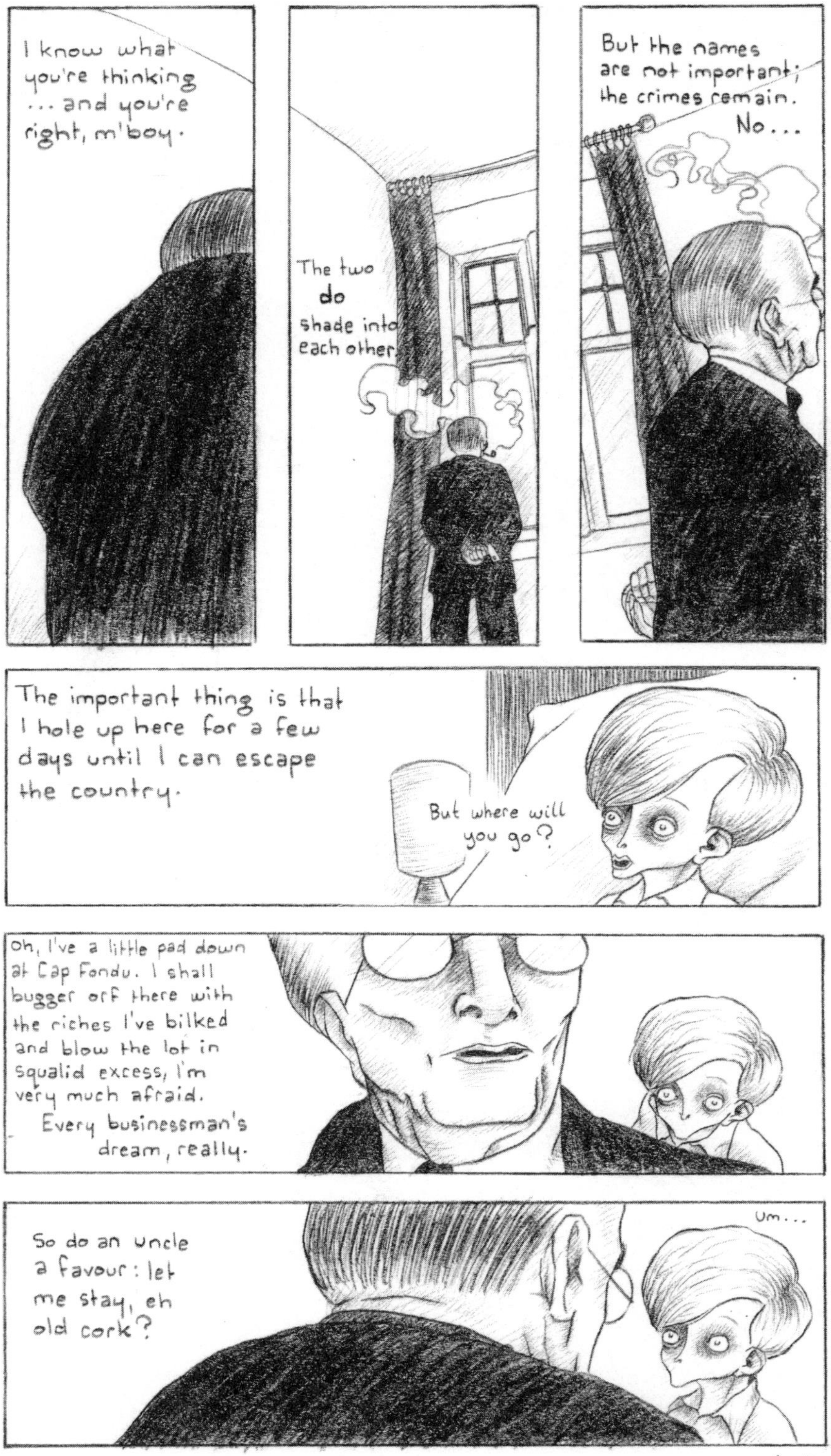
I know what you're thinking ... and you're right, m'boy.
The two do shade into each other.
But the names are not important; the crimes remain.
No...
The important thing is that I hole up here for a few days until I can escape the country.
But where will you go?
Oh, I've a little pad down at Cap Fondu. I shall bugger off there with the riches I've bilked and blow the lot in squalid excess, I'm very much afraid.
Every businessman's dream, really.
So do an uncle a favour: let me stay, eh old cork?
Um...

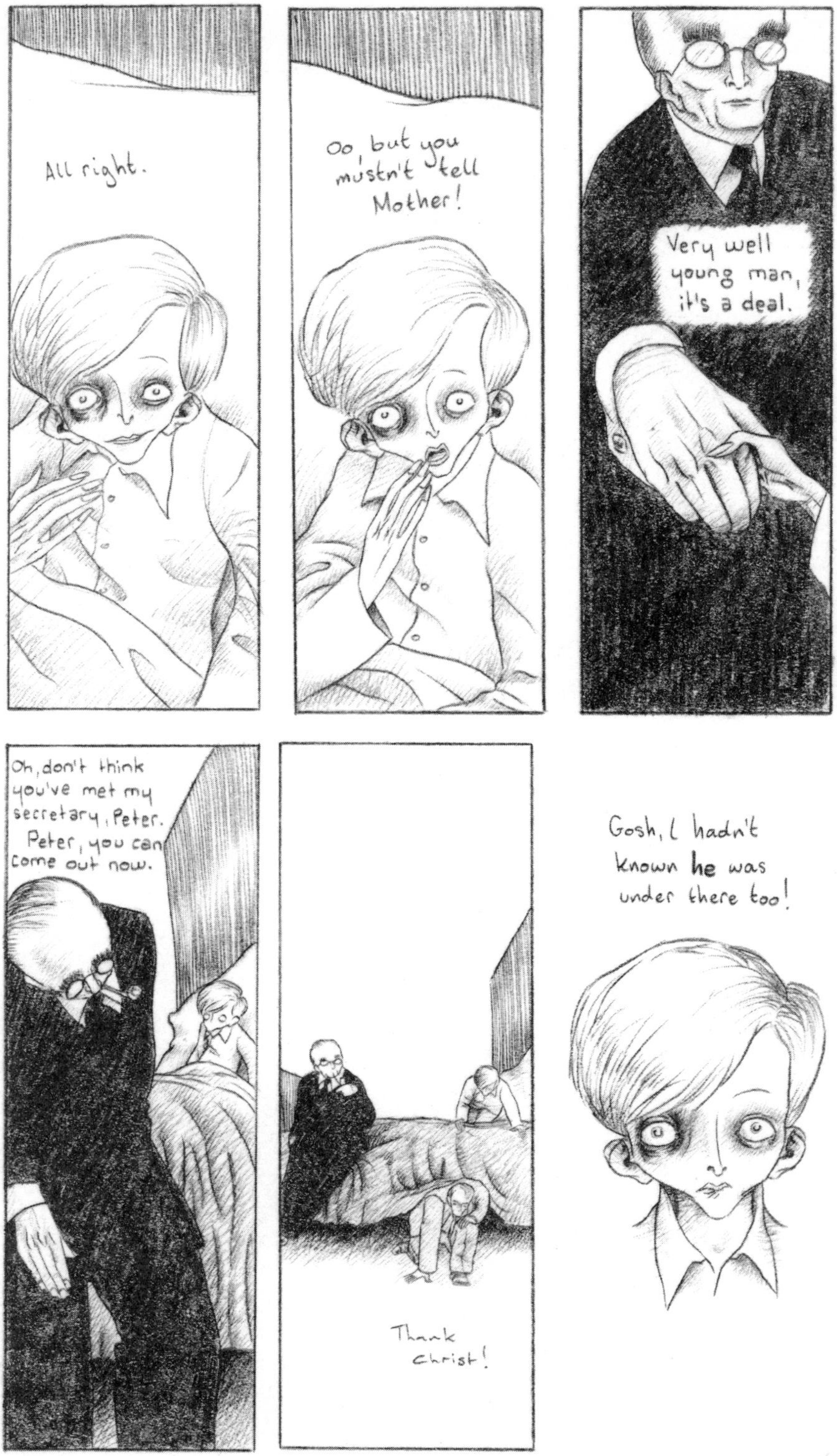
All right.
Oo, but you mustn't tell Mother!
Very well young man, it's a deal.
Oh, don't think you've met my secretary, Peter. Peter, you can come out now.
Thank christ!
Gosh, I hadn't known he was under there too!

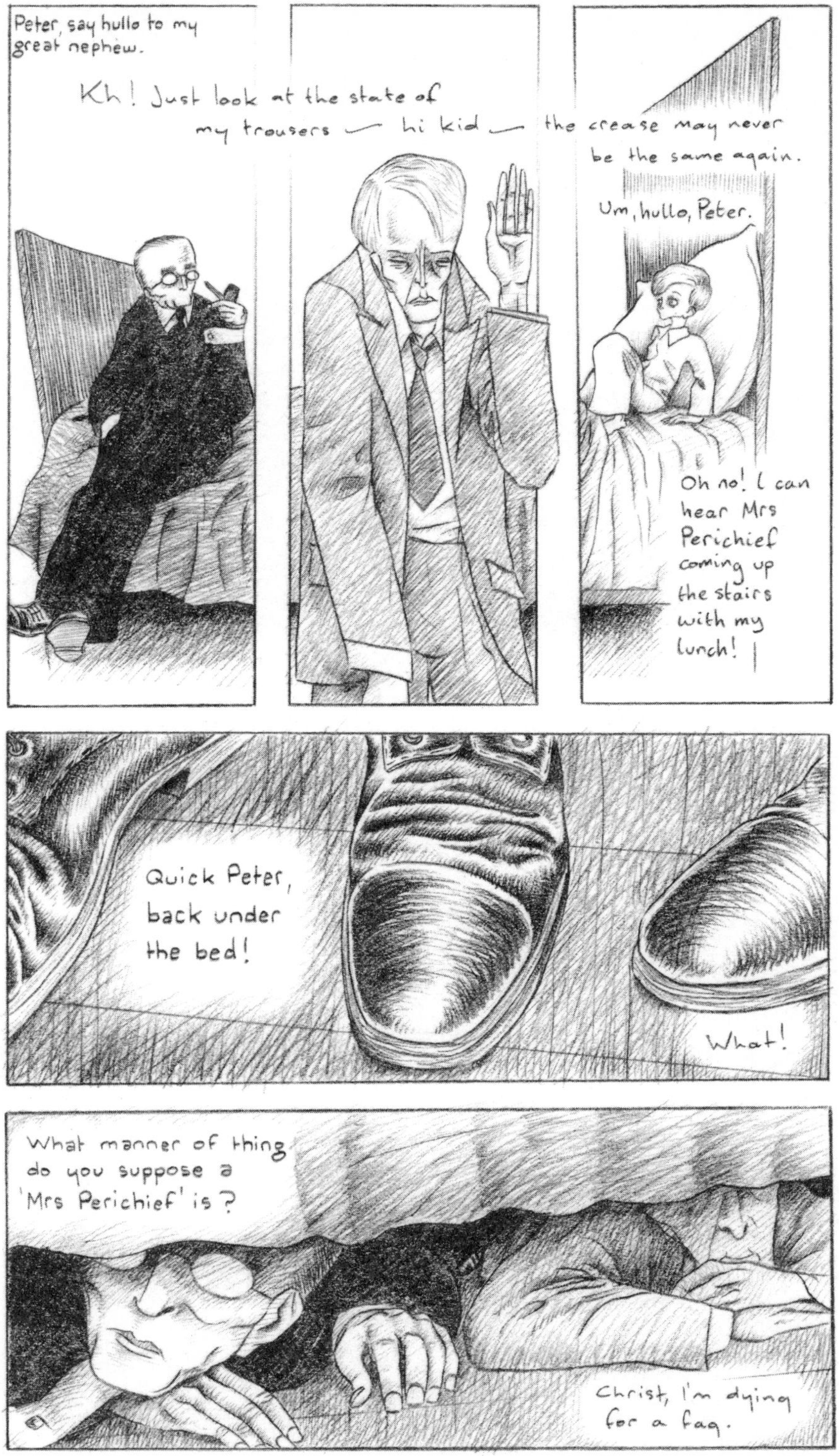
Peter, say hullo to my great nephew.
Kh! Just look at the state of my trousers — hi kid — the crease may never be the same again.
Um, hullo, Peter.
Oh no! I can hear Mrs Perichief coming up the stairs with my lunch!
Quick Peter, back under the bed!
What!
What manner of thing do you suppose a 'Mrs Perichief' is?
Christ, I'm dying for a fag.

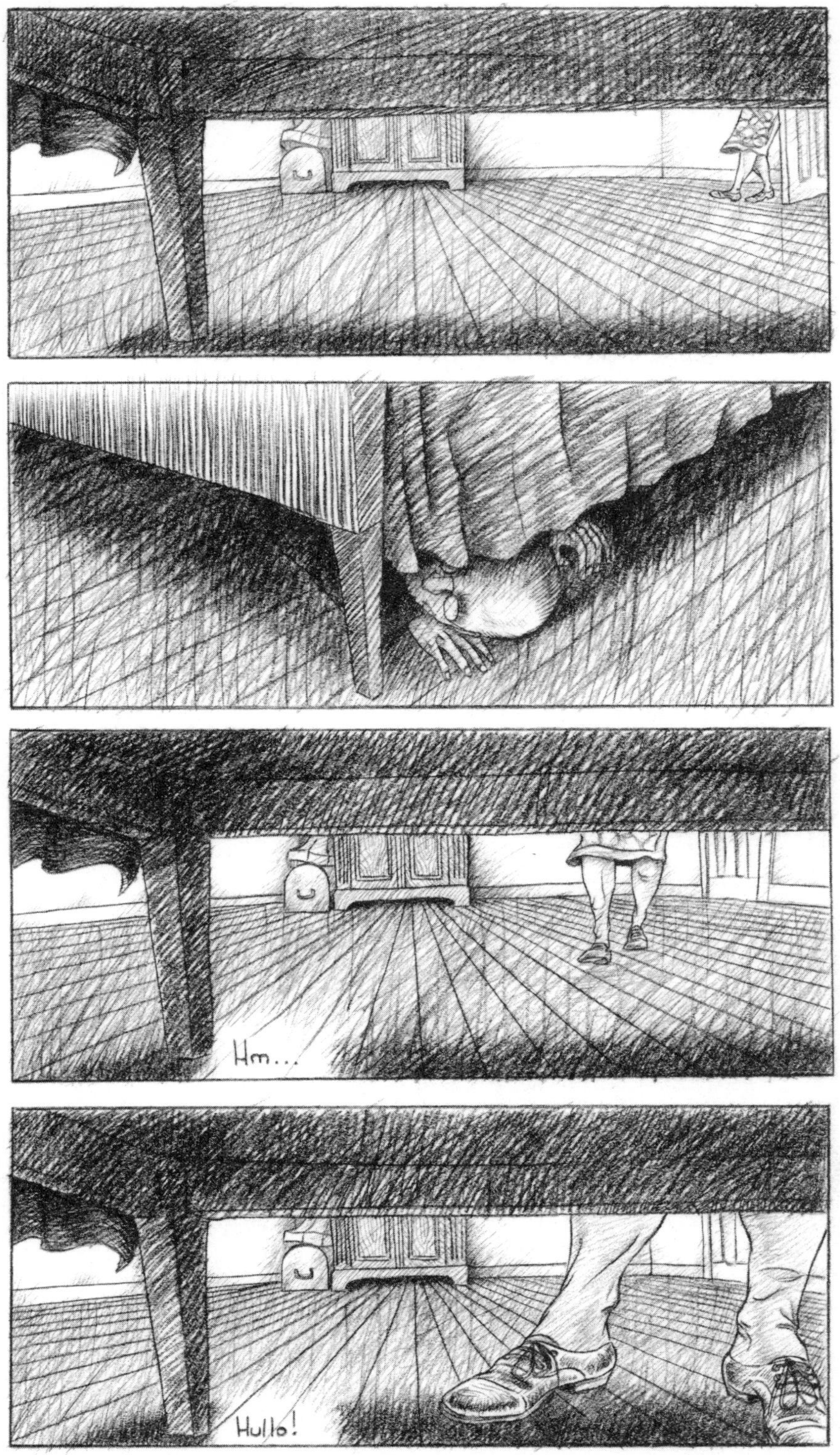
Hm...
Hullo!

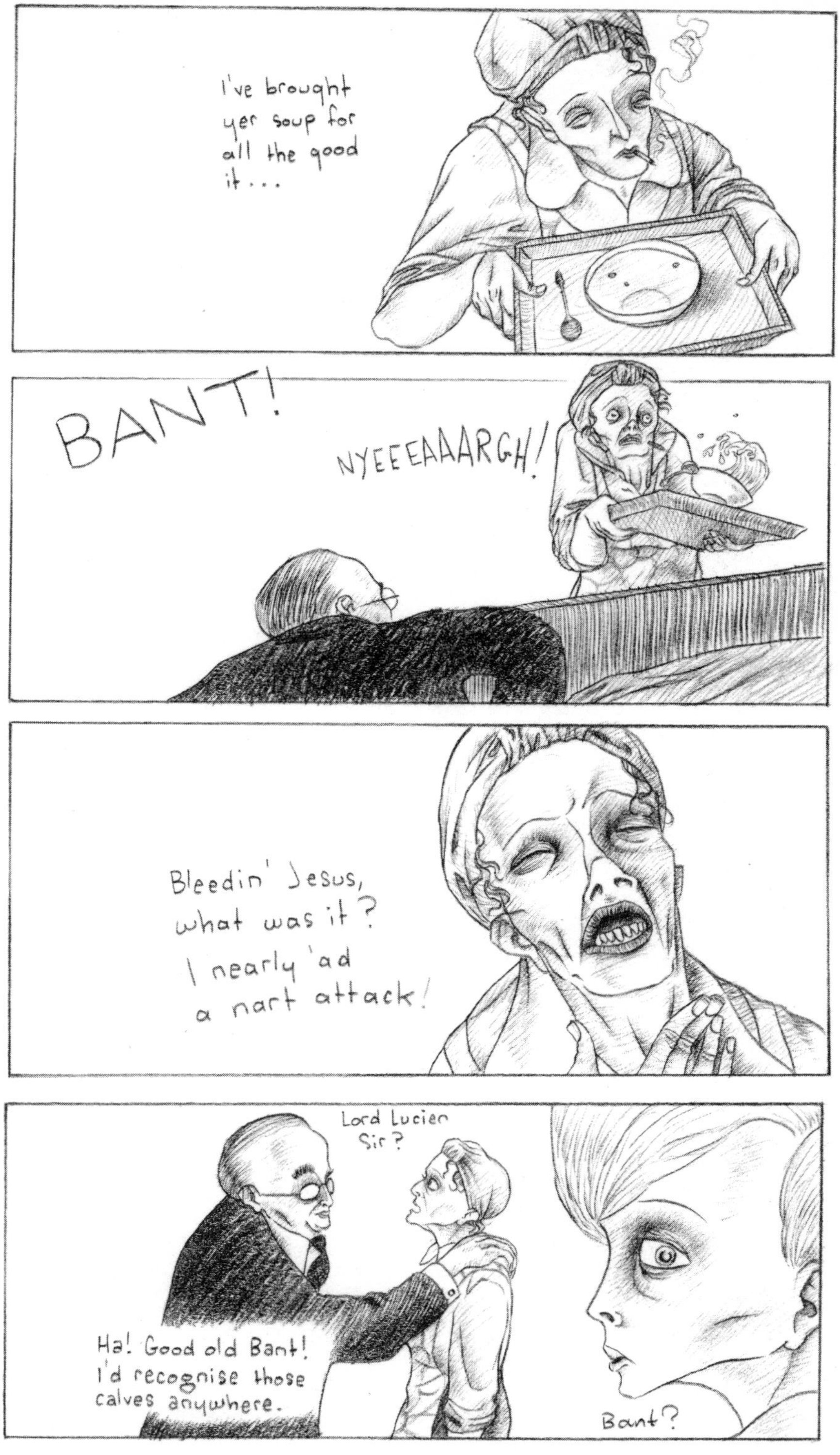
I've brought yer soup for all the good it...
BANT!
NYEEEAAARGH!
Bleedin' Jesus, what was it? I nearly 'ad a nart attack!
Lord Lucien Sir?
Ha! Good old Bant! I'd recognise those calves anywhere.
Bant?

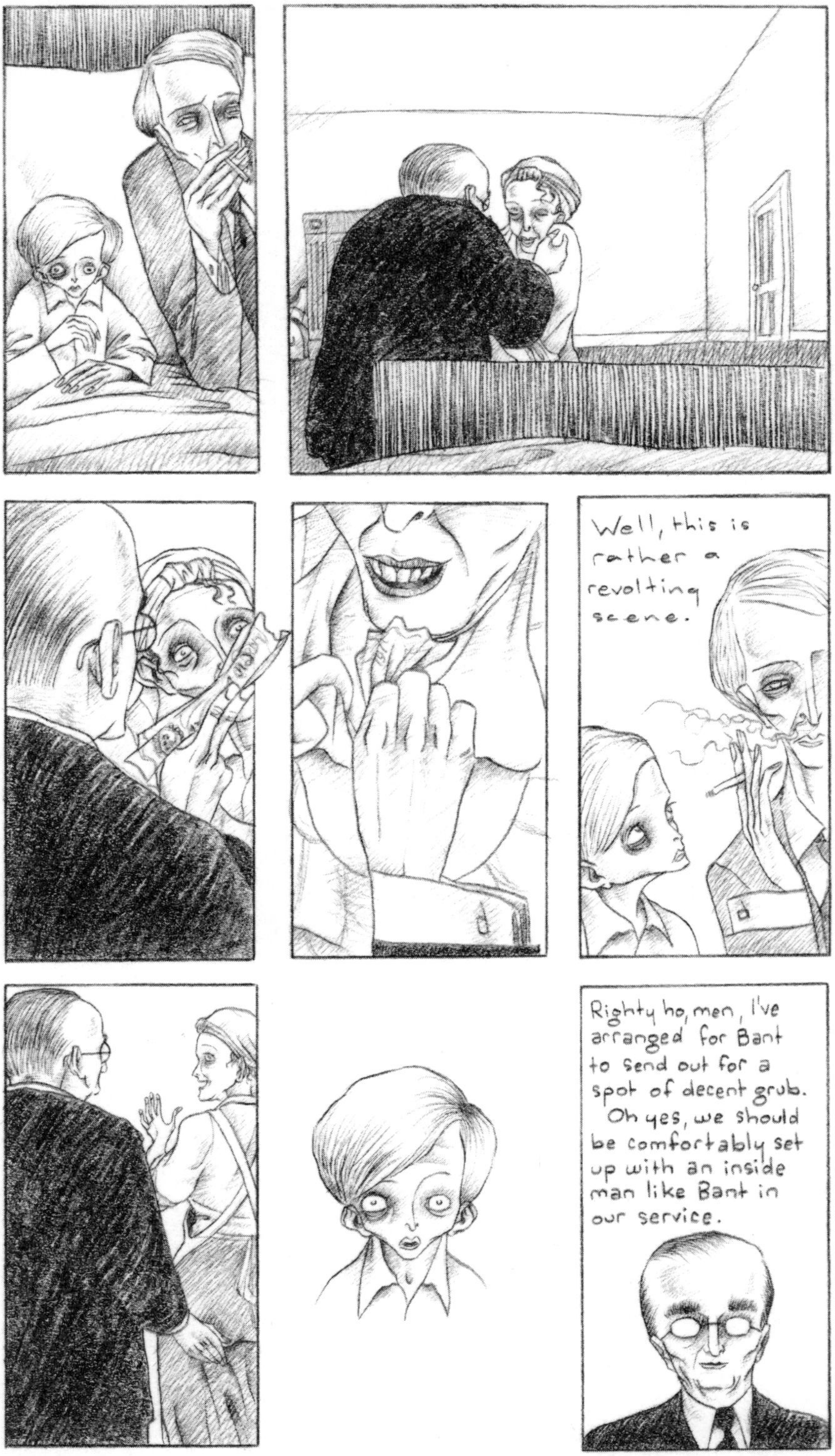
Well, this is rather a revolting scene.
Righty ho, men, I've arranged for Bant to send out for a spot of decent grub. Oh yes, we should be comfortably set up with an inside man like Bant in our service.

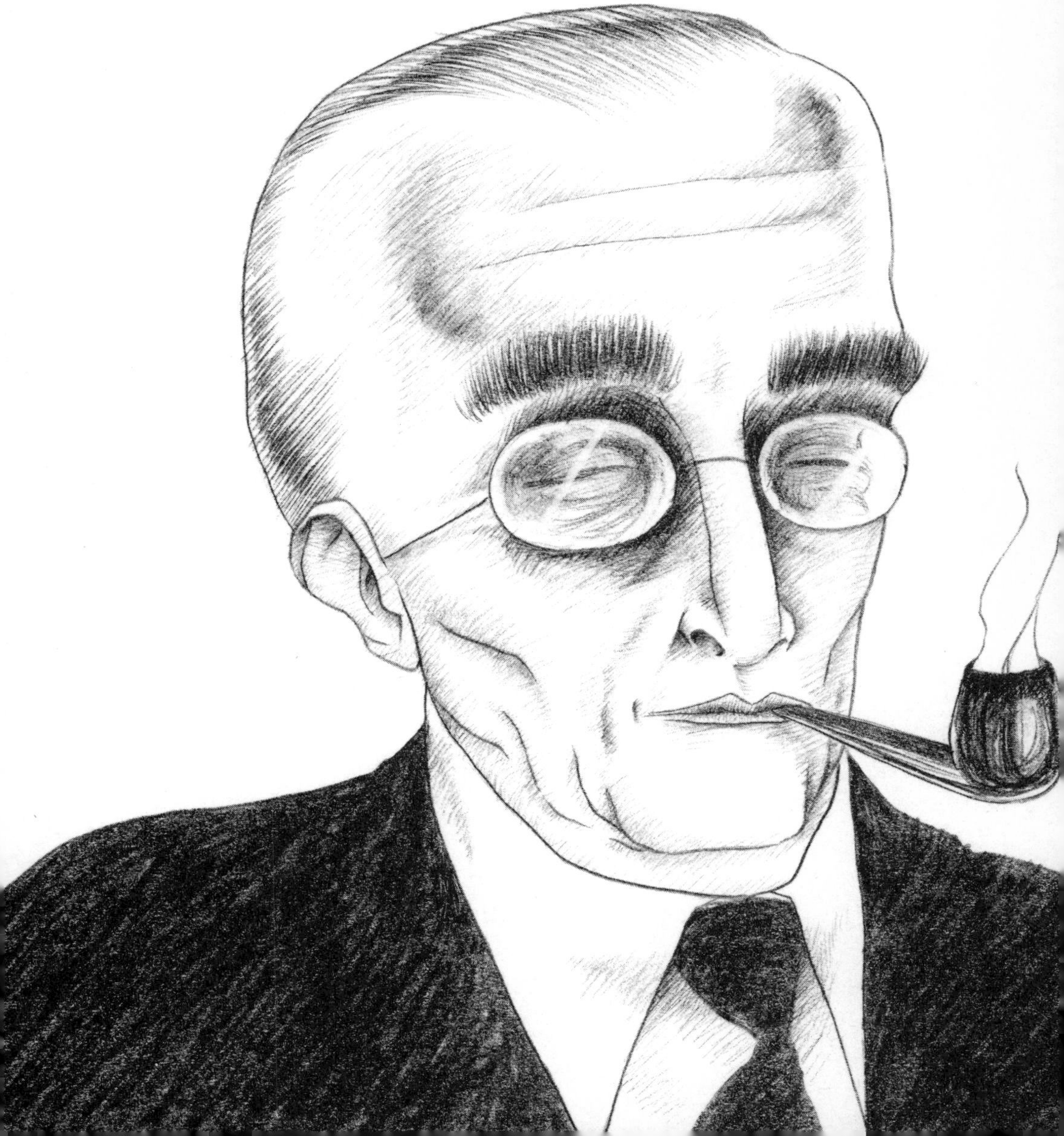

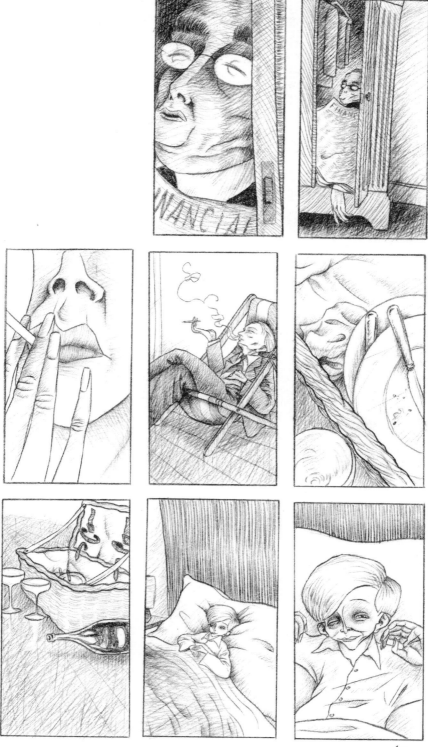

167

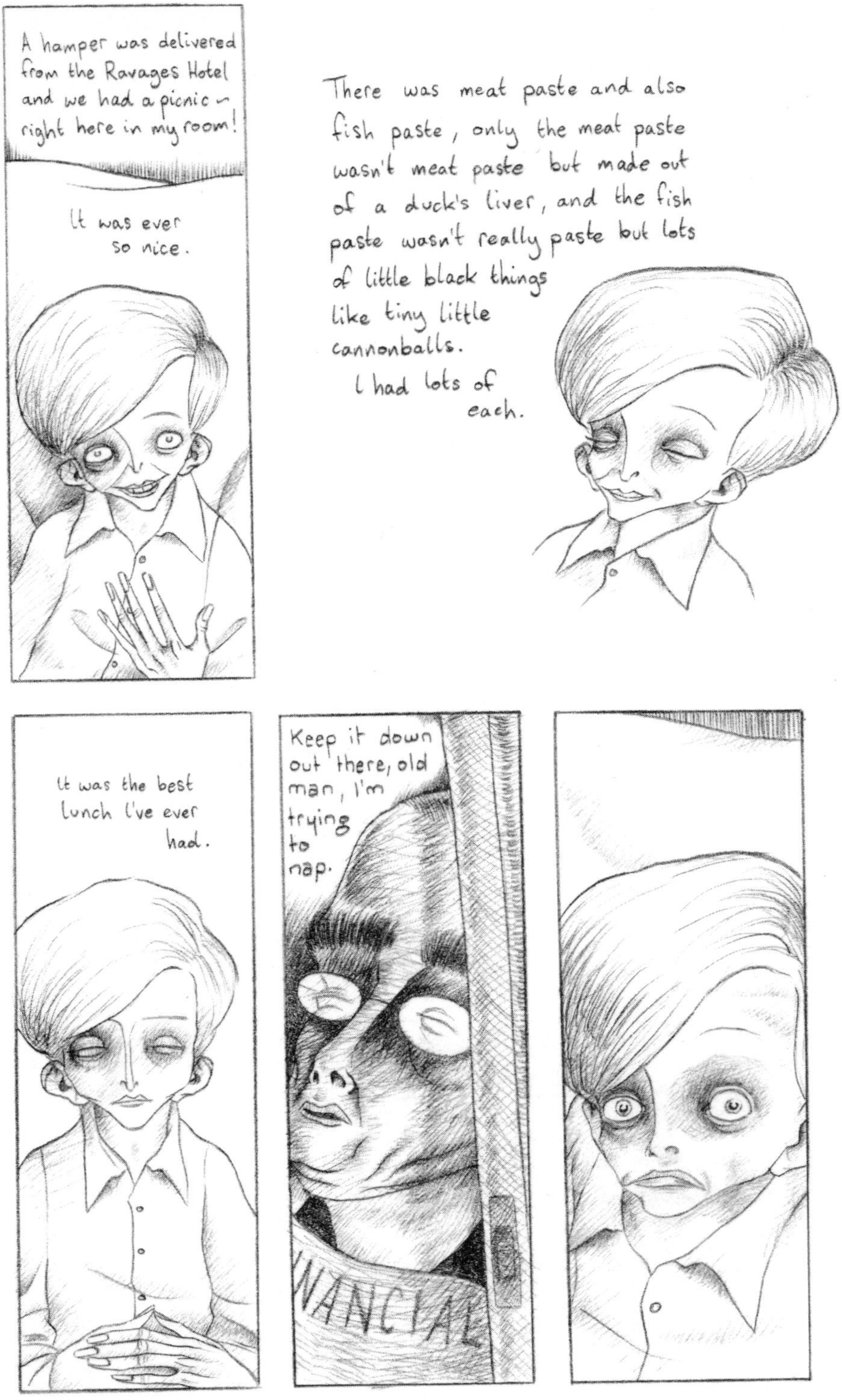
A hamper was delivered from the Ravages Hotel and we had a picnic – right here in my room!
It was ever so nice.
There was meat paste and also fish paste, only the meat paste wasn't meat paste but made out of a duck's liver, and the fish paste wasn't really paste but lots of little black things like tiny little cannonballs.
I had lots of each.
It was the best lunch I've ever had.
Keep it down out there, old man, I'm trying to nap.
NANCIAL

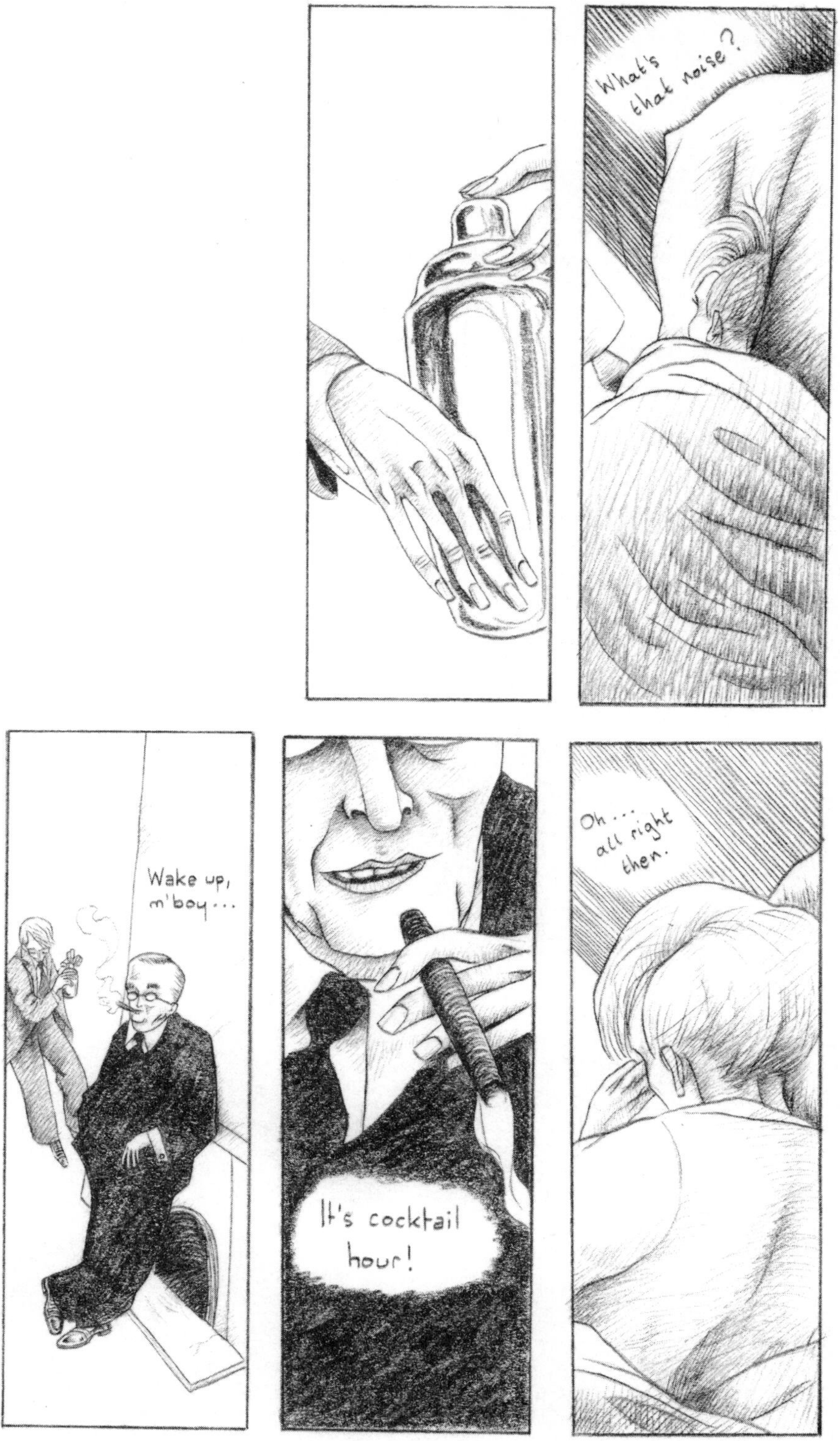
What's that noise?
Wake up, m'boy...
It's cocktail hour!
Oh... all right then.

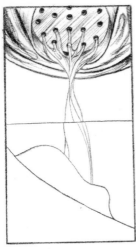

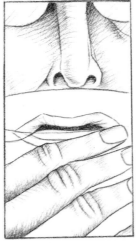

Ah! That hits the what's-it mm? I say m'boy, feelin' quite all right there?

I think so ...thank you.

Here...

...have the olives from my martini.

I'm not sure that I, uh, like olives.

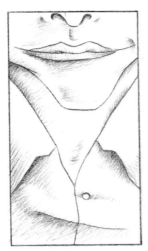

Oh, olives are much nicer when they've been in a martini, aren't they?

DINNAH!
... is served!

Dinner?

Just a few courses, old thing; stave off starvation till supper.

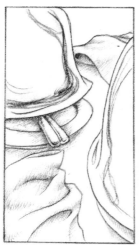

Ah! That filled a void. Now, to business ...coffee? Yes?

How likely a thing is an interruption by me niece or... er...that fellow she married?

Thank you, Uncle. I doubt we'll see Father but Mother... Mother could be in at any moment.

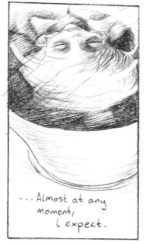

...Almost at any moment, I expect.

Um, Uncle Lucy? I...feel a bit sick.

171

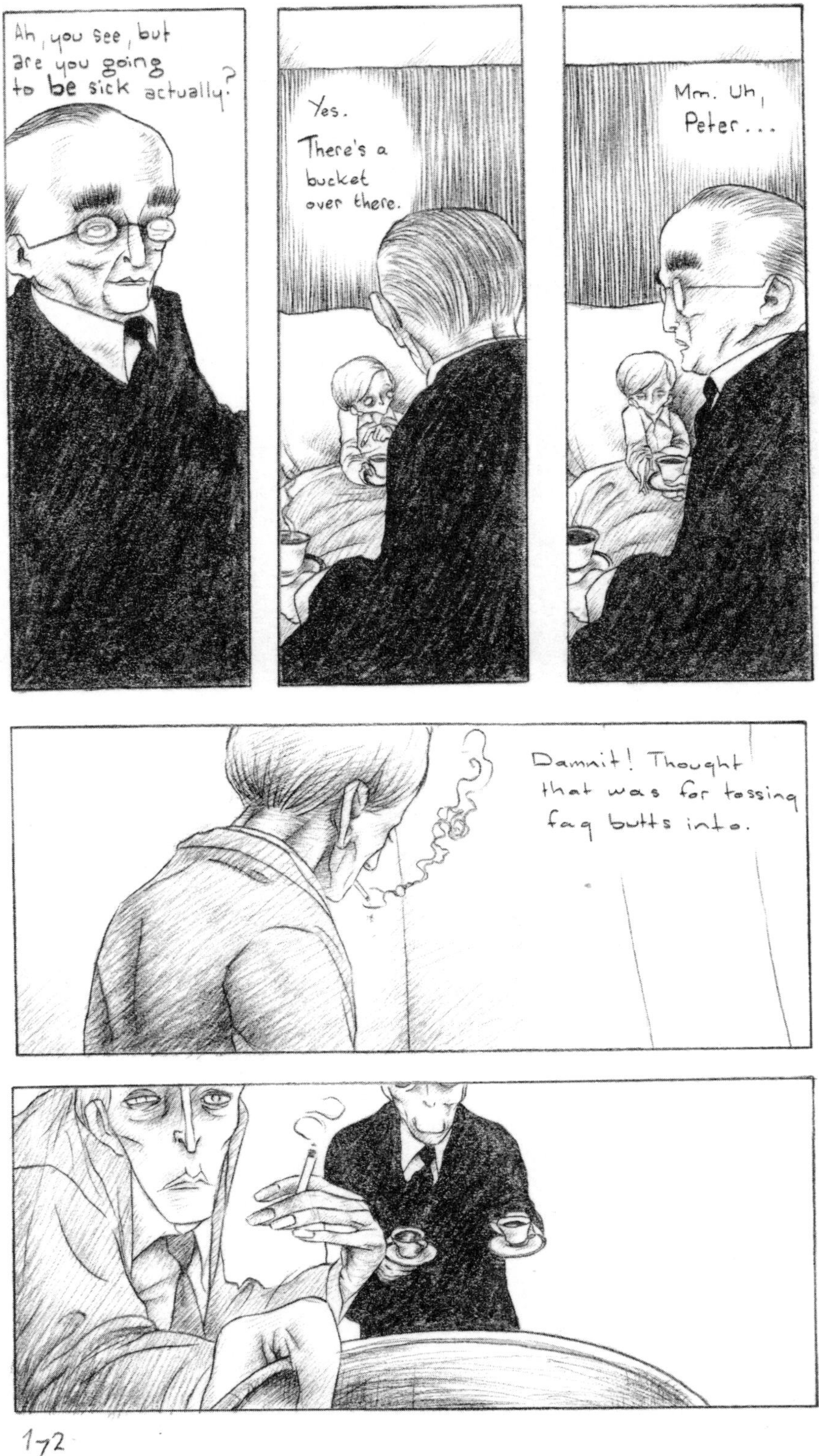
Ah, you see, but are you going to be sick actually?
Yes.
There's a bucket over there.
Mm. Uh, Peter...
Damnit! Thought that was for tossing fag butts into.

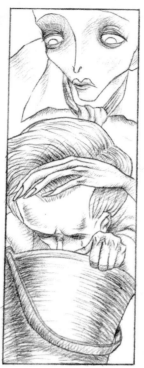

Is it over?

Hard to say.
Who'd have
thought the
little fellow
could hold
that much?

It's over!

Mm.
Better
empty that.
Covertly,
mind.

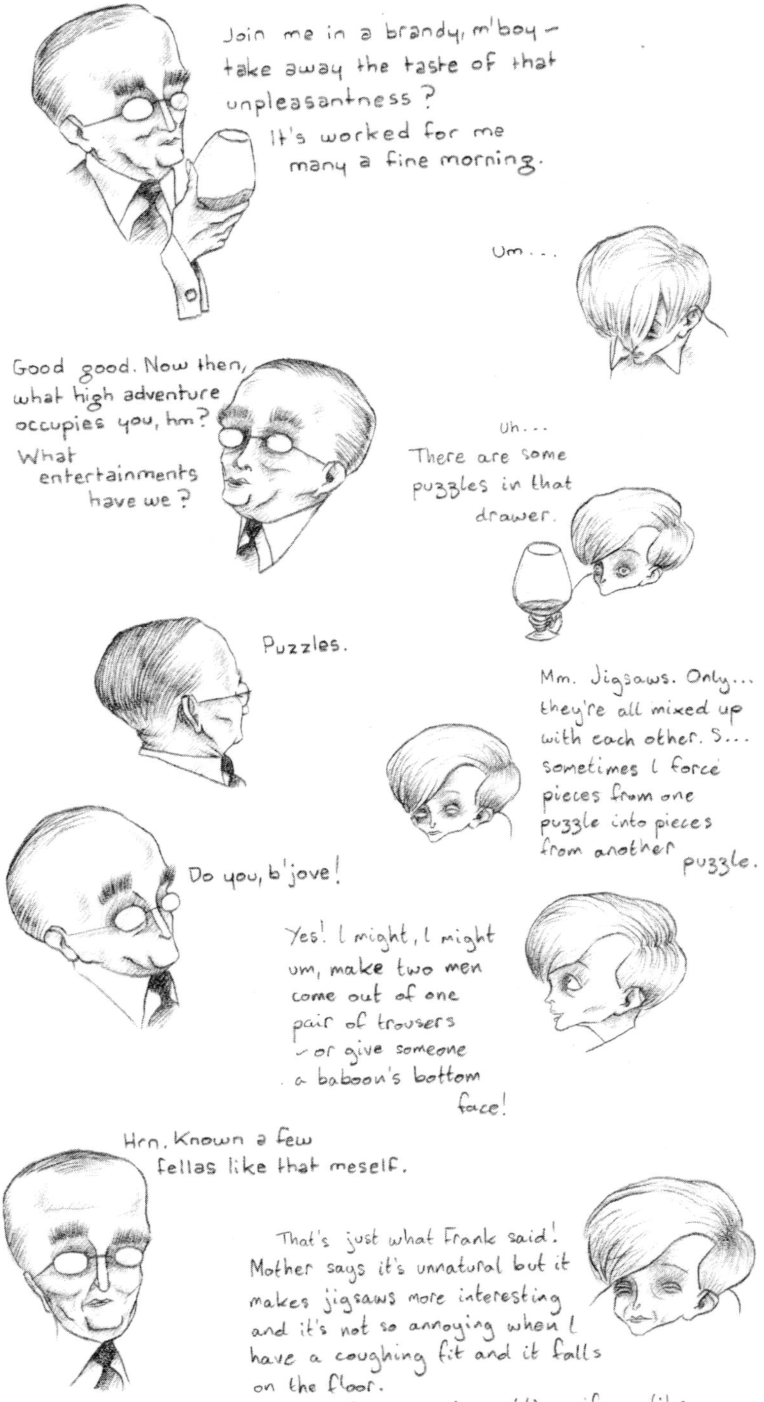

Join me in a brandy, m'boy —
take away the taste of that
unpleasantness?
It's worked for me
many a fine morning.

Um...

Good good. Now then,
what high adventure
occupies you, hm?
What
entertainments
have we?

Uh...
There are some
puzzles in that
drawer.

Puzzles.

Mm. Jigsaws. Only...
they're all mixed up
with each other. S...
sometimes I force
pieces from one
puzzle into pieces
from another puzzle.

Do you, b'jove!

Yes! I might, I might
um, make two men
come out of one
pair of trousers
— or give someone
a baboon's bottom
face!

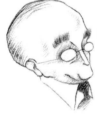

Hrn. Known a few
fellas like that meself.

That's just what Frank said!
Mother says it's unnatural but it
makes jigsaws more interesting
and it's not so annoying when I
have a coughing fit and it falls
on the floor.
Or there are toy soldiers if you like.

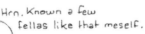

No games?

No.
There's not really
anyone to play
games with.

But for God's
sake, man, what
do you do from
hour to hour?

(... talk.

You talk!
To whom?
Yourself?
Imaginary
  friends?
Ju-ju man?

Imaginary friends?

I won't have
them in the house!

Then to whom?
Mm?
Speak up boy!

Do you know...
I don't really know.
Imaginary strangers,
     I suppose.

As long as
they **are**
imaginary...

Oh yes,
completely
made up.

175

Hm. What a spartan life you seem to lead.

Now, it so happens that I have with me a pack of cards. Know any card games?

oh! Um, like Three Inch Brag or, uh, Relentless Stud?

Ah, you play poker?

No... I just know the names.

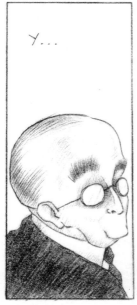

Y...

Mn.

Right. In that case I'll have to teach you. Don't worry, we'll play for low stakes to begin with.

176

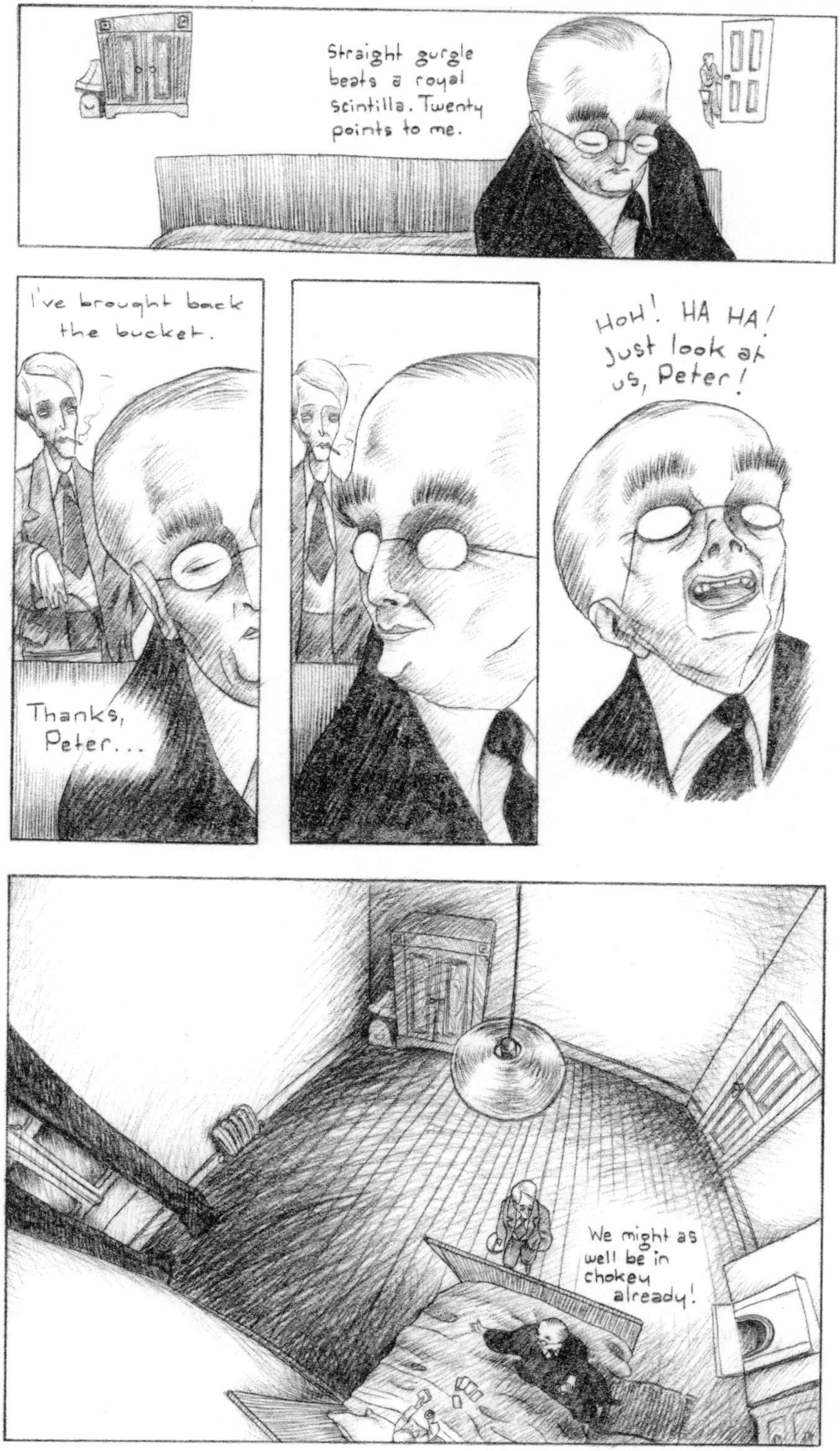
Straight gurgle beats a royal scintilla. Twenty points to me.
I've brought back the bucket.
Thanks, Peter...
HOH! HA HA! Just look at us, Peter!
We might as well be in chokey already!

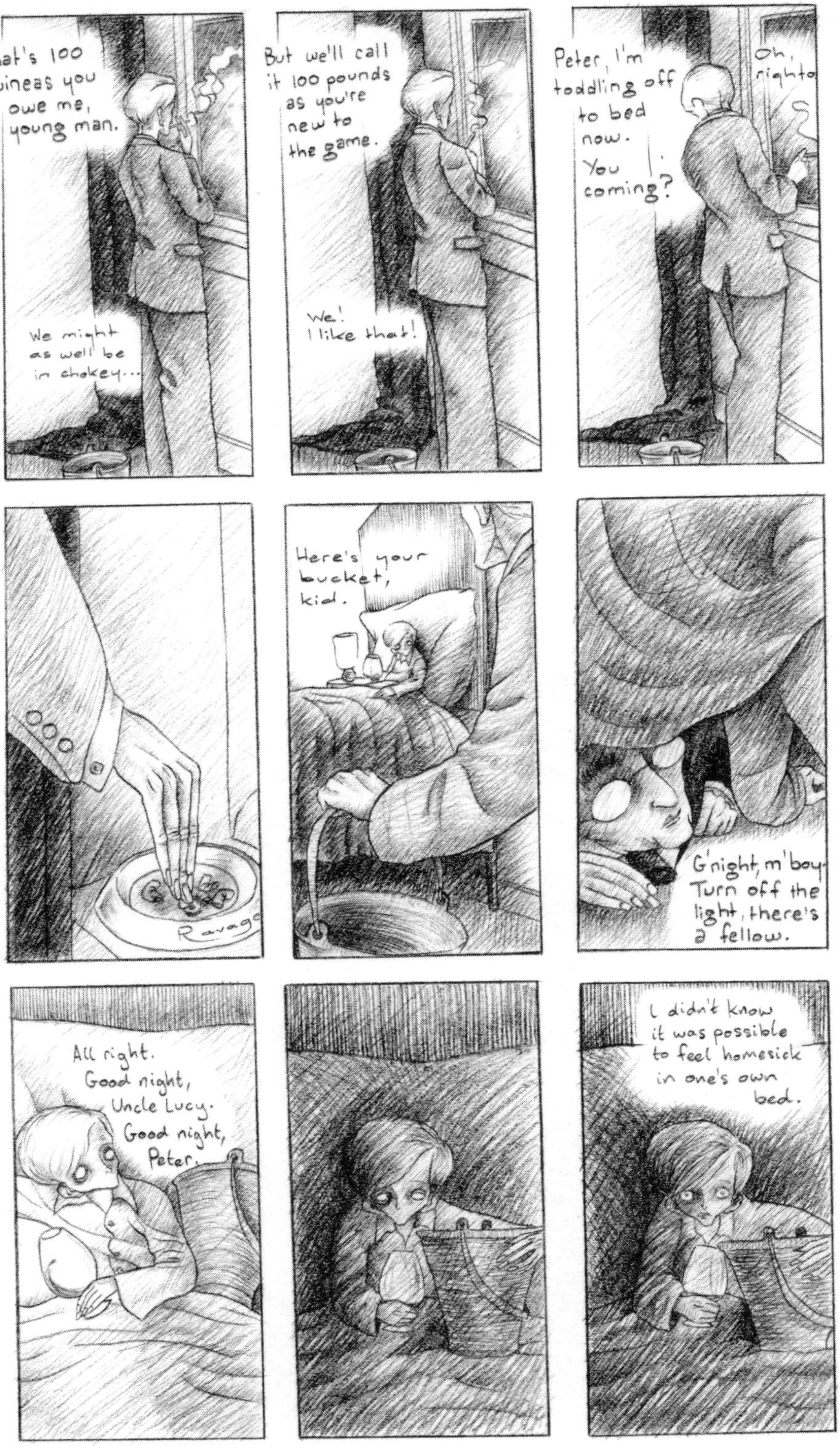

That's 100 guineas you owe me, young man.
We might as well be in chokey...
But we'll call it 100 pounds as you're new to the game.
We! I like that!
Peter, I'm toddling off to bed now. You coming?
Oh, righto
Ravage
Here's your bucket, kid.
G'night, m'boy. Turn off the light, there's a fellow.
All right. Good night, Uncle Lucy. Good night, Peter.
I didn't know it was possible to feel homesick in one's own bed.

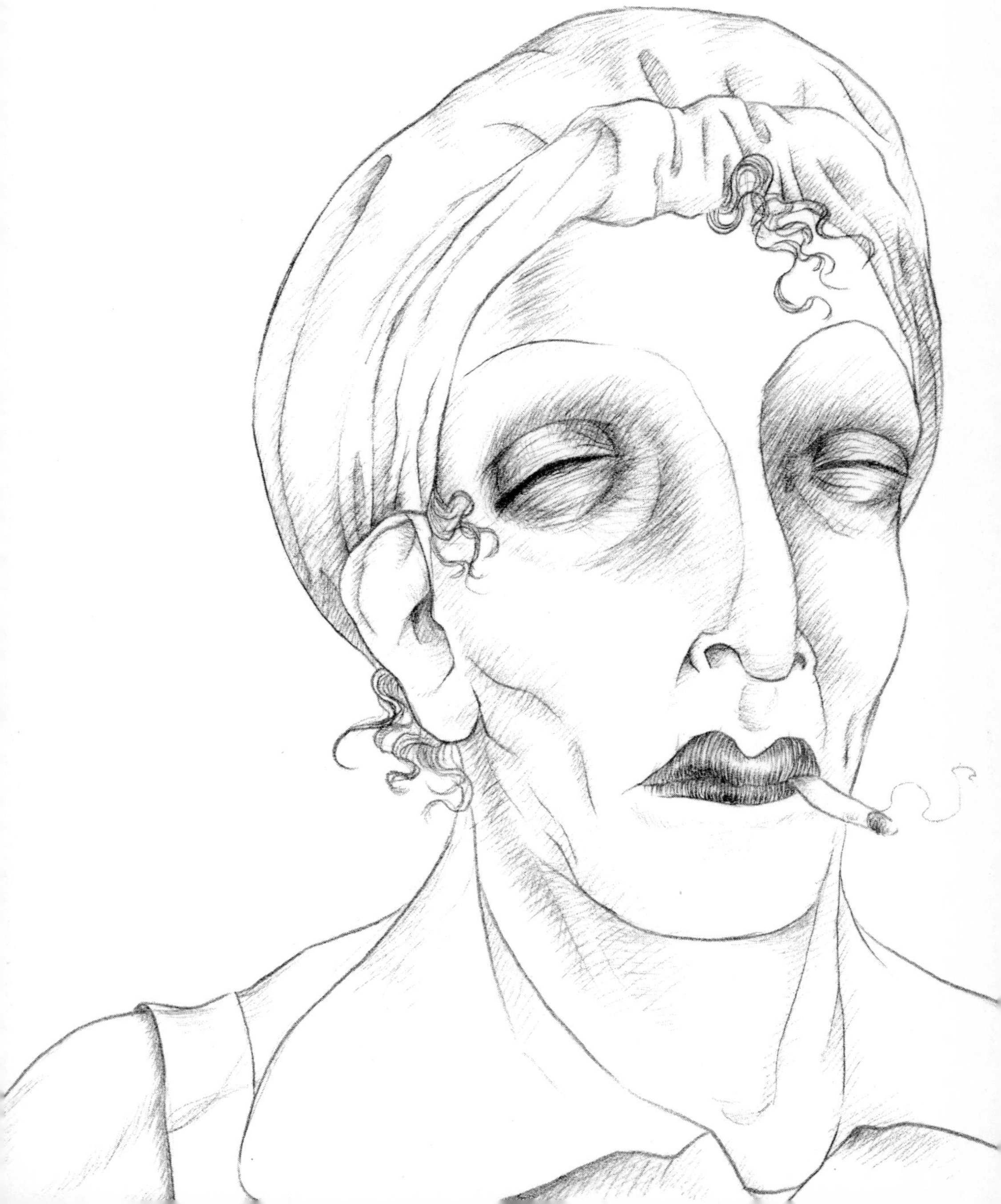

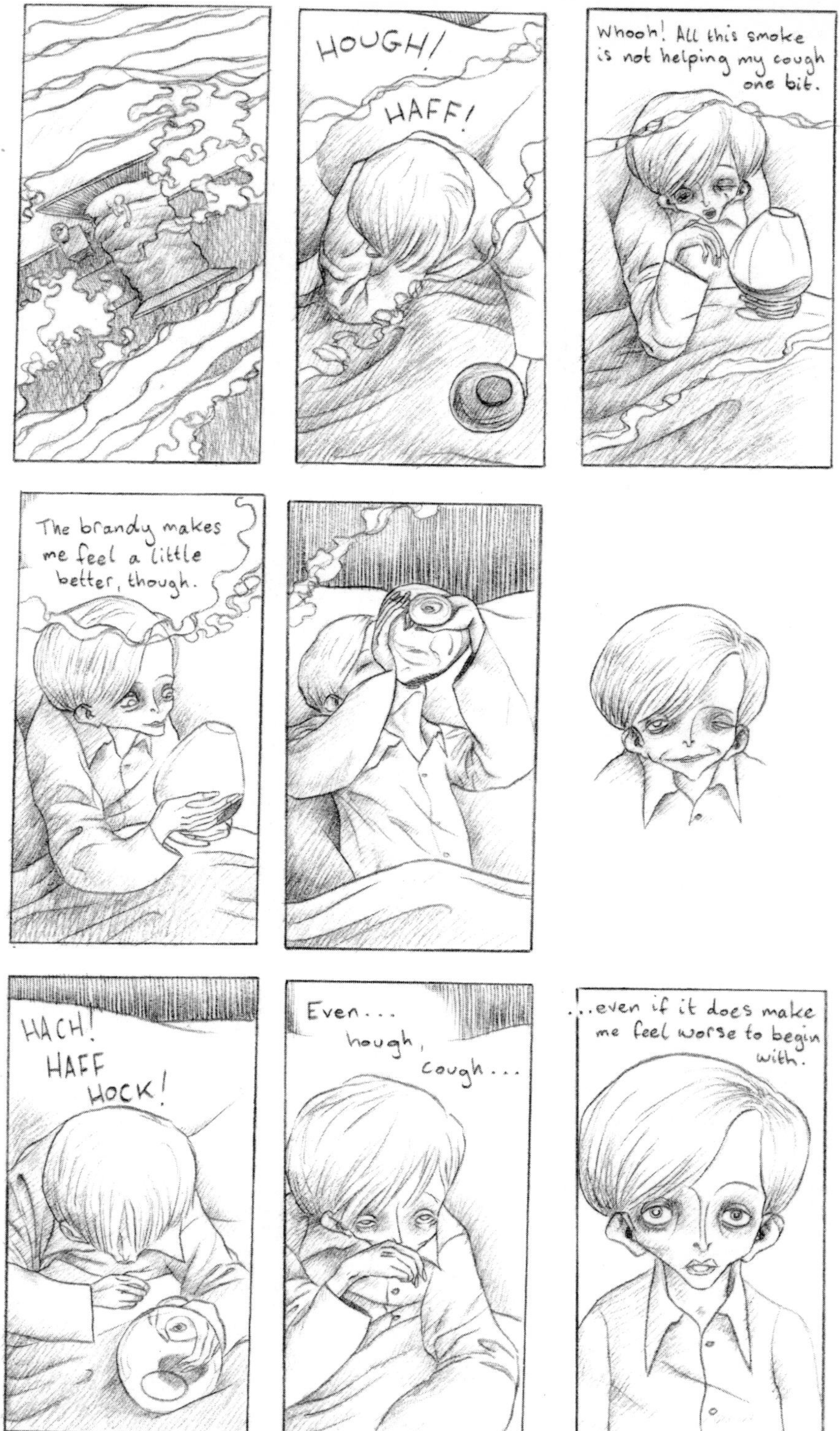
HOUGH!
HAFF!
Whooh! All this smoke is not helping my cough one bit.
The brandy makes me feel a little better, though.
HACH! HAFF HOCK!
Even... hough, cough...
...even if it does make me feel worse to begin with.

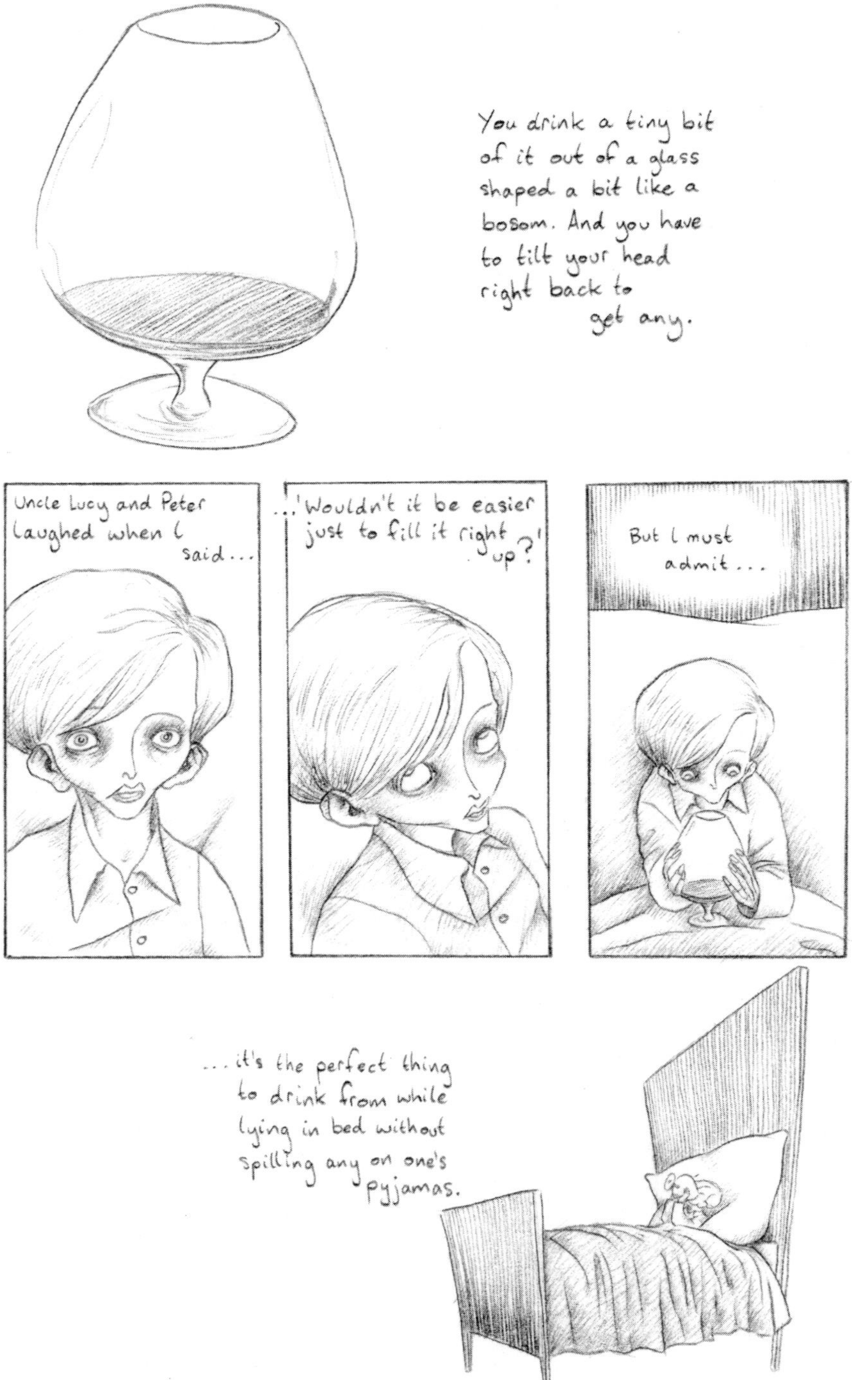
You drink a tiny bit of it out of a glass shaped a bit like a bosom. And you have to tilt your head right back to get any.
Uncle Lucy and Peter laughed when I said...
...'Wouldn't it be easier just to fill it right up?'
But I must admit...
...it's the perfect thing to drink from while lying in bed without spilling any on one's pyjamas.

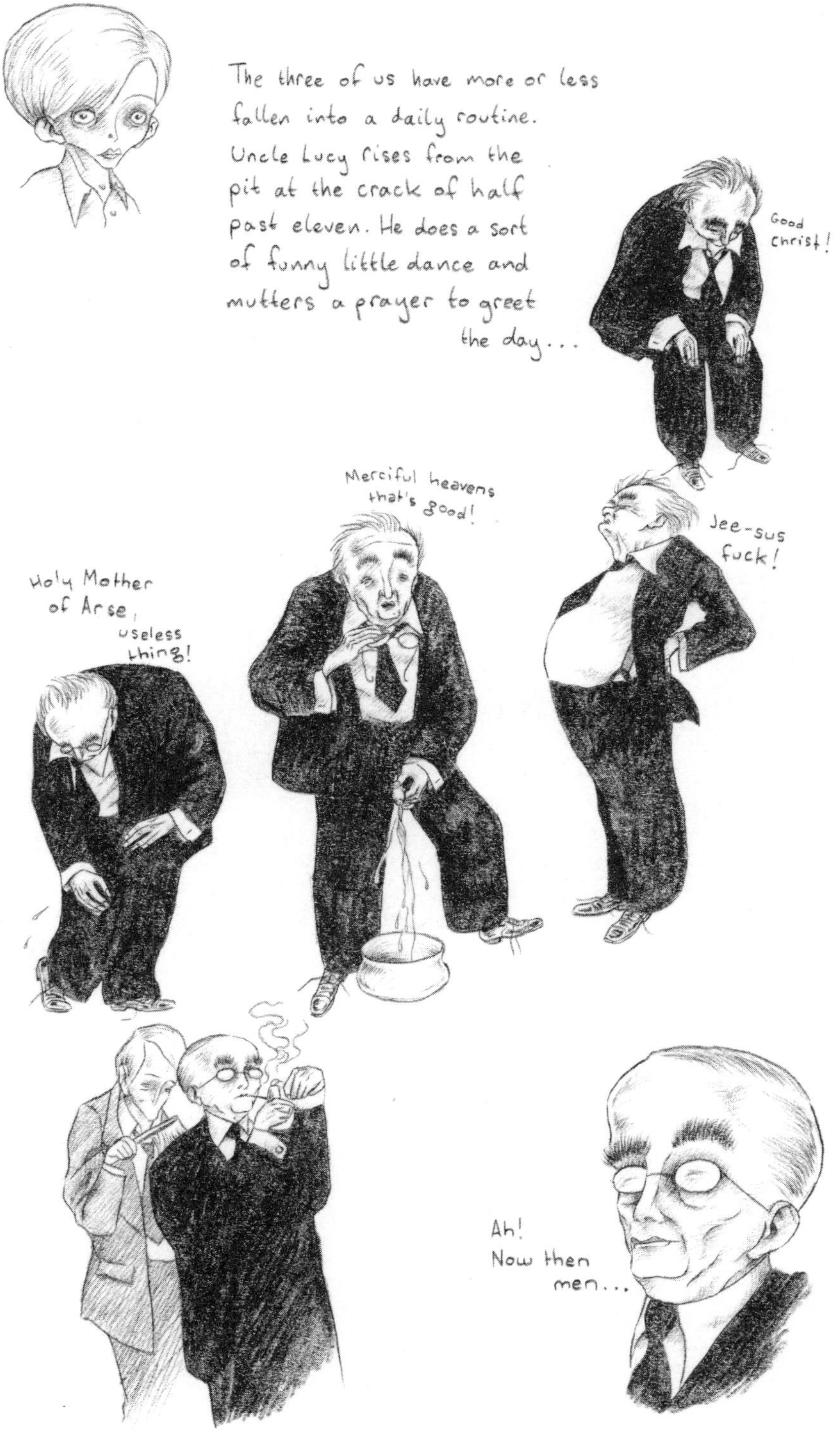
The three of us have more or less fallen into a daily routine. Uncle Lucy rises from the pit at the crack of half past eleven. He does a sort of funny little dance and mutters a prayer to greet the day...
Good christ!
Merciful heavens that's good!
Jee-sus fuck!
Holy Mother of Arse, useless thing!
Ah! Now then men...

After which he takes
his 'morning constitutional'.

Brrr! That's quite
enough of that.
Peter, hand me a...

...Bloody Mary.
Thanks, Peter.

And breakfast
is served.

Breakfast is followed almost
immediately by lunch, fresh
out of a hamper from
Ravages.

After lunch Uncle Lucy sits
in the wardrobe behind a great
big, duck-paste coloured news-
paper and says Harumph a
couple of times and falls
asleep.

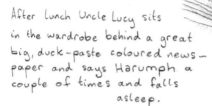

Peter tidies up, then
goes about his duties.

But if I think
I hear Mother coming...

...he shuts Uncle Lucy in the wardrobe
and dives under the bed.

It's usually a false alarm.
In fact, it's always
a false alarm.

Sometimes Uncle Lucy gets bored, or testy.
Once I asked him:

How is Aunty Euphemia,
Uncle Lucy?

I should keep your nose
where it belongs, boy:
on your face.

When Uncle Lucy gets bored, or testy,
his face sort of gathers up in the
middle. I said to Peter, I said:

He looks like
a stud on a
leather
armchair.

What!
Where?

I don't think he was
really listening.

186

But cocktail hour
always cheers us!

There's something about a martini
that escapes me just for the minute...
It's cool and it's clear,
makes me pleasantly queer,
but I've yet to discover what's in it.

Oh jolly good,
eh Peter!

Rather!
Jolly
jolly good!

Then it's dinner, of course, which comes out of a thing like a big shiny Aunty's hat.

I usually manage to keep most of it down but when Peter passes the port to the left, he passes my bucket to the right.

The bucket stops with you, m'boy.

Hoh!

Perhaps if he makes that joke every time I'll understand it one day.

After the port Uncle Lucy always gives me a chance to recoup my losses.

C'mon! Are we playin' cards here or jerking off!

I never do recoup my losses.

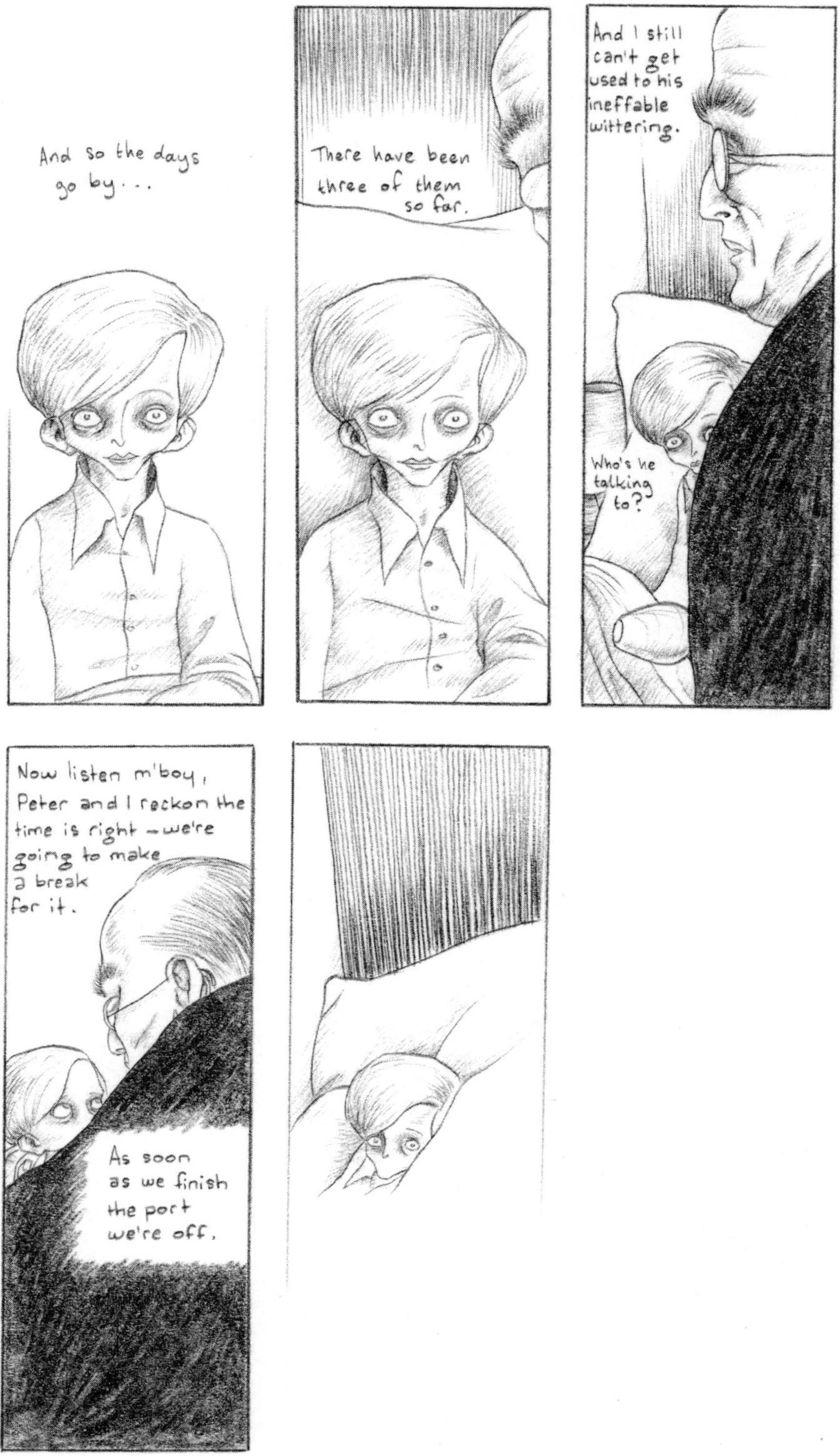
And so the days go by...
There have been three of them so far.
And I still can't get used to his ineffable wittering.
Who's he talking to?
Now listen m'boy, Peter and I reckon the time is right – we're going to make a break for it.
As soon as we finish the port we're off.

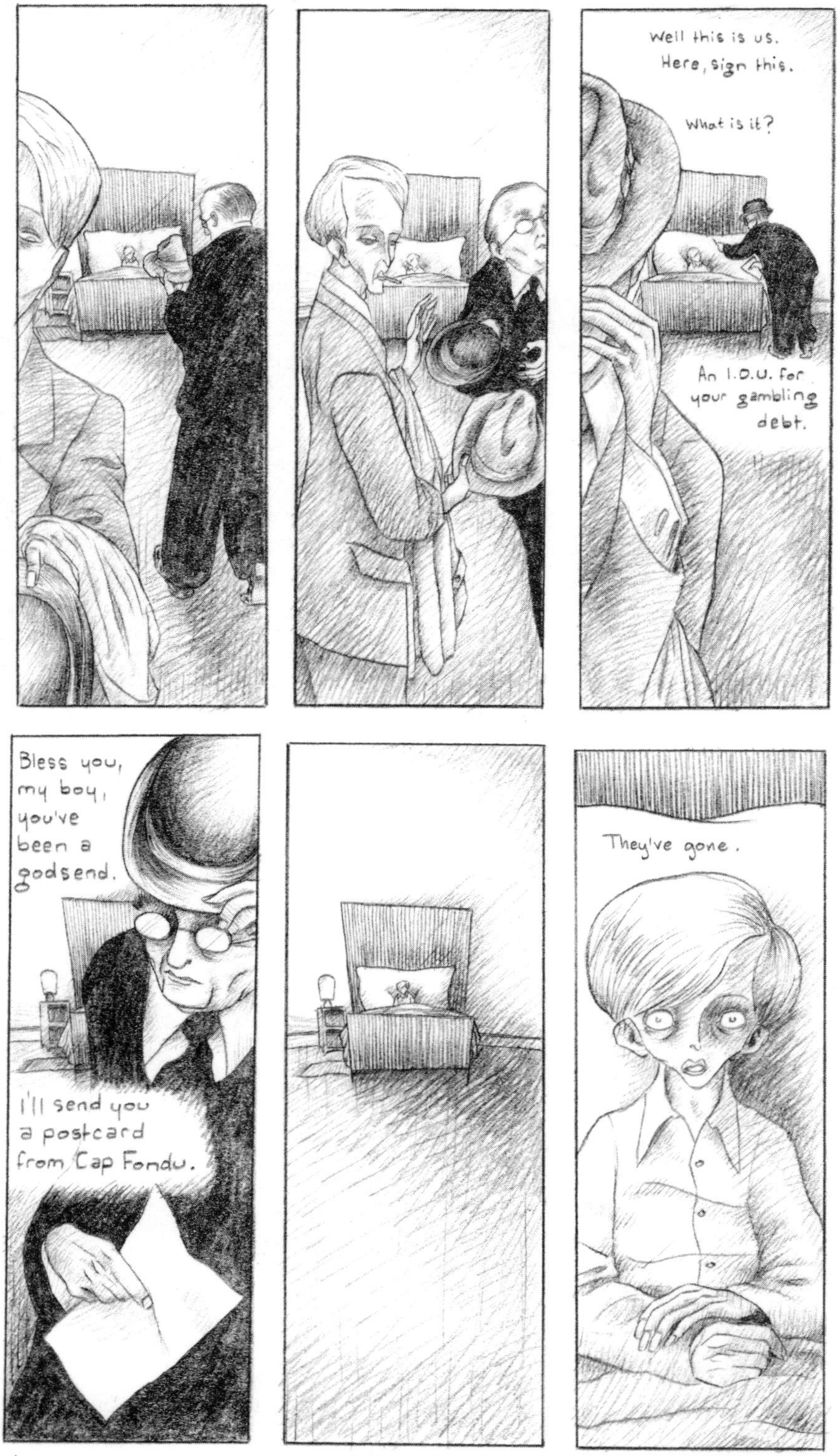
Well this is us.
Here, sign this.
What is it?
An I.O.U. for your gambling debt.
Bless you, my boy, you've been a godsend.
I'll send you a postcard from Cap Fondu.
They've gone.

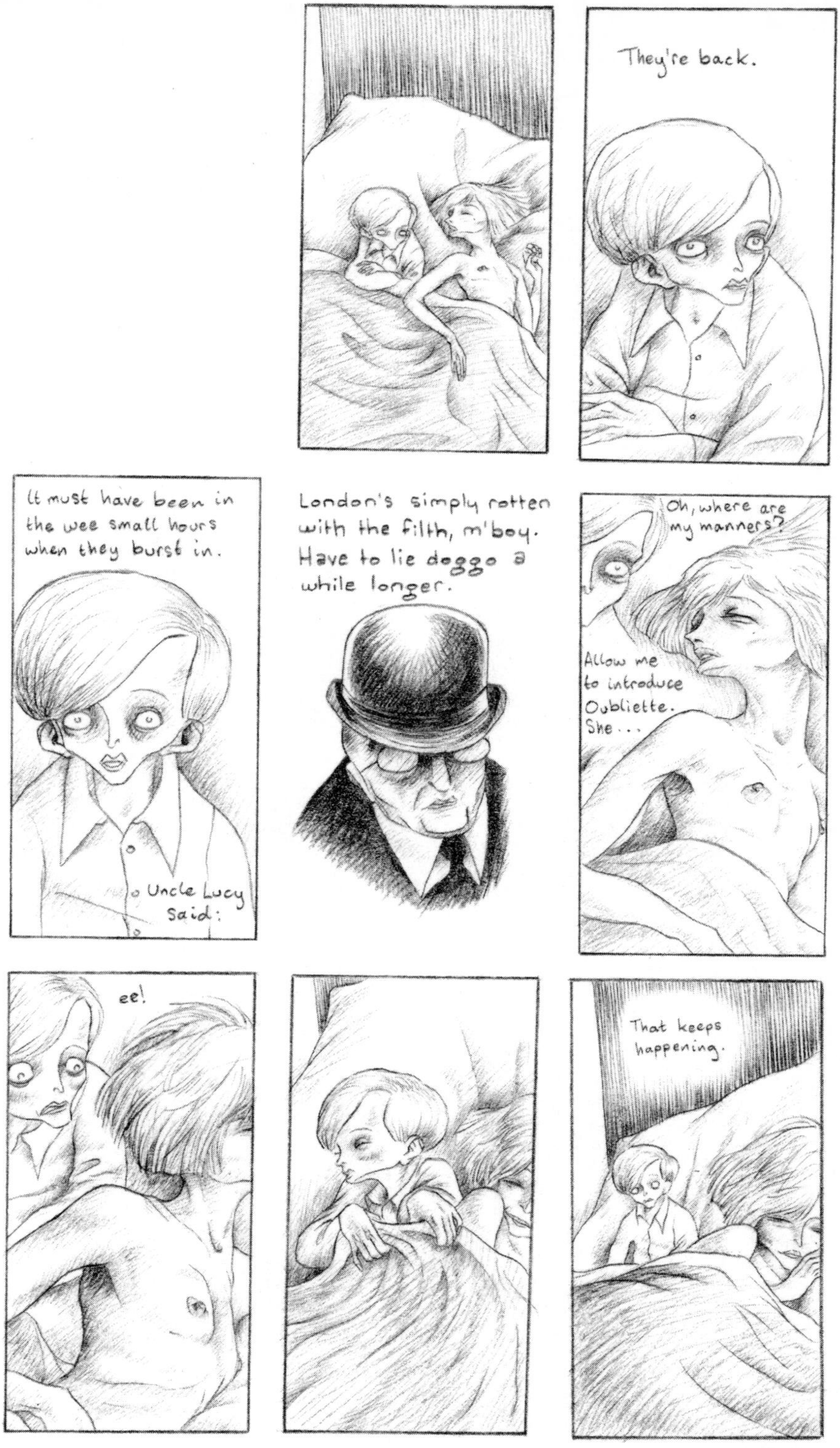
They're back.
It must have been in the wee small hours when they burst in.
Uncle Lucy Said:
London's simply rotten with the filth, m'boy. Have to lie doggo a while longer.
Oh, where are my manners?
Allow me to introduce Oubliette. She...
ee!
That keeps happening.

When they returned they had with them a very grand-looking lady and her lady's maid.

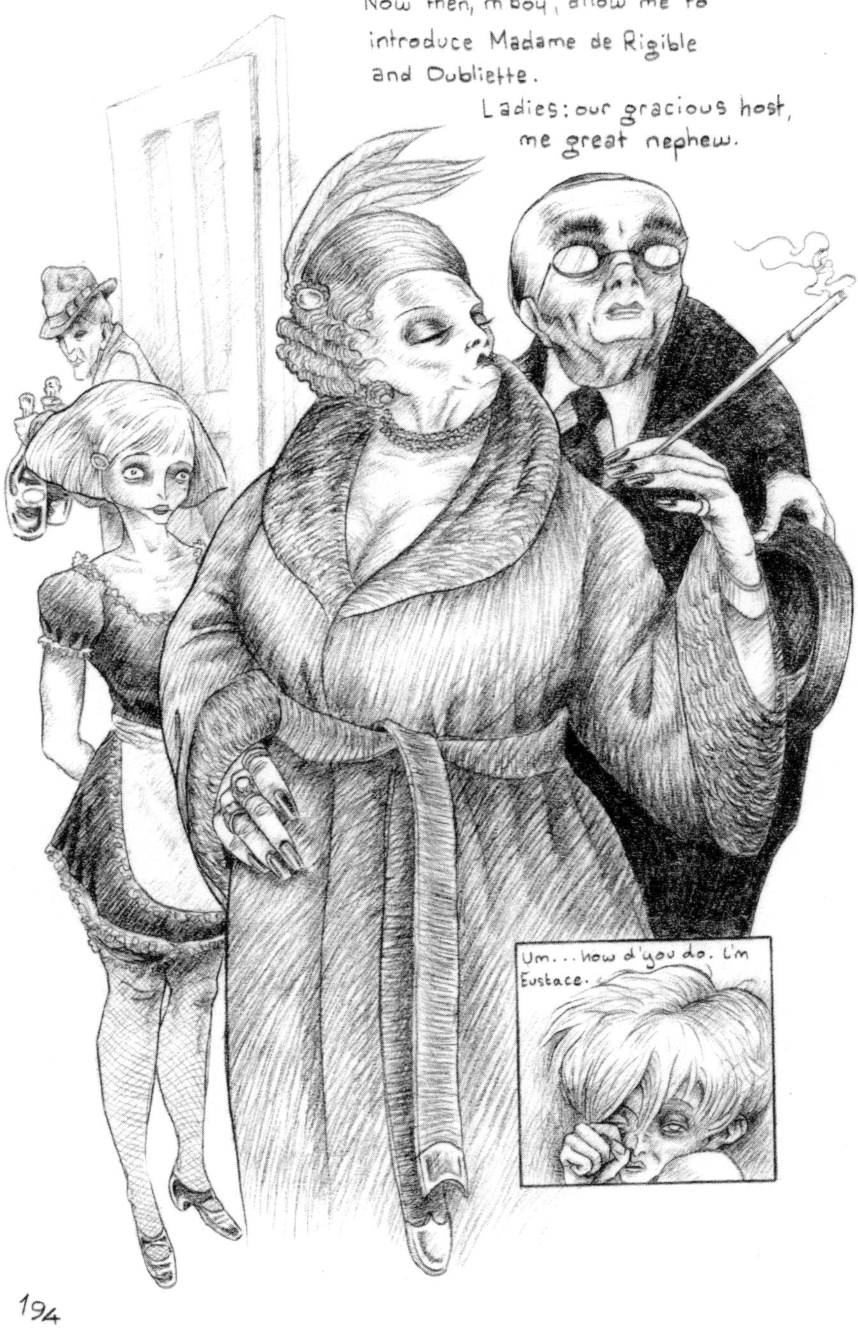
Now then, m'boy, allow me to introduce Madame de Rigible and Dubliette.
Ladies: our gracious host, me great nephew.
Um... how d'you do. I'm Eustace.

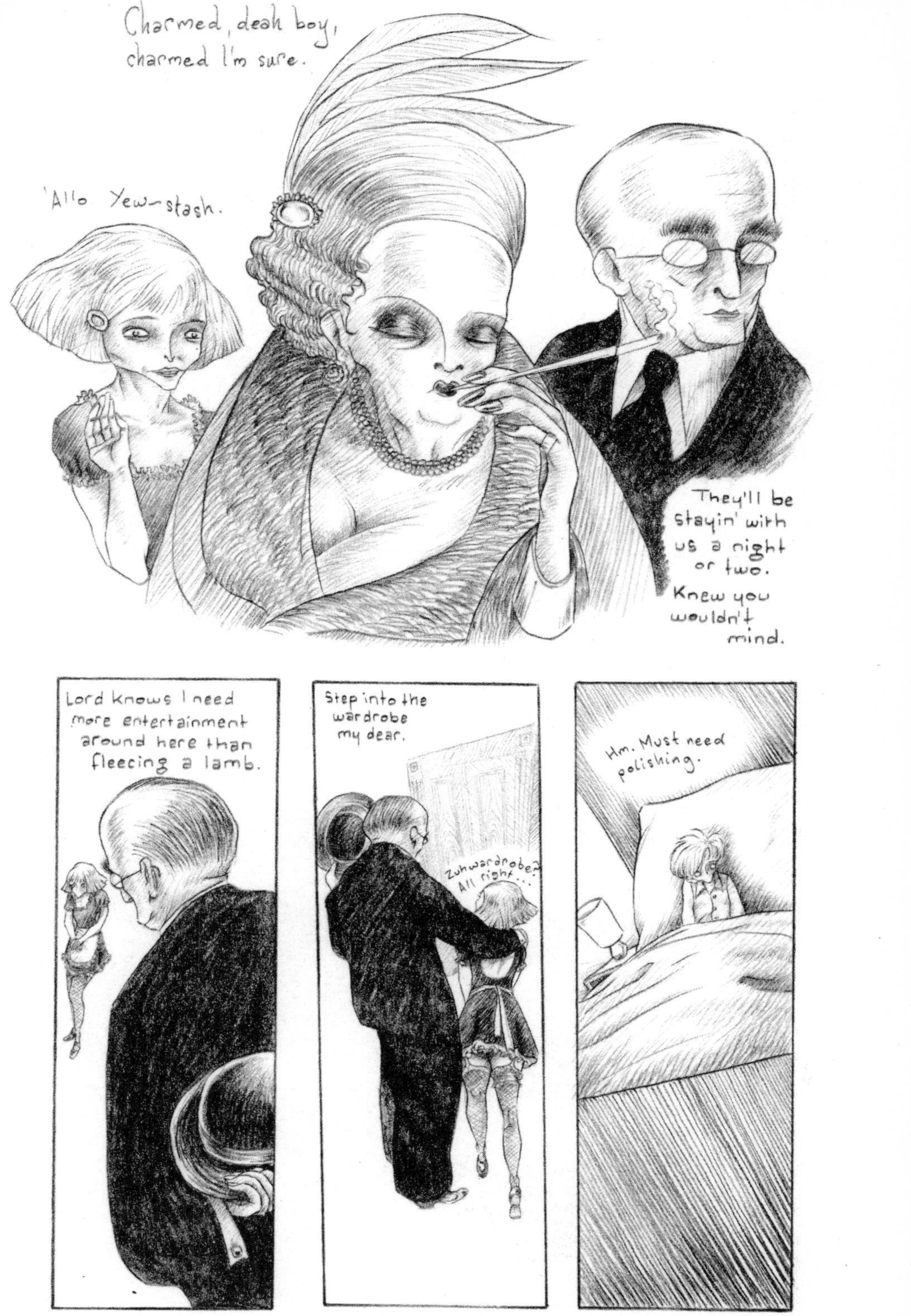
Charmed, deah boy, charmed I'm sure.
'Allo Yew-stash.
They'll be stayin' with us a night or two.
Knew you wouldn't mind.
Lord knows I need more entertainment around here than fleecing a lamb.
Step into the wardrobe my dear.
Zuhwardrobe? All right...
Hm. Must need polishing.

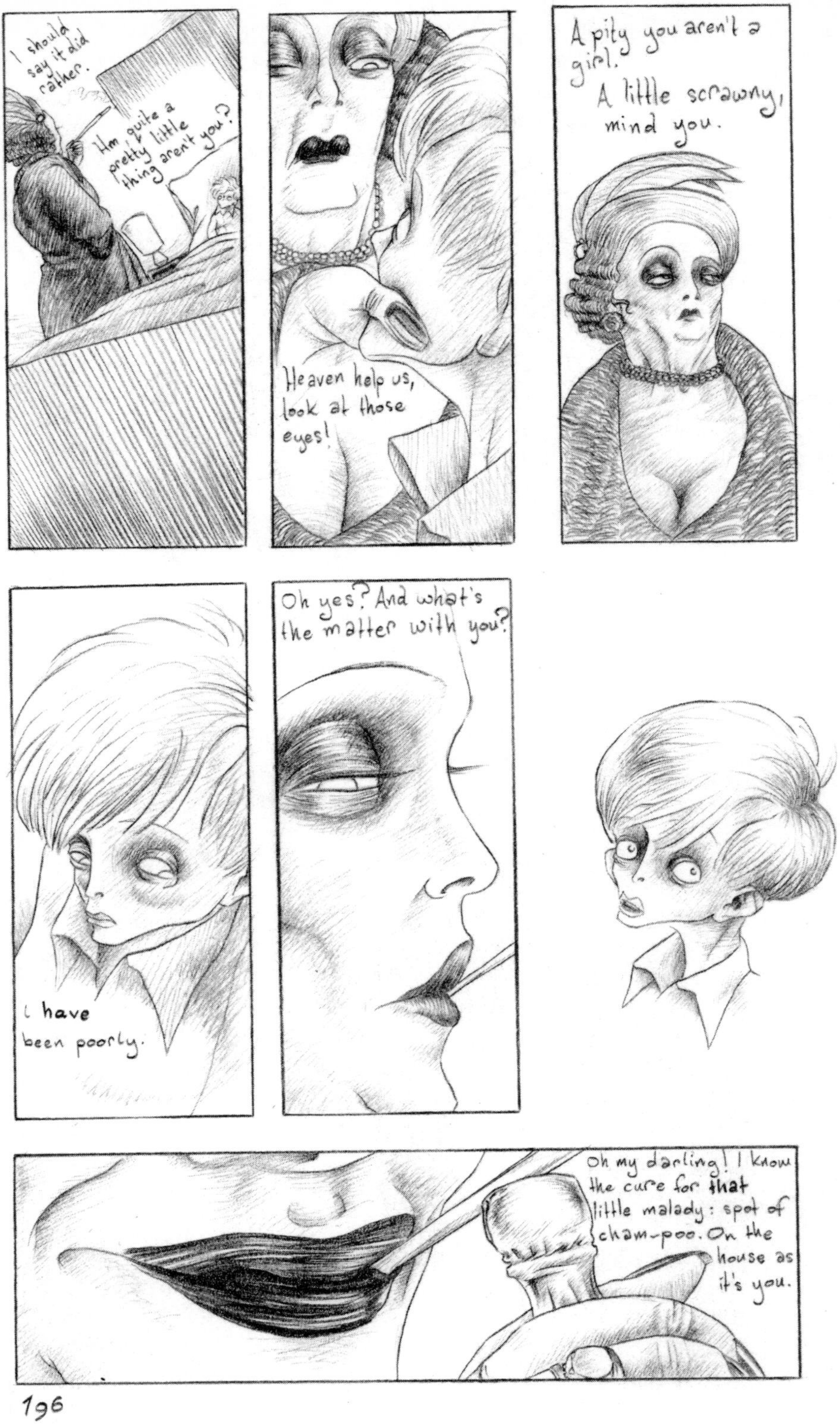
I should say it did rather.
Hm quite a pretty little thing aren't you?
Heaven help us, look at those eyes!
A pity you aren't a girl.
A little scrawny, mind you.
I have been poorly.
Oh yes? And what's the matter with you?
Oh my darling! I know the cure for that little malady: spot of cham-poo. On the house as it's you.

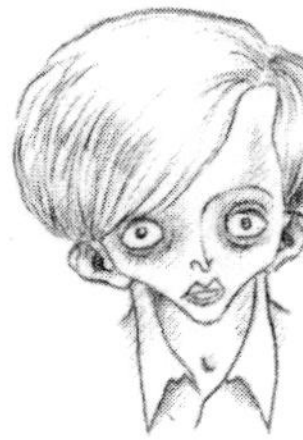

Uncle Lucy was a little while in
the wardrobe with Oubliette.
When they came out Oubliette
looked tired. I said to her...

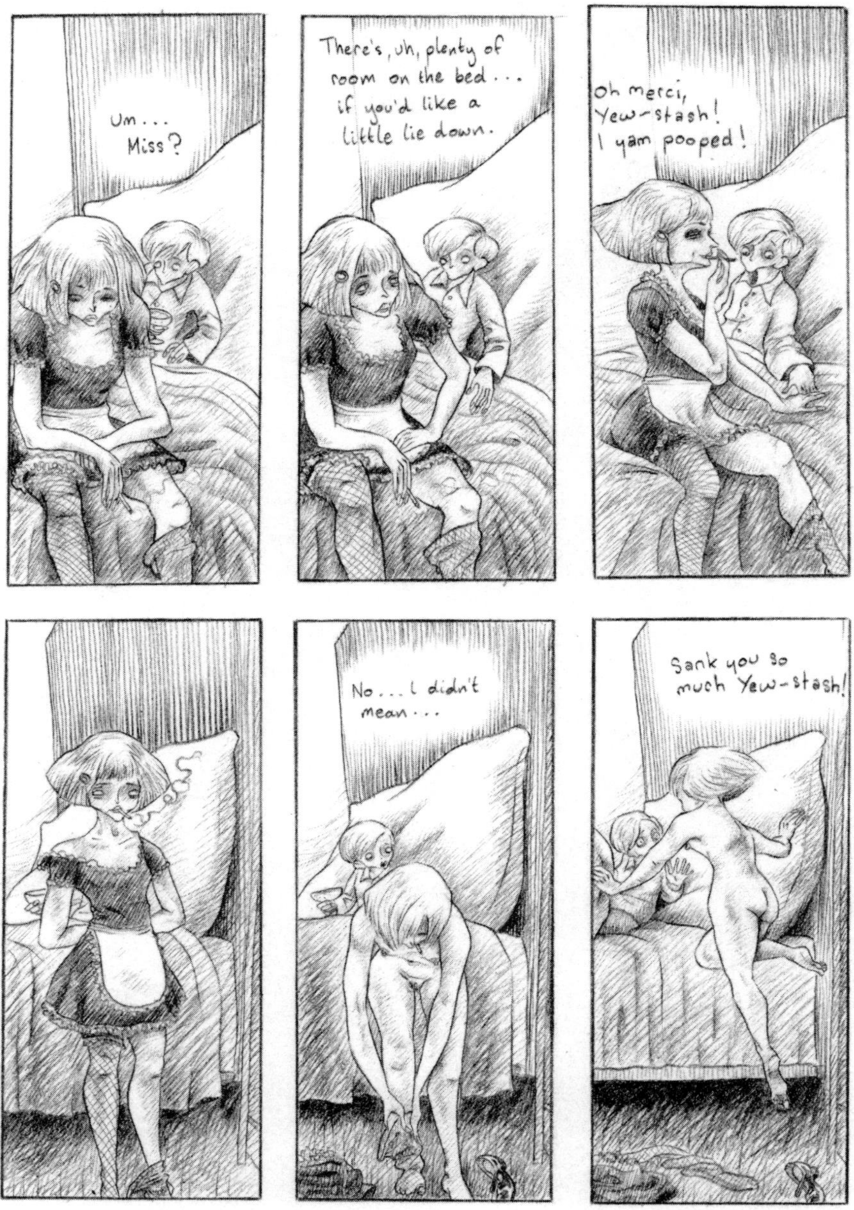
Um... Miss?
There's, uh, plenty of room on the bed... if you'd like a little lie down.
Oh merci, Yew-stash! I yam pooped!
No... I didn't mean...
Sank you so much Yew-stash!

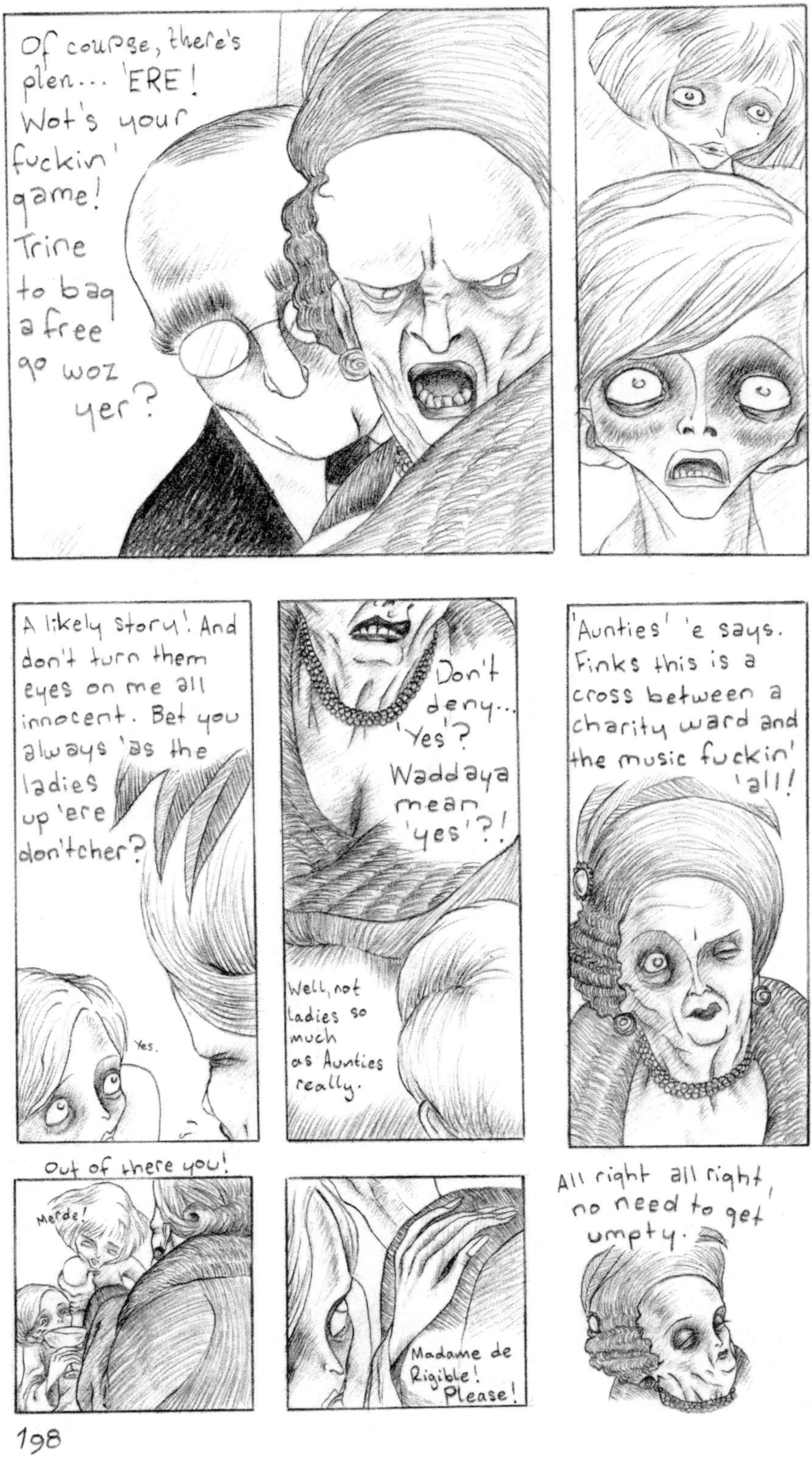
Of course, there's plen... 'ERE! Wot's your fuckin' game! Trine to bag a free go woz yer?
A likely story! And don't turn them eyes on me all innocent. Bet you always 'as the ladies up 'ere don'tcher?
Yes.
Don't deny... 'Yes'? Waddaya mean 'yes'?!
Well, not ladies so much as Aunties really.
'Aunties' 'e says. Finks this is a cross between a charity ward and the music fuckin' 'all!
Out of there you!
Merde!
Madame de Rigible! Please!
All right all right, no need to get umpty.

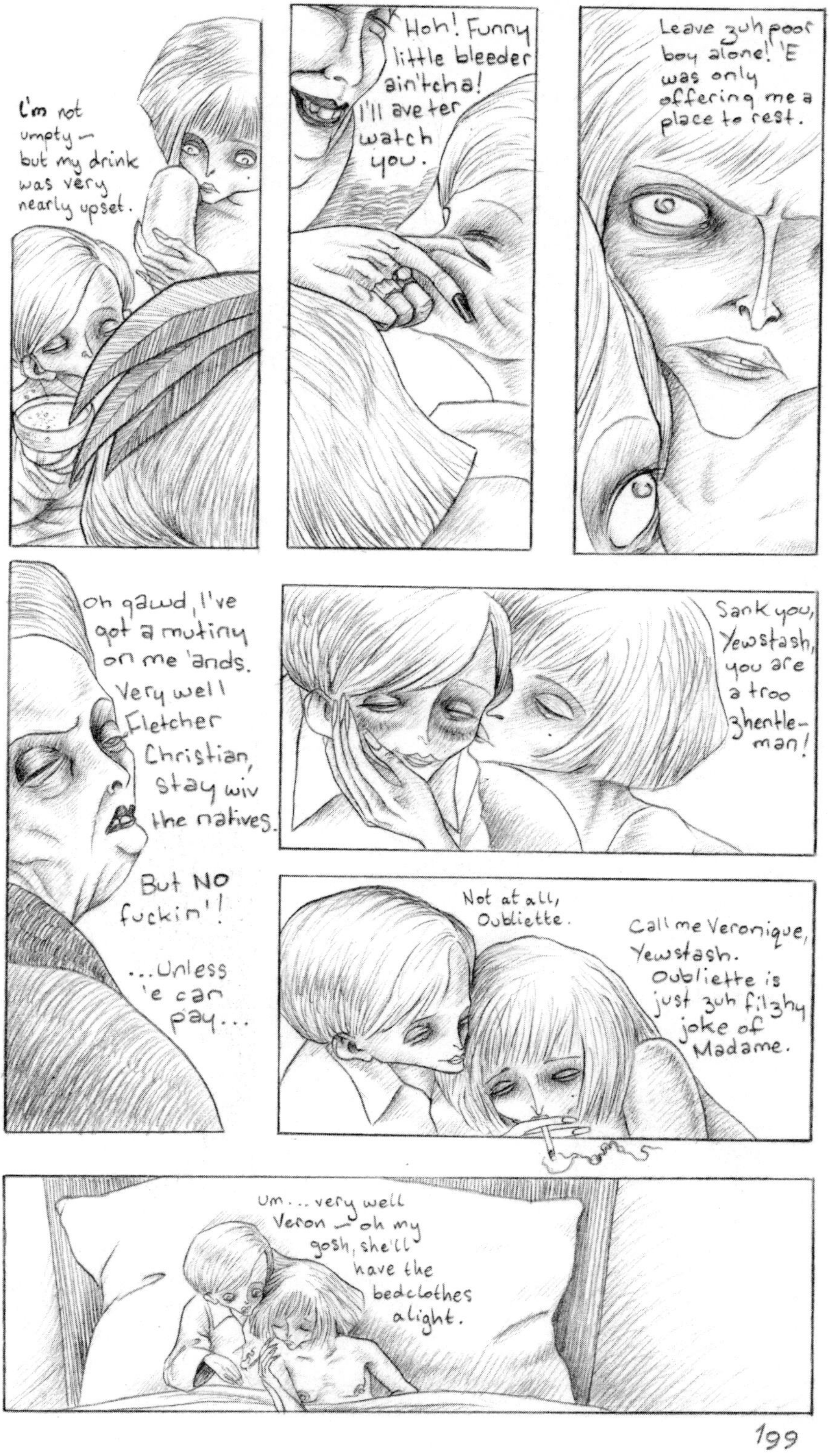
I'm not umpty — but my drink was very nearly upset.
Hoh! Funny little bleeder ain'tcha! I'll ave ter watch you.
Leave zuh poor boy alone! 'E was only offering me a place to rest.
Oh gawd, I've got a mutiny on me 'ands. Very well Fletcher Christian, stay wiv the natives.
But NO fuckin'!
...Unless 'e can pay...
Sank you, Yewstash, you are a troo zhentle-man!
Not at all, Oubliette.
Call me Veronique, Yewstash. Oubliette is just zuh filzhy joke of Madame.
Um... very well Veron — oh my gosh, she'll have the bedclothes alight.

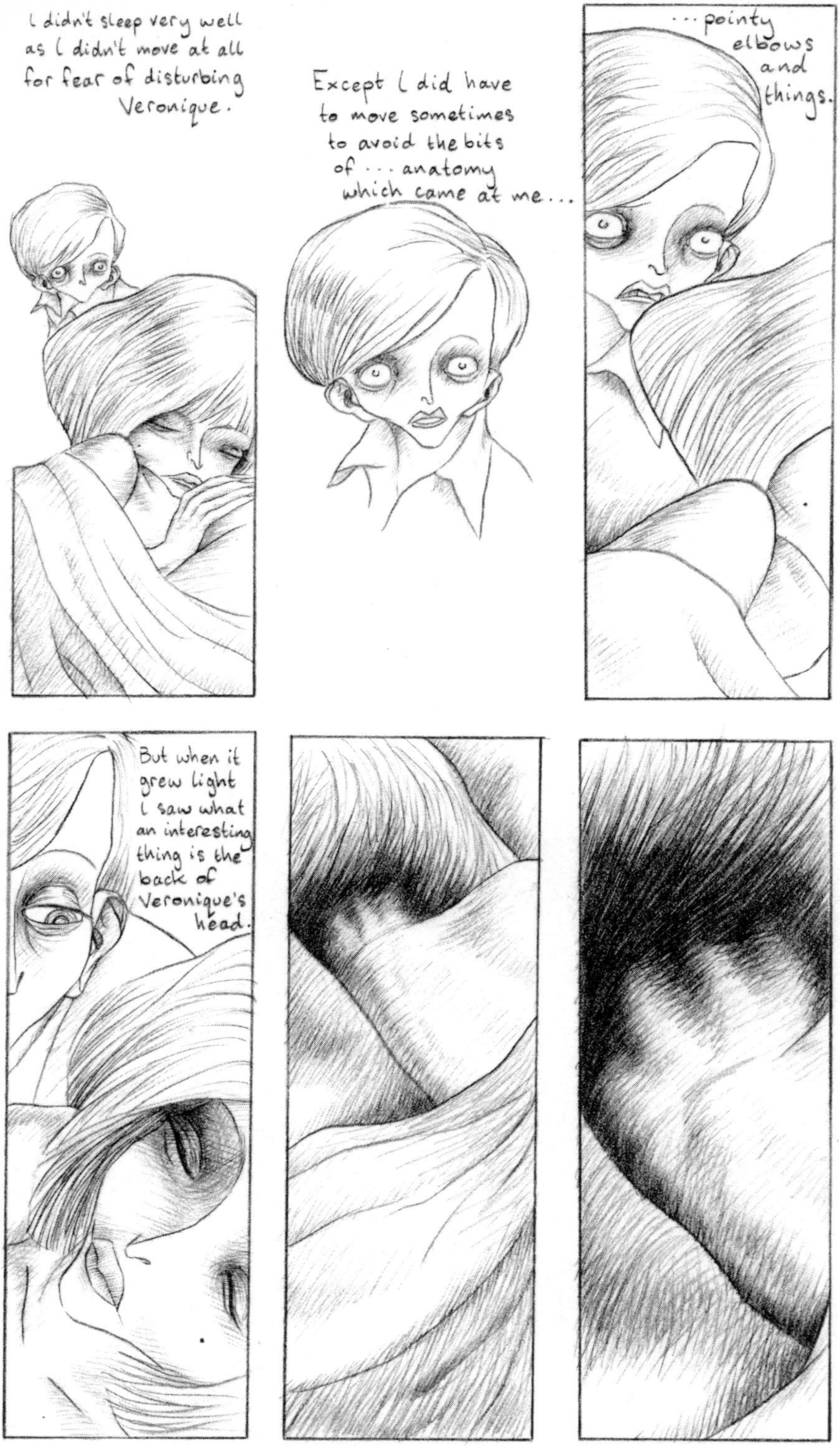
I didn't sleep very well as I didn't move at all for fear of disturbing Veronique.
Except I did have to move sometimes to avoid the bits of . . . anatomy which came at me . . .
. . . pointy elbows and things.
But when it grew light I saw what an interesting thing is the back of Veronique's head.

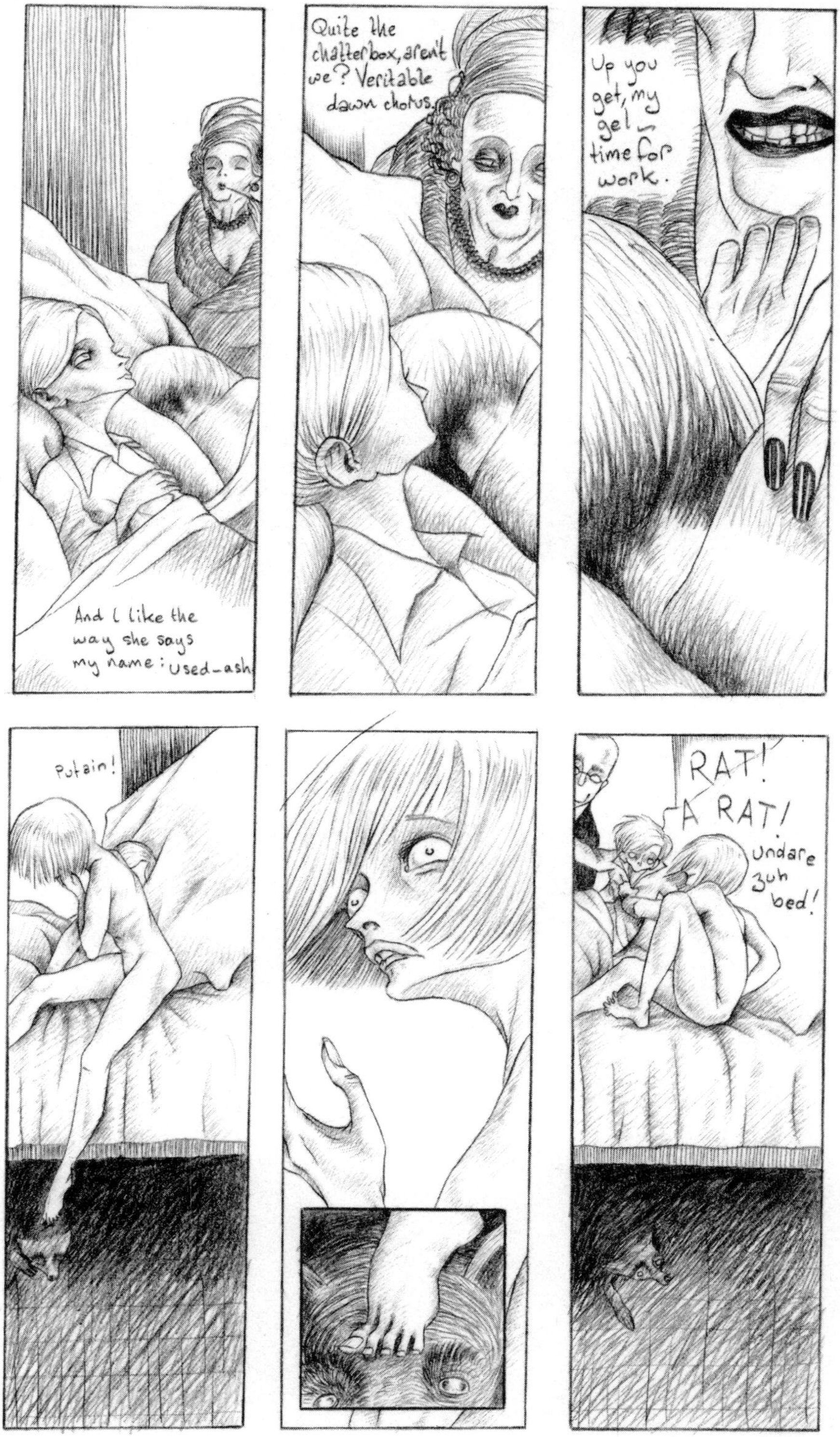
And I like the way she says my name: Used-ash
Quite the chatterbox, aren't we? Veritable dawn chorus.
Up you get, my gel – time for work.
Putain!
RAT! A RAT!
Undare 3uh bed!

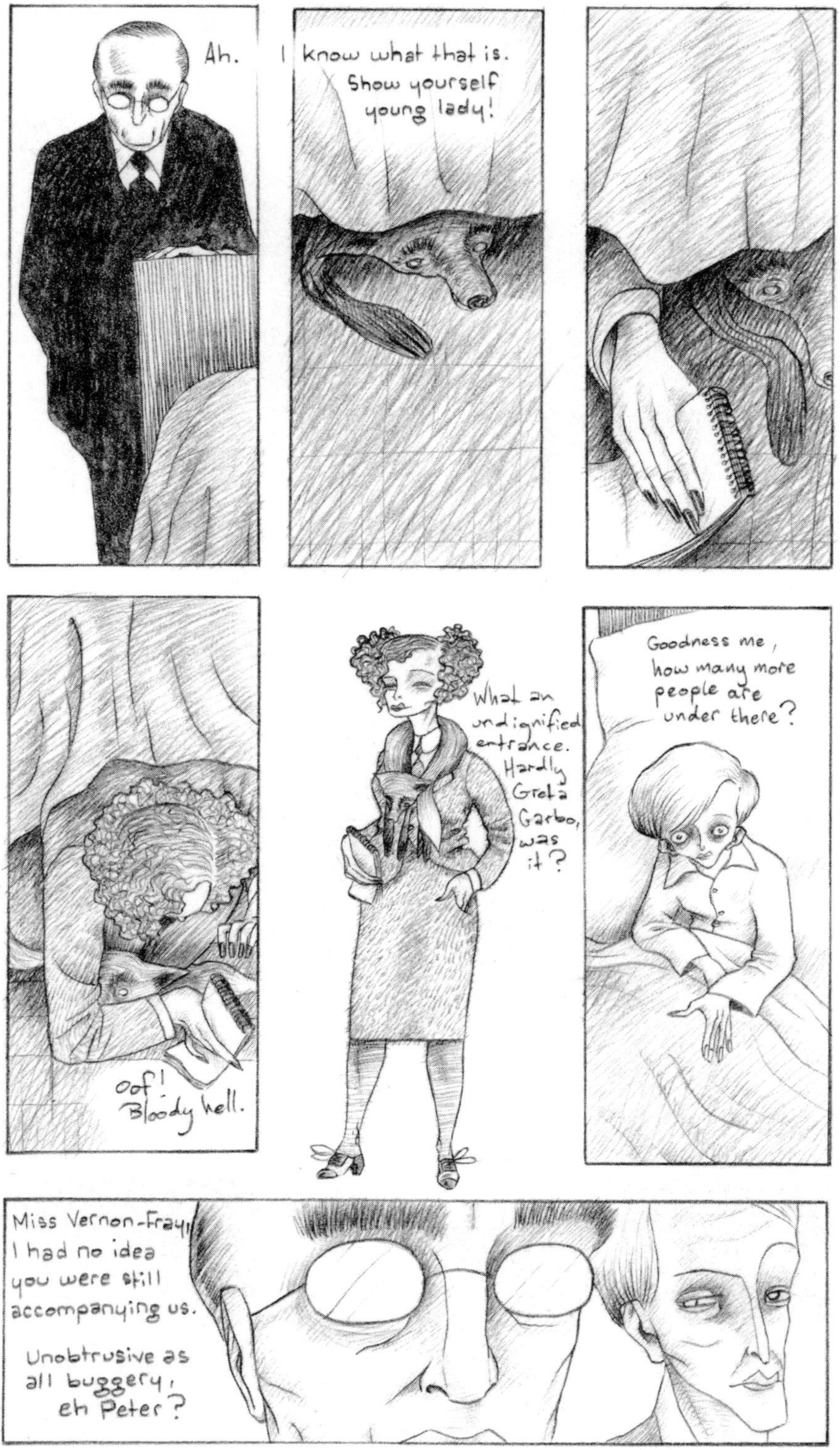
Ah.
I know what that is. Show yourself young lady!
Oof! Bloody hell.
What an undignified entrance. Hardly Greta Garbo, was it?
Goodness me, how many more people are under there?
Miss Vernon-Fray! I had no idea you were still accompanying us.
Unobtrusive as all buggery, eh Peter?

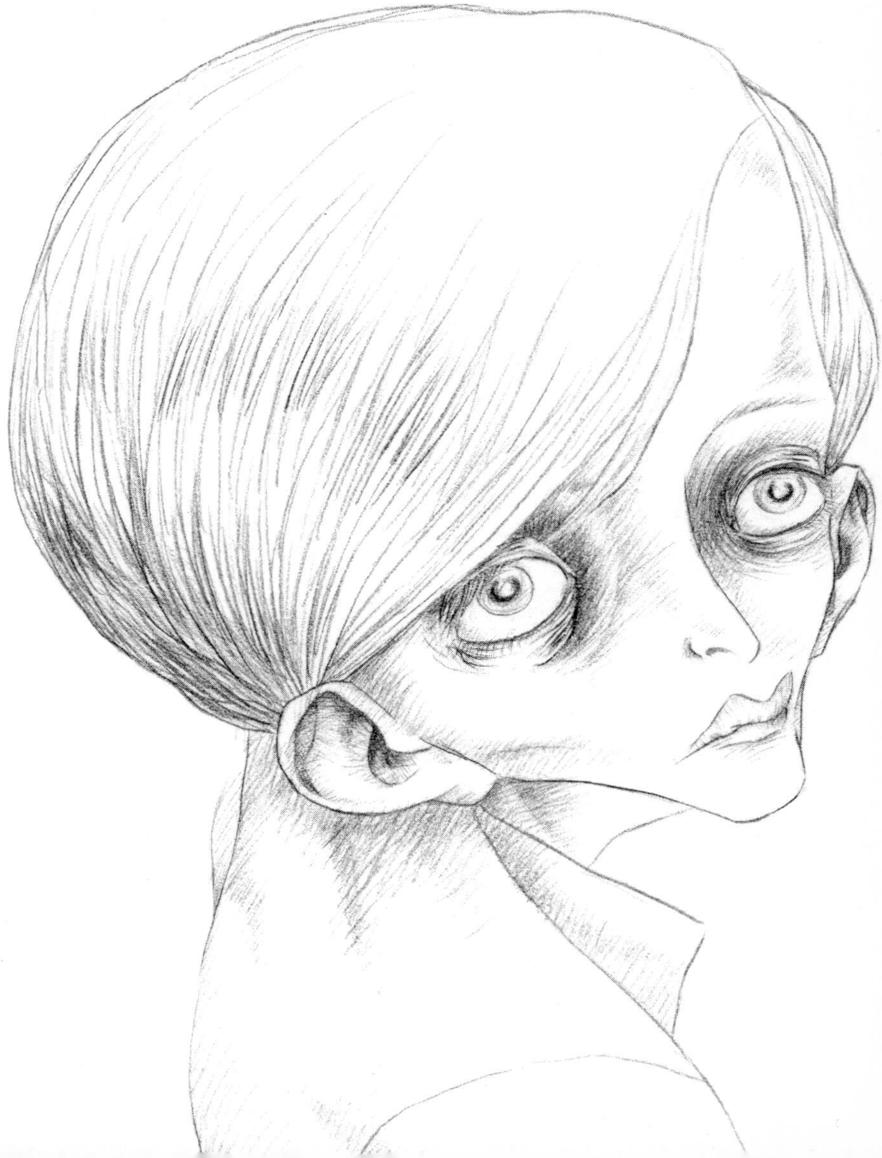

I say, has anyone a light? I'm parched.

Thanks awf'lly, doll face.

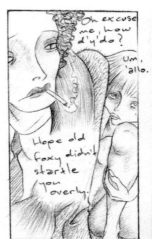

Oh excuse me, how d'y'do?

Um, 'allo.

Hope old Foxy didn't startle you overly.

Miss Vernon-Fray, may I have a word?

Oh. Yes... right. Rather.

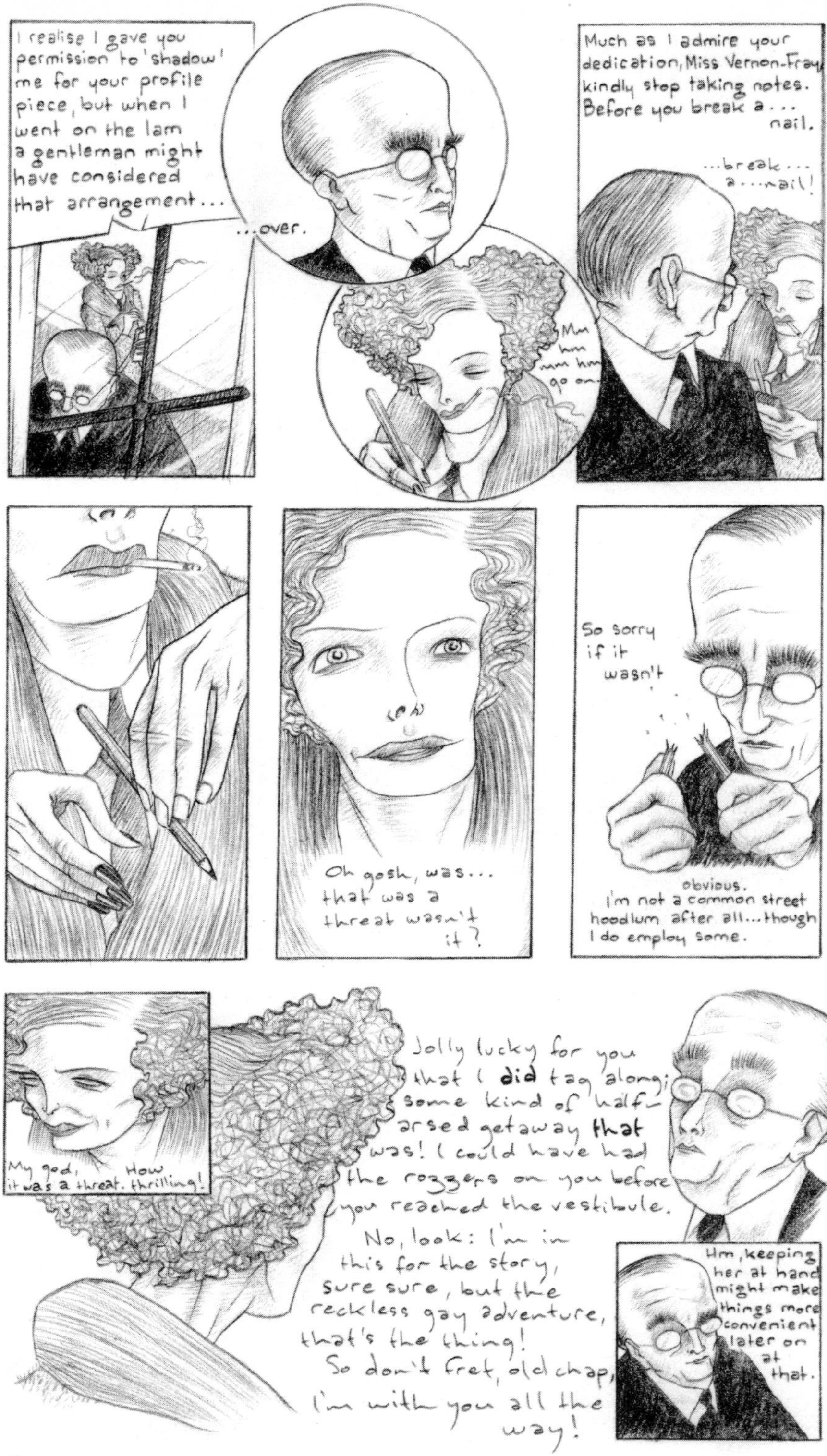
I realise I gave you permission to 'shadow' me for your profile piece, but when I went on the lam a gentleman might have considered that arrangement...
...over.
Mm hm mm hm go on-
Much as I admire your dedication, Miss Vernon-Fray, kindly stop taking notes. Before you break a... nail.
...break... a...nail!
Oh gosh, was... that was a threat wasn't it?
So sorry if it wasn't
obvious. I'm not a common street hoodlum after all... though I do employ some.
My god, it was a threat. How thrilling!
Jolly lucky for you that I did tag along; some kind of half-arsed getaway that was! I could have had the rozzers on you before you reached the vestibule.
No, look: I'm in this for the story, sure sure, but the reckless gay adventure, that's the thing!
So don't fret, old chap, I'm with you all the way!
Hm, keeping her at hand might make things more convenient later on at that.

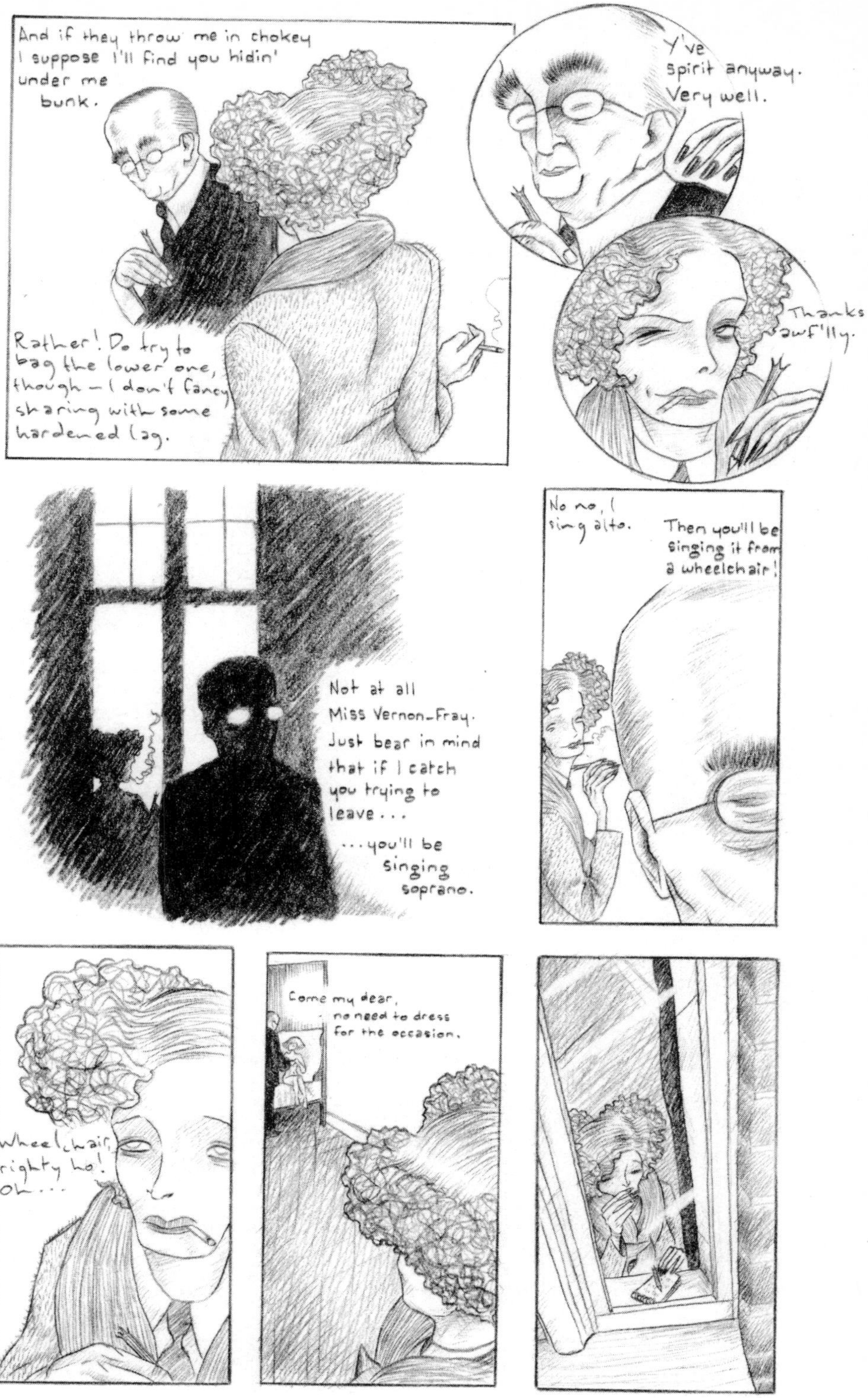
And if they throw me in chokey I suppose I'll find you hidin' under me bunk.
Rather! Do try to bag the lower one, though – I don't fancy sharing with some hardened lag.
Y've spirit anyway. Very well.
Thanks awf'lly.
Not at all Miss Vernon-Fray. Just bear in mind that if I catch you trying to leave...
...you'll be singing soprano.
No no, I sing alto.
Then you'll be singing it from a wheelchair!
Wheelchair, righty ho! Oh...
Come my dear, no need to dress for the occasion.

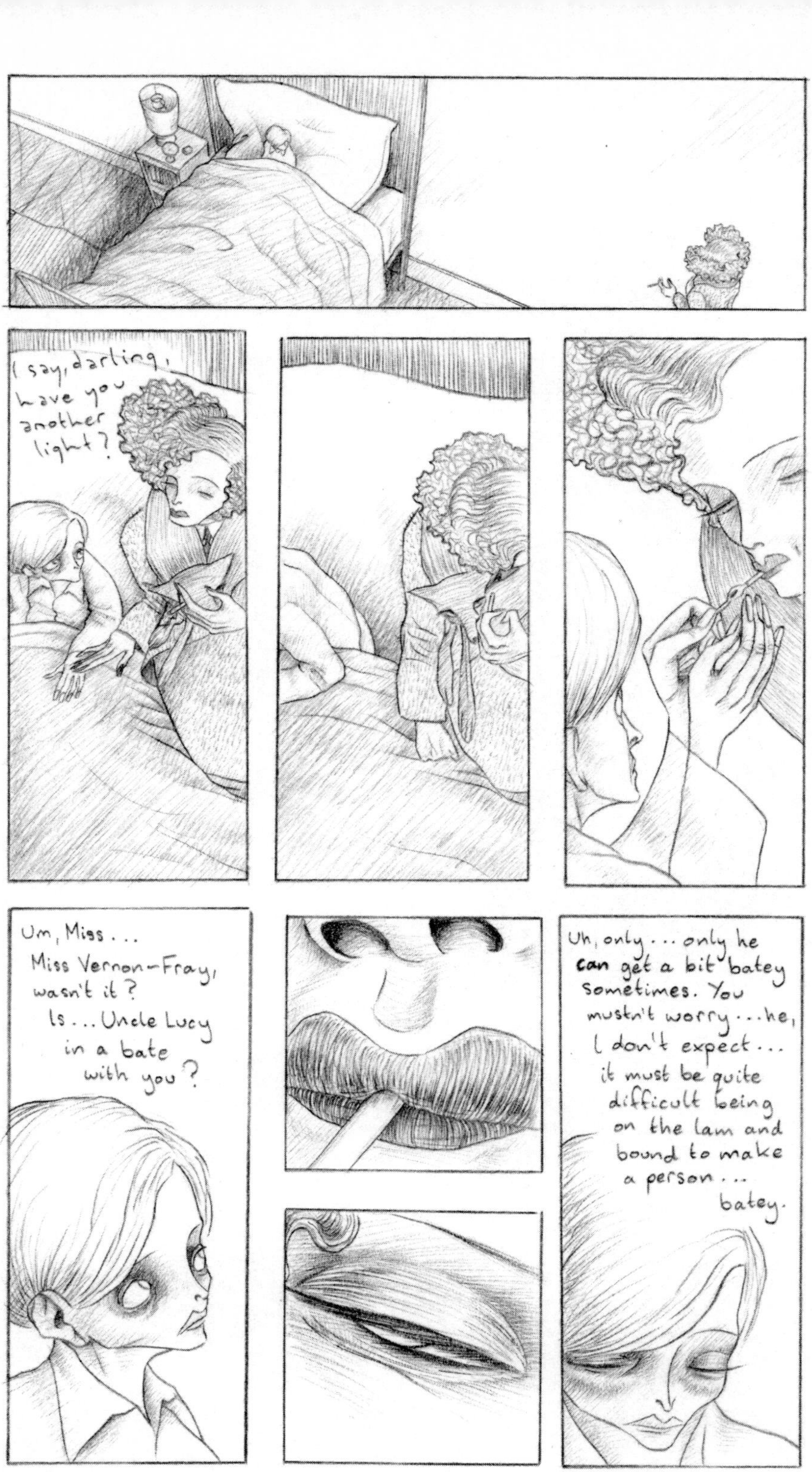
I say, darling, have you another light?
Um, Miss... Miss Vernon-Fray, wasn't it? Is... Uncle Lucy in a bate with you?
Uh, only... only he **can** get a bit batey sometimes. You mustn't worry... he, I don't expect... it must be quite difficult being on the lam and bound to make a person... batey.

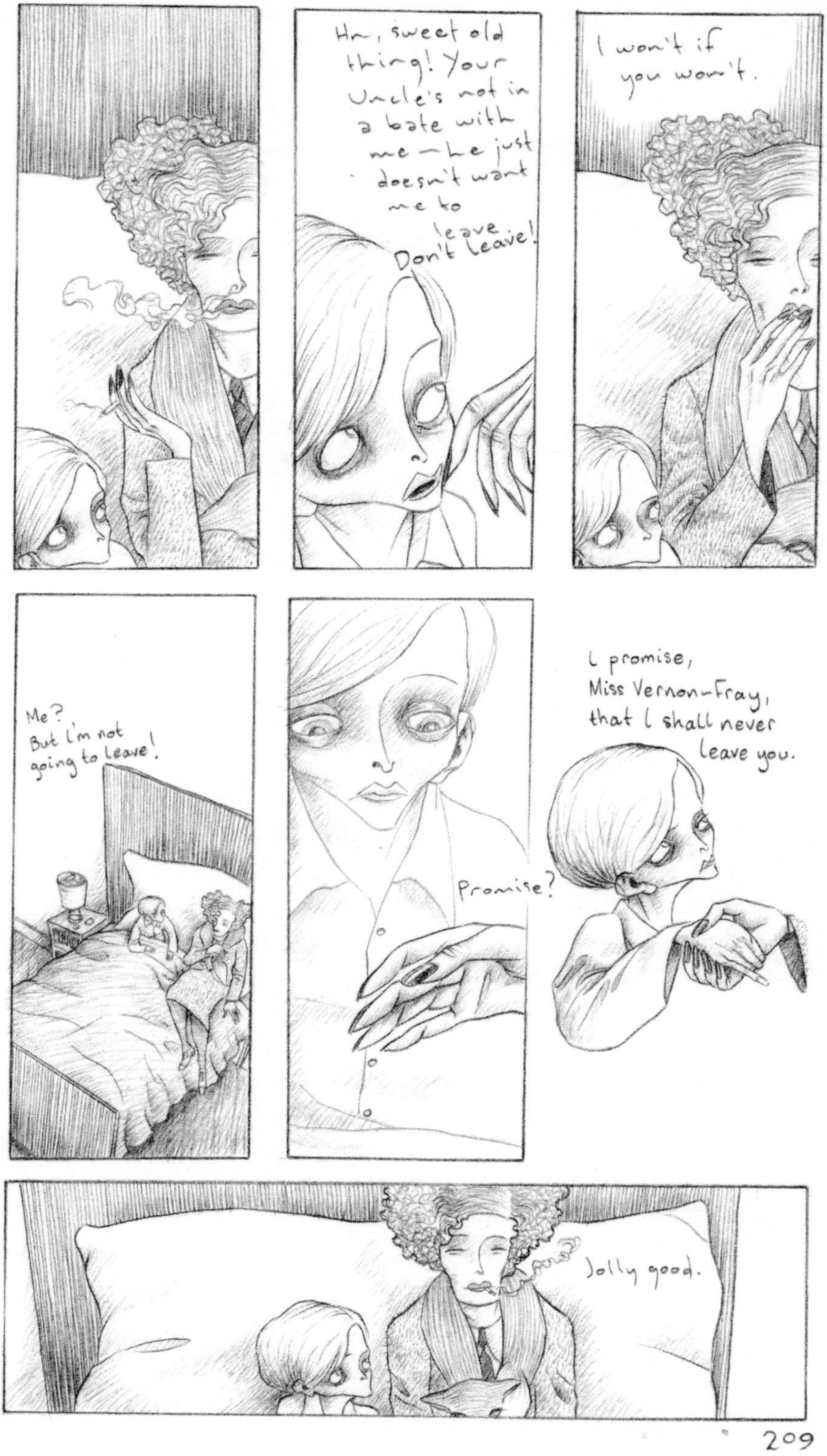

Hm, sweet old thing! Your Uncle's not in a bate with me — he just doesn't want me to leave
Don't leave!
I won't if you won't.
Me? But I'm not going to leave!
Promise?
I promise, Miss Vernon-Fray, that I shall never leave you.
Jolly good.

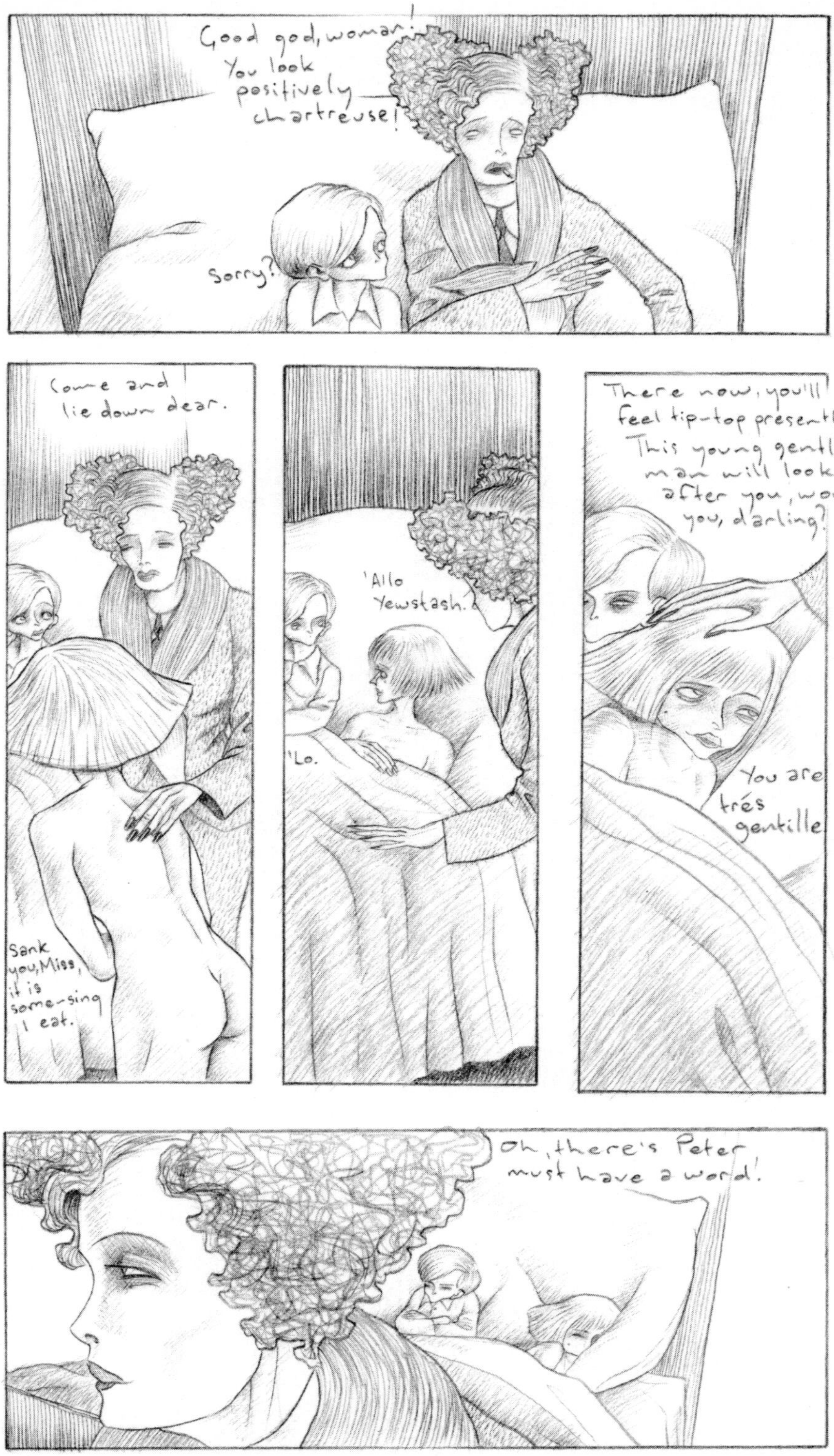
Good god, woman!
You look positively chartreuse!
Sorry?
Come and lie down dear.
Sank you, Miss, it is some-sing I eat.
'Allo Yewstash.
'Lo.
There now, you'll feel tip-top presently. This young gentle-man will look after you, won't you, darling?
You are trés gentille
Oh, there's Peter must have a word!

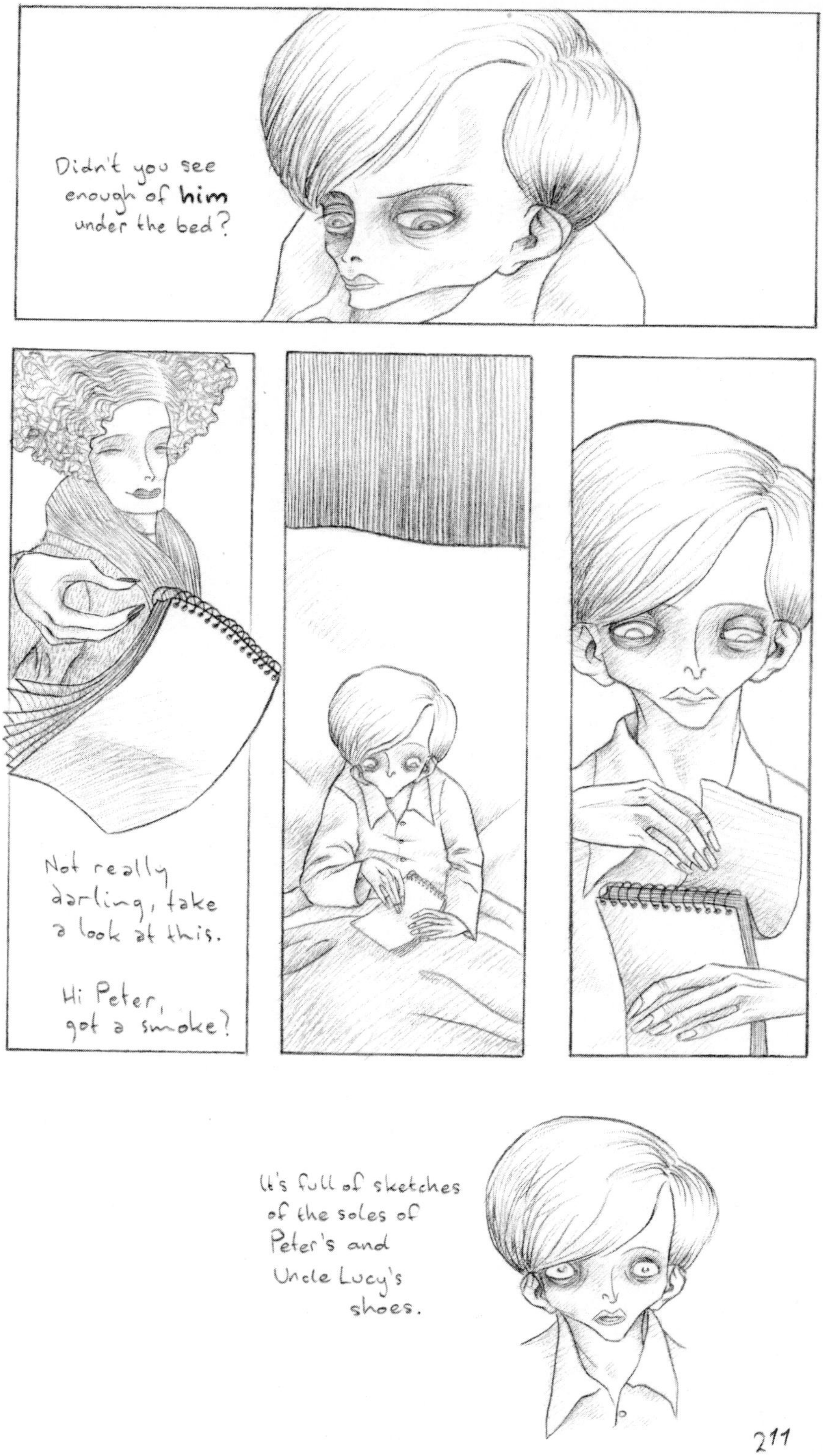
Didn't you see enough of **him** under the bed?
Not really darling, take a look at this.
Hi Peter, got a smoke?
It's full of sketches of the soles of Peter's and Uncle Lucy's shoes.

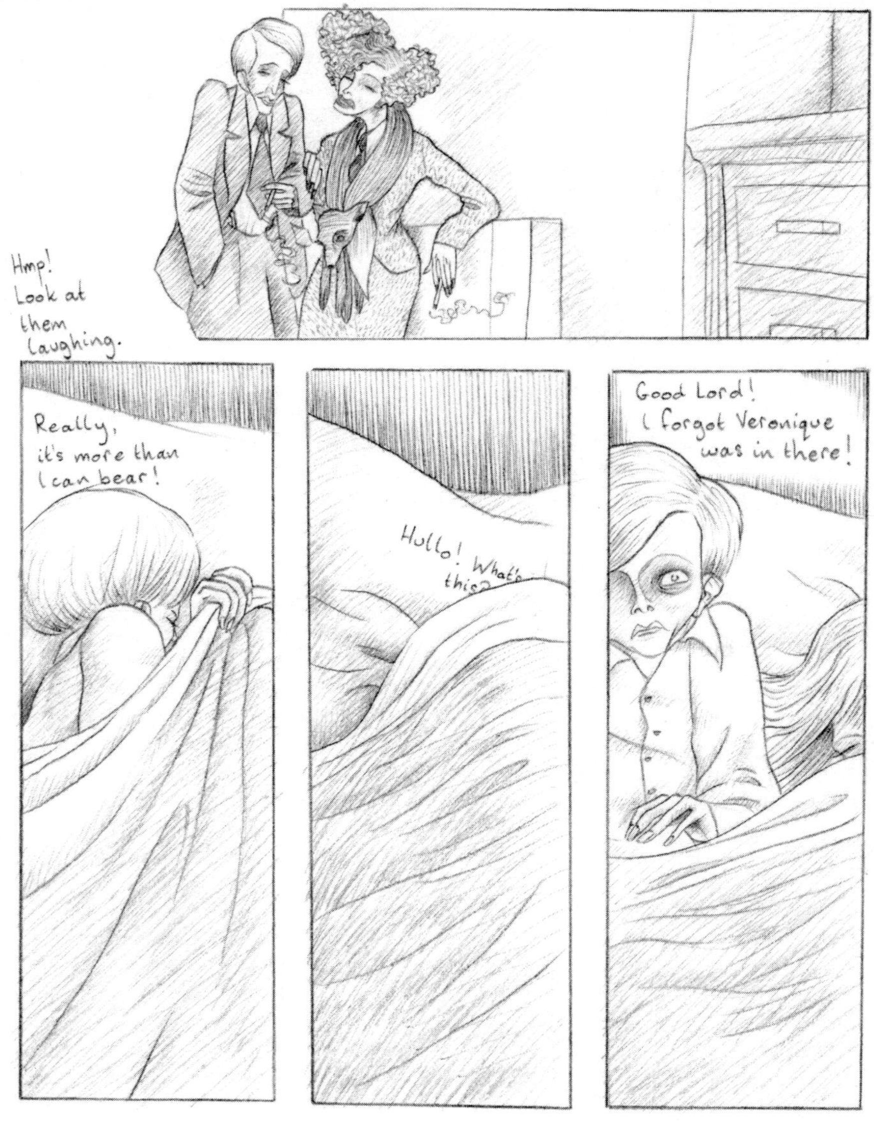
Hmp! Look at them laughing.
Really, it's more than I can bear!
Hullo! What's this?
Good Lord! I forgot Veronique was in there!

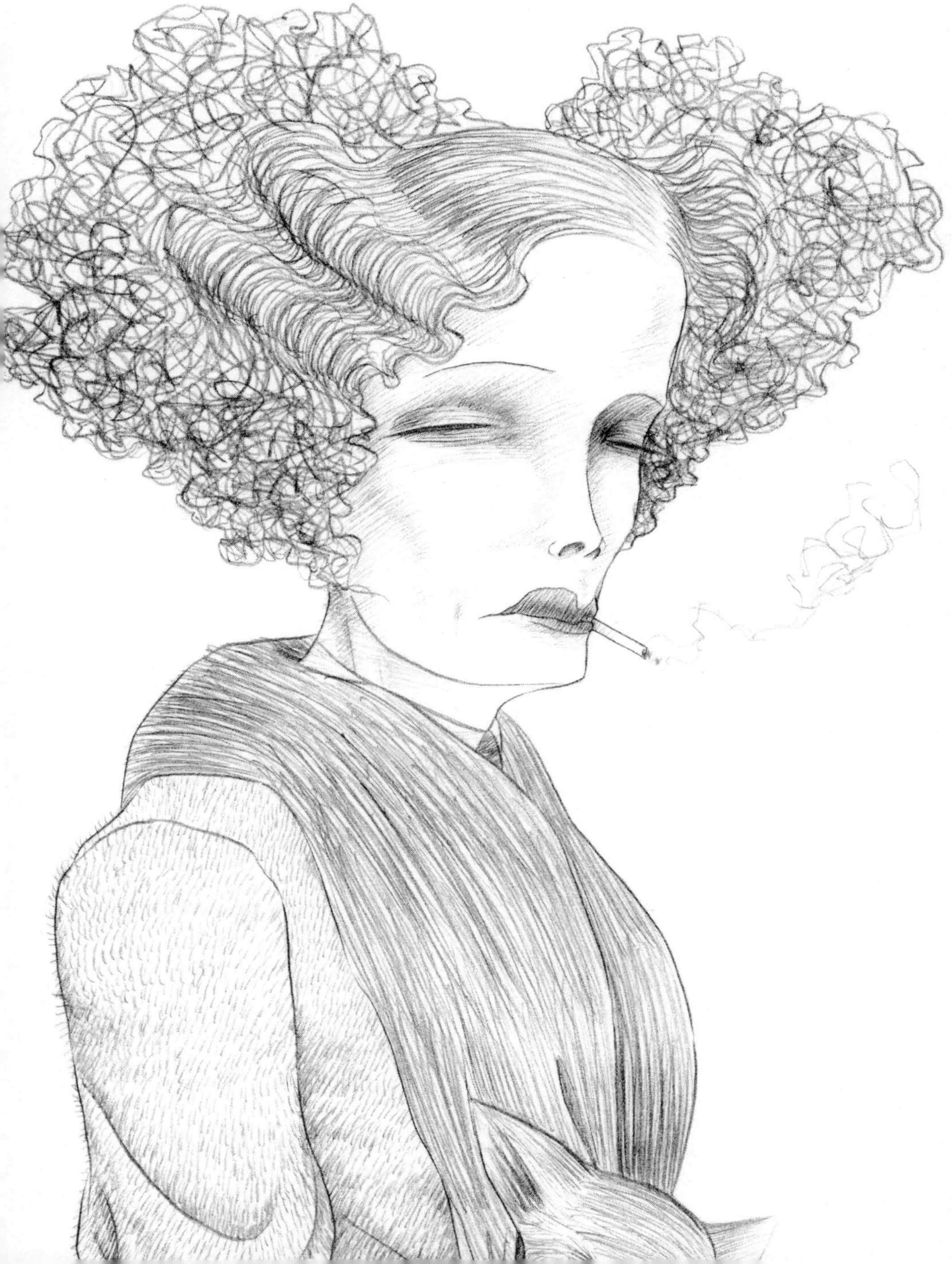

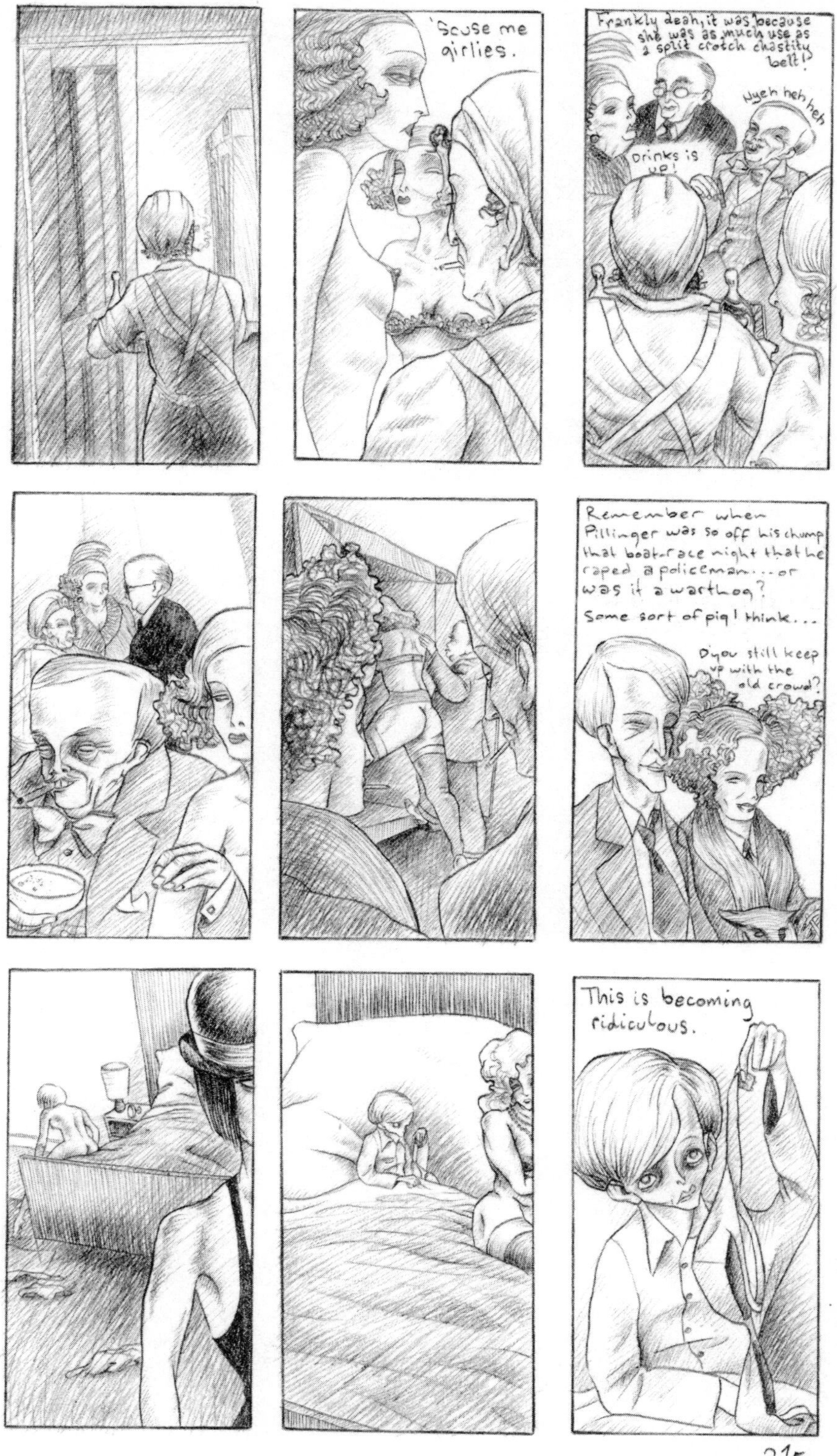
'Scuse me girlies.
Frankly deah, it was because she was as much use as a split crotch chastity belt!
Nyeh heh heh
Drinks is up!
Remember when Pillinger was so off his chump that boat-race night that he raped a policeman...or was it a warthog?
Some sort of pig I think...
D'you still keep up with the old crowd?
This is becoming ridiculous.

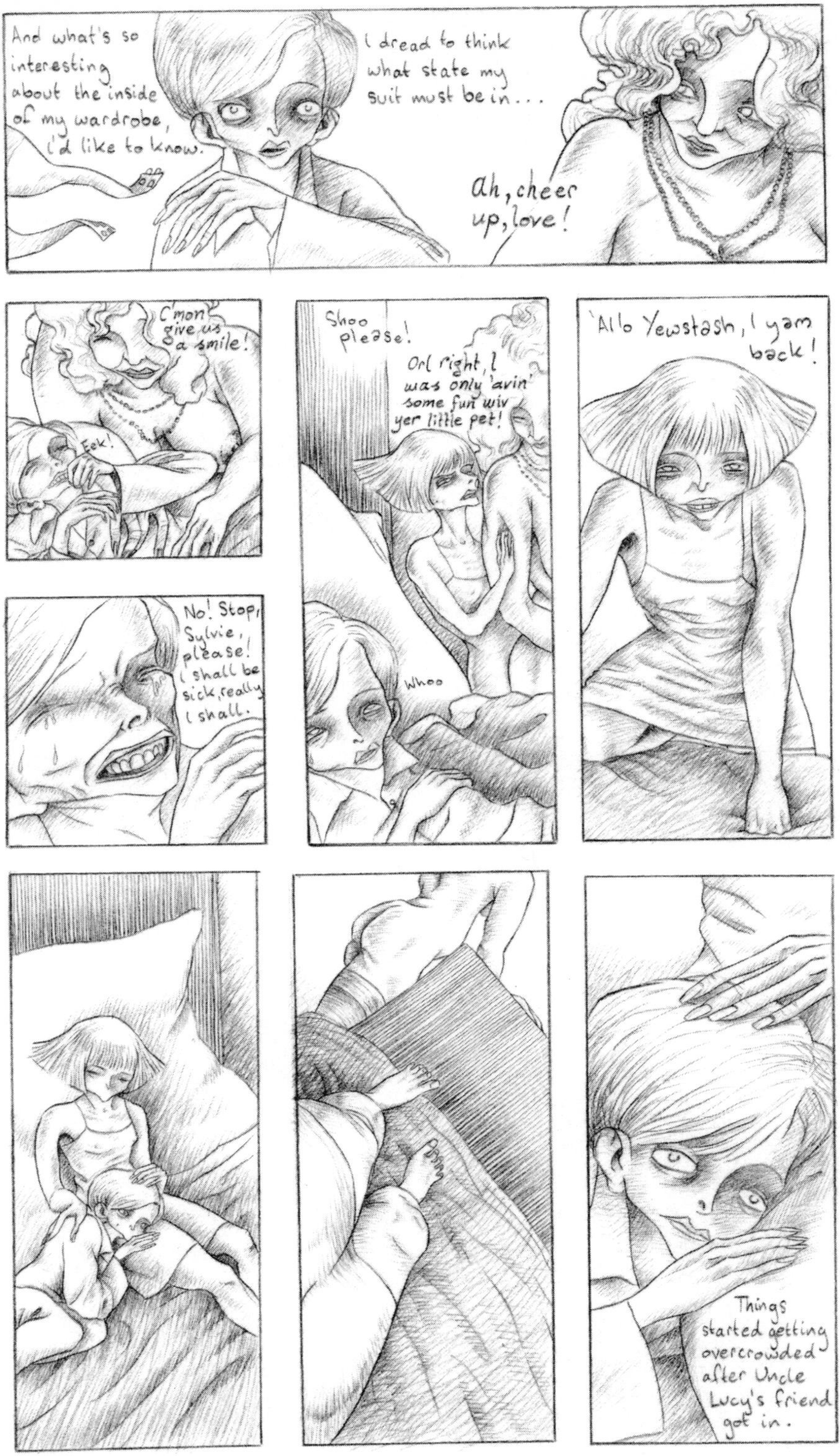

And what's so interesting about the inside of my wardrobe, I'd like to know.
I dread to think what state my suit must be in...
Ah, cheer up, love!
C'mon! give us a smile!
Eek!
Shoo please!
Orl right, I was only 'avin' some fun wiv yer little pet!
Whoo
'Allo Yewstash, I yam back!
No! Stop, Sylvie, please! I shall be sick, really I shall.
Things started getting overcrowded after Uncle Lucy's friend got in.

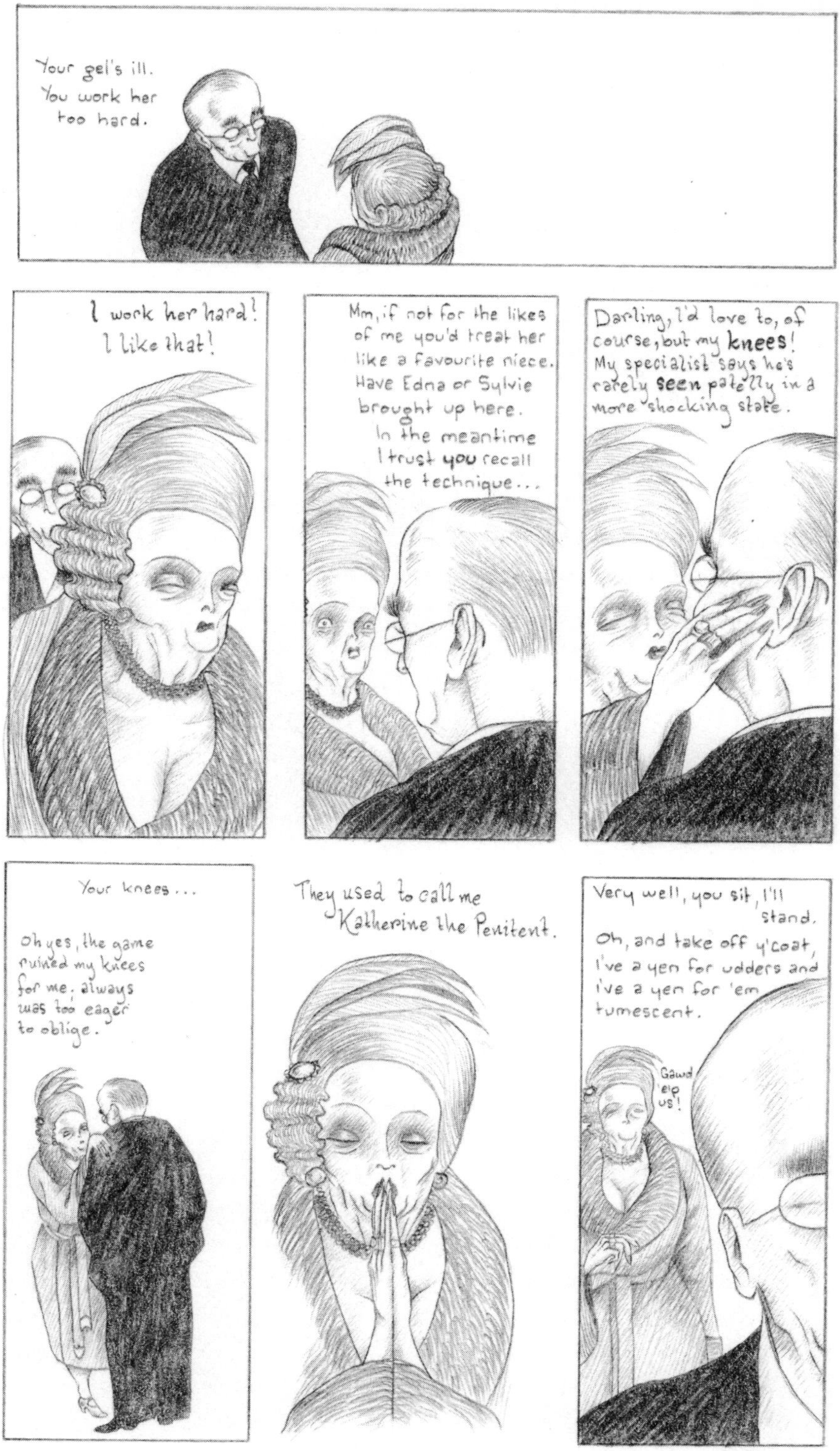
Your gel's ill. You work her too hard.
I work her hard! I like that!
Mm, if not for the likes of me you'd treat her like a favourite niece. Have Edna or Sylvie brought up here.
In the meantime I trust **you** recall the technique...
Darling, I'd love to, of course, but my **knees**! My specialist says he's rarely **seen** patelly in a more shocking state.
Your knees...
Oh yes, the game ruined my knees for me. always was too eager to oblige.
They used to call me Katherine the Penitent.
Very well, you sit, I'll stand.
Oh, and take off y'coat, I've a yen for udders and I've a yen for 'em tumescent.
Gawd 'elp us!

Them extra tarts is 'ere, Suh.

Goood, goood.

Only there's some bloke wiv 'em an' all.

Bloke! What bloke?

I dunno, 'Steve' sounded like.

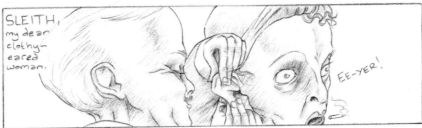

SLEITH, my dear clothy-eared woman.

EE-YER!

Raglan! Thank Christ: thought it was the rozzers!

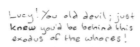

Lucy! You old devil; just **knew** you'd be behind this exodus of the whores!

Did you, Raglan, did...you weren't followed were you?

Followed? Not I! Too wily, old chap: walked backwards all the way!

Masterly, Raglan.

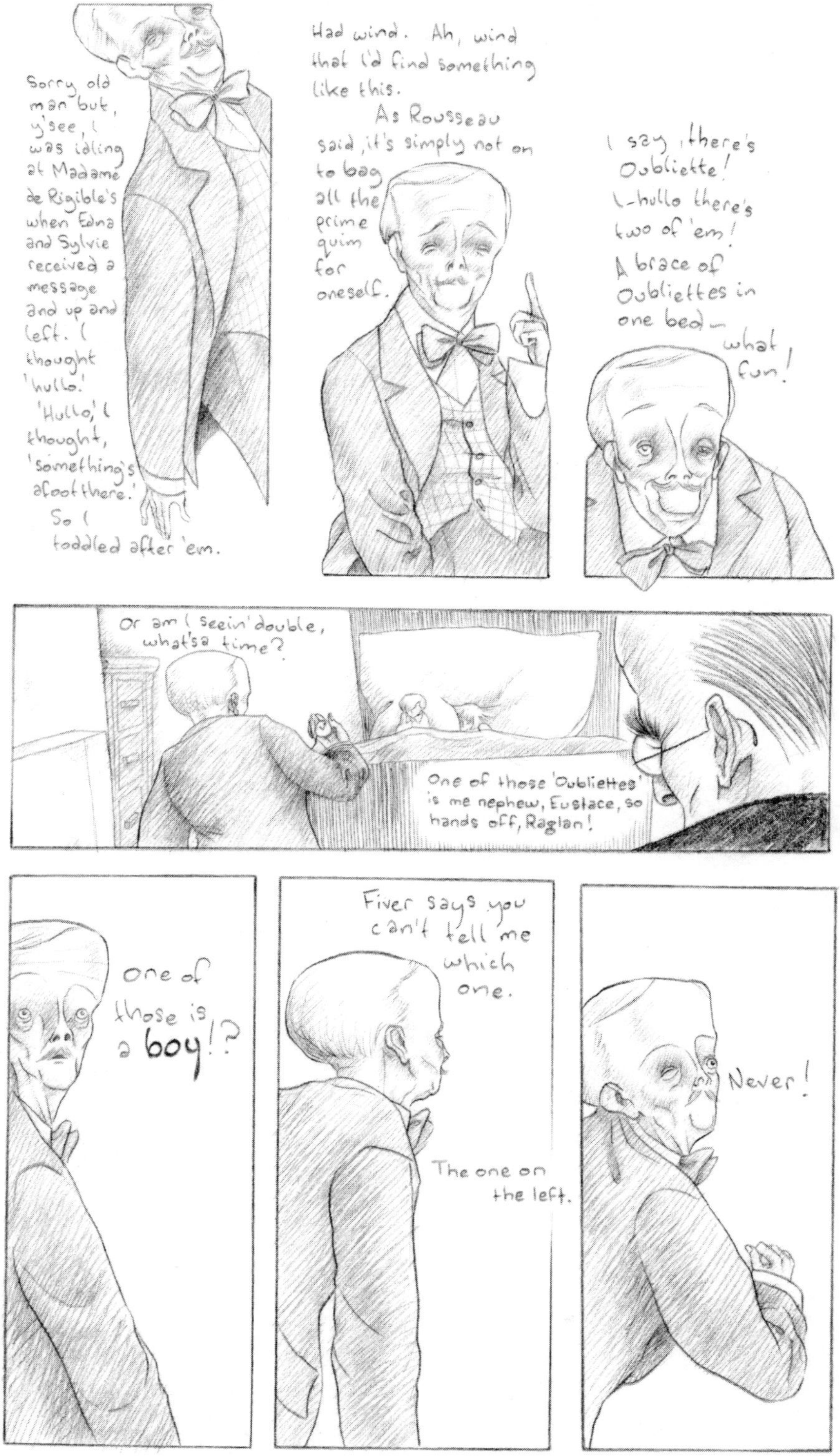
Sorry old man but, y'see, I was idling at Madame de Rigible's when Edna and Sylvie received a message and up and left. I thought 'hullo.' 'Hullo,' I thought, 'something's afoot there.' So I toddled after 'em.
Had wind. Ah, wind that I'd find something like this.
As Rousseau said, it's simply not on to bag all the prime quim for oneself.
I say, there's Oubliette! I-hullo there's two of 'em! A brace of Oubliettes in one bed — what fun!
Or am I seein' double, what'sa time?
One of those 'Oubliettes' is me nephew, Eustace, so hands off, Raglan!
One of those is a boy!?
Fiver says you can't tell me which one.
The one on the left.
Never!

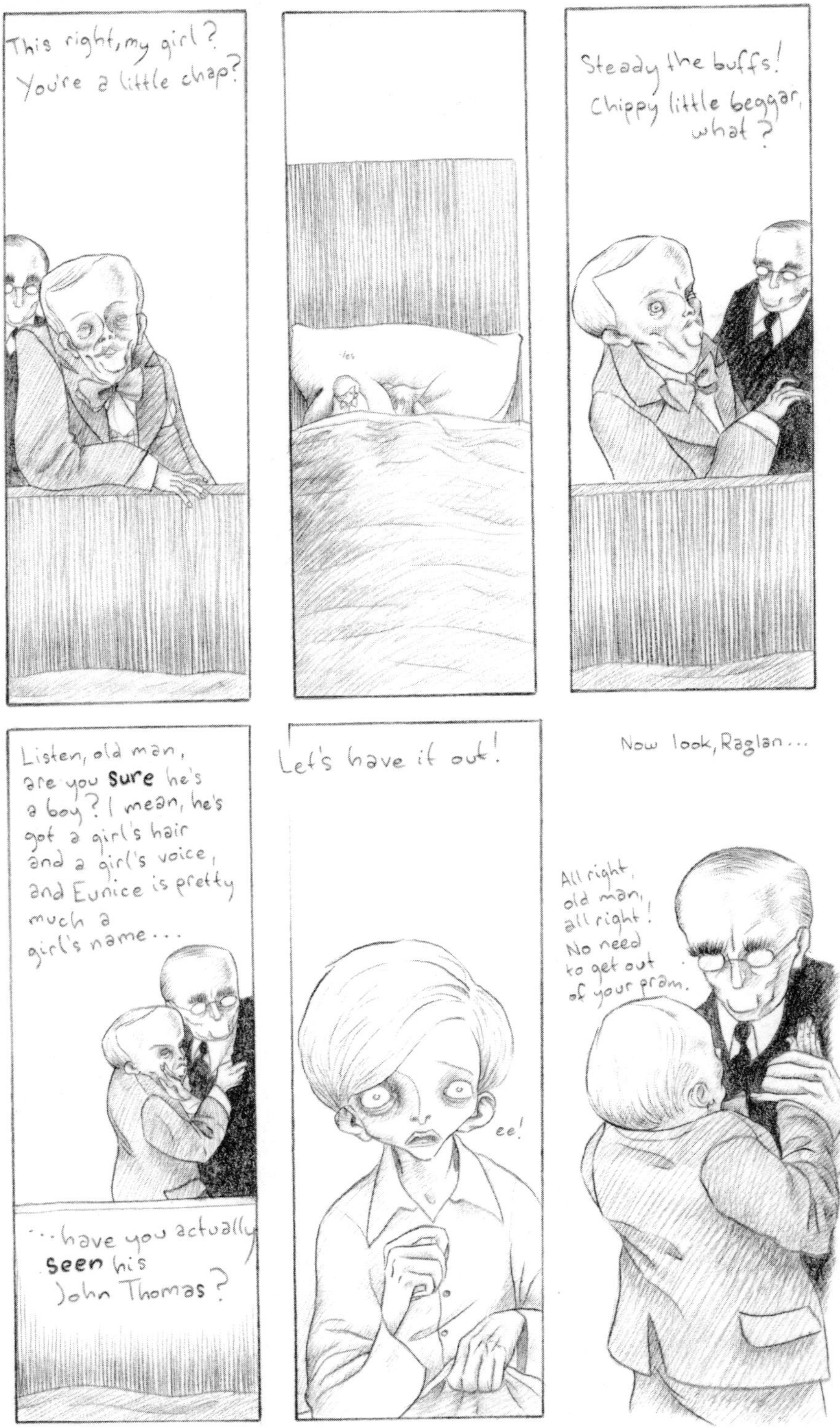
This right, my girl? You're a little chap?
Steady the buffs! Chippy little beggar, what?
Listen, old man, are you **sure** he's a boy? I mean, he's got a girl's hair and a girl's voice, and Eunice is pretty much a girl's name...
...have you actually **seen** his John Thomas?
Let's have it out!
ee!
Now look, Raglan...
All right, old man, all right! No need to get out of your pram.

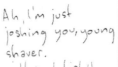

Ah, I'm just joshing you, young shaver.
Here, I lost the bet so you can have the fiver — nice crisp fiver!

oop

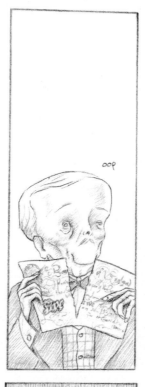

Yew got'ny thing to drink round here?

Unfortunately I require Mr Sleith to stay.
Send for more girls.

I don't think I like that Mr Sleith very much, Veronique.

Men. Zay are all much alike, yewstash — you are better off not being one.

221

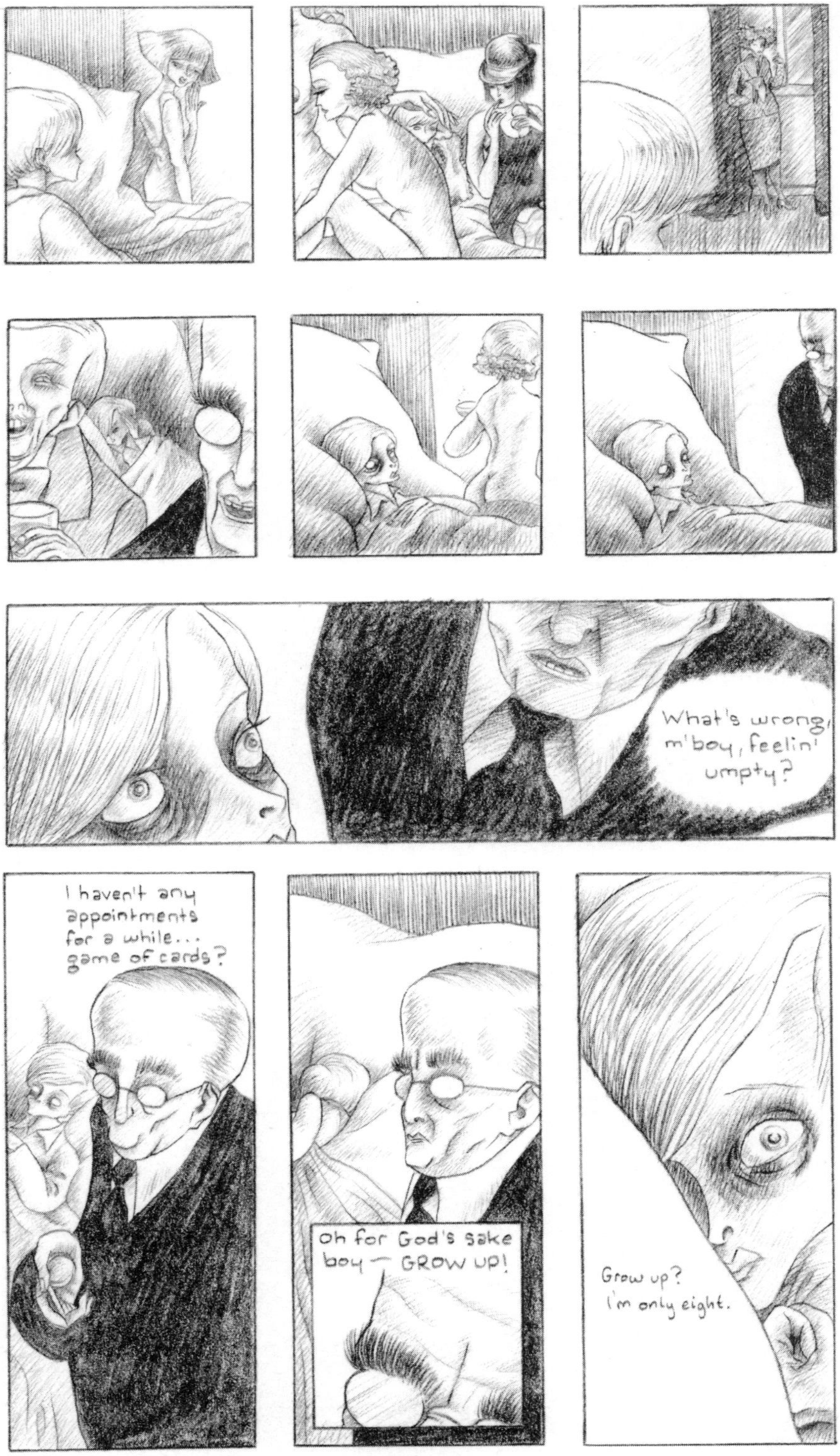
What's wrong, m'boy, feelin' umpty?
I haven't any appointments for a while... game of cards?
Oh for God's sake boy — GROW UP!
Grow up? I'm only eight.

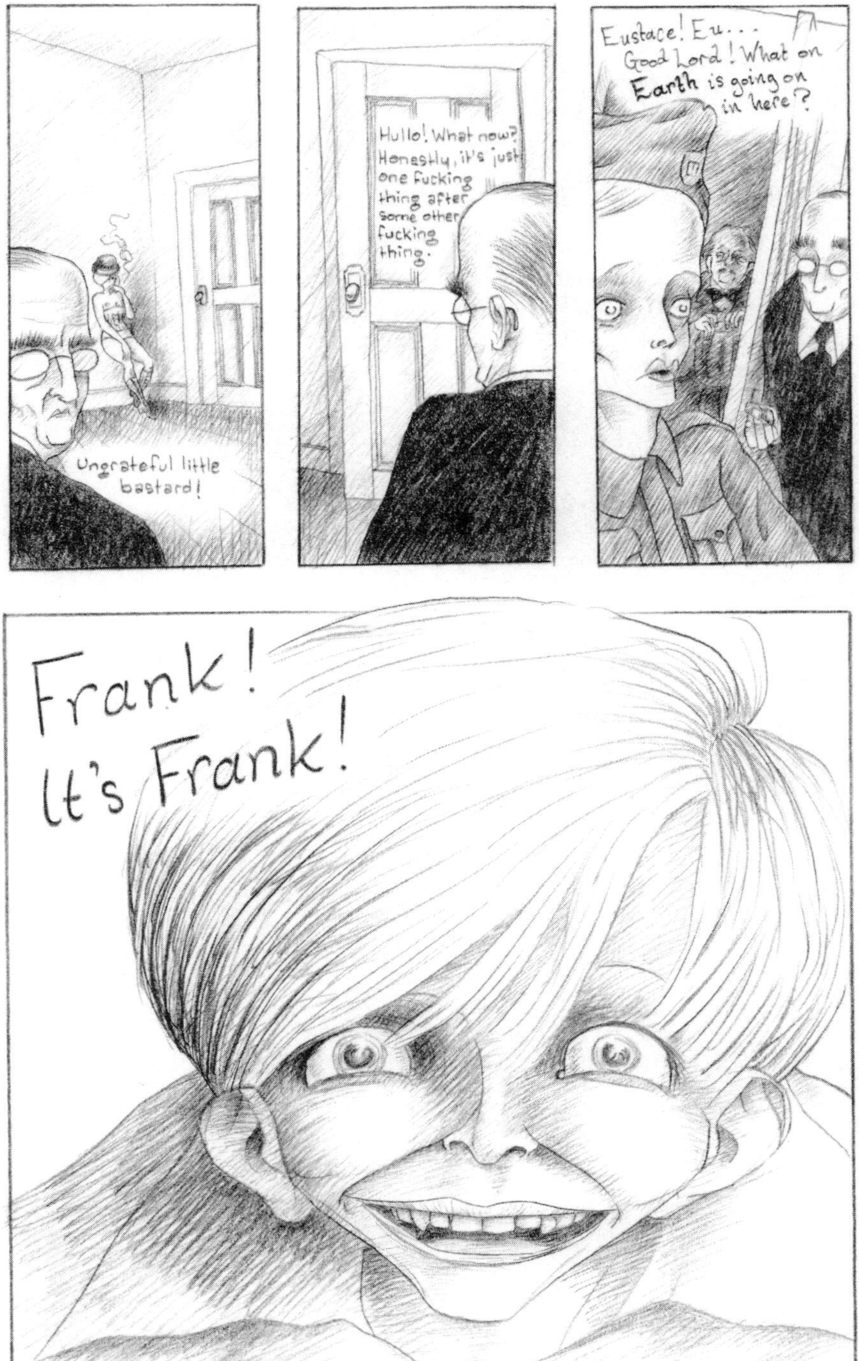
Ungrateful little bastard!
Hullo! What now? Honestly, it's just one fucking thing after some other fucking thing.
Eustace! Eu... Good Lord! What on Earth is going on in here?
Frank! It's Frank!

Frank m'boy! Welcome home!
Uncle Lucy?
Oo, 'allo sol-dier
Didn't Elbows tell me you'd disappeared?
Disappeared?!? Surely not: I'd have noticed.
But where's Eust—hullo who's this?
Ah, don't think you've met my secretary, Peter...
...Peter, this is me other great nephew, Frank.
Ahh...
How d'y'do... Frank.
H...
Tch

Frank, Frankie... oh excuse me Sir... Frankie darling, bubellah! I thought we were going to be alone, what is this place—I don't like it: it's full of koorvahs...

Let's leave!

Leave? My dear fellow, you've only just arrived! Come in, have a drink!

I hope your friend isn't going to be a nuisance m'boy. Please make it clear to him that we run a friendly establishment and it grieves us to see people leave.

I mean it! See to it that he doesn't leave or I will!

Yes, Uncle.

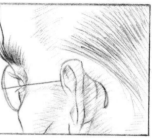

How could you bring him **here** anyway? You ought to have more respect for your family home!

Frank! Frank!

Frank, I'm over here!

Come with me, there's someone I want you to meet...

225

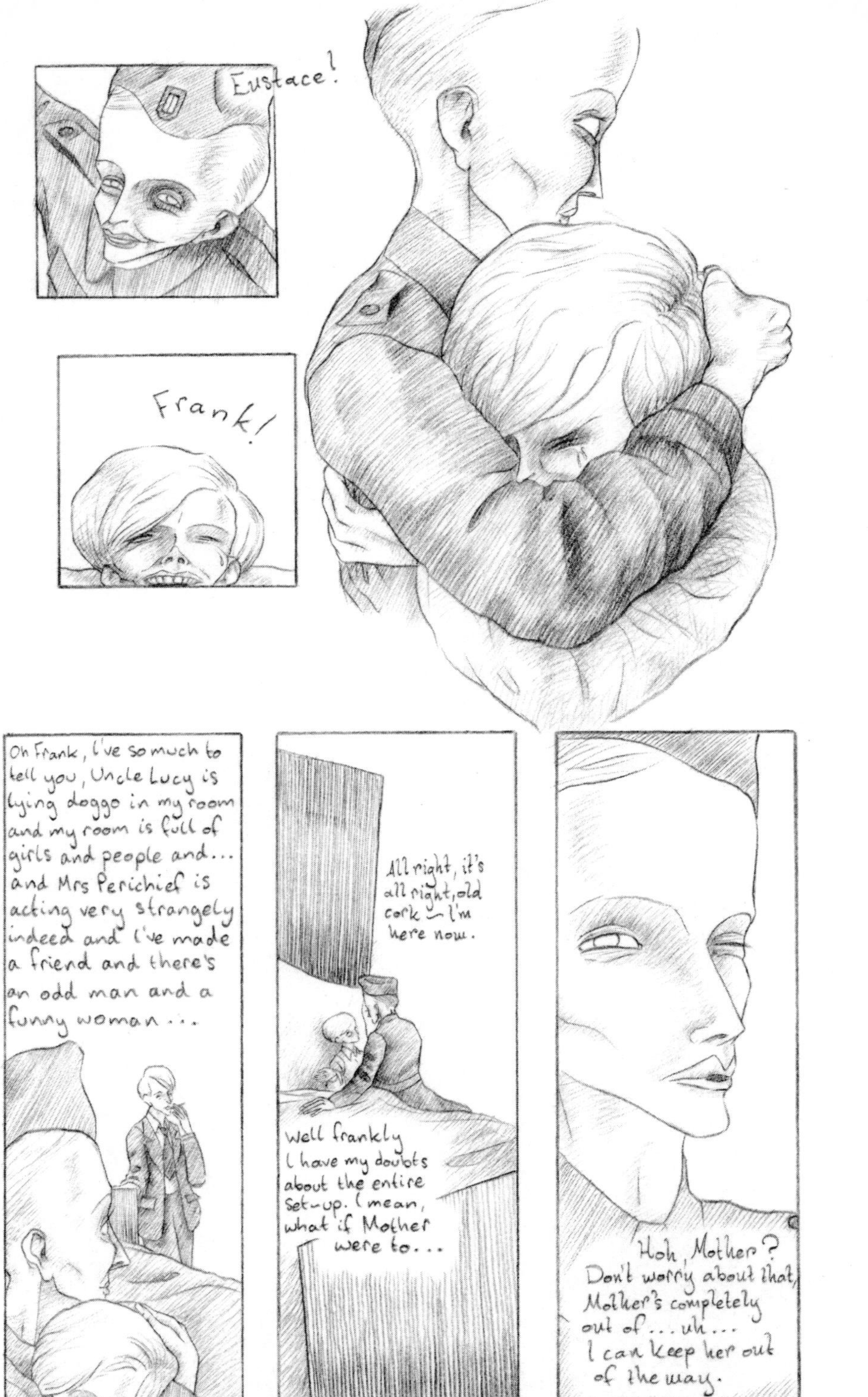
Eustace!
Frank!
Oh Frank, I've so much to tell you, Uncle Lucy is lying doggo in my room and my room is full of girls and people and... and Mrs Perichief is acting very strangely indeed and I've made a friend and there's an odd man and a funny woman...
All right, it's all right, old cork — I'm here now.
Well frankly I have my doubts about the entire set-up. I mean, what if Mother were to...
Hoh, Mother? Don't worry about that, Mother's completely out of ... uh ... I can keep her out of the way.

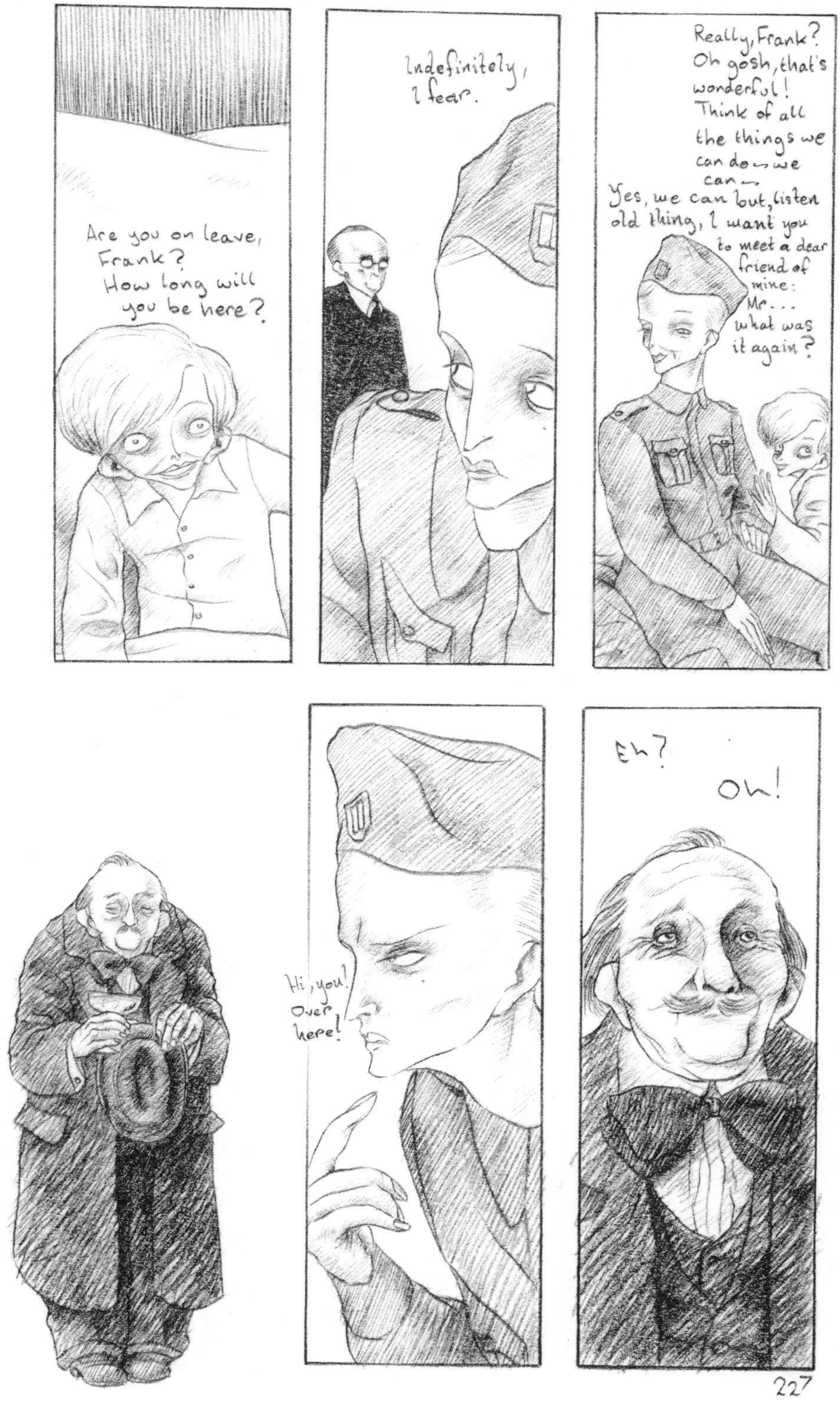
Are you on leave, Frank? How long will you be here?
Indefinitely, I fear.
Really, Frank? Oh gosh, that's wonderful! Think of all the things we can do — we can —
Yes, we can but, listen old thing, I want you to meet a dear friend of mine: Mr... what was it again?
Hi, you! Over here!
Eh?
Oh!

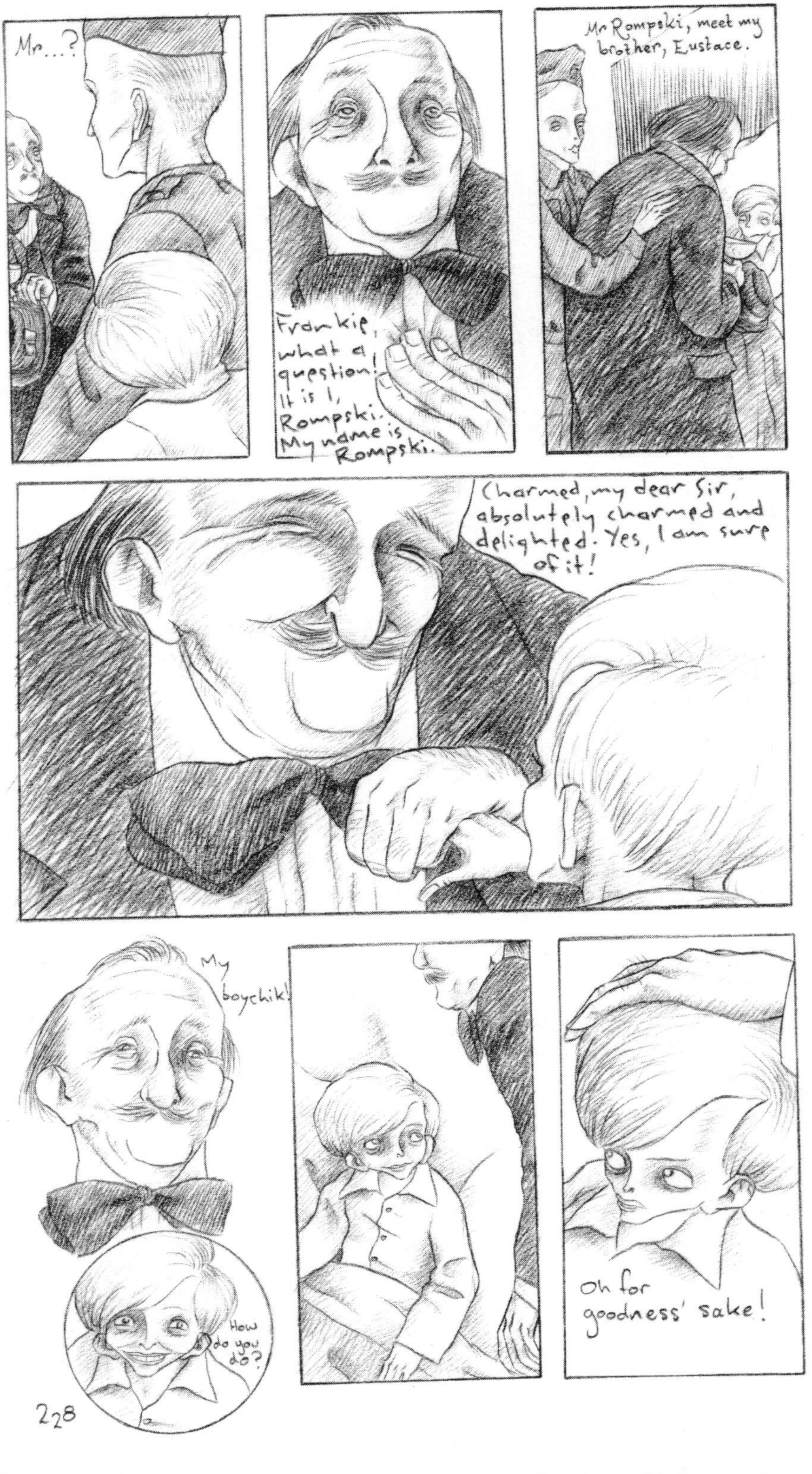
Mr...?
Frankie, what a question! It is I, Rompski. My name is Rompski.
Mr Rompski, meet my brother, Eustace.
Charmed, my dear Sir, absolutely charmed and delighted. Yes, I am sure of it!
My boychik!
How do you do?
Oh for goodness' sake!

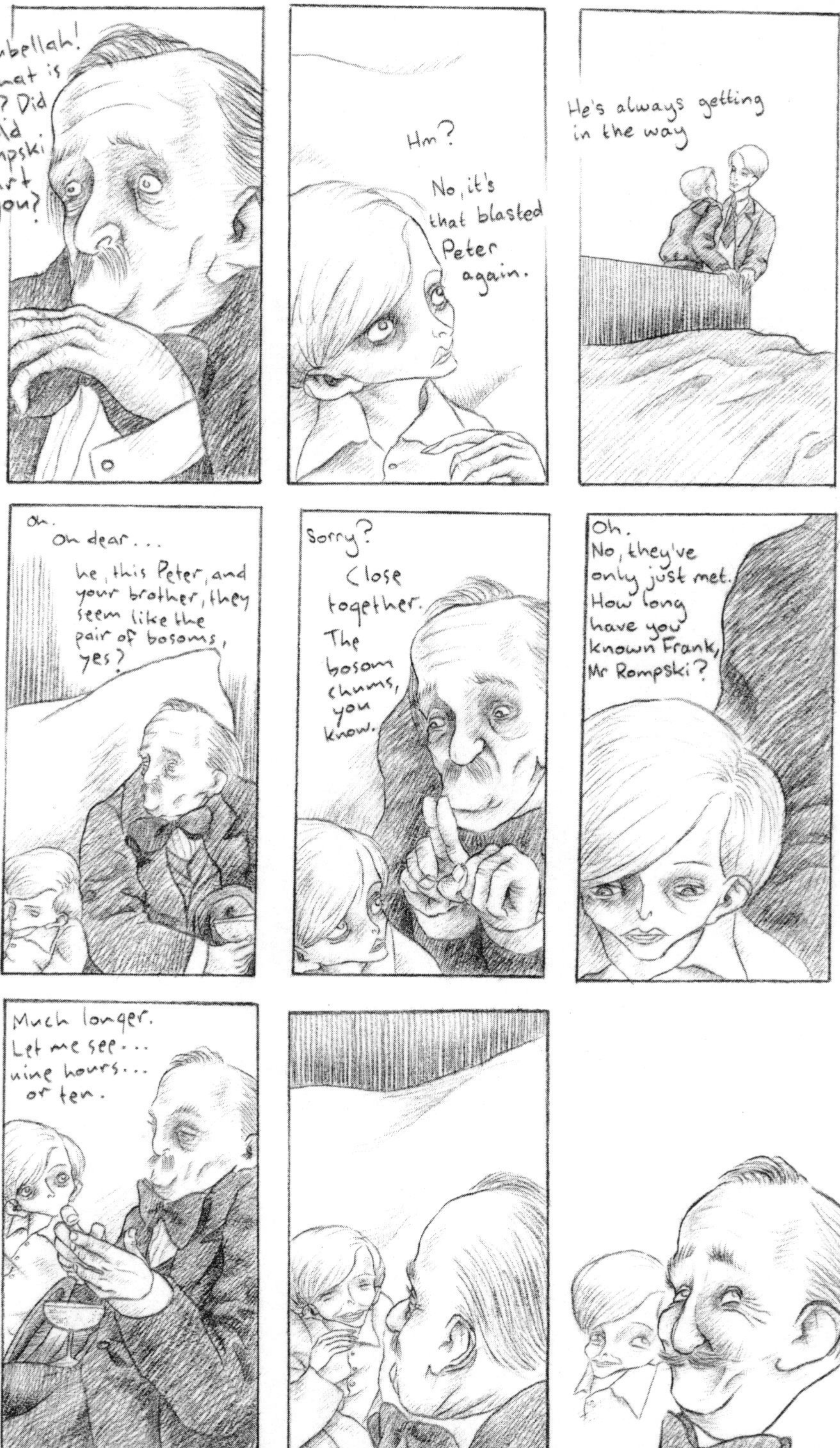
Bubellah! What is it? Did old Rompski hurt you?
Hm?
No, it's that blasted Peter again.
He's always getting in the way
Oh.
Oh dear...
he, this Peter, and your brother, they seem like the pair of bosoms, yes?
Sorry?
Close together.
The bosom chums, you know.
Oh.
No, they've only just met. How long have you known Frank, Mr Rompski?
Much longer.
Let me see...
nine hours...
or ten.

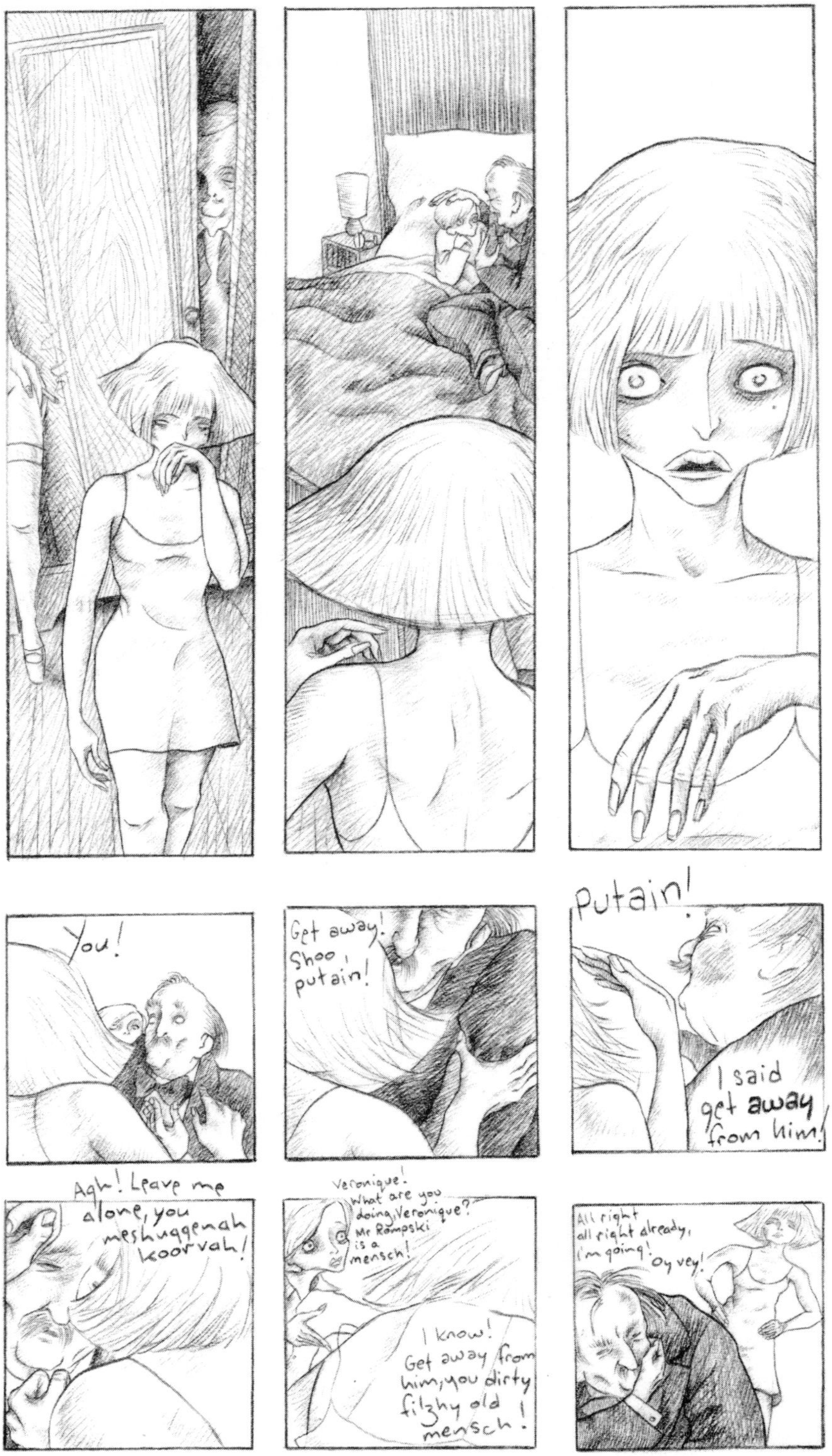
You!
Get away! Shoo, putain!
Putain!
I said get **away** from him!
Agh! Leave me alone, you meshuggenah koorvah!
Veronique! What are you doing, Veronique? Mr Rompski is a mensch!
I know! Get away from him, you dirty filthy old mensch!
All right all right already, I'm going! Oy vey!

Yewstash, are you all right?

What did you do that for, Veronique? Poor Mr Rompski!

Poor Monsieur Rompski nuzhing! He was touching you, Yewstash — I saw him! Where did he touch you?

What are you talking about? He only stroked my hair and my... what did he call it?

My lichtikeh punim!

MERDE! He licked your punim? Filzy devil, I cannot believe it! I should 'ave been 'ere to protect you.

I don't understand, Veronique — what's wrong?

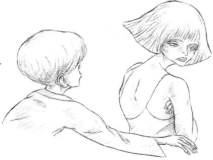

He didn't do anything that you or Frank don't do.

Yewstash, he shouldn't even 'ave done that.

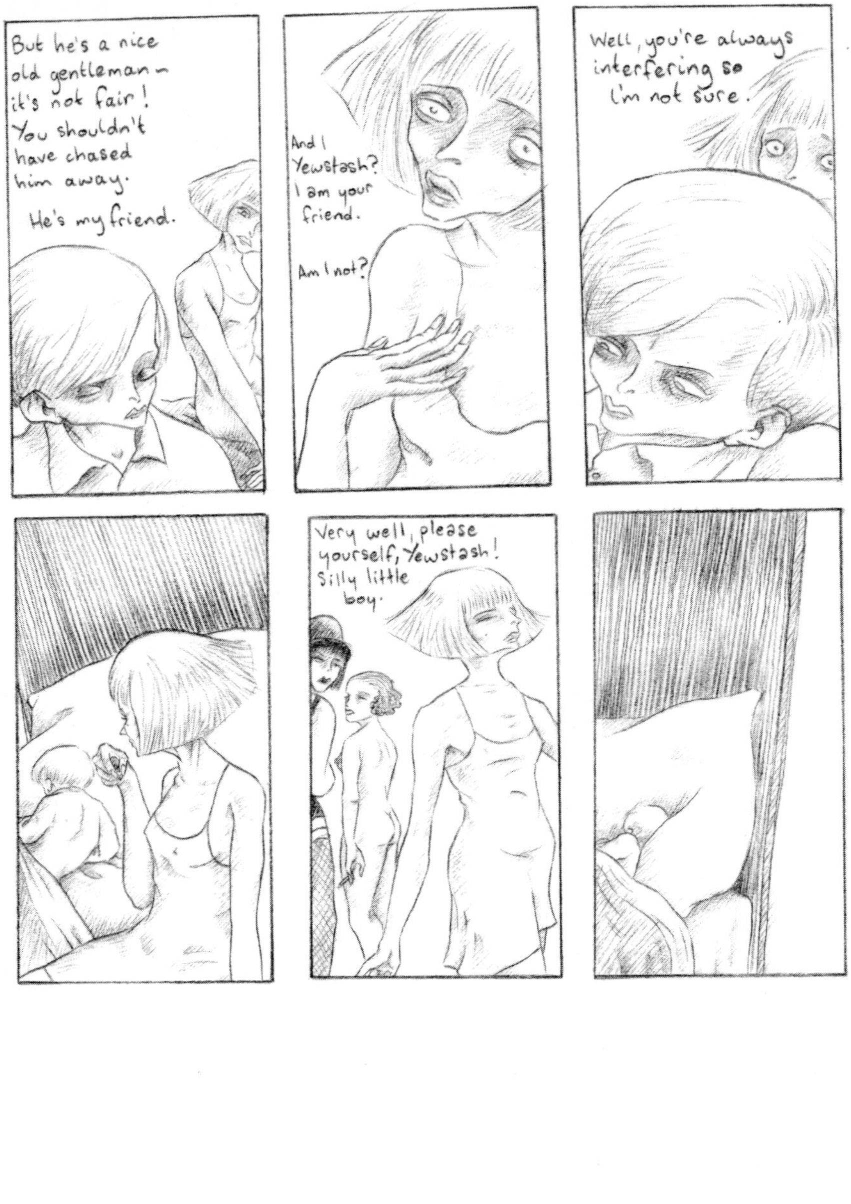
But he's a nice old gentleman – it's not fair! You shouldn't have chased him away.
He's my friend.
And I Yewstash? I am your friend.
Am I not?
Well, you're always interfering so I'm not sure.
Very well, please yourself, Yewstash! Silly little boy.

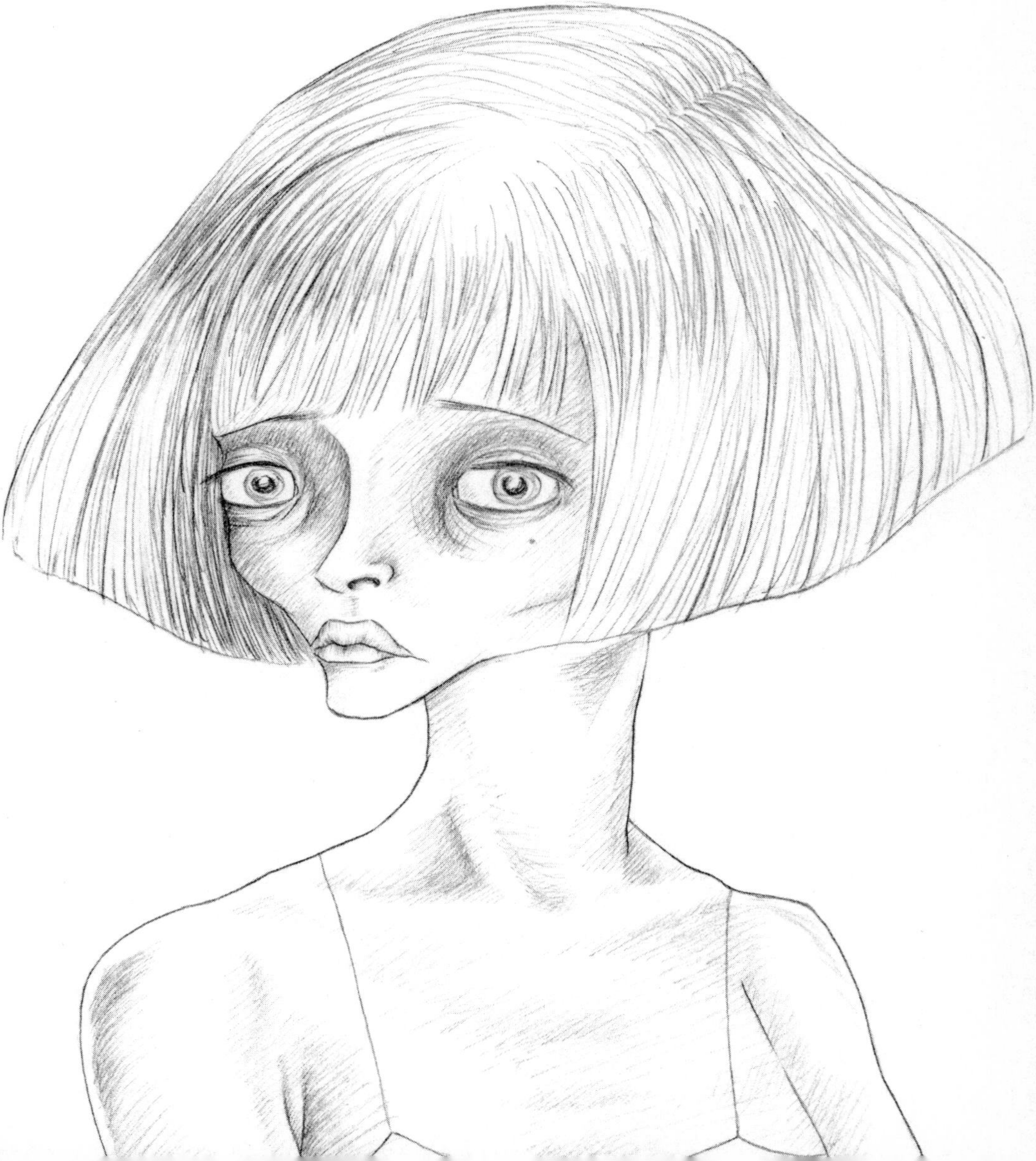

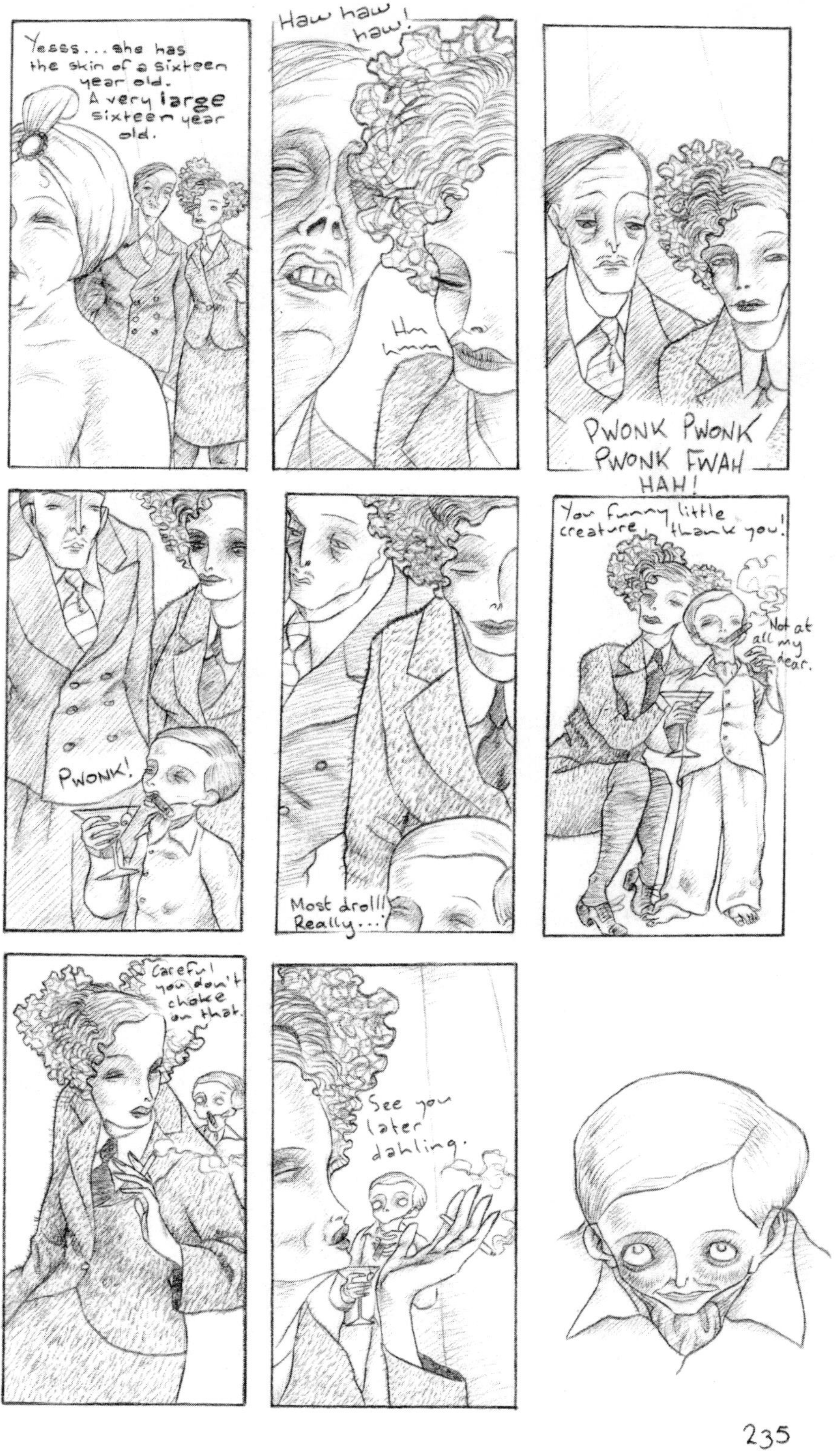
Yesss... she has the skin of a sixteen year old. A very large sixteen year old.
Haw haw haw!
Hm hmm
PWONK PWONK PWONK FWAH HAH!
PWONK!
Most droll! Really...
You funny little creature, thank you!
Not at all my dear.
Careful you don't choke on that.
See you later dahling.

Oh **hallay**! Haven't seen you in an **age**, my dear! Simply **everyone's** here. But then, perhaps you don't **know** everyone...

Stick with me, kid, and I'll introduce you around.

Afternoon, Edna, Matilda.

Awl right, love!

That was Edna. And Matilda.

Pru, Mimsy, Quartermain and Balthazar Wendling.

My dear sir, noble you certainly are; gaseous also.

Veronique you know of course.

'Lo, Yewstash

Mmph!

Bubellah! Where have you been?

over th...

I missed you, darling boy. Where's my kiss?

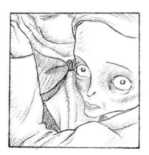

Bubellah! Where are you going? I get lonely.

See you later, dahling.

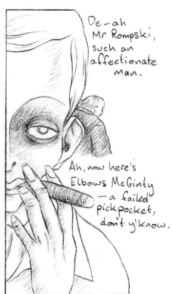

De-ah Mr Rompski, such an affectionate man.

Ah, now here's Elbows McGinty —a failed pickpocket, don't y'know.

Hullo Mr McGinty, have you any new tattoos today?

WAH HAH HAAH! I love this little fucker!

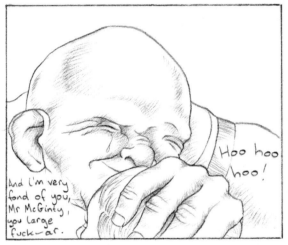

And I'm very fond of you, Mr McGinty, you large fuck—ar.

Hoo hoo, hoo!

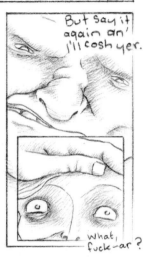

But say it again an' I'll cosh yer.

What, fuck—ar?

Ah hah, haaa! 'Ee's a boy, innee!

Ahh . . . if only me old mum could of 'eard that.

He misses his mother terribly. She died— when he throttled her.

238

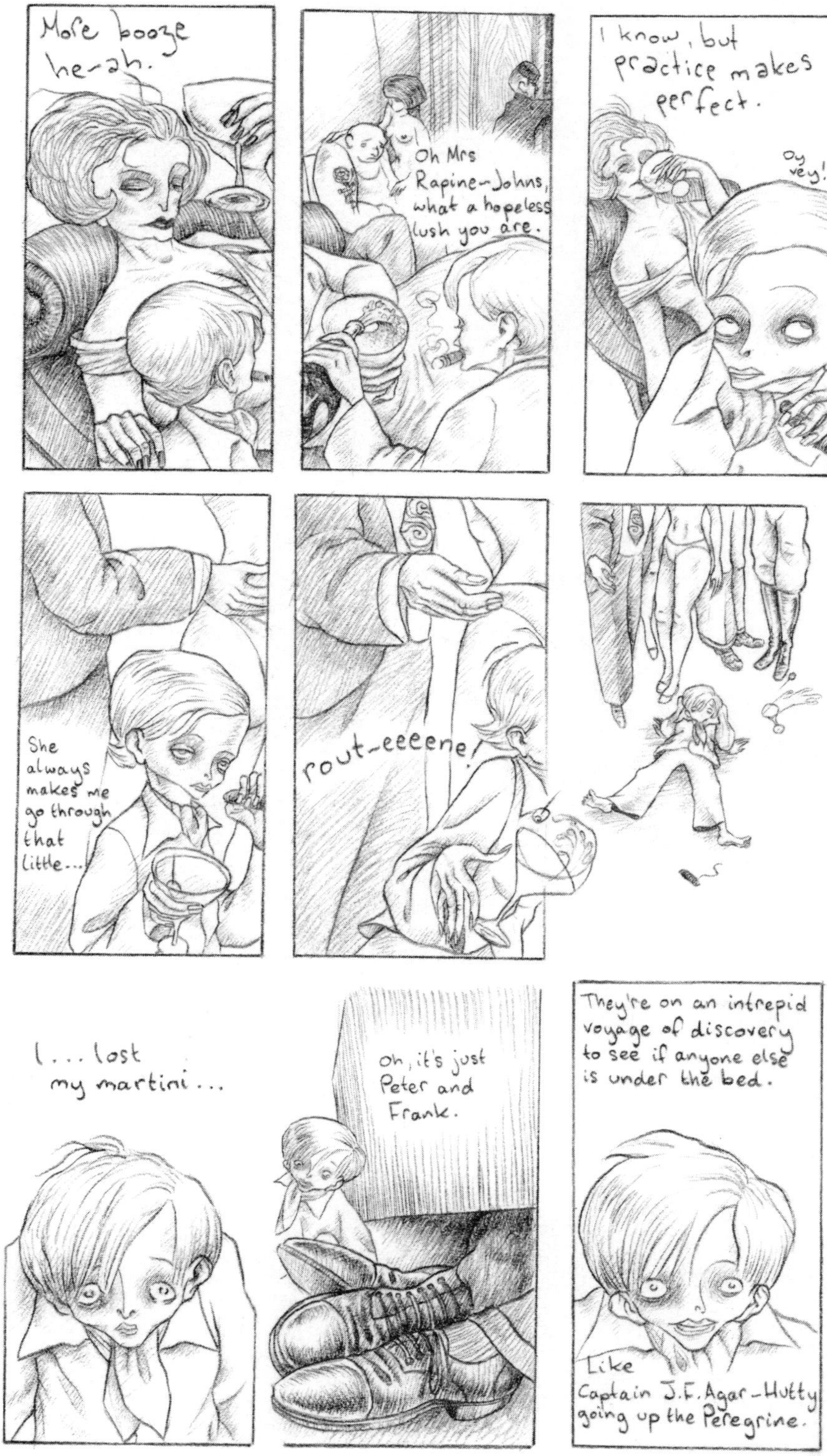
More booze he-ah.
Oh Mrs Rapine-Johns, what a hopeless lush you are.
I know, but practice makes perfect.
Oy vey!
She always makes me go through that little...
rout-eeeene!
I... lost my martini...
Oh, it's just Peter and Frank.
They're on an intrepid voyage of discovery to see if anyone else is under the bed.
Like Captain J.F. Agar-Hutty going up the Peregrine.

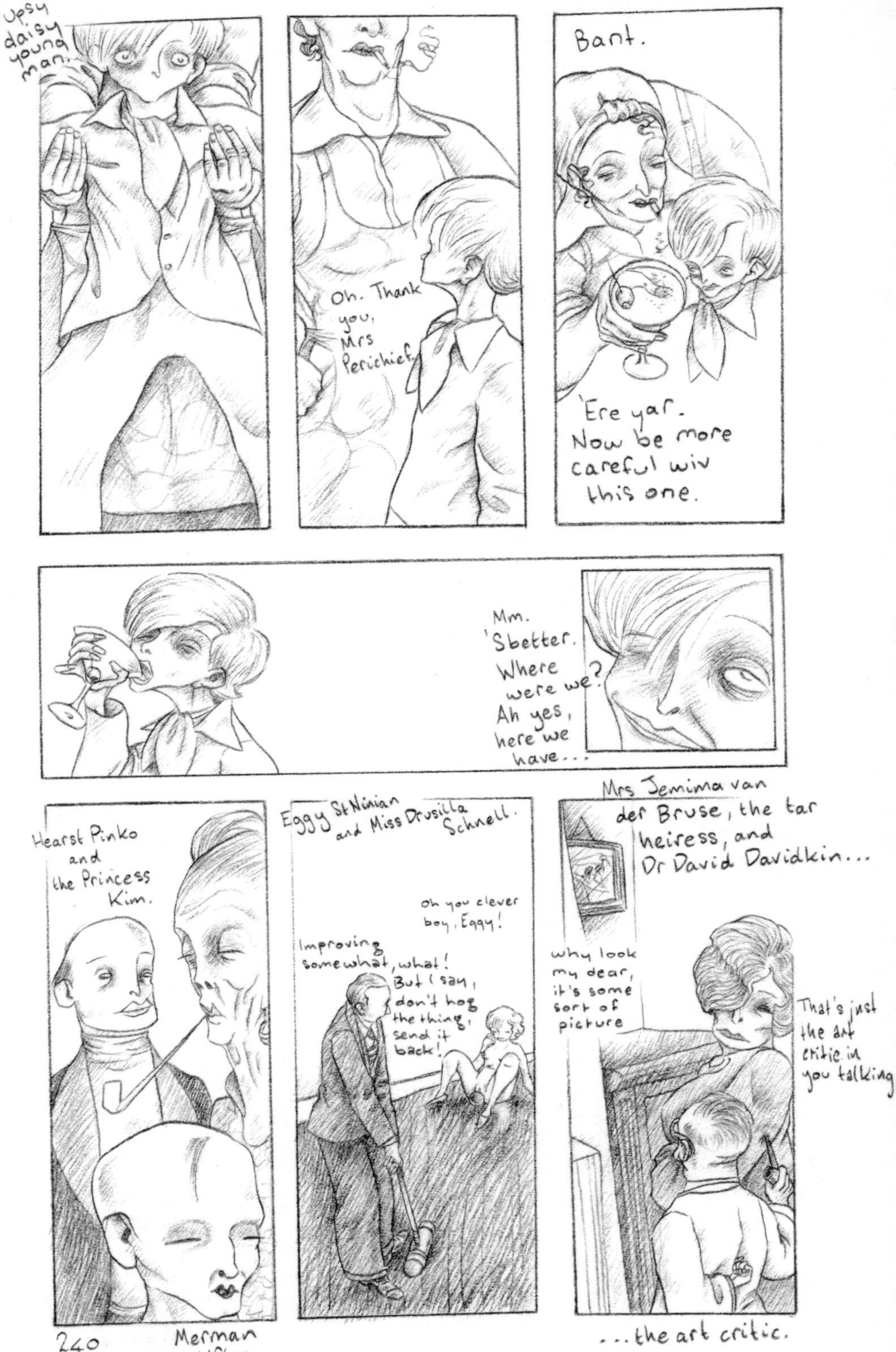
Upsy daisy young man.
Oh. Thank you, Mrs Perichief.
Bant.
'Ere yar. Now be more careful wiv this one.
Mm. 'Sbetter. Where were we? Ah yes, here we have...
Hearst Pinko and the Princess Kim.
Merman Ufton
Eggy St Ninian and Miss Drusilla Schnell.
Oh you clever boy, Eggy!
Improving somewhat, what! But I say, don't hog the thing, send it back!
Mrs Jemima van der Bruse, the tar heiress, and Dr David Davidkin...
why look my dear, it's some sort of picture
That's just the art critic in you talking
...the art critic.

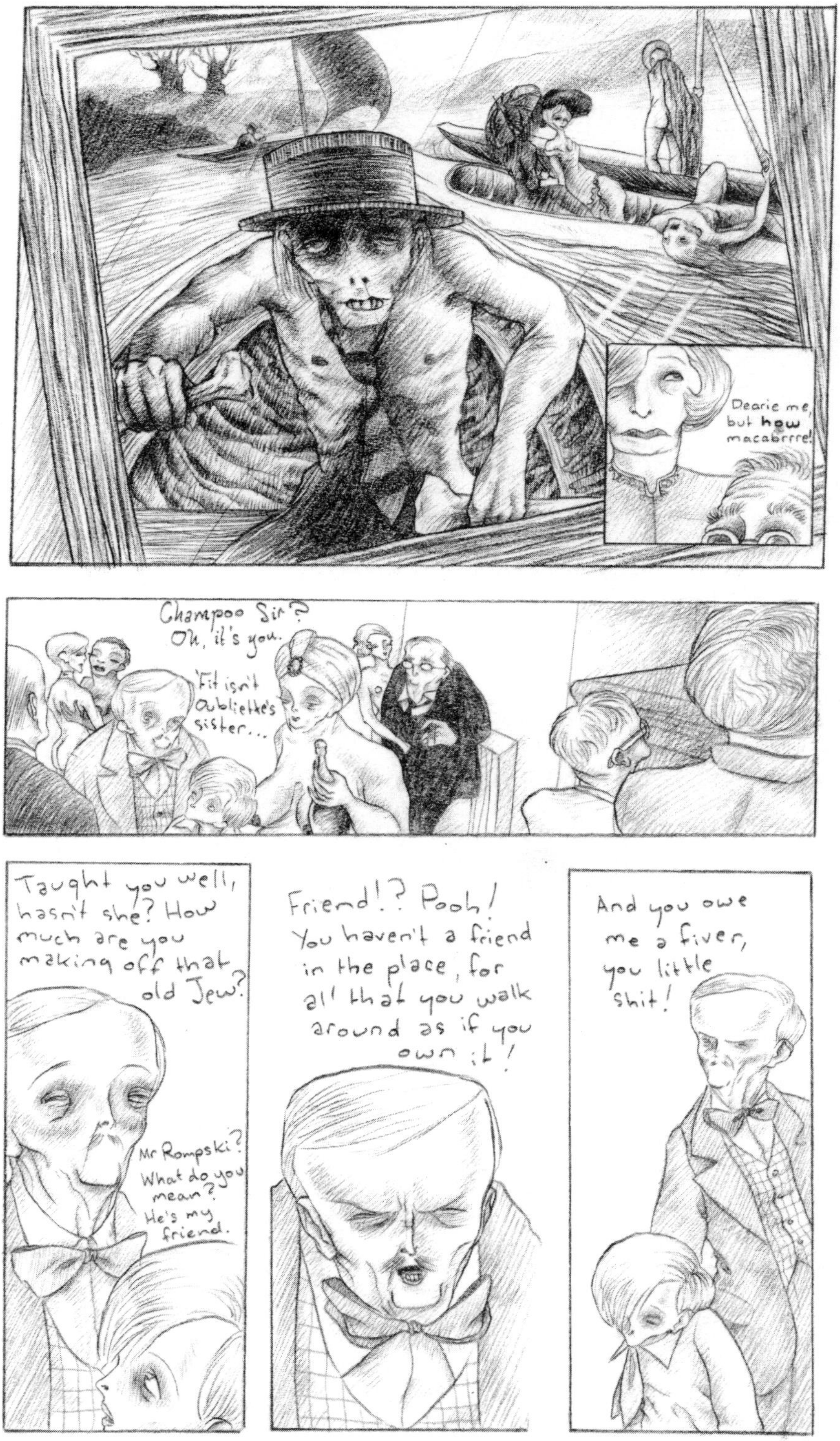
Dearie me, but **how** macabrrre!
Champoo Sir? Oh, it's you.
'Fit isn't Oubliette's sister...
Taught you well, hasn't she? How much are you making off that old Jew?
Mr Rompski? What do you mean? He's my friend.
Friend!? Pooh! You haven't a friend in the place, for all that you walk around as if you own it!
And you owe me a fiver, you little shit!

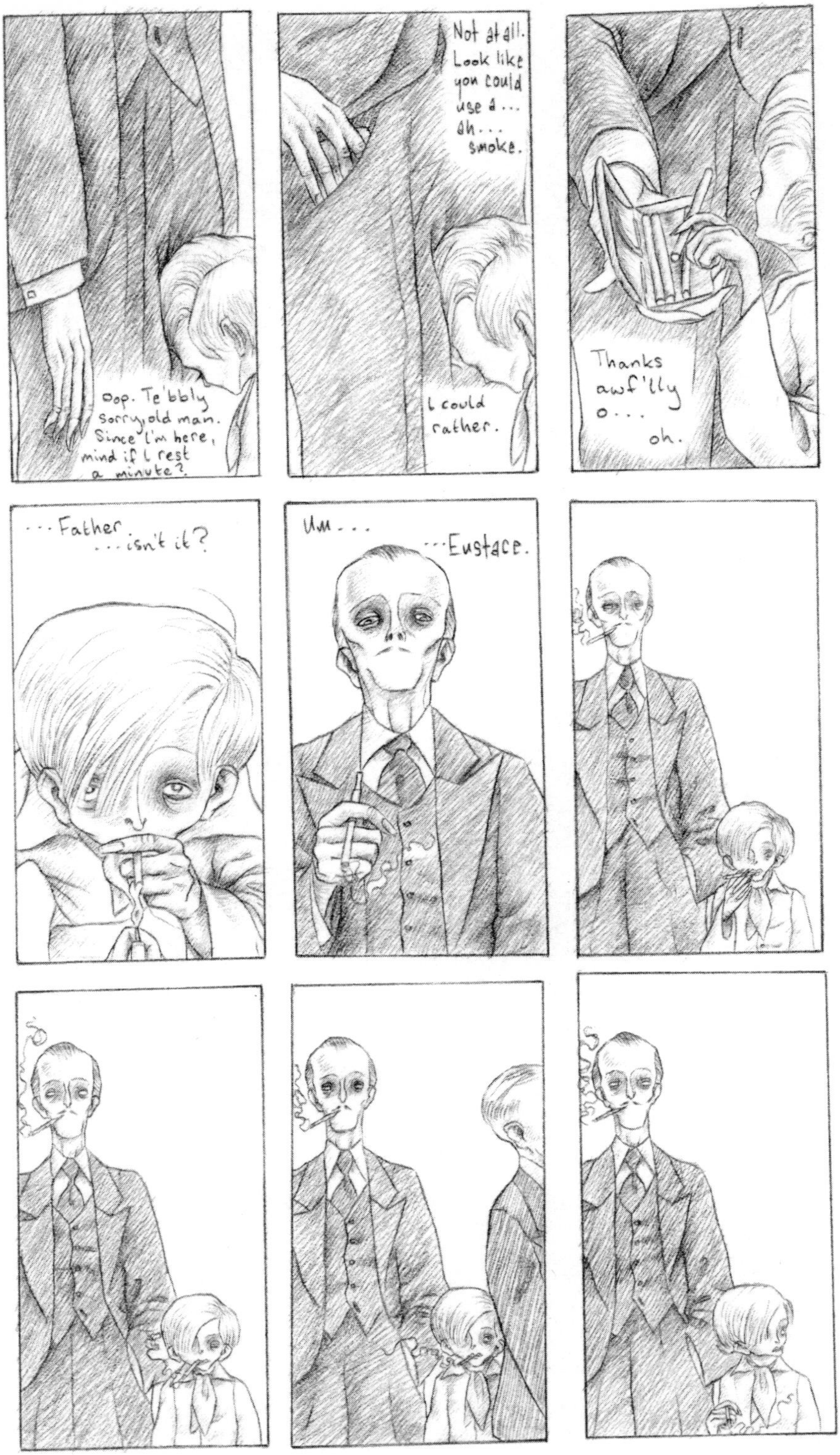
Oop. Te'bbly sorry, old man. Since I'm here, mind if I rest a minute?
Not at all. Look like you could use a... oh... smoke.
I could rather.
Thanks awf'lly o... oh.
...Father ...isn't it?
Um...
...Eustace.

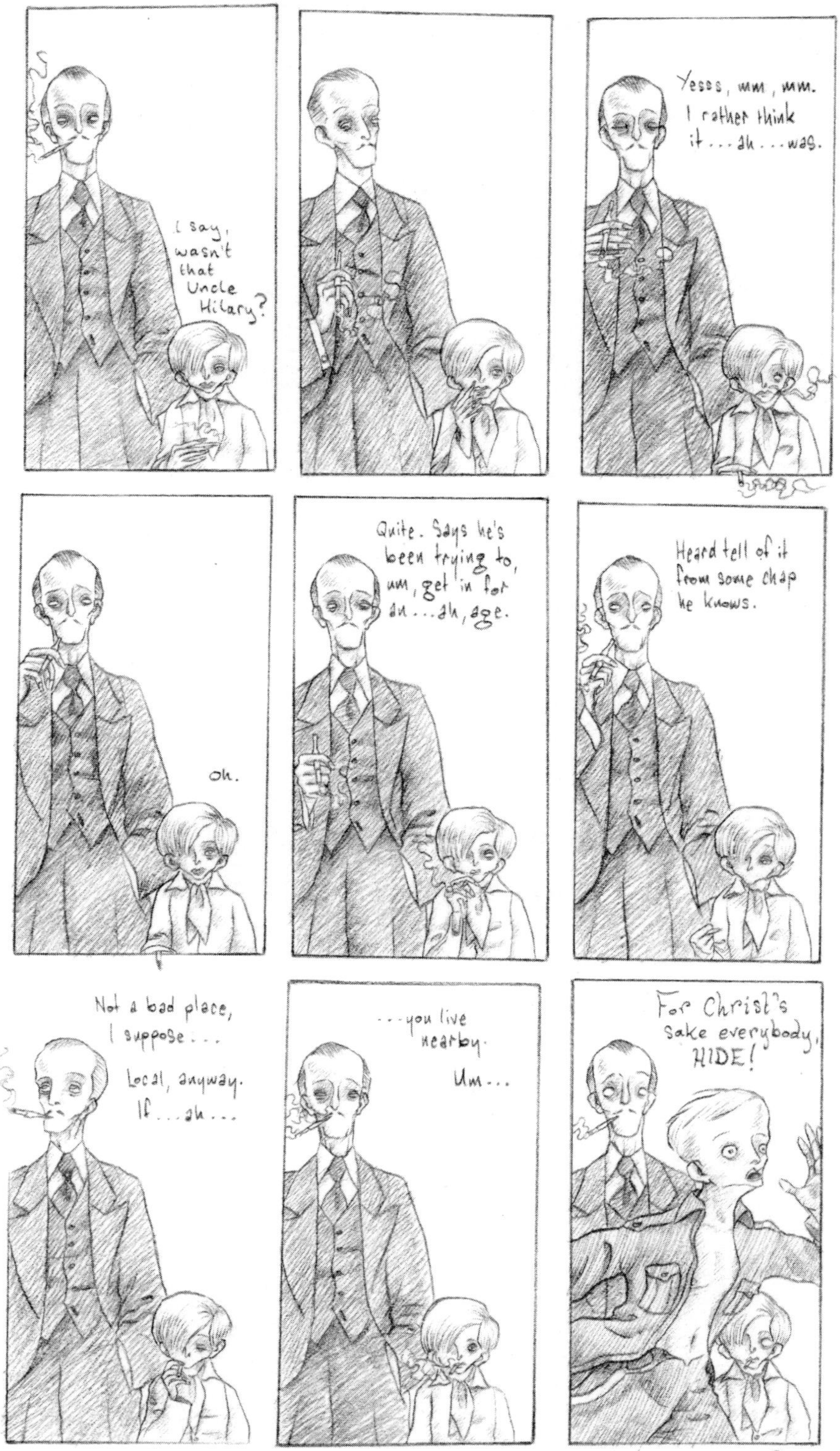
I say, wasn't that Uncle Hilary?
Yesss, mm, mm. I rather think it...ah...was.
oh.
Quite. Says he's been trying to, um, get in for an...ah, age.
Heard tell of it from some chap he knows.
Not a bad place, I suppose...
Local, anyway. If...ah...
...you live nearby.
Um...
For Christ's sake everybody, HIDE!

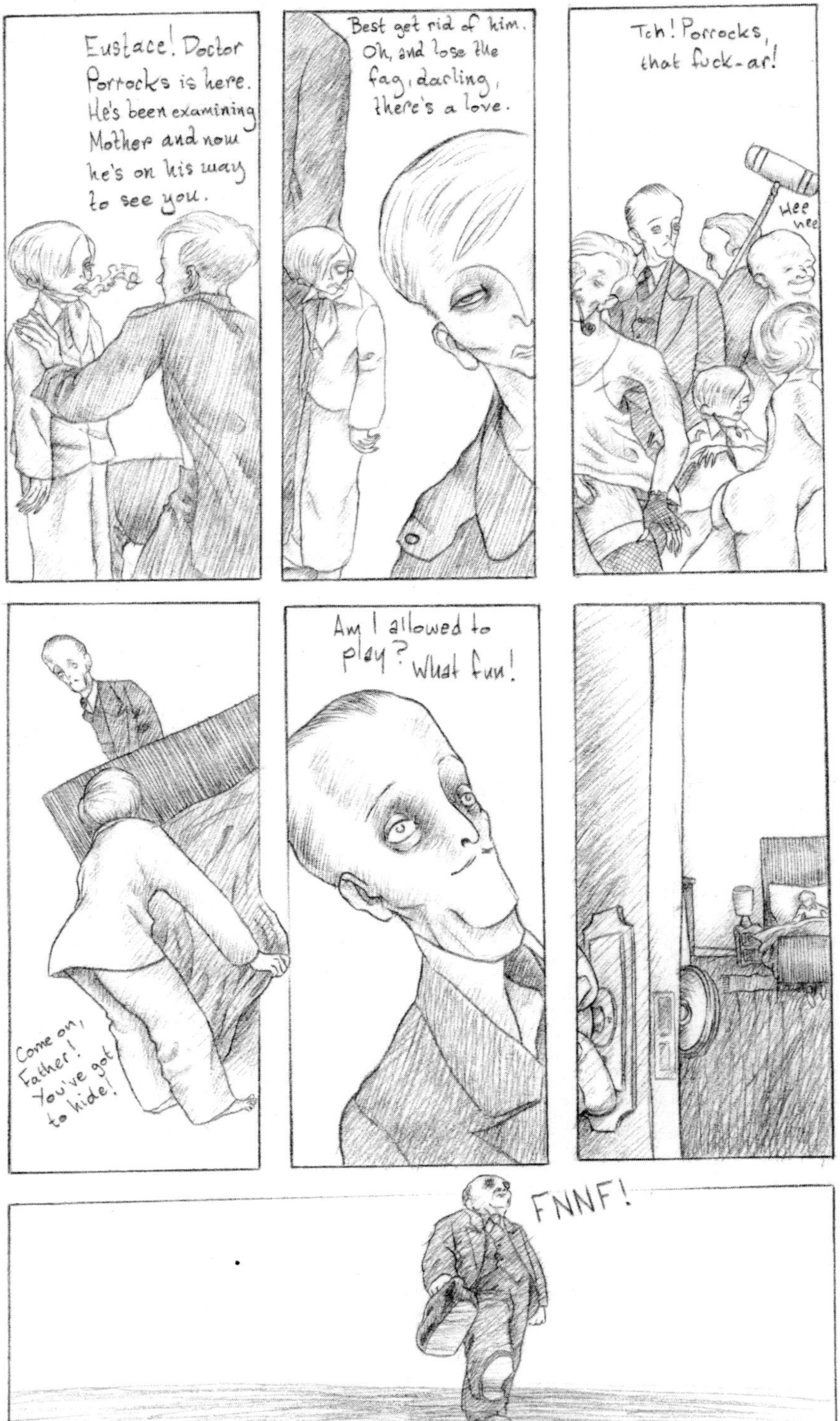
Eustace! Doctor Porrocks is here. He's been examining Mother and now he's on his way to see you.
Best get rid of him. Oh, and lose the fag, darling, there's a love.
Tch! Porrocks, that fuck-ar!
Hee hee
Come on, Father! You've got to hide!
Am I allowed to play? What fun!
FNNF!

FNNNF! Have yew bin Smokin', laddie?

Don't be ridiculous, man, I'm only eight.

Jih! Lissen here, yer mother is lying in there a wreck of a woman because of yerr she-nanigans! Aye, a husk, I tell ye!

A husk, sir, a husk? My mother a husk? No husk she!

And no wonder with what she's had to put up with with yer... malingering! There, you've made me say it!

And is that alcohol ah can smell on yerr breath?

If you're here to dish out some more, let's be having it and less of yere dialect.

If you haven't any then I bid you night night.

No? Then off you pop. D'ye ken?

No. It's jollop. Sticky black jollop.

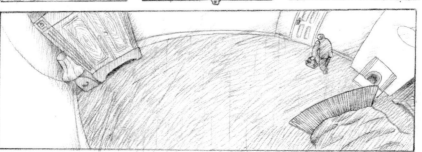

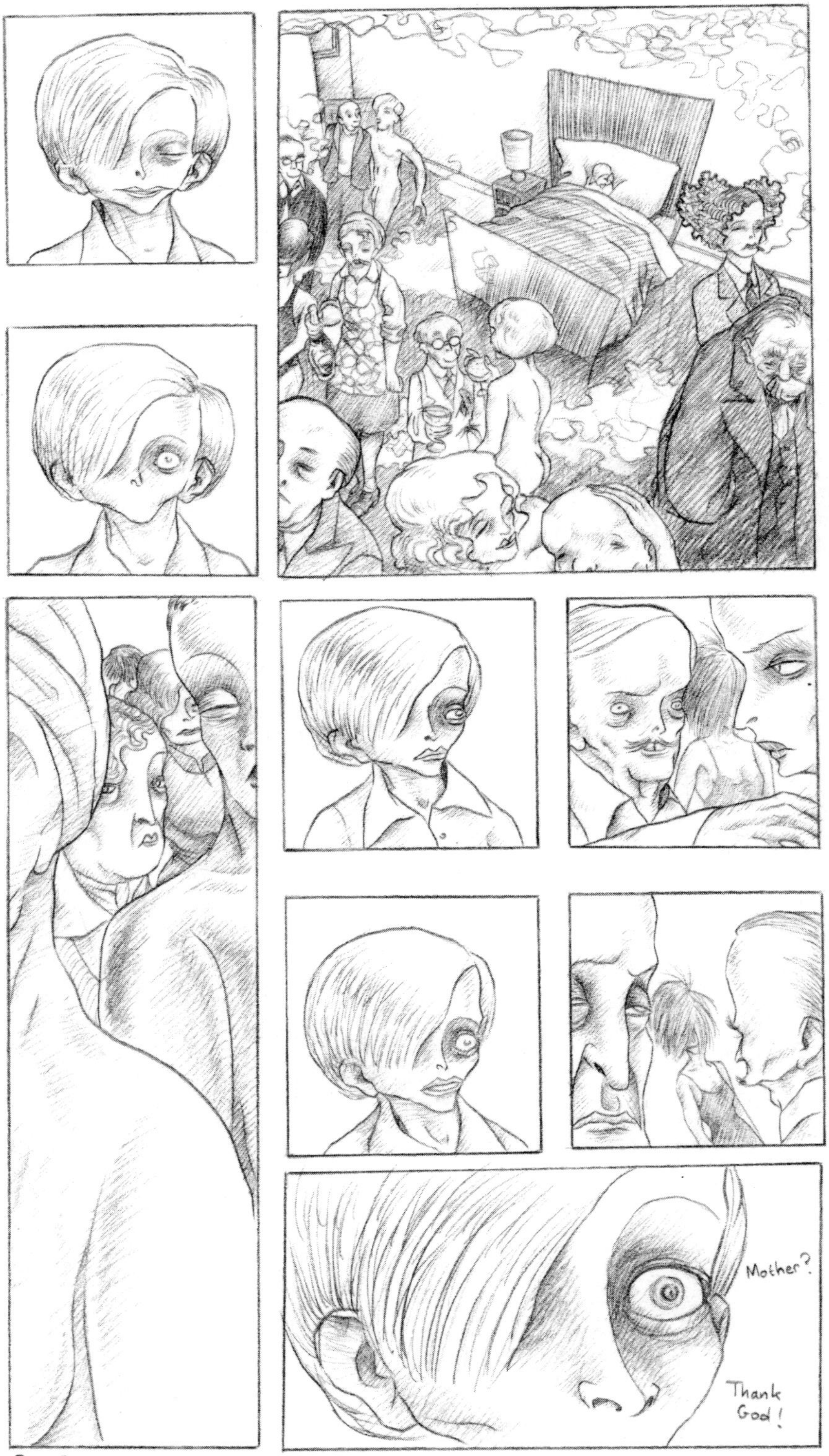
Mother?
Thank God!

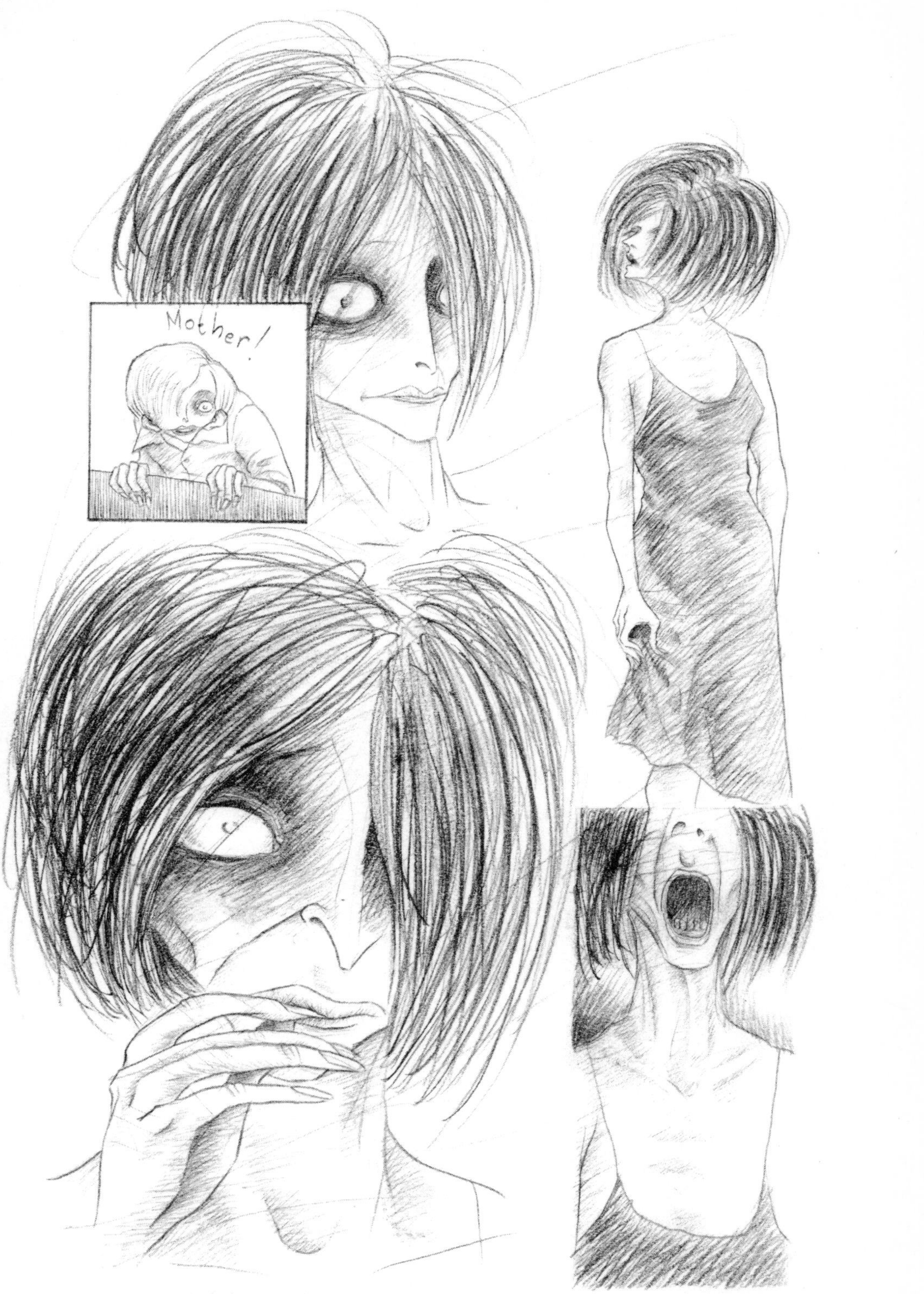
Mother!

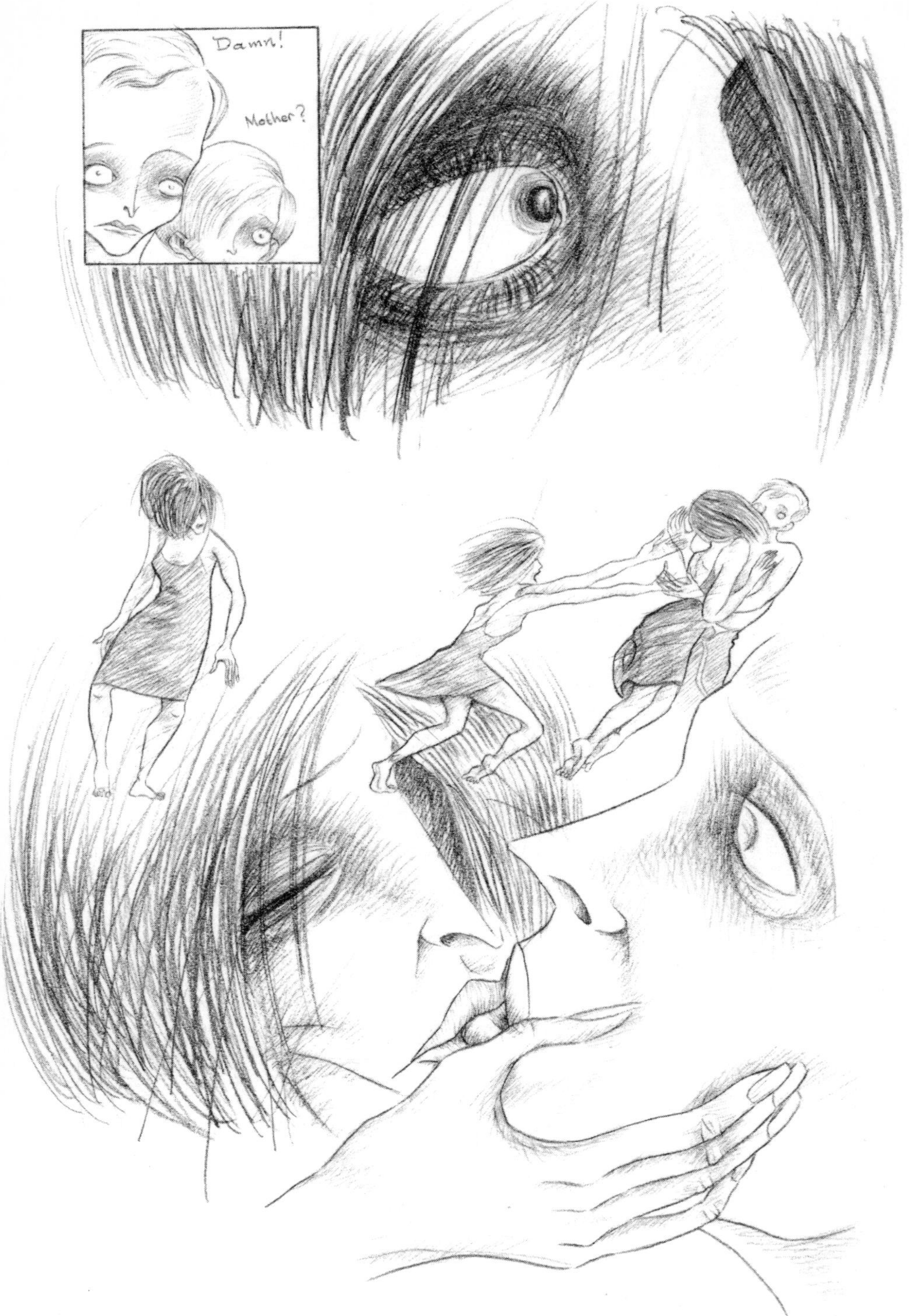
Damn!
Mother?

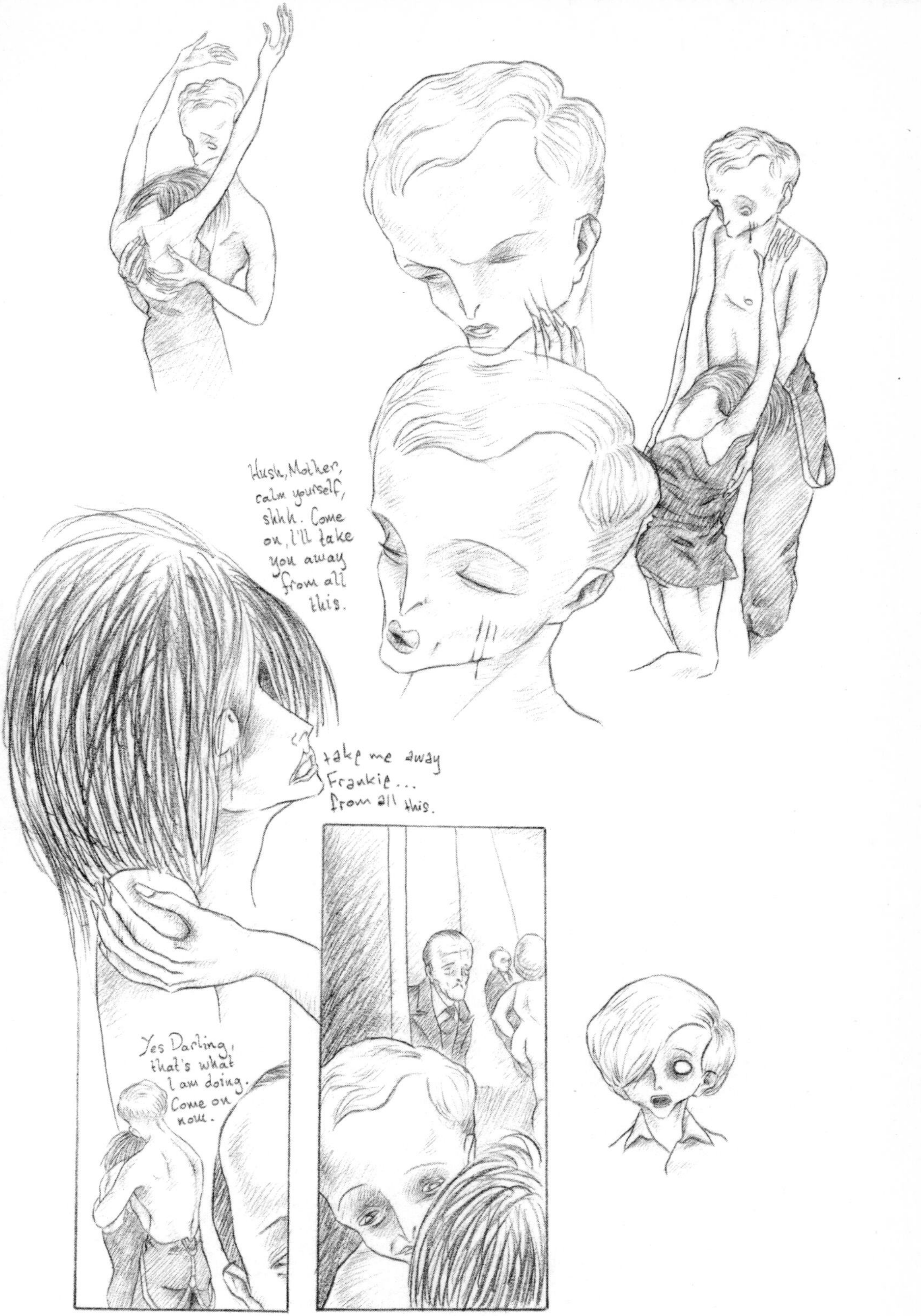
Hush, Mother, calm yourself, shhh. Come on, I'll take you away from all this.
take me away Frankie... from all this.
Yes Darling, that's what I am doing. Come on now.

Hullo old cork! And where might you be off to?

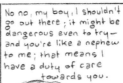

No no, my boy, I shouldn't go out there; it might be dangerous even to try— and you're like a nephew to me; that means I have a duty of care towards you.

Hm? Doesn't it? I must protect you.

Yes, at all costs.

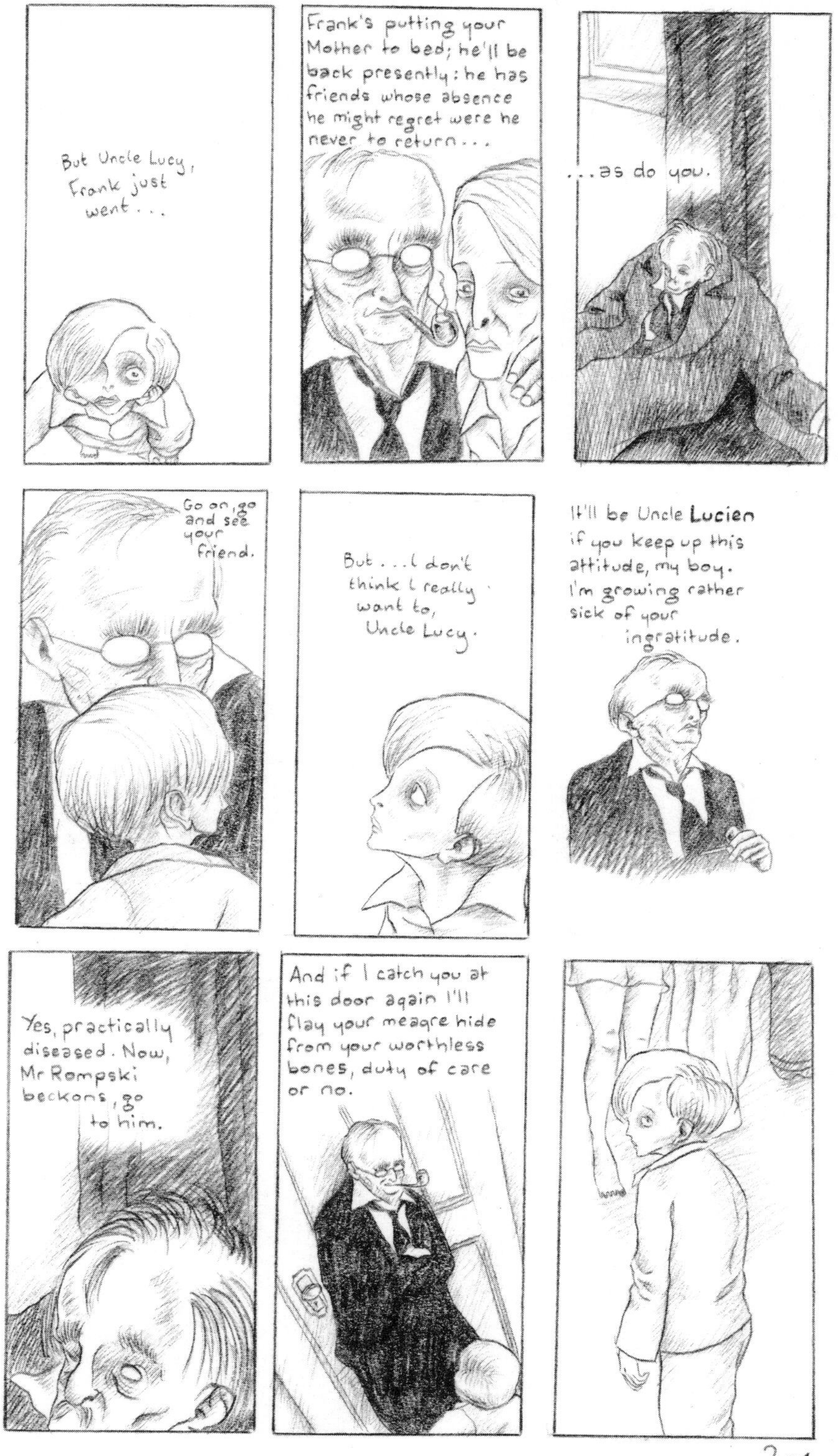
But Uncle Lucy, Frank just went . . .
Frank's putting your Mother to bed; he'll be back presently: he has friends whose absence he might regret were he never to return . . .
. . . as do you.
Go on, go and see your friend.
But . . . I don't think I really want to, Uncle Lucy.
It'll be Uncle **Lucien** if you keep up this attitude, my boy. I'm growing rather sick of your ingratitude.
Yes, practically diseased. Now, Mr Rompski beckons, go to him.
And if I catch you at this door again I'll flay your meagre hide from your worthless bones, duty of care or no.

Mr Rompski?
Uncle, I think he's asleep...oh.

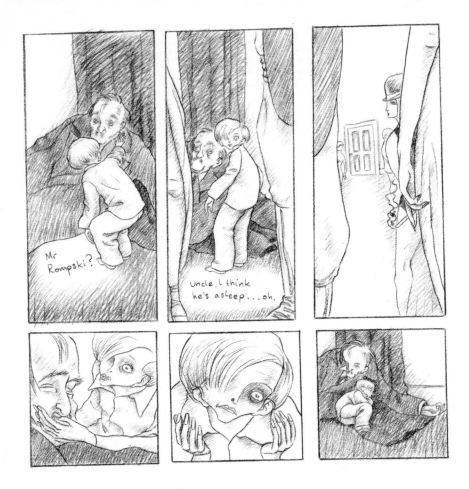

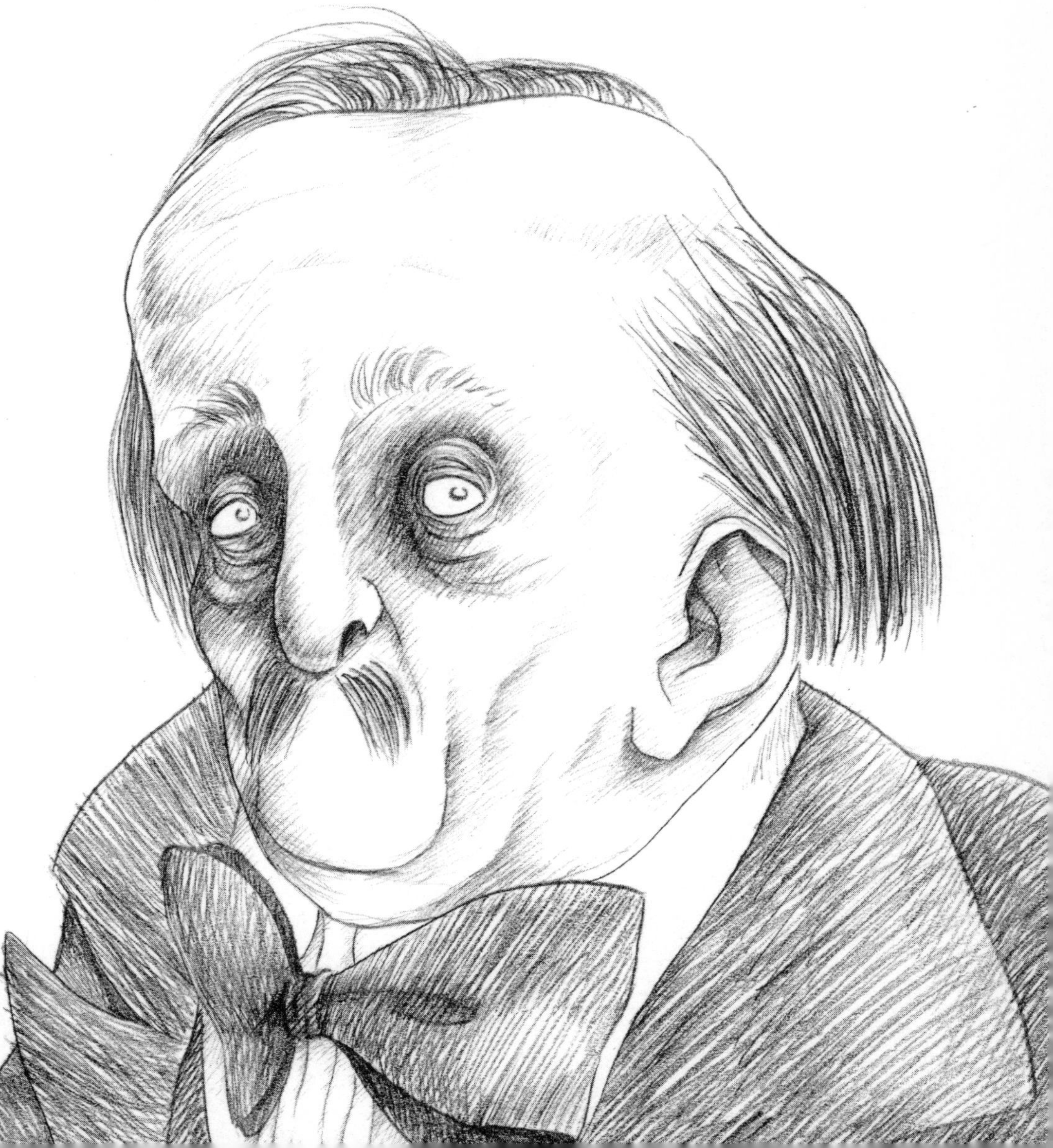

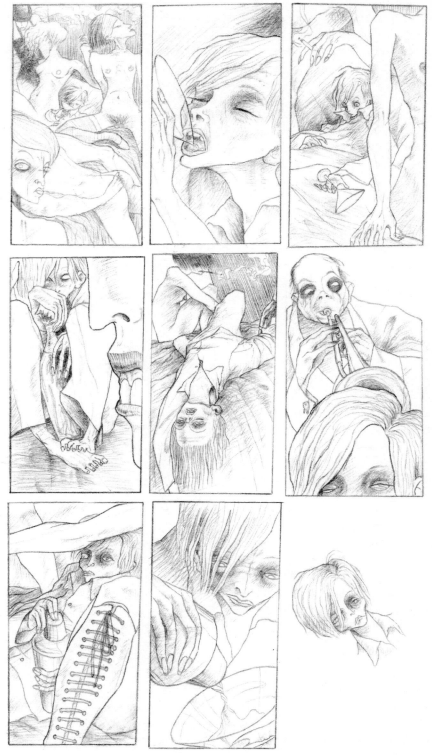

My head hurts
and and my mouth
tastes like a
wig and
my bed's full of
ladies
and it smells

of
ladies.

So under and over
the ladies I go,
goodness me,
I nearly put
my foot in
something
there.

No one talks to me
and I wish it was
just me again
'cos it's easier
not being talked
to when there's no one
to talk to y OH!
You silly fuck-ar! you've
spilt my drink!

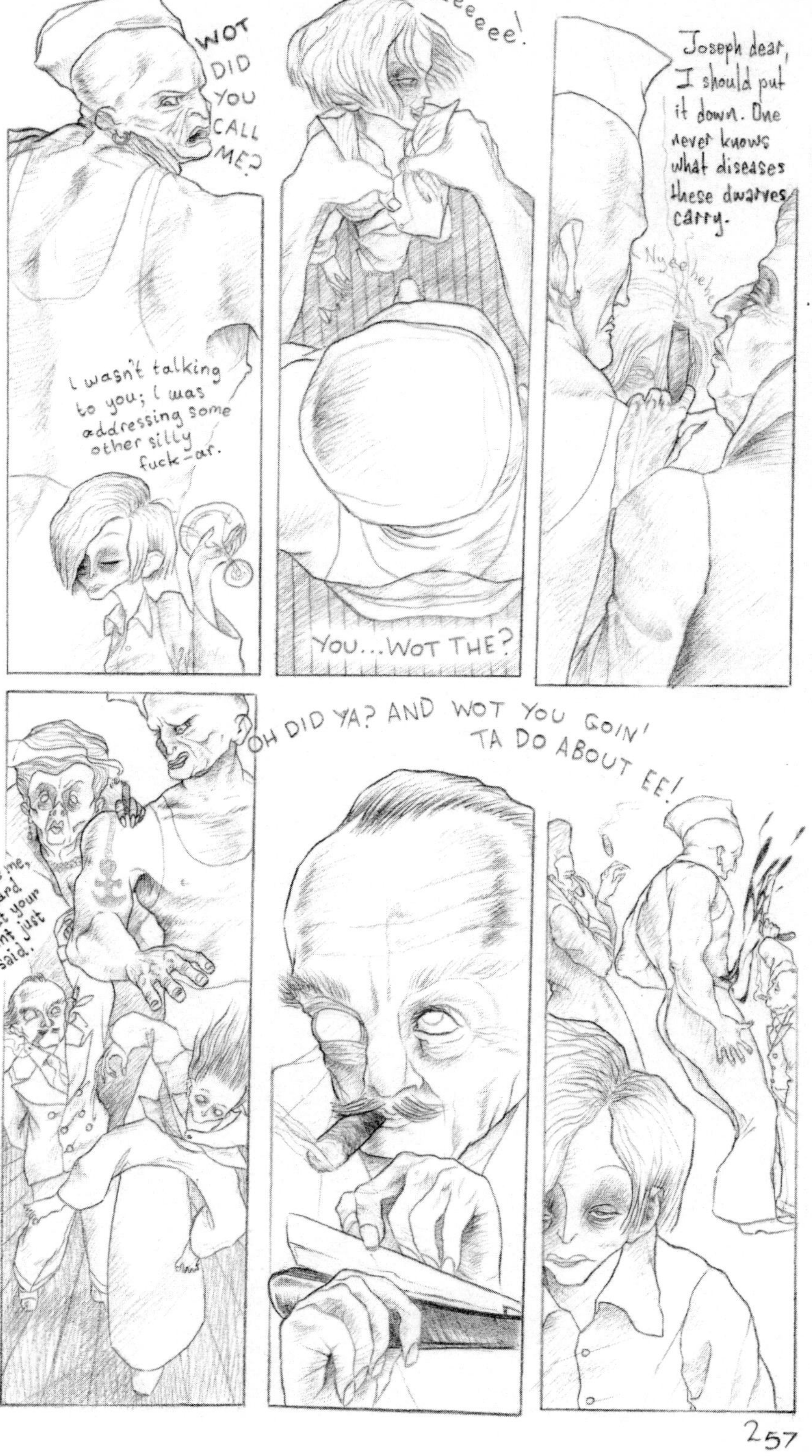
WOT DID YOU CALL ME?
I wasn't talking to you; I was addressing some other silly fuck-ar.
Weeeeeeee!
YOU... WOT THE?
Joseph dear, I should put it down. One never knows what diseases these dwarves carry.
Excuse me, I heard what your bint just said.
OH DID YA? AND WOT YOU GOIN' TA DO ABOUT EE!

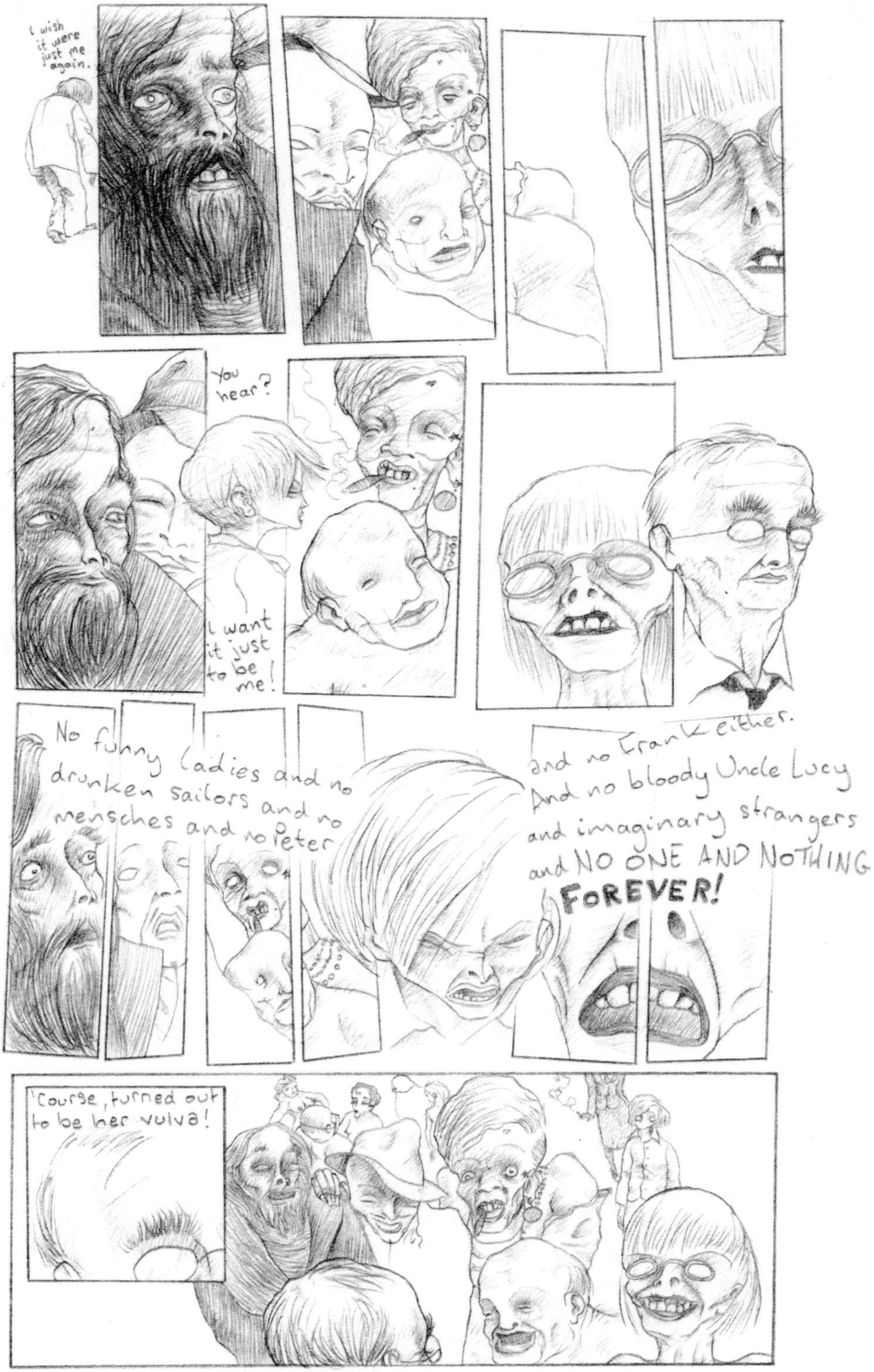
I wish it were just me again.
You hear?
I want it just to be me!
No funny ladies and no drunken sailors and no mensches and no Peter
and no Frank either. And no bloody Uncle Lucy and imaginary strangers and NO ONE AND NOTHING
FOREVER!
'Course, turned out to be her vulva!

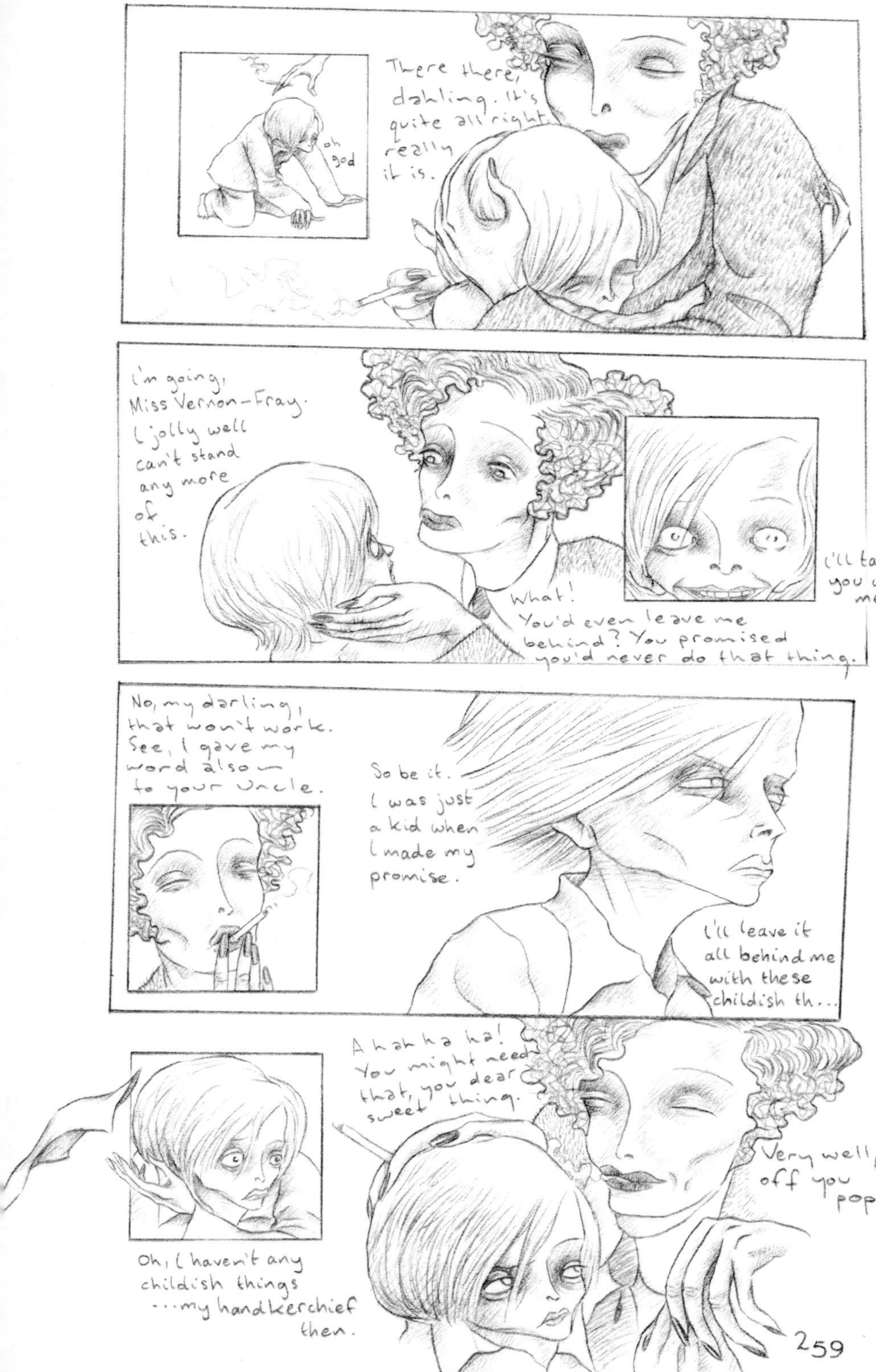
There there, dahling. It's quite all right really it is.
oh god
I'm going, Miss Vernon-Fray. I jolly well can't stand any more of this.
What! You'd even leave me behind? You promised you'd never do that thing.
I'll take you with me!
No, my darling, that won't work. See, I gave my word also — to your Uncle.
So be it. I was just a kid when I made my promise.
I'll leave it all behind me with these childish th...
Oh, I haven't any childish things ...my handkerchief then.
A hah ha ha! You might need that, you dear sweet thing.
Very well, off you pop.

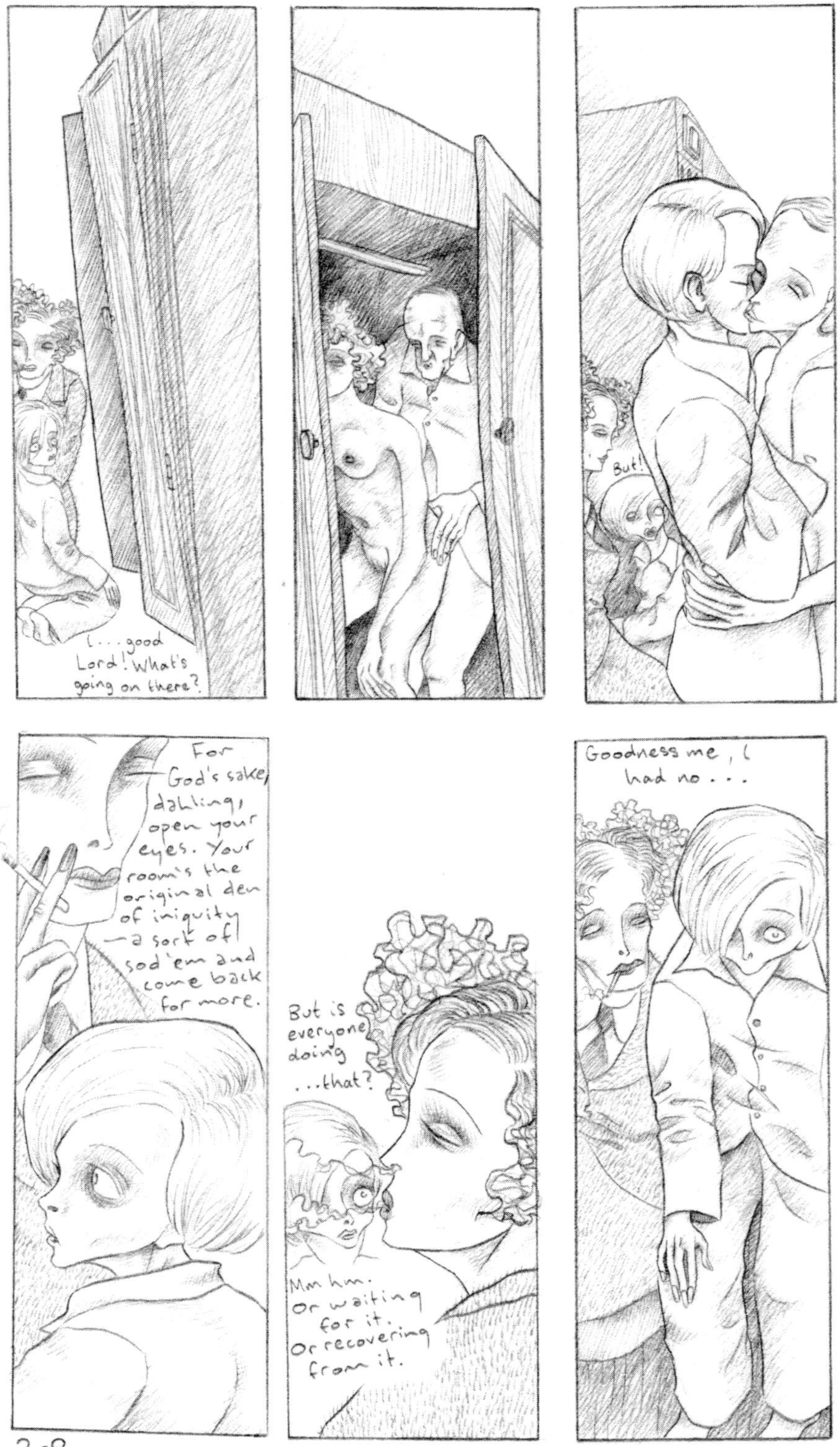
I . . . good Lord! What's going on there?
But!
For God's sake, dahling, open your eyes. Your room's the original den of iniquity — a sort of sod 'em and come back for more.
But is everyone doing . . . that?
Mm hm. Or waiting for it. Or recovering from it.
Goodness me, I had no . . .

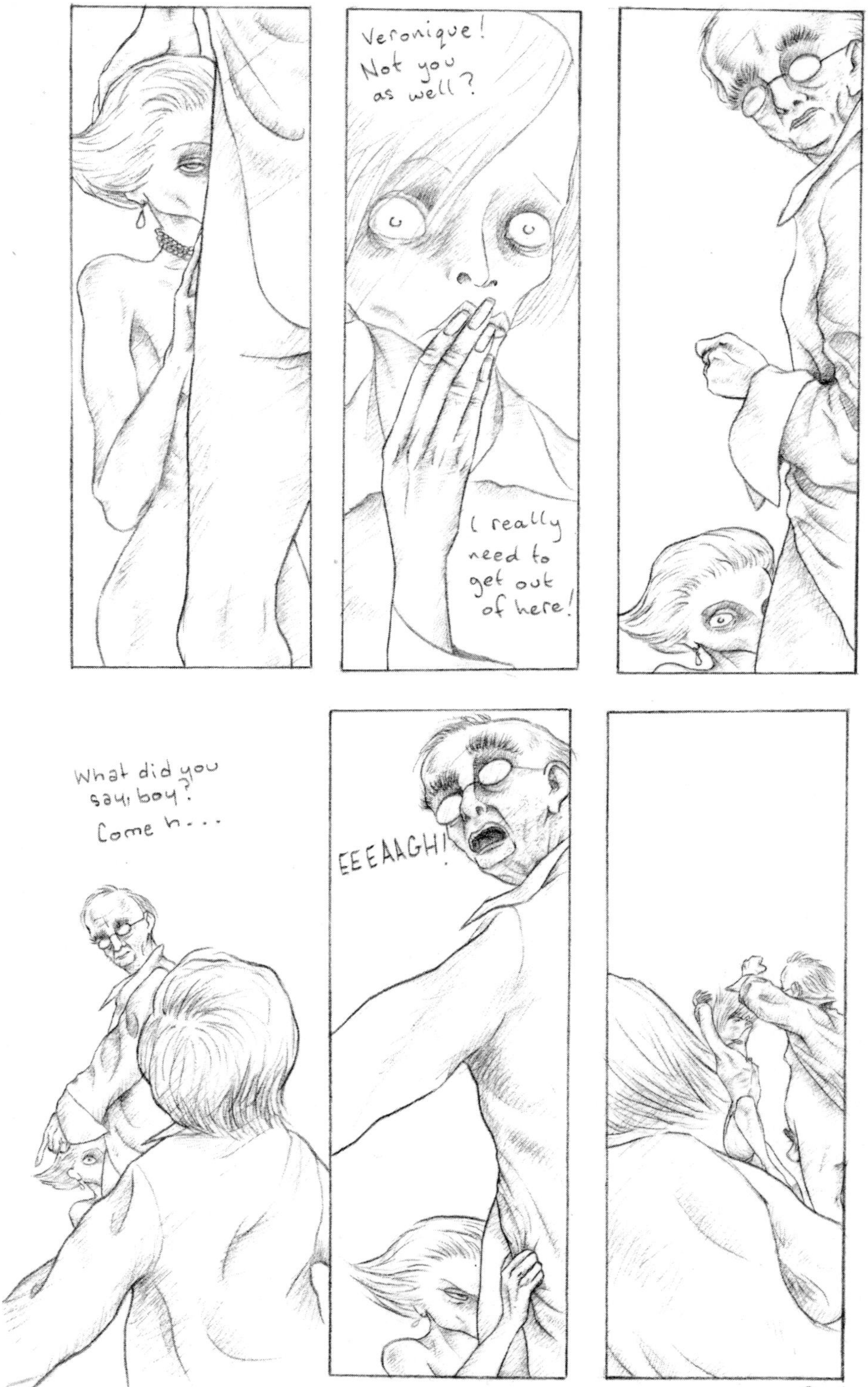
Veronique! Not you as well?
I really need to get out of here!
What did you say, boy? Come h...
EEEAAGH!

Um, excuse me please.

Yessss?
Oh, how exquisite! Have you come to play? Do let's!

Come here, you beguiling bitch and remove those pyjamas instanta!

So sorry, must dash.

I say, Malcolm, your little dwarfey's not playing ball.

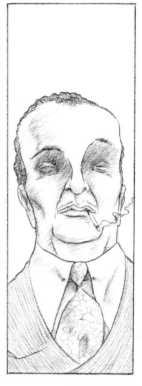

This ain't mine, this is one of Purvey Bothers' tarts.

262

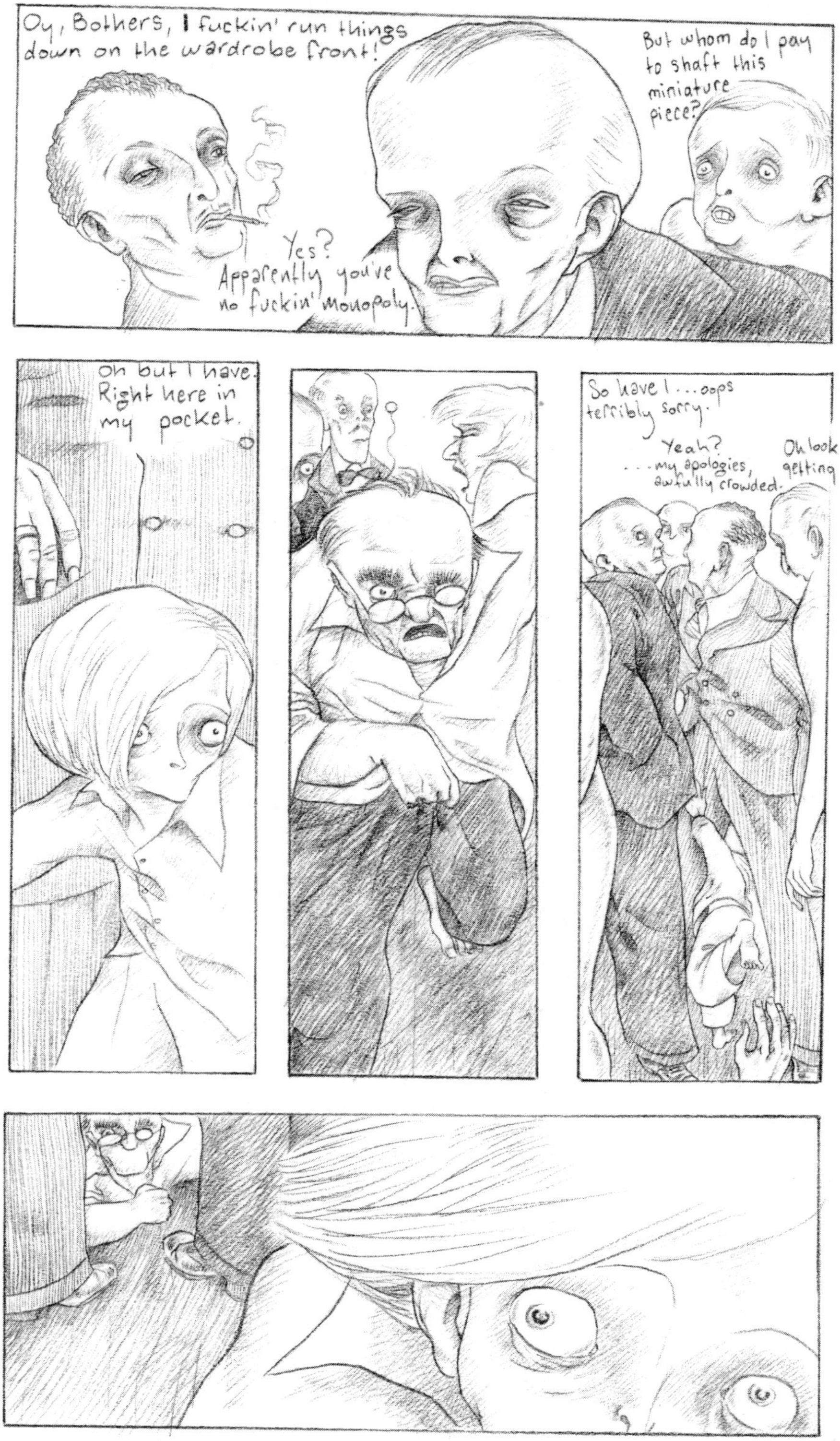
Oy, Bothers, I fuckin' run things down on the wardrobe front!
Yes? Apparently you've no fuckin' monopoly.
But whom do I pay to shaft this miniature piece?
Oh but I have. Right here in my pocket.
So have I... oops terribly sorry.
Yeah?
...my apologies, awfully crowded.
Oh look, it's getting awaaay!

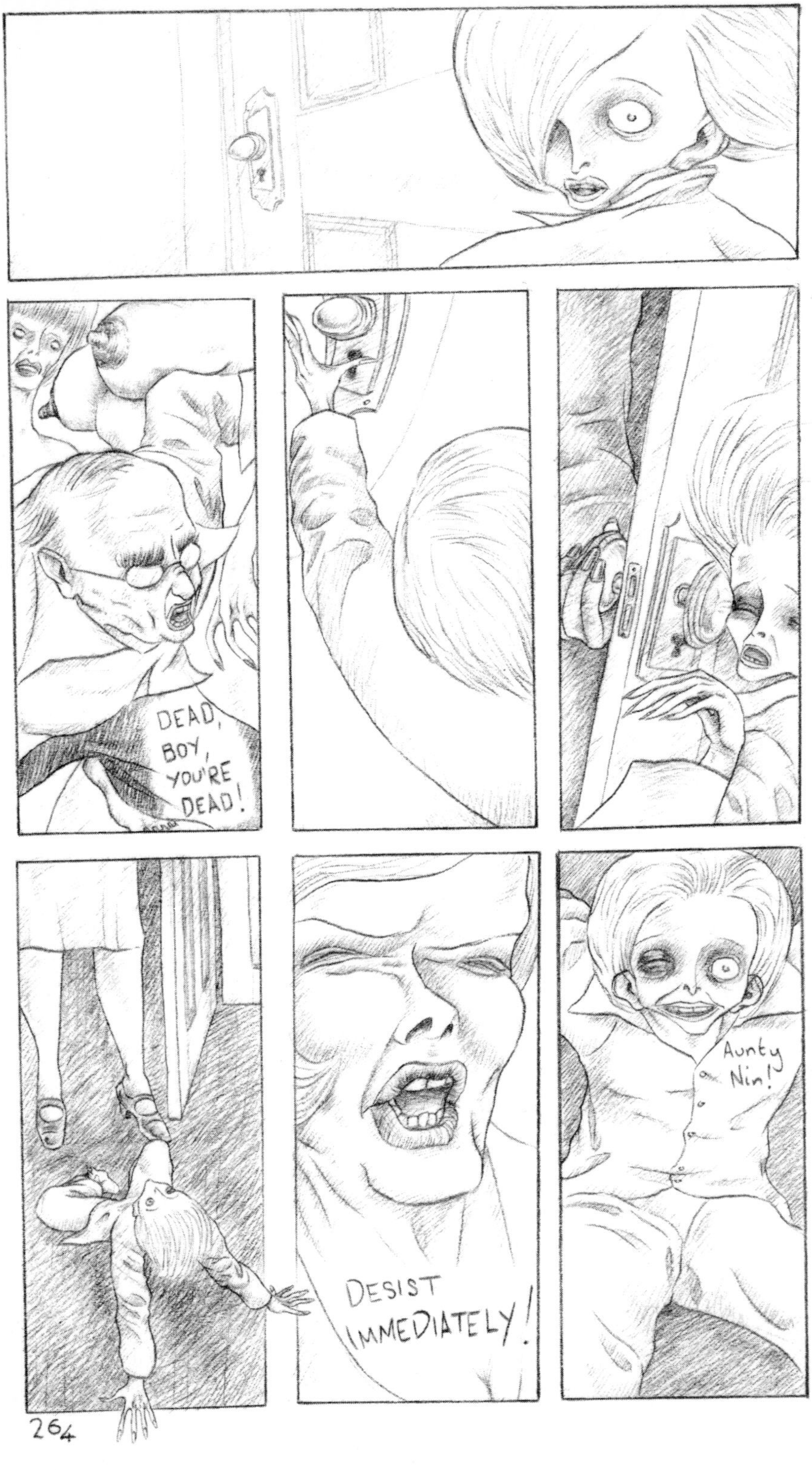
DEAD, BOY, YOU'RE DEAD!
DESIST IMMEDIATELY!
Aunty Nin!

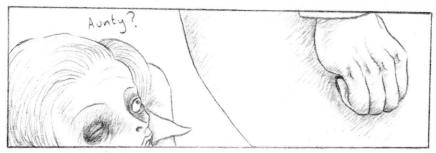

Aunty?

Oh my God, it's Nin!

Hilary! Put that sorry thing away and come home at once!

Oh no you don't!

I might have known this filthy hole would have something to do with you, Lucien.

Yes, well you just keep your nose out of my filthy hole! OW!

Stop struggling, Lucien dear.

Then let go, you mad bereted bitch!

Stop him!

265

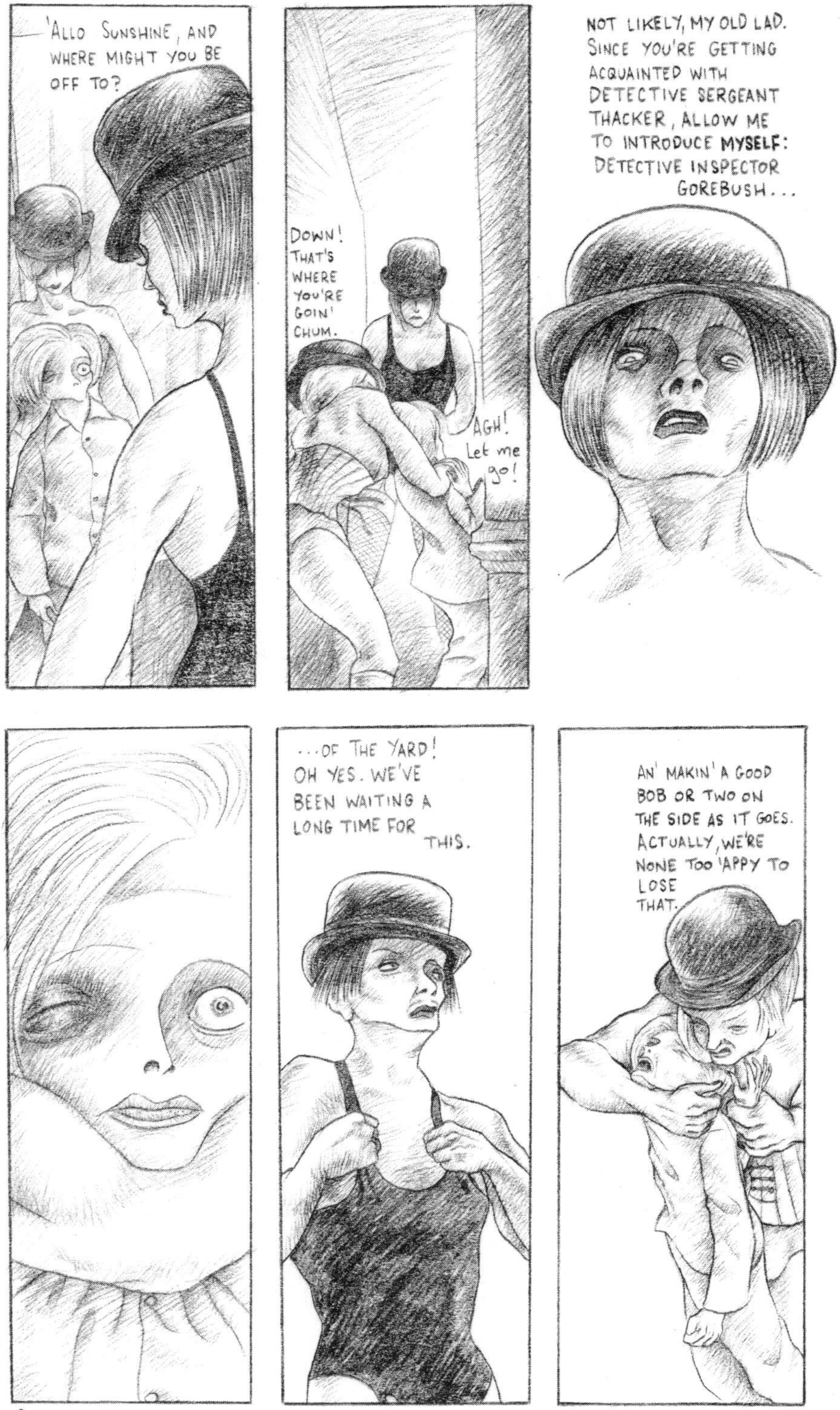
'ALLO SUNSHINE, AND WHERE MIGHT YOU BE OFF TO?
DOWN! THAT'S WHERE YOU'RE GOIN' CHUM.
AGH! Let me go!
NOT LIKELY, MY OLD LAD. SINCE YOU'RE GETTING ACQUAINTED WITH DETECTIVE SERGEANT THACKER, ALLOW ME TO INTRODUCE **MYSELF**: DETECTIVE INSPECTOR GOREBUSH...
...OF THE YARD! OH YES. WE'VE BEEN WAITING A LONG TIME FOR THIS.
AN' MAKIN' A GOOD BOB OR TWO ON THE SIDE AS IT GOES. ACTUALLY, WE'RE NONE TOO 'APPY TO LOSE THAT.

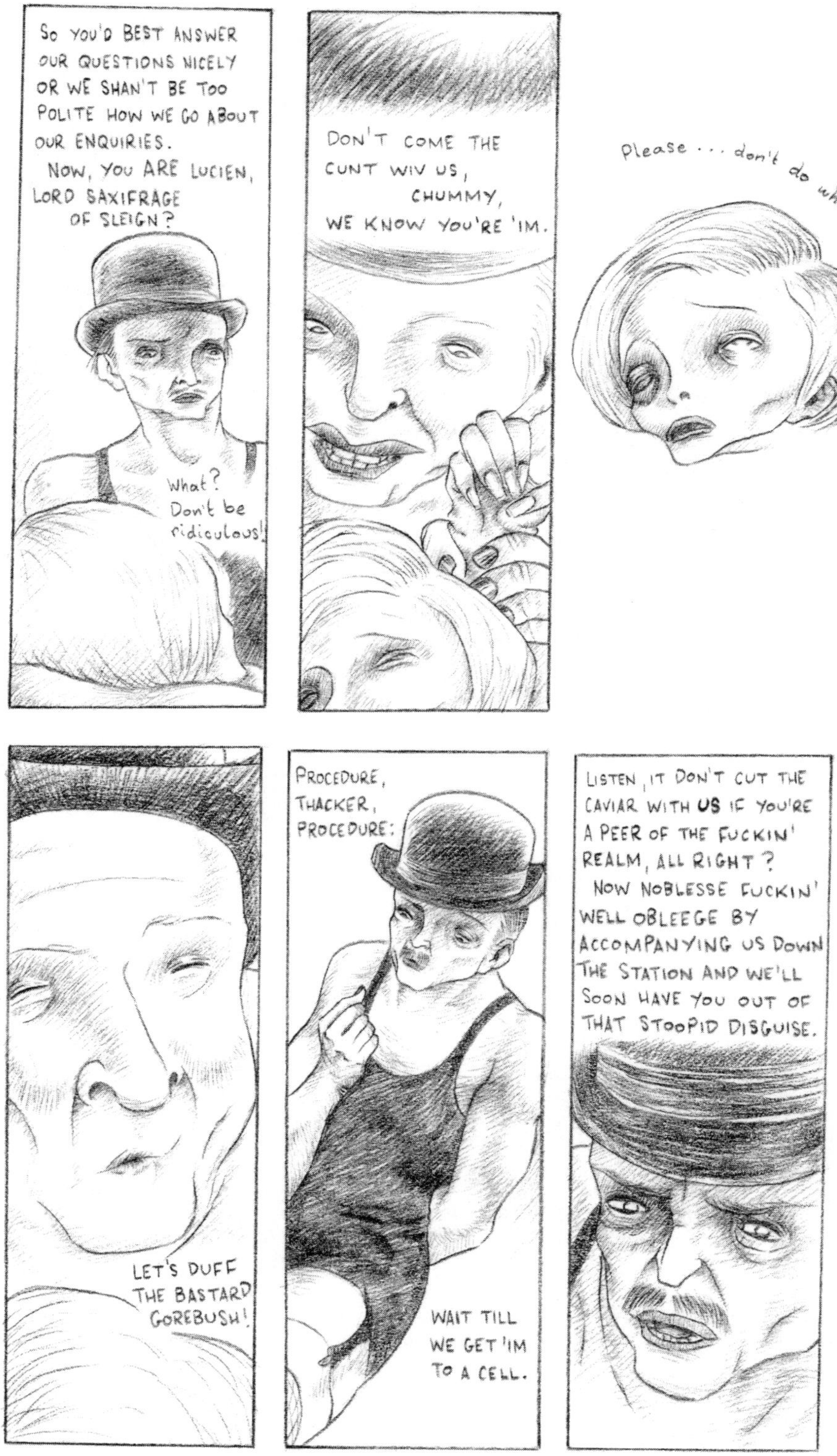

SO YOU'D BEST ANSWER OUR QUESTIONS NICELY OR WE SHAN'T BE TOO POLITE HOW WE GO ABOUT OUR ENQUIRIES.
NOW, YOU ARE LUCIEN, LORD SAXIFRAGE OF SLEIGN?
What? Don't be ridiculous!
DON'T COME THE CUNT WIV US, CHUMMY, WE KNOW YOU'RE 'IM.
Please . . . don't do what?
LET'S DUFF THE BASTARD GOREBUSH!
PROCEDURE, THACKER, PROCEDURE:
WAIT TILL WE GET 'IM TO A CELL.
LISTEN, IT DON'T CUT THE CAVIAR WITH US IF YOU'RE A PEER OF THE FUCKIN' REALM, ALL RIGHT?
NOW NOBLESSE FUCKIN' WELL OBLEEGE BY ACCOMPANYING US DOWN THE STATION AND WE'LL SOON HAVE YOU OUT OF THAT STOOPID DISGUISE.

Disguise? But I'm not...
CUFF 'IM, THACKER.
MY FUCKIN' PLEASURE.

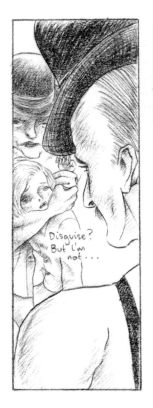

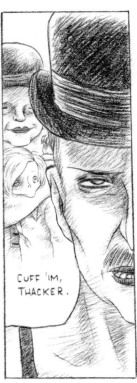

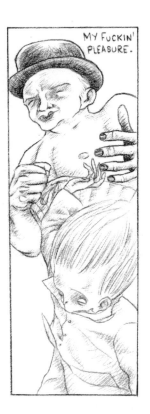

SAXIFRAGE EVADES LAW

New twist in case of renegade peer

Report by C.F. Vestry

Following our sensational report yesterday of the arrest by undercover policemen of renegade Lord, Lucien, Saxifrage of Sleign, Scotland Yard chiefs today admitted that they are reluctantly dropping charges of fraud and embezzlement against Saxifrage on the grounds that the man they arrested is not actually him but his eight-year-old great-nephew, Eustace Plender. The Yard was quick to add, however, that they are keen to prosecute for impersonation of a peer of the realm, suspected murder, running a house of ill repute, selling intoxicating liquors without a licence, supplying alcohol to a minor, illegal gambling, soliciting, pandering and wasting police time.

Shocking turn of events

Most shockingly, this turn of events means that Saxifrage remains at large, although police were downplaying the risk to the public. 'We are closing in and there will be no escape for Saxifrage; our net has no holes.' When asked how they had made the wrongful arrest a spokesman said, 'This was not a wrongful arrest. The suspect we have arrested is at the heart of London's underworld and is evidently a crimelord of no little power. It is therefore a rightful arrest, just a somewhat unexpected one. We had been watching this particular chummy with a fine-toothed comb and had every reason to believe he was Saxifrage. However, as he was suffering from contusions and internal bleeding which were self-sustained by resisting arrest, we were unable to question him directly upon reaching the cells to ascertain his true identity. We have since established that he is in fact a blood relation of Saxifrage which, I believe, goes a long way towards our vindication. The public may rest assured that we always get a man.'

Ruse

Since his imprisonment last night, Saxifrage's great nephew has contracted pneumonia, perhaps as a ruse to escape trial. Nevertheless, police are adamant that he will be brought to justice in due course, even if posthumously. Meanwhile, the search for Saxifrage continues.

Before the fall: the pre-scandal Saxifrage in happier times

Extract from 'The Daily Grind', 20th March 1936

Published by Jonathan Cape 2013

2 4 6 8 10 9 7 5 3 1

First published in Great Britain in 2013 by
Jonathan Cape
Random House, 20 Vauxhall Bridge Road,
London SW1V 2SA

www.vintage-books.co.uk

Addresses for companies within The Random House Group Limited can be found at:
www.randomhouse.co.uk/offices.htm

The Random House Group Limited Reg. No. 954009

A CIP catalogue record for this book is available from the British Library

ISBN 9780224093583

The Random House Group Limited supports The Forest Stewardship Council (FSC®),
the leading international forest certification organisation. Our books carrying the FSC label
are printed on FSC® certified paper. FSC is the only forest certification scheme endorsed by
the leading environmental organisations, including Greenpeace. Our paper procurement
policy can be found at: www.randomhouse.co.uk/environment

Printed and bound by MPG Books Group Ltd, Bodmin, Cornwall